Accidental Incest, Filial Cannibalism, & Other Peculiar Encounters in Late Imperial Chinese Literature

Harvard East Asian Monographs 304

Accidental Incest, Filial Cannibalism, & Other Peculiar Encounters in Late Imperial Chinese Literature

Tina Lu

Published by the Harvard University Asia Center
Distributed by Harvard University Press
Cambridge (Massachusetts) and London 2008

Printed in the United States of America

The Harvard University Asia Center publishes a monograph series and, in coordination with the Fairbank Center for Chinese Studies, the Korea Institute, the Reischauer Institute of Japanese Studies, and other faculties and institutes, administers research projects designed to further scholarly understanding of China, Japan, Vietnam, Korea, and other Asian countries. The Center also sponsors projects addressing multidisciplinary and regional issues in Asia.

Library of Congress Cataloging-in-Publication Data

Lu, Tina.

Accidental incest, filial cannibalism, & other peculiar encounters in late imperial Chinese literature / Tina Lu.

p. cm. -- (Harvard East Asian monographs ; 304)

Includes bibliographical references and index.

ISBN 978-0-674-03156-2 (alk. paper)

1. Chinese literature--Qing dynasty, 1644–1912--History and criticism. 2. Social conflict in literature. I. Title. II. Title: Accidental incest, filial cannibalism, and other peculiar encounters in late imperial Chinese literature. III. Series.

PL2297.L76 2008

895.1'090048--dc22

2008035458

Index by the author

♾ Printed on acid-free paper

Last figure below indicates year of this printing

18 17 16 15 14 13 12 11 10 09 08

To

Tovah, Natalie, Eli—

and

Adie, who snuck in under the wire

Acknowledgments

The winds have to be favorable for a book to be written. I am glad to have a chance to thank the many friends and colleagues who played a part in this book's completion.

I have had the opportunity to present the research that became this book in many different venues: on multiple occasions and panels at the annual Association for Asian Studies meetings; at various universities, including the University of California (at Berkeley and at Los Angeles), Cornell University, Yale University, and Harvard University; and also to my own students at the University of Pennsylvania. At those talks, many colleagues and friends asked questions and provided insights that led me in new directions. I am grateful for all those comments and ask for forgiveness if I omit some of those who helped me: Robert Ashmore, Allan Barr, Peter Bol, Kang-I Sun Chang, Maram Epstein, Si-yen Fei, Paul Goldin, Robert Hegel, Rania Huntington, Wilt Idema, Keith McMahon, Michael Puett, Haun Saussy, David Schaberg, Shang Wei, Sophie Volpp, Stephen West, Ye Yang, Judith Zeitlin.

An earlier version of Chapter 3 appears in *Trauma and Transcendence in Early Qing Literature*, ed. Wilt Idema, Wai-yee Li, and Ellen Widmer. I thank the Harvard University Asia Center for allowing me to include a newer version of that essay here and for the comments of the anonymous reviewers for that volume. An earlier version of Chapter 4 appeared in *Late Imperial China* (June 2003) as "*Zhaoshi bei* 3 and the Boundary Problem in Late Imperial Narrative."

Grants from the Center of East Asian Studies from the University of Pennsylvania and research leave from the university allowed me valuable time to think and to write.

Other colleagues generously read portions of the manuscript. They offered up invaluable suggestions, patched up holes in my learning, and many times saved me from myself: Eileen Chow, Wai-yee Li, Stephen Owen, Matthew Sommer, and Ellen Widmer. I am grateful to them all, as well as to the two anonymous readers who evaluated the book for the press. My partner in all things, Stuart Semmel, tirelessly listened, read, proofread, rebuilt my desktop, and gently mocked my bibliographic failings. As with all my projects, this book is part his.

This book was written in fits and starts over the past decade, joyfully delayed by the births and infancy of my four children. When I married, I wrote a book about marriage. This book concerns a world with many generations: how the world looks, not as an individual, but as a member of a family. I thank my children for transforming my perspective into one much more recognizable to a premodern Chinese sensibility and, also, for enriching my world immeasurably.

T.L.

Contents

Maps and Figure

Maps

Figure

Accidental Incest, Filial Cannibalism, & Other Peculiar Encounters in Late Imperial Chinese Literature

ONE

The Play as Map of the Empire

In that Empire, the Art of Cartography attained such perfection that the map of a single Province occupied the entirety of a City, and the map of the Empire, the entirety of a Province. In time, those Unconscionable Maps no longer satisfied, and the Cartographers Guilds struck a Map of the Empire whose size was that of the Empire, and which coincided point for point with it. The following Generations, who were not so fond of the Study of Cartography as their Forebears had been, saw that that vast Map was Useless, and not without some Pitilessness was it, that they delivered it up to the Inclemencies of Sun and Winters. In the Deserts of the West, still today, there are Tattered Ruins of that Map, inhabited by Animals and Beggars; in all the Land there is no other Relic of the Disciplines of Geography.

Suárez Miranda, *Viajes de varones prudentes*, Libro IV, Cap. XLV, Lérida, 1658
(Jorge Luis Borges, "On Exactitude in Science," from *In the Maker*, 1960)

What would it mean to map a premodern empire? The cultural theorist Jean Baudrillard takes this short story by Borges—quoted above in its entirety—and turns it into a meditation on representation, using the map as an example of a representation so all-encompassing that it can take the place of the original. I take Borges's story (whose fictional date of 1658 places it almost dead center chronologically of the texts discussed in this book) to mean something else entirely—as a meditation on the difficulties of representing an early modern empire.

The sort of imperial map we imagine now—something like those marble inlaid maps installed by Mussolini to glorify the old Roman empire, with Rome a central mass coming to spread over more of the Mediterranean basin and Europe—is an artifact of a modern conception of imperial power; for all his lofty intentions, Mussolini's Roman empire is still nothing but *primus inter pares*, one polity (admittedly the biggest and most powerful), surrounded by others. But contemporary Roman jurists and political thinkers had something grander in mind. Not only was Rome civilization itself, but, as the intellectual historian Anthony Pagden writes, part of the imperial project was "to include everyone there was in the world."[1] What borders would such a map have? How to depict it against the backdrop of the rest of the world, if it *is* the rest of the world? Mapping the reach of the Catholic Church, say, with its promise of universality, presents something of the same problem.

In some sense, the geopolitical map cannot represent such an empire, whose space is not normal space. The frustration of Borges's cartographers—and the escalation of their efforts—is understandable: perhaps a map as large as the empire itself could avoid the pitfalls of imperial representation. Nonetheless, with the universal promise of the Spanish Empire, or the Catholic Church, or the Qing Empire, any map—no matter how vast—might seem Useless, inadvertently pointing to the Empire's limitations. And what to do with the map then? It is a double of what cannot be doubled, and it can only be consigned to the Wilderness, an imaginary, entirely uncontested location, filled with the stateless, the "Animals and Beggars" of which Suárez Miranda writes.

Midway through Li Xuanyu's *Qingzhong pu* (Registers of the pure and loyal), written around the time of the Ming dynasty's fall (1644) about a popular uprising in 1626, it seems that the evil eunuch Wei Zhongxian and his supporters have won the day. The eunuch's faction has killed or driven to death a number of its enemies, including our hero Zhou Shunchang, innocent of any crime except the choice of his friends. Zhou has already been murdered in prison, while his son (who has managed to sneak into his cell) watches. In Act 20, the ghosts of those killed gather together and head toward the capital to seek vengeance.

The angry ghosts make their way to Beijing in what seems to the modern reader like an airplane ride spanning a great swathe of the mighty empire. As they fly above Suzhou and head northward, they cross the Yangzi. Singing in chorus, the ghosts look down and describe the vista beneath them: "The Yangzi River rolls, its waves striking the heavens/But still unable to wash clear the enmity of

Yunyang." And then looking downward, using ancient appellations for some of the locations, they name each of the regions between Suzhou and the capital: "In one gaze there is bustling Wei and Yang; / The obscure Huai River and Anhui / Tiny Qingdao and Qi / And arid Mo and Yan."[2]

To arrive in the capital, the ghosts make a journey of eleven hundred kilometers or so as the crow (or spirit) flies—many more if on foot, horseback, or boat to take advantage of the roads, courier stations, and the Grand Canal that a terrestrial traveler would have to have used. Even under the most optimistic of conditions, such a journey in the seventeenth century would have taken a month. But the ghosts' journey takes place in a moment; and unlike a trip in an airplane, the whole landscape beneath is taken in all at once, the whole mighty empire comprehended in "one gaze."

There is a similar moment in *Changsheng dian* (Palace of everlasting life; 1688), one of the most famous plays in the canon. In it, the Qing playwright Hong Sheng presents his version of one of the most compelling episodes in Chinese history: the disastrous consequences of the love affair between the Tang emperor Xuanzong and his concubine Yang Yuhuan. Pining for her even after she has hanged herself at the behest of rebelling troops, the emperor orders her body disinterred, only to find the grave empty. In Act 43, a shaman seeks her out in the spirit world, leaving his body among the living while his soul soars to the immortals.

What the shaman sees as he begins his journey resembles the flight of the ghosts in *Qingzhong pu*. The actor playing the part of the shaman mimes the act of flying on the winds. He starts off in the known world: "Securely treading on the lightness of the white clouds, / Opportunely taking advantage of the high winds' convenience, / I stride over the bowl-like blue sea. / When I gaze back, where does the realm appear? / Pale and fading out, nine spots of floating mist."[3] The "nine spots" are *jiuzhou* 九州, the nine lands that make up the emperor's realm, here so reduced by distance that they—immense territories filled with great cities and populated by millions—almost fade to nothingness. In one glance, *yiwang* 一望, the ghosts can see the entire area between Suzhou and Beijing; the shaman outdoes them, seeing at once all of the nine lands.

Still, the shaman's journey has only begun: "In speaking I have already come to the eastern end of the sea, / With its peaks of ten thousand cubits. / These are the three islands and the ten islets each piercing through to the heavens. / I'll just circle around the high and lofty garden of the immortals, / To the beautiful palaces."[4] The "three islands and the ten islets" refer to a mythical landscape, the island homes of the immortals. Carefully numbered and named just like the nine lands the shaman looked back on before, these "three islands and ten islets" are of a different order from the nine lands. If the ghosts' journey could have been undertaken, albeit with more difficulty, on conventional modes of transportation, the shaman's journey depends on the altered states of dreams, trance, and death with which *Changsheng dian* abounds.

Within the context of the late Ming and early Qing, these moments can surely not be detached from a late imperial interest in maps and mapmaking. The shaman of *Changsheng dian* and the ghosts of *Qingzhong pu* fly over landscapes that might as well be giant maps that gesture toward encompassing the whole of the mighty empire, or perhaps even the whole universe. These isolated moments conceive of all imperial space as a whole; more broadly, however, one might see the genre of *chuanqi*—long dramas based on southern performance traditions—in this light, since the very form of the genre represents imperial space.

Even though for centuries *chuanqi* have been experienced largely as excerpts, one structural feature all *chuanqi* plays share emerges only when one reads the plays in their entirety.[5] All *chuanqi* are situated in a precise moment in historical time and are obliged to violate the Aristotelian unity of place. None can take place in a single locale; instead, at least some characters must move from one part of the empire to another, and actions taking place in one locale are shown to have an impact on others taking place at a great distance. Such a generic demand is remarkable, since in late imperial times travel itself was anomalous: women were expected to remain at home, and the vast majority of men traveled very little. (Travel's ubiquity in *chuanqi* reflects the genre's close ties to the elite, since journeys of officials from post to post are not only a mainstay of the genre but also among the few perfectly sanctioned travels of the time.) Every *chuanqi* creates an imagined empire. The stage turns into a window on the empire at large, with its many provinces, many spheres of human existence, and many simultaneous actions all adding up to a single play with a unified narrative arc.

—

Simultaneity across space not only characterizes the generic norms of the *chuanqi* drama but also serves as a fundamental way of conceiving of an empire connecting far-flung locations. In writing on nationalism, Benedict Anderson famously discusses the impact that the novel and the newspaper had on how time was imagined in late eighteenth- and early nineteenth-century Europe and its colonies;[6] both of these forms allowed readers to tie their own existences to those of others distant from them in space but inhabiting the same moment. For the same reason, calendars, which allowed for ritual action to be coordinated across space, were imperially sponsored projects.[7] Consider, for example, Act 8 in Tang Xianzu's *Mudan ting* (The peony pavilion; 1598), in which the local official Du Bao supervises the first planting of the season; that moment, just as much as the invasion of the barbarian prince that takes place later, is meant to invoke simultaneity of action across the sweep of the empire.

In *chuanqi*, events taking place at the same time also tie together the spheres of the political and the domestic, whose unity was the essence of the Confucian empire. What seems in its outlines to be a simple romantic comedy or a domestic drama cannot find full resolution in the confines of a household, or even the borders of a single county or a single province; instead, action inevitably spills out into the empire at large. Sometimes this is because local matters and great affairs of state are shown to be linked causally: in one of *Changsheng dian*'s most famous scenes, couriers hurrying lychees from the far south to the north to indulge Concubine Yang's whims trample a blind fortuneteller to death. What happens at court affects even the humblest of countrypeople and vice versa.

But even more so, it is specifically the case that the domestic and the global are shown to be one. If romantic comedies and tragedies eventually turn political, plays concerned explicitly with history or court politics show how the forces that tear apart an empire eventually find their way into the fabric of personal life. In Ruan Dacheng's

Yanzi jian (The swallow letter; 1645), for example, a love triangle involving a young man, a courtesan, and an official's daughter requires no less an event than the An Lushan Rebellion to resolve. What might appear distant or lofty—factional struggles or a political quarrel—inevitably infiltrates the sphere of the family. How domestic can a play about the evil eunuch Wei Zhongxian's downfall be? *Qingzhong pu*'s hero incurs the wrath of Wei through the most domestic of all actions, the arrangement of his daughter's marriage. In betrothing her to the son of Wei's enemy, he sets up a chain of actions that leads to his own death and ultimately that of Wei.

In the early Qing dynasty, the Kangxi emperor commissioned the Jesuit missionaries Joachim Bouvet and Jean-Baptiste Régis to head a surveying team, which would take twenty years to prepare a map of the entire empire, meticulously measuring distances both through travel and through state-of-the-art astronomical observations. The final product, the 1718 *Huangyu quantu* (Complete map of the empire), was of unprecedented size and detail and included not just all of present-day China but extended even to present-day Nepal's Mount Everest, its height carefully surveyed. Like Suárez Miranda's, the Jesuits' map is an ideal form, more comprehensive and more encompassing than the debased reality of the empire itself.[8]

The next few generations witnessed other ambitious projects that also aimed at total comprehensiveness. In the 1730s, the Qianlong emperor commissioned the *Daqing tongli* (Complete Qing rituals), a collection prescribing proper ritual behavior for every milestone in life, from birth to death. The *Siku quanshu* (Complete library of the Four Treasuries), the Qianlong emperor's project to gather together and classify all the writings of the Chinese tradition, also attempts to encompass the whole of the empire. Like the map representing the empire, which might be rolled up and stored away, which might be more real than what it showed, so too the two-thousand-year-old literary tradition might be fully comprised.

Although a number of scholars have studied the structure of ideas that buttressed the creation of empires in early modern Europe, historians of China have tended to assume (or even to argue) that such a complex of ideas was unnecessary for the Chinese state.[9] When territorial expansion was debated, as at the Kangxi court in the case of Taiwan, the focus was not theoretical—whether there was a point beyond which the empire should not expand—but instead purely expedient. No minister wondered whether the empire was exceeding its rights. Public debates like those that took place in Spain in 1551 between Juan Ginés de Sepúlveda and Bartolomé de las Casas regarding the moral justifiability of the Conquest would have been unimaginable. Just as the Qing dynasts claimed, the borders to a state governed by benevolent behavior might not exist at all, as the traditional appellation *wuwai* 無外 (without an outside) indicates. States defined by a shared language or a shared history have built-in limits. But the empire was different. Why should the whole world not fall under a single Confucian rule? All it would take would be allegiance to the emperor and adopting proper beliefs about the family. If the Empire is characterized not by a people, nor even a language, but an idea, then why should it not extend infinitely, covering all worlds and cultures?[10]

We can consider plays in the context of imperial ideology—both as reinforcement and as challenge. If *chuanqi* dramas might be thought of as windows onto a doubled empire that always stands in complex relationship to the original, they are an ideal version, more whole, more encompassing, more certain, than the real empire ever was. The early Ming emperors carefully censored the presence of emperors in their stagings of *zaju* (or northern-style drama, which was very popular from the Yuan into the middle of the Ming); they recognized the challenges that a duplicated emperor could present to the singular one. A doubled empire might have a similarly threatening impact on absolute claims of singularity. In relating the final fall of the Song dynasty and the general Wen Tianxiang's principled resistance to and death at the hands of the Mongol conquerors, the eighteenth-century playwright Jiang Shiquan's *Dongqing shu* (The evergreen tree; 1781) thematizes the problem of the doubled empire, one half terrestrial and one half heavenly. Loyalty's very essence is that it brooks no relativism and allows for no substitutes. Nonetheless, the scene of Wen Tianxiang's execution is necessarily broken by a chiasmus in which two separate worlds are depicted, and the general's place in both shown. The first half of the act shows his defiance up to the very moment when he is killed, and the second half, unseen by any of the characters in the first half, shows the Dragon Emperor's commendation of him.

Wen Tianxiang's ultimate apotheosis is beyond question—yet throughout the play, we have hints that his martyrdom is complicated: perhaps others who surrendered to the Mongols had good reason; perhaps Wen's motivations have been selfish; and indisputably the mandate of heaven has passed from the Song. Wen's last words even include a benediction to the new Mongol emperor, urging him to do his best, a tacit acknowledgment of the new monarch's legitimacy. Nonetheless, Wen Tianxiang's reward after death removes all such subtle moral shadings; the Dragon Emperor speaks from an absolutist, universalist position that is incontrovertible. In *chuanqi*, the immortal world present in each play bequeaths something of its own certainty to the imperial order, even when, as in *Dongqing shu*, the play otherwise explores the contingent, imperfect, morally ambiguous nature of imperial power.

—

The empire is more than the commingled spheres of domestic and global, or the world of men and that of gods. Modern readers have noted critically that *chuanqi* plots depend on coincidences that strain belief; virtually all demand accidental encounters in some strange location between characters who appear to each other to be strangers, but who are actually closely connected in some direct or indirect fashion. Friends, acquaintances, relations, friends of friends, run into each other. That these encounters can take place at all suggests that this empire, enormous though it might be, is not of infinite scope and utterly without borders.

In *Xilou ji* (The western tower; 1610), by Yuan Yuling (1592–1670), the young man Yu Juan accidentally encounters a friend at an inn on his way to the examinations. Yu Juan reveals that he has not died of lovesickness—but he also learns, incorrectly, that his beloved has been driven to suicide by the persistent attentions of a powerful official's son. This conversation between the two friends is in turn overheard by a third man, a stranger who vows to avenge the two lovers. Even though the play's action takes place in cities across the Jiangnan region, we are expected to believe that an eavesdropper might know enough about all parties concerned to be able to put his plan into action; the play's dénouement depends on not one but two vanishingly improbable encounters.

Here the world is imagined politically, as a finite network of acquaintances. By politics, I do not mean various authors' associations with various contemporary political cliques, although much important scholarship has dealt with such matters.[11] Instead, this book is concerned with politics in another sense. As the anthropologist Arjun Appadurai puts it, "what creates the link between exchange and value is *politics*, construed broadly."[12] Writers of late imperial fiction were, I propose, deeply engaged with profoundly political questions like: What ties individuals together? To what extent are these ties permanent, or do they remain contingent and circumstantial? What transforms individual families or couples into a society? These questions were often addressed, as Appadurai suggests, through the problem of exchange, specifically through the interface between commodities and persons.

The book that follows draws heavily on anthropological scholarship—some ethnographic description but especially theoretical explorations of kinship and exchange—because the drama and fiction of this period wrestle with very similar problems. I am not suggesting in any way that late imperial Chinese literature can be used as raw data for ethnographic description. Instead, obsessed with questions we consider anthropological and highly self-conscious in its discussion of economy and society, of exchange and kinship, the literature itself is actively engaged in staking out and exploring these questions. In effect, the authors are themselves the anthropologists of what they saw around them.

One might just as easily see things the other way; from my perspective, twentieth-century anthropologists seem deeply engaged in problems that engrossed Chinese writers of the late imperial period. Take, for example, the following position on one of the most important questions in Chinese philosophy: "what makes man really different from the animal is that, in mankind, a family could not exist if there were no society: i.e., a plurality of families ready to acknowledge that there are other links than consanguineous ones, and that the natural process of filiation can only be carried on through the social process of affinity."[13] One could hardly come up with a better one-sentence summary of late imperial Confucianism, and yet the author of the above quotation is no premodern, nor a sinologist; rather, he is instead the twentieth-century French anthropologist Claude Lévi-Strauss, in an essay on the nature of the family.

In fact, this problem—the relationship between society and family—has been a hallmark of Chinese thought from its beginnings. How do the parallel structures of individual human families combine to form a society? The *Daxue* (Great learning), one of the Four Books studied by all participants in the examination system, presents one answer to Lévi-Strauss's question about how the family might form a part of a greater human collective. According to the *Daxue*, the state is simply the family writ large; in both family and state, order is to be imposed and taught: "The ancients who wished to illustrate illustrious virtue throughout the kingdom, first ordered well their own states. Wishing to order well their states, they first regulated their families. Wishing to regulate their families, they first cultivated their persons. Wishing to cultivate their persons, they first rectified their hearts" (1.3).

But the *Daxue* is only a jumping-off point to questions that reach a new level of sophistication and prominence in the Ming and Qing dynasties. Is it the case that, as Lévi-Strauss suggests (but the *Daxue* does not), the family is a more natural structure than a society? Many scholars have suggested that the place of ritual changed over the course of the Ming, with increasing numbers of thinkers arguing that it served to express emotion rather than create it. Perhaps that philosophical shift implies a belief that ultimately artificial institutions must somehow accommodate natural human sentiment. What, then, is the connection between those institutions and seemingly natural human relationships? How are the ties of the state related to familial relationships? Or more broadly, what is it that ties people together as a community beyond what connects two individuals together in a relationship? In late imperial China, writers of drama and fiction addressed these questions head on.

—

In Meng Chengshun's enormously influential tragic romance *Jiaohong ji* (translated by Cyril Birch as *Mistress and Maid*; ~1640), Wang Jiaoniang's father initially refuses to permit a match between the girl and her first cousin. The father cites the commands of the state. When presented with the proposal, he sings angrily: "What you say is ignorant./To make a good match/One must act according to the principles of human relations. Nowadays the court has established the law:/Maternal cousins are not allowed to marry. They call each other brother and sister/How can they become related by marriage?"[14] Her father argues that marriage between the two cousins (who do not share the same surname) would offend *renlun* 人倫, "the principles of human relations," first because it has been forbidden by the court, and second because, since the two cousins already stand in relation to each other as brother and sister, they cannot also be husband and wife.

Renlun consists of five relations: that between father and son, between ruler and subject, between husband and wife, between elder brother and younger brother, and between friends. Jiaoniang's father sees a conflict between two of these ties, so that loyalty to the state stands in the way of the young people's marriage. By allowing the match to take place, the father would at once sanction incest and disobey the strictures of the state—two offenses against *renlun* with one blow. Of all human relations, a love affair between cousins, since they in some sense belong to the same family, seems perhaps the most confined and the easiest to keep within the family's walls. Why does this matter need to spread outside, much less to the state, as Wang Jiaoniang's father suggests? He points to another way in which the empire is connected together. To her father, all five human relations are interrelated, to the point that there is no fulfilling the moral imperatives of one while ignoring the others. Far more than any dream of flying or of travel, variations on this notion of the empire as a network of relationships were extraordinarily powerful and pervasive throughout the late imperial period.

Dramatizations of the fundamental unity of the five relations had been part of the cultural repertoire for centuries. Qiu Jun's didactic play *Wulun quanbei* (The Five Normative Relations perfected and completed; mid-fifteenth century) tells of a concubine captured by a barbarian invader and then commanded by her mother to kill herself. Katherine Carlitz writes of Yao Maoliang's southern drama *Shuangzhong ji* (Two great loyalists; fifteenth century), which in enacting the unity of the *wulun* renders the state as natural as a family. In this play (a precursor to the *chuanqi* genre), a general whose troops are under siege comes up with the idea of feeding his loyal concubine (in the form of a soup) to his starving troops. Fortunately for him, the concubine volunteers her body, sparing him from having to commit murder. Her sacrifice, which demonstrates her commitment not only to her master but to the polity as a whole, inspires the troops to fight on. Immediately thereafter, his brother general's young servant boy makes the same vow. Once they are eaten, the concubine and the servant are literally integrated, as much as anybody can be, into the body politic, which is shown to us to be a seemingly natural entity built on individual, incontrovertible loyalties: the love of a woman for her husband, the gratitude of a servant to his master.[15]

Even though the equation between sexual love and loyalty—two of the *wulun*—dates back at least as far as the *Chuci*, the trope takes on a new urgency in the late imperial period and is made obliquely and explicitly in lyric poetry, as Kang-i Sun Chang explores, and in both fictional and nonfictional prose. In the wake of the Ming dynasty's fall, it became a commonplace to draw complicated correlations and equivalences between love for a courtesan and loyalty toward the doomed state.[16]

Shuangzhong ji is not the only late imperial text to propose an organic body constructed of filiality, loyalty, and chastity; other texts suggest that an individual might embody all the familial and political virtues. In an encomium to Shen Yunying, the daughter of a deceased Ming general, Mao Qiling (1623–1716) articulated the same fantasy. Once again, these virtues can be fully incorporated within a single body only through the sacrifice of a female body. After her father's death in battle, Shen Yunying took over as general of his troops, killing numerous bandit soldiers and reclaiming her father's body for burial. Later on, after the Manchus defeated the Ming, she prepared to take her own life by drowning (but was stopped by her mother). Mao praises her: "Loyalty, filiality, chastity, and virtue—all gathered in one woman's person, this is something that since the ancients has not existed."[17]

At the same time, the female body also holds the promise of true debauchery. In *Jingzhong qi* (The banner of loyalty; seventeenth century), a Jurchen prince brags that his concubines now include the Song emperor's own ladies, as well as the captive wives and daughters of high ministers at the Song court. But the most notorious of his mistresses is none other than the traitor Qin Gui's own wife; the prince says, "His wife Ms Wang from the beginning has come in and out of my bed curtains, and we have often shared banquets."[18] Capable of even worse than the infamous Qin Gui is his wife, precisely because she can embody adultery as well as treason.

Perhaps this fantasy—that all the virtues (or their equivalent vices) might be gathered together into the same body, never to be torn asunder again—is prevalent precisely because the potential fissures among the *wulun* are all too real. The community is always capable of dissolving into loving husbands who are not filial sons, inseparable brothers who do not see themselves as servants of the same state, and friends who are perfidious.

Jiaoniang's father refuses to give the two young lovers permission to marry for two reasons: first, so they might act in accordance with the law, and also so they might continue as proper sister and brother. He does not give priority to either tie, but he does choose the conflation of two of the *wulun*—vassal and sibling—over that of two others—spouse and sibling. In other words, the fantasy that all normative relations might be expressed at once, variously articulated by so many writers of this period, is itself uncomfortably close to another nightmare, that of *luanlun*, that all the relations might be gathered together, in a daughter who is also a wife, or brother and sister who are also husband and wife. One of the themes this book traces is the fear of incest, which, practiced collectively, allows for a way to imagine the relation between each and every household in the empire, all equals in the same position. The imagined community in premodern China has much to do with imagining other families, all assiduously avoiding endogamy.

—

The movement of people, as they join new households, divide up inheritances, and engage in trade, can hardly be separated from the circulation of objects. The chapters that follow explore these two models, of people as members of interlocking families and as participants in the exchange of objects, in a variety of different fictional texts. Constant flux marks both the families and the ownership of the objects. Any family unit is temporary, constantly being destroyed that it might be perpetuated. And with objects—exchanged, traded, bought, and sold—it is not so much their static ownership that is important as their motion across time and space.

Among other historians, Craig Clunas has analyzed the late Ming craze for collection and the rise of the cult of the antique (and the concomitant rise of the forgery). One collector, the belle-lettrist Lu Shusheng (1509–1605), writes about his love for inkstones. How can it be, he wonders, that even the opinions of authorities differ so on the best inkstones? He muses:

> Perhaps there is simply no fixed value for things, and their worth is to be decided only through the mouths of literati? In that case, how can anyone know whether those in my collection are superb, or not? If, in my hobby of collecting inkslabs, I'll take nothing but the very best ones, then among rare antiques in the world, aren't there a myriad things other than inkslabs? As for rare antiques, men in power can surely acquire them, but often they have to snatch them from the possession of others.[19]

Lu Shusheng rejects all notion of gentlemanly collectors of rarefied objects whose hobby allows them to escape the dusty struggles of the world. Instead, in the picture he paints, ownership of material possession is always tenuous, subject to the desires of others, whether those who determine value or those who determine ownership. Even more than inkstones, it is value that circulates: created by some, desired by all, seized by a few. The inkstones provide an arena for connection and competition among people.

Chuanqi titles suggest that one might read the plays in this context, of objects that are the center of competing desires. The plays feature not only the travels of people but also those of their objects, which must pass through the ownership of many before they find a final, proper resting place. These two interlocking sets of journeys can invite a form of mapping. Many *chuanqi* are named after the play's emblematic object, and in some sense plays trace the tokens' movements, as they circulate through various economies—whether powered by lust for sex, for profit, or for vengeance. For example, Wang Jide's *Tihong ji* (Written on red; ~1623) hinges upon a maple leaf with a poem written on it that travels between lovers; Gao Lian's *Yuzan ji* (Story of the jade hairpin; ~1575) tells of how an engaged couple—and their engagement gifts, a jade hairpin and a fan pendant—are reunited.

In *Yipeng xue* (A handful of snow; ~1640), Li Xuanyu introduces an object much like Lu Shusheng's inkstones, whose ownership invites violence and even murder. The eponymous "handful of snow" is a priceless antique cup owned by the cultured, aristocratic Mo Huaigu. Yan Song, son of the real-life corrupt prime minister Yan Shifan, catches wind of this treasure and makes plans to seize it. Instead of giving it up, though, Mo Huaigu secretly has a copy made and turns it over to Yan Shifan instead of the original. When Yan Shifan finds out, he authorizes a search of Mo's property; a loyal steward is able to sneak the cup out, and Mo Huaigu, his concubine, and the steward all flee to the protection of a friend stationed on the frontier. They are followed, and Yan Shifan authorizes Mo Huaigu's beheading and the exile of all his family. But the same loyal steward takes his master's place and is decapitated in his stead. Later, Mo Huaigu's only son survives because his own manservant takes his place in going into exile. In other words, this play revolves around substitutions, sacrifices, and trades: a fake antique that passes for a real one; a steward who dies for his master, who in turn is said to have died for the sake of the cup; another servant who takes the name of the family's single heir.

The cup is simply an outward manifestation of value that circulates; in this play, people and objects are alarmingly fungible. As

Appadurai writes, "commodities, by virtues of their exchange destinies and mutual commensurability, tend to dissolve the links between persons and things."[20] The play revolves around two scales of value, two precious invaluable objects whose continuity and existence are threatened, both characterized by extreme singularity: the antique cup, passed down within the Mo family for countless generations, and the aristocratic family itself, dwindled to the only son Mo Huaigu and his only son Mo Hao. And yet, although substitutes ultimately cannot be found for either of these and all the fakes are uncovered, both the cup (missing for much of the play) and the Mo lineage (whose last heir spends much of the play under a different surname) survive by investing their value elsewhere. As the anthropologist Igor Kopytoff suggests, biographies of things and those of people can never quite be sorted out properly; as we see with the cup and the Mo family, commodities dissolve the lines bounding people from things.[21]

In fact, the presence of these objects is absolutely critical to maintaining the human community, as becomes obvious when people circulate in the absence of objects. The belles-lettrist Ji Yun (1724–1805) suggests one reason that *chuanqi* so often revolve around things. In one anecdote from *Yuewei caotang biji* (Random jottings from the Cottage of Close Scrutiny), he tells of a real-life girl whose experiences closely resemble those of a character from a play. After the girl's dying parents sell her for the price of two coffins, she enters Ji Yun's grandfather's house as a servant. All that the little girl—renamed Liangui by the lady of the house—remembers of her origins is that she comes from Shandong; she cannot remember the name of her village or its county, only that it is near a postal route.[22] Finally, she knows she is betrothed to a neighbor boy named Hu and that his family, too, had to flee to avoid starvation.

Some years later, when she is married, her groom—whose last name is Liu—turns out to have been adopted from a family whose surname is Hu. And, moreover, he hails from Xintai, in Shandong, right on the postal route. In other words, his story is a perfect fit for Liangui's own, and the whole thing sounds as if comes right out of literature: "It seemed rather like the story of Princess Lechang's mirror, in which a couple was first separated and then reunited." Ji Yun regrets, though, that the union does not measure up to a literary one: "My late uncle Lifu said, 'With a little embellishment, this incident could be made into a *chuanqi*. Unfortunately, this girl was a stupid hick who only cared about eating and sleeping and would be unworthy of such embellishment. What a pity!'"

In other words, Liangui and her husband lack the signature object which would certainly have played an important role in a drama with the same plot. Ji Yun writes: "Hard evidence (*xianzheng*), however, was lacking." He refers specifically to *hard* evidence, that which manifests itself, here a material object to be used in exchange, like a mirror, a fan, or a painting. Where the real Princess Lechang was reunited with her husband because each carried half of a broken mirror, Liangui lacks such a token, leaving her and her husband as unmoored from their identities in marriage as they were before. Human beings, roaming around, joining and rejoining each other, are insufficient unto themselves in forming a society or even a play; without a token, Liangui is—in Ji Yun's own words—not too much more than an animal, interested only in the bodily functions of eating and sleep. The circulations of people must be accompanied by the movement of objects, which must have the capacity to circulate independently. Ji Yun is right that *chuanqi* dramas address these concerns: how a mirror, or a fan, or a painting can return to its rightful owner poses questions about the finitude of a population, how we are moored to our own identities, and whether humans have places where they properly belong.

—

In *Writing and Authority in Early China*, Mark Edward Lewis argues that China's great contribution to world history—the worldwide empire, managed by classically trained bureaucrats—was above all else a speech act, created by words. Rather than viewing texts as the means by which the empire perpetuated itself, Lewis argues, we might turn things around and see the empire as the means by which the texts perpetuated themselves. Lewis concerns himself with origins, but some of the critics of *Writing and Authority in Early China* ask whether the argument does not in fact apply better to a period later than that covered by most of the book. Lewis closes the book with a comment about the future of the civilization whose beginnings his book traces:

that the empire's textual double—on stage—continues to survive even now, long after the demise of its offstage counterpart.[23]

This introduction has centered on that staged empire. The rest of this book moves on to the imagined spaces and communities in short narrative and then concludes with the long novel. The book as a whole examines three different kinds of text, and not just the empire they create, but other communities and institutions as well. This is, in short, a book largely about genre. Different genres—operating simultaneously, often the product of the same pens—allow for radically different arguments about the nature of society. (I hasten to add that in no way are all major genres of late imperial literature represented here. Among others, I have omitted lyric, *tanci*, and all sectarian literature; even though I am concerned with the literary theme of comprehensiveness, this book in no way makes the same claim.) I have begun with the *chuanqi*, the most totalizing form of late imperial literature and the one inseparable to its core from the imperial system. In the chapters that follow, I turn to short and then to long fiction.

Of course, our understanding of genre may not perfectly coincide with that of the late imperial period. For example, the following chapters juxtapose discussions of various short classical narratives with their counterparts in the vernacular, although the classical tale was in many ways an entirely separate form. Even within short classical narratives there existed multiple internal divisions as well: the more fictional *chuanqi* set against the less fictional *zhiguai*; long, complex narratives as opposed to short anecdotes. So even as this book turns on genre theory—which in itself was in many ways the centerpiece of late imperial literary criticism—I am myself guilty of sometimes muddying generic waters.

And a final stipulation: do not let these texts' sharing the same library shelf or the volumes of a single writer's oeuvre deceive you. To speak of genre seems to imply parallelism, but the three main forms I discuss in this book—*chuanqi*, short narrative, and long prose narrative—were not parallel forms of expression; instead, as scholarship makes increasingly clear, they occupied radically different positions within the culture. They varied wildly in the size of their readership. For the late Ming and the first decades of the Qing, in urbanized Jiangnan especially, but in urban areas elsewhere as well, *chuanqi* dominated cultural life in a virtually unprecedented way, with arias and plots part of the texture of life, not just for the elite, but for anyone with pretensions to literacy—and even some without. The status of these genres was reflected in their positions vis-à-vis the literary market: *huaben* were intended for sale; *chuanqi*, not; some long novels were, and others decidedly not. *Chuanqi* were written under the playwrights' own name; fiction, under a pseudonym. The texts I discuss even differed in their relationship to the law (the novels were almost always banned).

Despite these differences, the critic Fredric Jameson's point holds equally true for all three: "Genres are essentially literary *institutions*, or social contracts between a writer and a specific public, whose function is to specify the proper use of a particular cultural artifact."[24] So much of the literary output of the late imperial period, and especially that of the late Ming, took place in the form of literary criticism, especially in collating, anthologizing, and editing earlier works. Literary criticism—and especially genre theory—could approach policing, with constant re-evaluations of the borders and careful scrutiny of the interiors to make sure that unworthy specimens had not infiltrated. One might even say that genres were constantly in the process of being created and recreated.[25]

In other words, I fully recognize that what follows is necessarily a simplification, a still photograph of the always dynamic process through which individual texts inhabit a genre. In each of the chapters that follows, individual texts sometimes chafe against generic constraints. Nonetheless, as a whole, these different genres invite radically different ways of conceiving the polity. The connections that structure *chuanqi* are deeply problematized in fiction, both short and long, and these are the subject of this book. When Ji Yun—in his *zhiguai* writings—reflects on how the real world differs from the world of *chuanqi*, this is a comment on his own chosen genre of *zhiguai* and even prose narrative more broadly.

In another anecdote, he tells of a married couple, driven apart by circumstance. Mr. Li's mother falls ill after her son has been married for only one month; the young bride and groom care for her solicitously until her death seven or eight months later. After her death, they obey the demands of ritual and do not share a bed for three years. Once the period of mourning concludes, husband and wife are driven by poverty to turn to her family, where the house is so cramped that the couple cannot share a room, and the wife sleeps with her mother. Finally, her brother takes the family to Jiangxi in an effort to make his fortune; Mr. Li plans on rejoining his wife at a later occasion but then receives word that his wife has died.

He gets a job as a scribe for a bandit with island headquarters. There, he frequently sees one of his boss's concubines, who bears an astonishing resemblance to his own dead wife. Actually, it turns out that on the way to Jiangxi, the family had been waylaid by bandits and his wife kidnapped. To hide the shameful matter, her family then bought a cheap coffin and sent it home empty. In other words, she is alive—and is in fact the woman who so resembles his dead wife. These two gaze at each other longingly, but neither has any idea of the other's true identity. After six or seven years, government troops approach. In hiding, Mr. Li sees the bandit chief's concubines dragged off, weeping and trembling. Once he makes his way home, Mr. Li decides to buy a better coffin for his wife with the proceeds of his work for the bandit chief, but first he insists upon seeing the bones of his dead wife. His wife's uncle is forced to confess the deception, and, heartbroken, Mr. Li realizes that the woman on the island must have been his wife. Despite all his efforts, he cannot track her down. He never remarries, and eventually he becomes a Buddhist monk.

As is always the case with Ji Yun's writing, one cannot tell the extent to which the events described are fictional, but here he goes out of his way to make this account into a literary matter, as if life were an opera except for its lack of songs: "This matter could really be made into a *chuanqi*. It's too bad that there's no conclusion at the end, but it's really the peer of *Taohua shan* [the seventeenth-century romance]. Though we never see the songs, [the rest]—the mountains and greenery on the river, the constant tenderness in the midst of unending lakes—it really can't help but increase one's sadness."[26]

Scholars from multiple disciplines have observed that the imperial state—lacking a modern infrastructure, with a staff that was minuscule—was nonetheless able, in an almost unparalleled way, to penetrate fully all layers of lived culture, making it almost impossible to conceive of alternative cosmologies, much less political organizations. In this chapter, we have seen how this is the case with the long southern drama, whose very form argues the central tenets of the neo-Confucian state. In these plays, the domestic and the political are one, and both imperial state and family are utterly natural. The course of the play involves the repair of both; neither can be fixed without the other.

The relationship between the state and other forms of human community is much more complicated in the other texts I address in the chapters after this. In short and long fiction, the human community's relationship to the state is neither natural nor immune from interrogation. For that matter, the human community itself often appears contorted and estranged from itself. The narratives in the chapters that follow treat superficially unusual situations that do not reflect the reality of late imperial life—perfect doubles who are strangers, accidental incestuous encounters, improbable family reunions. These hypothetical situations are a kind of seam in the faith that a family and the state are fundamentally at unity, a place where the two have obviously and perhaps clumsily been joined. In other words, the absence to which Ji Yun elliptically refers—that renders a reunion imperfect, that makes a round-trip journey different from simply staying still, that in short distinguishes fiction from the *chuanqi* drama—is much of the subject of this book.

TWO

The Geography of Exchange

The following four chapters treat short narratives—some in classical, but most in vernacular Chinese—and how these stories delineate the borders of the human community. Sometimes these concerns take relatively obvious forms. For example, a number of the tales in Pu Songling's late seventeenth-century *Liaozhai zhiyi* (Stories of the strange from Make-Do Studio) set up situations that resemble thought problems to test the precise limits of the community of people and its place with regard both to the natural order and to the supernatural order. Can a ghost bring a suit against a human? Can humans marry ghosts and foxes? Questions about the borders of the human community have obvious, political relevance, particularly at a time when the Manchus were reinventing the empire. In a world in which the Qing legal code expanded to cover numerous, far-off jurisdictions, it does not seem ridiculous for a woman to seek redress from human courts after a tiger devours her son.

In vernacular stories, those questions are posed from a different angle. So often the focus in these texts is on the resolution of a superficially gift-like, reciprocal exchange. Other than gifts, these "replacements" include, among others, round-trip journeys (in which travelers return to their starting point); family reunions (which bring a separated family together again, sometimes with its original members, but sometimes not); and wife-swappings (which reunite husbands with their original spouses). Since the conclusion often recapitulates the status of the beginning, how is what has happened different from nothing having happened at all?

In the 1925 *Essai sur le don* (translated in English as *The Gift*), the anthropologist and social theorist Marcel Mauss famously wondered what a gift exchange was. He posed a similar question to the one I have just asked of the late imperial short story: if a person gives away one object as a gift and then later receives a similar object as another gift, perhaps even from the original recipient, what, if anything, has changed? How, if at all, does what has happened—two matching transactions, one that gives and one that receives—differ from no transaction at all?

Mauss's answer sets gift-giving apart from other transactions because gifts call into question not just ownership, but all the other ways in which persons interact with commodities:

> One could say that it [the gift in premodern societies] partakes of all kinds of legal principles that we, more modern, have carefully isolated from one another. It is ownership and possession, a pledge and something hired out, a thing sold and bought, and at the same time deposited, mandated, and bequeathed in order to be passed on to another. For it is only given you on condition that you make use of it for another or pass it on to a third person, the "distant partner."[1]

Gift-giving and gift-receiving, in other words, enhance solidarity, and what seems initially like nothingness itself, the giving of one thing and the receiving of another, forces a general re-evaluation first of the world of things—of what it is to own something—and also of the world of people—of what it is that sets us apart from others, but also ties us to others.

Mauss provides another opening as well. Chinese literature of this period deals in enormously sophisticated ways with dyadic relationships, the ties between two people, forged either by voluntary exchange or by involuntary obligation. How is that relationship to be extended to a third party, what Mauss calls a "distant partner"? Or beyond that, how is the relationship to involve many more, whether a small community or the infinite host of the empire? The vernacular short story, and the classical tale as well, closely scrutinize these matters.

By the late Ming, travel had become increasingly central in the cultural imagination. Books of route maps, travel essays, and geographical speculations all circulated widely. Many of them reflected a mercantile attitude to geography, meaning that travel was perceived as a means to earn money. This chapter concerns a number of fictional seventeenth-century journeys, all of them from *huaben*, or vernacular short stories. Some of these journeys—undertaken mostly by traders, usually in pursuit of profit—are considerable in length, and all of them feature a high degree of geographical specificity. All the protagonists leave and return, inscribing a loop on the map. (In an age when travel was considerably more dangerous than in our own, the return was by no means a foregone conclusion. The historical record is full of merchants who leave but never return.)

To what extent are these journeys real? Or, to pose the question slightly differently, what would a late Ming reader have known about geography, and how would that reader have conceived of the relation between two locations in space? To what extent would such a reader have understood one journey as fantastical and another as realistic? I suspect that some readers might have been able to plot the characters' journeys on a mental route map; others might even have had a fairly good sense of the relation of each province to the others. The real-life version of one of these fictional traders might have carried a Wanli-era route book something like *Shangcheng yilan* (Merchant routes at a glance). The opening page of the first *juan* showing how locations are connected to one another indicates one way a contemporary traveler or a reader might imagine the connections between locations (see Fig. 1).

The abundance of route books suggests that readers of the *Sanyan* (Feng Menglong's *Three Words*, the three anthologies of *huaben* dating from the 1620s, which reimagined the genre) would have had fairly detailed knowledge about their own region, the lower Yangzi river delta. Whereas route books presented a single route to connect most locales, in the lower Yangzi delta, a potential traveler could choose from among many different paths and shortcuts, suggesting a sophisticated spatial understanding. In other words, a relatively

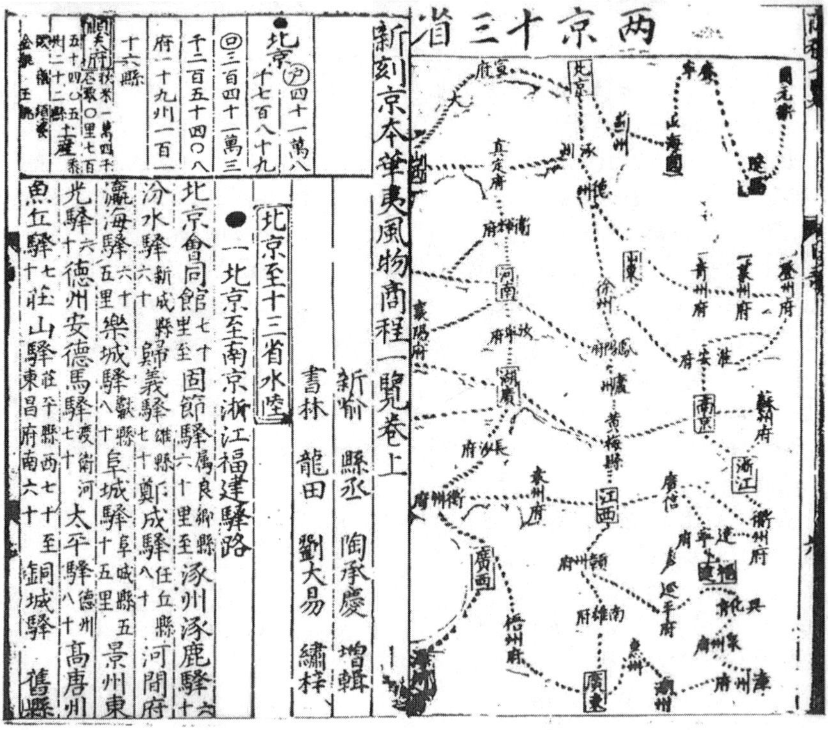

Fig. 1 Wanli-era map of routes connecting major points in the Ming empire, from the merchant handbook, *Shangcheng yilan* (Merchant routes at a glance).

well-to-do resident of Suzhou would probably have known not just the distance to Hangzhou, but even its approximate location, and how far beyond that one would have to travel to reach lesser towns such as Chun'an and Xinghua. Readers' knowledge of farther-flung locations, like Hepu district, the most distant locale in "The Pearl-Sewn Shirt," was probably much more tenuous.

In this chapter, I treat the journeys literally—in the sense that I map them and try to imagine them as they might have been traveled—but there is no question but that these journeys are intrinsically fictive. They do not resemble contemporary records of real-life journeys; instead, they reflect on the *idea* of travel (hence, the reasonableness of depicting the journeys as impossible straight lines). The *huaben* spaces I treat are not figured in such a way as to highlight regional differences (whether of culture, or of consumer goods, or even of tourist sights). Local color is decidedly not the point; instead, these texts, though deeply engaged with space and distance, treat them as abstractions.

In *Atlas of the European Novel*, Franco Moretti proposes an equally abstract political reading of geography: "The novel functions as the symbolic form of the nation-state . . . and it's a form that (unlike an anthem, or a monument) not only does not conceal the nation's internal divisions, *but manages to turn them into a story*."[2] According to Moretti, Jane Austen's novels, for example, represent a breakthrough. Instead of conceiving of distance as absolute—with a loved one who is Here, or Away, as he puts it—Austen's heroines discover concrete, relative distance.[3] Moretti sees these distances in fiction, which mark the world of the landowners from that of the bourgeois, or that of the city from that of the country, as an important way in which the nation was imagined.

The primary focus in these Chinese stories is not with the nation, but instead with another sort of community, created first and most obviously by circulations of goods and of people, but also by circulations of karma. With their tight narrative construction, *huaben* constantly contend with the question of whether economies of money or populations of people can admit new value or new members. Readers of *huaben* know that a stranger met on a journey always turns out to be someone familiar, whether a relative or another close connection; an item picked up in travels always turns out to be either one's own possession or otherwise of karmic importance. The story's end involves the tying up of all threads. We might consider *huaben* to pose questions at the heart of social thought: Can new value be introduced, or old value disappear? Or, one might ask, is the human community essentially open or closed? *Huaben* suggest that these kinds of questions—economic, political, literary, anthropological—are actually one and the same.

In reading these vernacular stories, we are intruding on a complicated conversation. Partly, it concerns retribution (or compensation), one of the most important themes of the late Ming. Wilt Idema has written of how the theme of compensation shapes narrative at its most basic level, first by imposing a temporal sequence, but also by inserting an internal calculus that determines how we interpret every action. As Idema puts it, "Heaven is not anymore an inscrutable power that arbitrarily destroys and saves but is now described as an impersonal, automatically operating abacus."[4] If such are the workings of existence itself, then the primary task of these short narratives—especially when they concern businessmen and their accounts—must be to show how it is that things come out even. *Huaben* themes venture closely to various means of record-keeping, sometimes through examining the fairness of a set of transactions or by showing how—to choose two of the themes explored by this book—the family reunion and the round-trip journey might perfectly restore balance.

—

To a traveling merchant, a landscape might appear to be a series of obstacles to traverse, preferably as quickly and safely as possible.[5] A merchant earned money by transporting goods across what was potentially a treacherous and certainly a tedious distance. In other words, distance might figure as value, so that one might map out any journey with distance measured not in *li*, but in value added. In *Guangzhi yi* (Notes on the Guang region), a geography of the southern reaches of the empire based on its author's real-life travels in the late years of the Wanli reign, the official and belle-lettrist Wang Shixing describes the metal trade in the far southwest. He writes: "The resources of Dian [present-day Yunnan] include copper and tin. There one *liang* of copper costs only thirty cash, whereas in other provinces it is worth two or three times that."[6] The merchant is the middleman, and if he can get the metal from Dian, he will have earned the price differential. Or we might map the distance from Yunnan to Wuling in Guangxi Province as the 300 percent markup in the prices of copper and tin.

There are perfectly sound reasons that a *liang* of tin costs so little in one place and so much more in another. Wang Shixing goes on to explain what a merchant must do to transport that metal from Dian to Wuling: "From Dian to Zhengyuan there are more than twenty stations in all, through each of which everything has to be carried on the backs of either people or horses. From Zhengyuan, one can take a boat down the Yuan River; to get to Wuling there are another twenty stations." Wang explains that the river curves so much that the land journey is less than a third the length of the journey on water: "So when officials take a boat, they often get off at Chengxi; but merchants laden with heavy goods can't abandon their boats—but, then, what with the shoals, rocks, and hazards they fear that their boats will sink." On water, as a merchant burdened with tin and copper must travel, the journey to Wuling takes at least a month. Distance is shorthand for visualizing the hazards of such a venture.

Perhaps this is why late imperial writers suggest a parallel between the careful accumulation of a fortune through prudent thrift and the plodding journeys of a traveling trader. In the thirty-fifth story of *Xingshi hengyan* (Constant words to awaken the world; 1627), "Old Retainer Xu Saves the Family out of Righteous Indignation" (a title Patrick Hanan abbreviates as "Old Retainer"), journeying is virtually synonymous with profit. The anonymous author, whom Hanan calls Langxian, makes such trading the métier of the morally impeccable servant Xu Aji. The story of Aji, told by many late imperial writers,[7] has usually been studied for its take on loyalty and servitude; as a trader, Aji accumulates a significant fortune but keeps none of it, turning over every cent to an ungrateful mistress. However, my focus is on the short portion of this story that recounts how Aji makes his fortune.

After the youngest brother of a wealthy family dies, his two older brothers conspire to split the estate, lest they be forced to contribute to the upkeep of the youngest brother's widow and his children. The two older brothers take the best fields, the horse, and the cow, leaving the youngest brother's family the worst fields and the elderly slave Aji and his wife (whom the elder brothers regard as worth less than the two beasts of burden).

Aji resolves to secure the livelihood of his mistress, Ms Yan, and her children. She sells her few ornaments and hands him twelve taels of silver, and with that modest sum he sets off from their home in a village called Jinsha in Zhejiang province. After a little consideration, he heads to nearby Mt. Qingyun, where he buys some lacquer; from there he goes to the mouth of the Xin'an River and takes a boat not to Hangzhou but further on to Suzhou, in hopes of making a larger profit. Suzhou happens to be experiencing a shortage of lacquer. After reaping a healthy profit, he invests in the grain that Suzhou is awash in; heading from there to Hangzhou—which is suffering from drought—he sells his rice and discovers that lacquer actually turns out to be pricier here than in Suzhou. Since all the lacquer dealers had assumed that they would get a better price in far-off Suzhou, scarcity has driven prices up precipitously in Hangzhou. Aji makes a quick journey to Mt. Qingyun for more lacquer and returns to Hangzhou.

From there he goes back to Mt. Qingyun, leaving some of his profits there as a surety for one of his middlemen before hurrying home to update his mistress on his progress. After that, he quickly returns to Mt. Qingyun to collect his money and to buy more lacquer, which he then sells in Xinghua, a more distant destination than Suzhou or Hangzhou, and consequently one where lacquer is selling for higher prices. Xinghua also happens to be experiencing a surplus of grain, and Aji takes the grain he buys there and sells it in Hangzhou where there is still a grain shortage. From there, he once again goes back to Mt. Qingyun to buy more lacquer. By now, having profited from each journey, he possesses 2,000-odd taels of silver, and, bringing back these hard-won proceeds by boat and on horseback, Aji returns home with the silver that will guarantee the future of his mistress's family.

On the map, Aji's journeys are clearly fairly tight circuits. (See Map 1.) Any success is made to seem the result of industry, rather than of destiny. At no point in his trading does Aji realize a fantastic profit. Instead, he manages to double his capital after selling all his lacquer, and then after buying sixty loads of rice, he makes a profit of 20 percent. The relatively modest profits are reflected in the distances Xu Aji travels; his longest journey, from Mt. Qingyun to Xinghua, located near Yangzhou, is still a little under 400 kilometers. (In fact, these distances are so small that Xu Aji's travels cannot be mapped legibly at the same scale as the other journeys described in this chapter, as we can see in Map 2.) Even though under Ming conditions, such journeys could not have been easy ones for

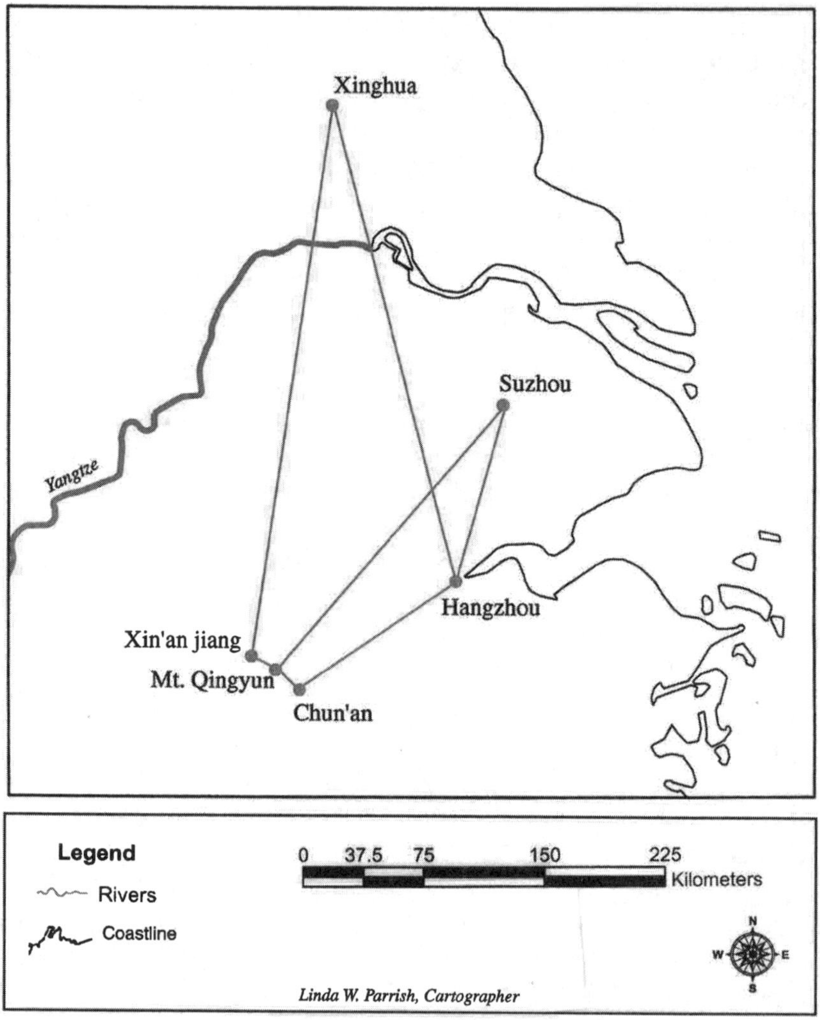

Map 1 Xu Aji's travels in *Xingshi hengyan* 35

the sixty-year-old Aji, the areas through which he passes were among the best developed in imperial China. A 1570 route book published by the Huizhou merchant Huang Bian describes how someone could cover much of the terrain Aji does, traveling from Yangzhou all the way to the border between Zhejiang and Nanzhili quickly, easily, and cheaply.[8]

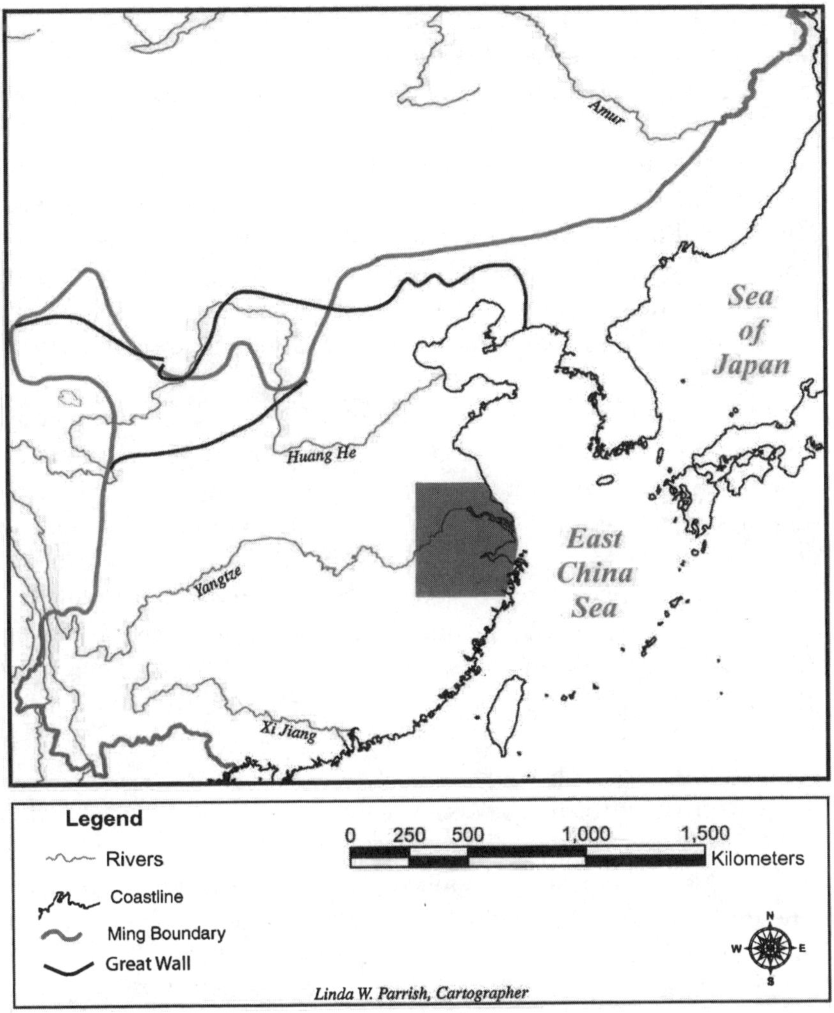

Map 2 Xu Aji's travels

Only the sheer number of his journeys, each with a modest but healthy profit, interest compounded on interest, makes his fortune. Aji is remarkable only for his exceptional industry. He deals in only two commodities, grain and lacquer, but other commodities are circulated in similar ways. He buys what is abundant in one locale and then travels to another where it is lacking. Aji himself, and other merchants working simultaneously alongside him, actually create the closed circuits we see on the map. On one journey, he decides to go to nearby Hangzhou instead of far-off Suzhou because he has heard he will get a better price in Hangzhou for his lacquer; however, once there, he is unable to buy goods to sell for the return trip. His old philosophy—distance and value correspond—is confirmed: "Next time I'll still choose the far-off place."[9] Since Aji's success depends on a faith that what is overabundant in one locale *must* be lacking elsewhere and then on his selection of a location with complementary supplies, Aji can travel only along the discrete, closed loops we see on the map.

After Aji turns over the proceeds from his travels to his mistress, she uses the silver to buy the estate of a wastrel gambler. The gambler wants to sell his lands for 3,000 taels of silver, but since even the wealthiest local families do not have so much liquidity, he ends up settling for the 2,000 that Aji has earned in the course of his travels. It is no coincidence that the plodding trader supplants the gambler. These two have based their economic life on two opposing but complementary principles, both of which are grounded on the behavior of others. Whereas Aji seems to take as an article of faith that a surplus in one place necessarily implies a lack elsewhere, the gambler's behavior seems to indicate quite another *credo*. A few decades later, Li Yu opens the eighth story of *Wusheng xi* (Silent operas; 1654) with a discussion of the illogical behavior of gamblers, each of whom behaves as if he were firmly convinced that he will hit the jackpot, and none of whom sees the obvious truth that all the others believe the same thing—but only one of them can be correct. There is only a finite amount of money, and each one can win only if the others lose. How, Li Yu wonders, can anyone think that different rules will govern everyone else? He asks: "The world's money all ends up someplace (*zhaoluo* 著落). If it doesn't end up here, then it's there. If you say that neither side gets it, could it be that a ghost made off with it?"[10] How can a gambler believe that he alone will defy this implacable logic and that he alone will beat the house? Gamblers are solipsist antitravelers; the *zhaoluo* of money will fall on them, they believe, without their having to travel for it. Working in concert, merchants, by contrast, can all make money.

It should be pointed out that once opened, the loop that Aji creates resists closure. After all, why should Aji not continue his journeying infinitely and so increase his mistress's wealth infinitely? The story must provide an answer to this question, lest the increasingly aged Aji continue traveling forever:

> I am an old man traveling alone, carrying so much money. But that's not the important point. If there is a crash, then all my work will be for naught. Plus, the year comes to an end, and everyone at home must be wondering where I am. I might as well go home and negotiate a good price to buy some land to be our capital (*genben* 根本). Then we can take the rest out to do business.[11]

No matter how cautious Aji has been, trading is still a more risky business than farming. Aji travels to trade staple commodities like grain and lacquer; he cashes out to pursue the even more fundamental enterprise (*benye* 本業) of agriculture. In this way, he contrasts again with the gambler whose land Ms Yan purchases. If gamblers are anti-merchants, they are even more fundamentally anti-farmers in their belief that money will emerge from their stationary positions—not by creating wealth, as agriculturalists do, but by taking someone else's. Having earned his fill, Aji settles down back at home, no permanent networks of exchange having been created by his journeys, and no place fundamentally different from any others.

—

But what if elsewhere really is fundamentally different, in a way that goes beyond a temporary shortage of grain or lacquer? If we measure distance as profit, then the greater the distance, the greater the possibility for profit. Aji's unexceptional journeys—taking place within the confines of Jiangnan—realize a modest but substantial estate of 3,000 taels of silver. What about a journey to an infinitely distant location? What would such a journey to an almost unimaginably distant location do to value? For truly great differences, one might imagine the profit as infinite, so that what is worthless at home might elsewhere be a priceless jewel, and vice versa. The rare trader who could navigate such distances could achieve immeasurable wealth. Crossing the borders of the immense empire, in other words, intimates the possibility not only of a boundless world but also of one in which all goods—no matter how seemingly insignificant, not just rice and lacquer—could come to signify riches.

Economic wish fulfillment that depends on the foreign and exotic animates the first story of the collection *Paian jingqi* (Slapping the table in amazement; 1628), whose title Hanan translates as "The Tangerines and the Tortoiseshell." The author, Ling Mengchu, writes of a business failure named Wen Shi, who is asked by a friend to come along on an overseas voyage. As they prepare for the journey, all the other crewmen bustle about buying things that they can sell when they reach faraway parts, but Wen Shi spends his only tael of silver—a charitable gift from the rest of the crew—on an enormous quantity of cheap tangerines. He plans to share them with his shipmates as a treat for their kindness.

These men are so eager to go abroad because enormous profits await those who venture abroad, as the narrator explains:

> Now it seems that when goods from China were brought here, you could sell them at three times cost. If you then traded for goods native to here, the same was true when you brought them back to China. With one round-trip, it might be that you'd get eight or nine times interest—so everyone did their best to take this route.[12]

A similar loop allows Aji to make his mistress a wealthy woman, but this time there is no perspicacity or even diligence involved. Instead, it is crossing over and returning itself that gives rise to profit. Naturally, the hardships of such a journey are entirely elided. If Wang Shixing writes of arduous portages and treacherous rapids and Langxian writes of mundane matters like Aji's need for raingear and good shoes, Ling Mengchu's sailors are practically teleported to a land of fantastic profit.

When Wang Shixing describes the passage of the metal ore, space is perfectly continuous, measured by one official station after another ("the waters then pass through the stations of Yingkou, Zhuzhan, Qianyang, Hongjiang, Anjiang, Tongwan, and Jiangkou"). If the traders stopped halfway, one guesses, the value of the ore would have increased in precise proportion. In contrast, in Wen Shi's world, distance is discontinuous, with a radical break marking the difference between two locations, one here—which can be mapped—and one over *there*—which cannot. This radical discontinuity almost figures a linguistic difference, with the mediation between two systems of value a displaced translation.

When they stop at an island-nation, Wen Shi brings his tangerines out. None of the natives has ever seen such an exotic fruit, and what is so common at home is snatched up as if it were a great treasure. What is even better is the peculiar currency of the kingdom of Jiling: all their coins are of the same weight in silver, but are differentiated in value from one another because of their stamps (dragons, animals, trees, and, for the least valuable coins, water plants). Chinese coins, in contrast, are bronze. (Silver in the Ming dynasty was never coined and was instead valued strictly by weight: a tael of silver signifies that unit of weight.)

Since he is Chinese, Wen Shi naturally wants to charge by weight (to be exact, the enormous sum of one *qian*, or one-tenth of a tael, for a single tangerine). Both parties are delighted; Wen Shi because of the profit he is making, and the natives of Jiling because as far as they are concerned they too are making out like bandits:

> Just now, all those who had bought tangerines had used the water plant coins, thinking that they'd bought this fine thing with lesser quality money, so they were all satisfied. Just like Chinese people, they were happy to have derived this small profit.[13]

This fantasy, familiar from European history, involves a new world with gold-paved streets and natives eager to trade for worthless baubles, but here it takes a considerably more innocuous form, since the story insists that both parties profit through the exchange. Far from being absolute, Chinese values—that the tangerines are essentially worthless, and silver is valued according to its weight—are not even given priority. Cultural translation and monetary exchange are figured so similarly here that Ling Mengchu's insistence on equity allows us to surmise that in the age's great fiscal policy debate, Ling must have been a cartalist rather than a metalist; even the gold standard of value, silver, does not possess value in and of itself but instead derives its value from authority and cultural context.

As the supplies of fruit dwindle, the customers begin paying more. Wen Shi asks his customers to pay him not with one of their coins of large denomination, but instead with many coins marked with water plants. Within the borders, if we conceive of all as belonging to an organic unity, gain for one can only spell loss for another (most gamblers lose, so that a few can win, and lacquer that is overabundant in one place is lacking in another). But across borders where value itself is defined differently, the zero-sum game no longer holds and both parties might profit.

Wen Shi is flooded with silver; returning to the ship, he weighs one of the thousand coins he ends up with; it turns out to be eight *qian* and seven *fen*. We were told earlier that one tael's worth of goods taken abroad would earn "eight or nine times interest"; can it be coincidental that the tangerines he means to sell for one *qian* earn him between eight and nine times that amount? Wen Shi's profits far outstrip that initial prediction. The bushel of tangerines bought for one tael have earned him 870 or so taels.

And his good luck has just begun. After they set off to sea, the ship runs into a huge storm and is forced to seek refuge at a small, uninhabited island. Everyone else stays on board, but Wen Shi decides to explore. On top of a hill, he finds an enormous turtle shell, big as a bed. He has no idea what he will do with it, but he lugs it back nonetheless. When the ship returns to China, a Persian trader evaluates all the goods brought back by the traders. Focusing his attention on the shell that Wen Shi thought might merely be a curiosity, he offers Wen Shi the unbelievable sum of 50,000 taels of silver for it. Ecstatic, Wen Shi agrees, wondering why anyone would want to pay such money for the oddity. After the deal is sealed, the trader explains that the turtle shell was shed by a larval dragon, but only after twenty-four ribs were fully formed, with one enormous, luminous pearl inside each. The Persian intends to bring the pearls back to his own country, where each pearl will bring the price he paid for the entire shell.

This transaction differs from the one involving the tangerines in that its model is not translation; the Persian trader, the narrator is careful to tell us, has lived in China for so long that in clothes and behavior he is indistinguishable from someone Chinese, and the trader's perfect Chinese carries over in other realms as well. The Persian and the Chinese share identical indices of value—to both men,

50,000 taels is a staggering price, but an entirely appropriate price for a gigantic, glow-in-the-dark pearl. The two sets of transactions that make Wen Shi's fortunes are perfectly symmetrical: this time he plays the part of the men of Jiling. From his perspective, he has profited handsomely—but the small advantage he derives is entirely dwarfed by the unfathomable riches the same shell brings the Persian.

Wen Shi pays nothing for the shell, and the Persian trader tells the Chinese traders that he will be selling the pearls for 1,200,000 taels of silver. But then the financial picture grows murky. The Persian showers not just Wen Shi but all of his shipmates with largesse, gifts that are not part of the price of the shell: each is given two rolls of silk and a string of pearls, and Wen Shi himself is given eight rolls of silk and four strings of larger pearls. And even if we might calculate the value of those gifts, the Persian trader concludes by giving Wen Shi temporary use of his house. This deluge of gifts confuses any calculation of profit, suggesting instead a fountain of wealth emerging from this curiosity of a shell, found on a hillock. Truly, travel to other lands suggests infinitude, and not just in a geographical sense of an infinitely large world.

The tangerines speak of a dream exchange, a fantasy of cultural exchange, but the shell speaks of another sort of fantasy. Promised an astounding profit of eight or nine times, Wen Shi outdoes this prediction: instead, both he and the Persian trader have grown unimaginably wealthy from what was free for the taking on a hilltop. Something regarded by others as worthless has become instead the source of virtually infinite wealth.

Unlike Xu Aji's journeys—or those of the real-life merchants of whom Wang Shixing writes—Wen Shi's trip defies any mapping. As the Persian trader explains, no one knows where the infant dragon will next shed its shell; even if they could find out, the Chinese crew—blown serendipitously to the island during a storm—could not repeat their journey. Nor, I suggest, can we map the Kingdom of Jiling's position with regard to the Chinese heartland, to pin down forever the location where tangerines are such a rare treasure. If the empire were ever to expand to include the Kingdom of Jiling, tangerines would then be worth exactly what it cost to bring them from the south of China. It is only the impossibility of mapping Jiling that allows Wen Shi to become wealthy. In fact, one suspects that to Ling Mengchu, the Persian trader himself hails from a land so distant as to stand in for the unfathomably exotic, and even Persia would defy mapping.[14]

—

The first story in *Gujin xiaoshuo* (Stories old and new; 1620) by Feng Menglong, "Jiang Xingge Re-encounters His Pearl Shirt" (translated by Cyril Birch as "The Pearl-Sewn Shirt"), features a pair of traveling merchants. This most famous of all *huaben* exemplifies the genre's treatment of travel, karma, and profit—but also shows how these themes have deeper implications for how we think individuals ought to interact in a family, and in society at large.

Jiang Xingge and Chen Dalang are merchants who make their living by specializing in trade along a specific route; business is referred to repeatedly by one of its Ming names, *daolu* (道路, or literally "route"). Jiang Xingge's business takes him between unspecified locations in Guangdong and his own home in Zaoyang, near Xiangyang in Huguang province; Chen Dalang's takes him between Xiangyang and his hometown of Xin'an in Anhui province. In other words, one of the first things this story establishes is that these merchants—unlike Xu Aji, for example—regularly take long journeys that span many provinces. From Zaoyang to the provincial seat of Guangzhou, Jiang Xingge has to journey about a thousand kilometers, as the crow flies, and we will have reason to believe that he makes many stops and detours along the way. Chen Dalang's route between Xin'an and Xiangyang takes him—again, as the crow flies—about 700 kilometers, but when he stops to trade grain near Nanjing, his overall journey—taken twice a year we are told, once there and once back—stretches out to 900 kilometers. (It makes sense that the more prosperous Jiang Xingge has a slightly longer route and also deals in luxury items like pearls, tortoiseshell, and exotic woods.) A contemporary trader might easily imagine Jiang Xingge's and Chen Dalang's intersecting routes. (See Map 3 and Fig. 1.)

After a few years of blissfully happy marriage with his wife, Wang Sanqiao, Jiang Xingge must resume his travels. He entrusts her with

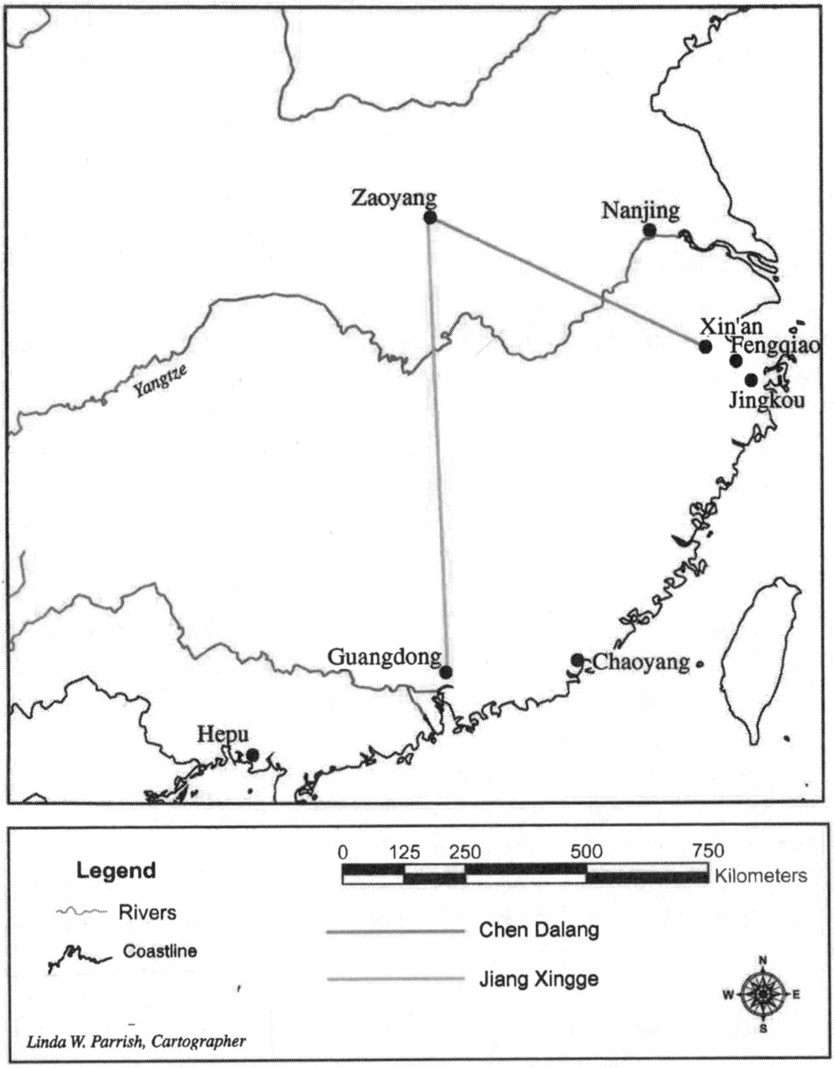

Map 3 Jiang Xingge's and Chen Dalang's routes

the pearl-sewn shirt, a family heirloom, and sets off for Guangdong, promising to return in a year. His young wife misses him dreadfully, and she consults a fortuneteller, who assures her that Jiang is on his way home already. In looking out for him, Sanqiao accidentally attracts the notice of another traveling merchant, Chen Dalang, who seduces her with the help of a go-between. When he in turn leaves on business, she sends him off with the pearl-sewn shirt as a love token. Chen Dalang stops in Fengqiao, where he befriends a fellow merchant, to whom he confesses everything about the love affair in which he is embroiled. That merchant turns out to be Jiang Xingge himself, traveling under a pseudonym and horrified to learn that his wife has taken a lover.

When he divorces her, he also wordlessly sends along the love tokens entrusted to him by Chen Dalang, a length of silk and a hairpin, broken by Xingge in a fit of rage. Sanqiao concludes that her husband means for her to commit suicide, but her mother saves her. Later, Sanqiao remarries and becomes the concubine of an official named Wu Jie on his way to an official posting.

Meanwhile, after his return home, Chen Dalang's peculiar behavior with regard to the pearl-sewn shirt arouses the suspicions of his own wife, Ms Ping; she hides the shirt from him, and after a big fight, he leaves home, heading back to Zaoyang. On the road he is robbed and arrives at Zaoyang penniless, only to discover that Sanqiao was divorced and married off again long ago. There, Chen Dalang falls ill but manages to send a letter home. By the time his wife reaches Zaoyang, he is already dead; after her servants rob and then desert her, she is penniless and stranded. To raise funds for Chen Dalang's funeral, she is forced to remarry. Her new husband is her dead husband's erstwhile rival, Jiang Xingge.

Once again, Jiang Xingge ventures out to do business; in Hepu, he is charged with murder after he is involved in a dispute over a pearl, over which an old man named Song dies. Coincidentally, Wu Jie has been promoted and is now the magistrate presiding over Jiang Xingge's case. Sanqiao pleads her former husband's case to her new husband; when Wu Jie sees how much Sanqiao and Jiang Xingge still care for each other, he allows the two to reunite. Finally, all three—Jiang Xingge; his senior wife, Ms Ping; and his now junior wife, Sanqiao—live happily ever after.

The events of this *huaben* span a large part of the entire settled space of the Ming empire, from the far east coast all the way into

Hepu, less than a hundred kilometers from the Annam border. All the major characters—Jiang Xingge, Chen Dalang, Ms Ping, Sanqiao, and Wu Jie—make major journeys that intersect with one another in multiple ways. (See Map 5.) Even if, like Aji, both Dalang and Xingge start off traveling simple circuits for the sake of making money, each continues journeying for other reasons. Jiang Xingge stops off in Suzhou to see the sights, and Chen Dalang, of course, returns to Xiangyang to see Sanqiao.

Characters run into each other, not in major metropoles, although locales like Nanjing and Suzhou do figure, but in relatively humble towns like Zaoyang, Fengqiao, and Hepu. These are not population centers but places for trading, precisely set up for the intersection of these paths: Hepu is where pearls are harvested and sold to the merchants who will take them eastward, and Fengqiao is "a gathering place for middlemen in the rice and firewood business."[15] These places allow for not one serendipitous meeting, but many. Xingge and Dalang become acquainted in Fengqiao; Ms Ping is married off to Xingge in Zaoyang; Xingge finds himself in trouble with the law in Hepu, where Sanqiao's new husband, Wu Jie, happens to be magistrate. All these locations participate in the exchange of goods and in the transfer of women from one family to another.

Just as one might map out the journeys of the major characters, one might also chart the movement of some important objects. The eponymous pearl-sewn shirt, for example, is entrusted to Sanqiao by Xingge; she then gives it to Chen Dalang, who in turn has it stolen by his wife Ms Ping, who then returns it to her new husband Xingge. Or one might instead chart the shirt's motion across space: from Zaoyang to Fengqiao near Suzhou to Xin'an, and then back again to Zaoyang. (See Map 4.) Or we might even conceive of the travels of the women as similar transferals of property; Sanqiao passes from Jiang Xingge's hands to Chen Dalang's to Wu Jie's and then back again to Jiang Xingge's. (In this sense, it is very significant that the go-between's business is referred to a number of times as *yahang*—she is as much a middleman as Jiang Xingge or Chen Dalang, though the commodity in question is not grain or pearls, but Sanqiao.)

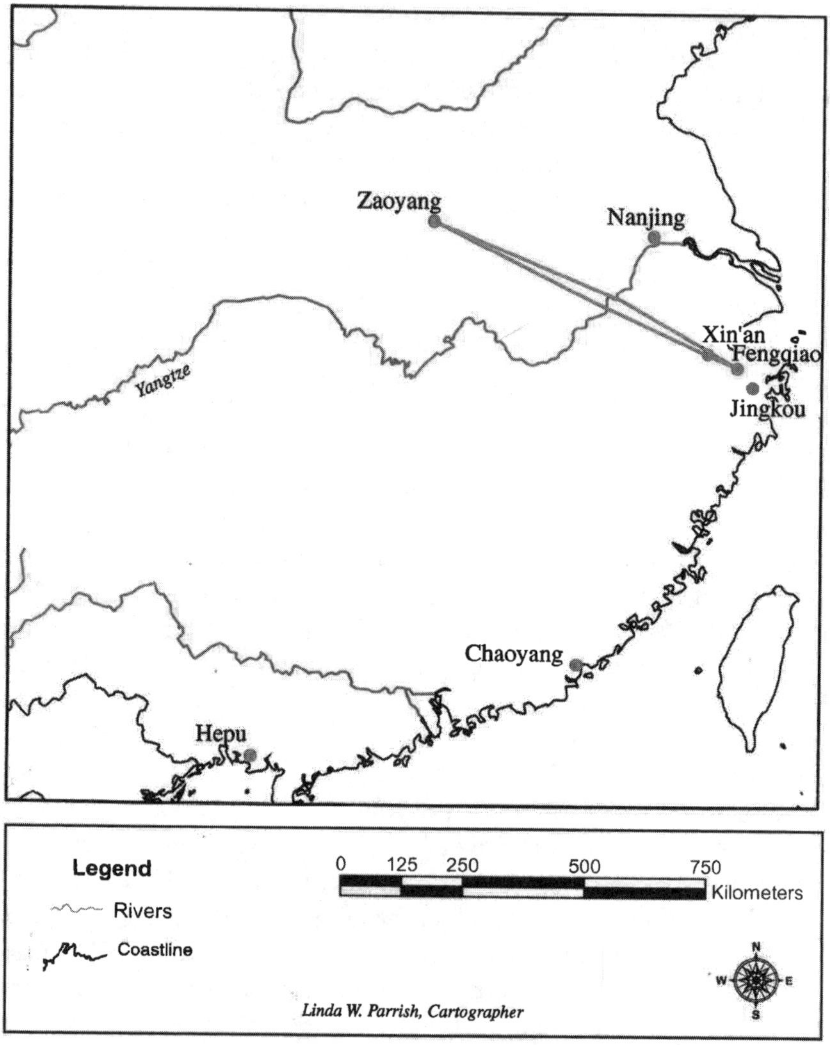

Map 4 The journey of the pearl-sewn shirt

We can even see how the sixteen trunks that hold Sanqiao's dowry might stand in for the woman herself, as they are passed from her parents to Jiang Xingge, back to her parents, then to Wu Jie, and finally back again to Jiang Xingge.

Sometimes we trace not a single, individual object but a category, most notably pearls. The pearl-sewn shirt, of course, is entrusted to

Sanqiao by Jiang Xingge and then given as a love token to Chen Dalang; but there are also the pearls the go-between Granny Xue shows to Sanqiao to entice her; and finally there is the pearl in Hepu, over which Jiang Xingge becomes involved in a fight. Just as much as people, pearls make their way through the empire. Our characters—Sanqiao included (her first interaction with Granny Xue reveals Sanqiao's eye for jewels)—are all middlemen, with commodities passing through their hands, as they and these goods circulate. What at first glance is a map of people moving throughout the empire turns out also to be a chart of pearls doing so—and also a suggestion that one might tell this story from the perspective not of the people but of the objects.

The pearl-sewn shirt itself—and to a lesser extent, the other pearls too—seem sacred objects, not perfectly alienable from the person with whom they are affiliated. Old Mr. Song dies over a pearl; and of the shirt itself, it hardly seems right to call Jiang Xingge the owner since he *cannot* dispose of it at will. Even if Xingge passes the shirt to his wife, who then gives it to her lover, the shirt itself is destined to find its way back to its proper place. (Like the karmic link between husband and wife, the connection between the shirt and Jiang Xingge cannot be severed, despite the intentions of Sanqiao and Chen Dalang.)

There is a mysterious economy of pearls in the story: over pearls, Xingge's wife is seduced; over a pearl-sewn shirt, Xingge loses his wife; over yet another pearl, Xingge regains his wife. Is the story's subject Jiang Xingge and Sanqiao or the circulation of pearls, mediated by humans? Mauss writes of similar exchanges, with objects that seem similarly imbued with agency. Among Native Americans in the Pacific Northwest, copper objects, according to Mauss, function much as pearls do in our *huaben*: they "have a power of attraction that is felt by other copper objects, just as wealth attracts wealth. . . . They are alive and move autonomously, and inspire other copper objects to do so."[16] (Accordingly, we can trace the travels of the Pearl-Sewn Shirt itself, as in Map 4.)

But there are other ways to ground the actions of the story as well. The journeys mesh with a surprisingly detailed timeline, not simply a sequence of events. In a seminal article on early *huaben* (those that circulated before the publication of the *Sanyan*), Hanan remarks on how carefully vernacular fiction marks time.[17] The events of the main story—from Jiang Xingge's departure from Zaoyang to his eventual reunion with Sanqiao in Hepu—take just about five and a half years. The author scrupulously lards the story with temporal hints, both relative and absolute: among many other details, in the second month, Xingge points at a flowering tree and promises that he will return again when the tree blossoms again; Dalang's seduction of Sanqiao takes place on the seventh day of the seventh month, *qiqiao*; by the time Dalang returns to Zaoyang, Sanqiao has been divorced for one year; at the very end, Sanqiao's husband Wu Jie almost gratuitously mentions the length of their marriage, three years. These events map out so neatly not because any absolute temporal positioning is important, but because what is being expressed here is simultaneity over distance. To read this story is to imagine men and women traveling throughout virtually the entire empire, exchanging goods and commodities with one another, with women joining, leaving, and then rejoining families as they move through space and time. (One can visualize this easily in Map 5.) It is a powerful vision of a human community, five individuals who are a miniaturized cosmos.

"The Pearl-Sewn Shirt" rewrites in vernacular Chinese a classical tale from 1612 by Song Maocheng, "Zhushan," which Hanan renders "The Pearl Vest." That earlier version of the story integrates the two concluding plots—Xingge's marriage to Ms Ping and his reunion with Sanqiao—considerably less intricately than Feng Menglong's version. Rather than weaving simultaneous plots together, Song Maocheng narrates first the reunion between husband and wife and only then concludes separately with what he treats as an incidental matter of hearsay: "The second wife of the Chu merchant [i.e., Jiang Xingge of "The Pearl-Sewn Shirt"] was none other than this Xin'an man's wife [i.e., Chen Dalang]."[18] In the vernacular version, the perfect aptness of the story's resolution is not afterthought, but instead front and center: Chen Dalang, who took someone else's wife, now has his widow marry someone else, and Jiang Xingge, who had his wife taken, is returned his own and takes Chen Dalang's.

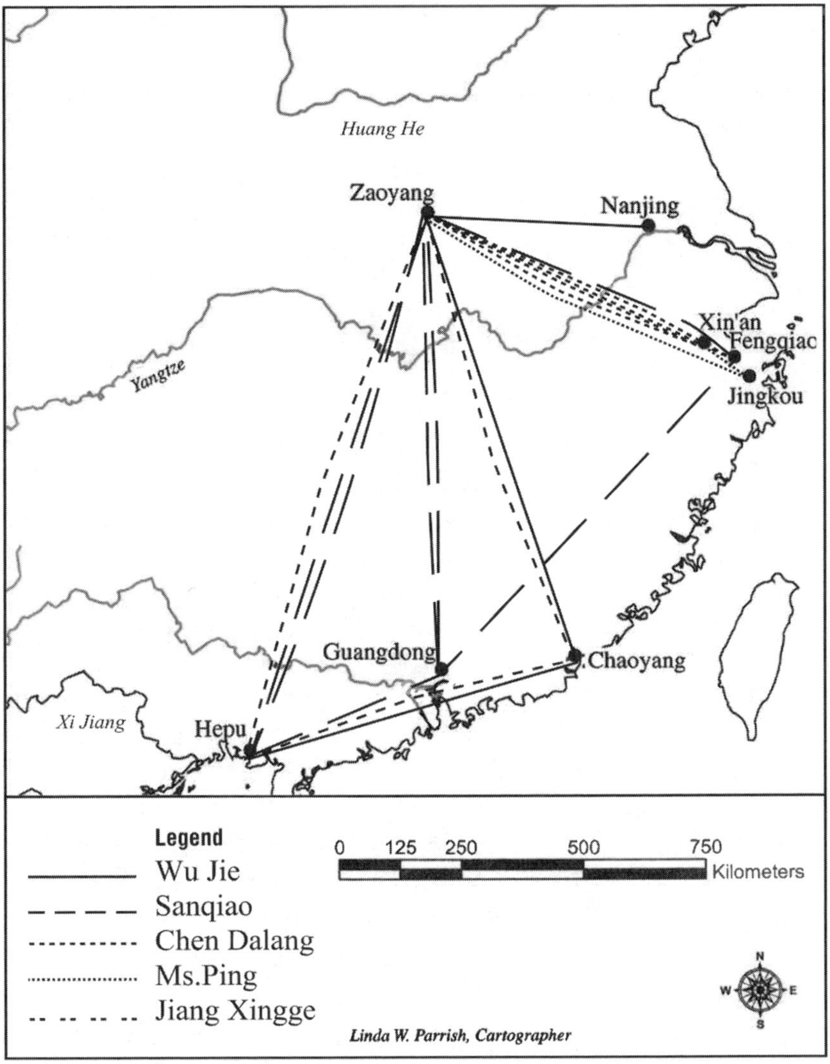

Map 5 Journeys in *Gujin* 1

Even the barebones of the resolution leads Song Maocheng to marvel at how perfectly everything has worked out: "The Recluse comments: If this is true, the Way of Heaven is simply too close, governing us in everything!"[19] In other words, the web of simultaneity spreading over the entire empire is only partially what is going on. Just as important is that Chen Dalang's perfidy and Jiang Xingge's generosity are each requited in as few strokes as possible and that these complicated exchanges and widespread travels create a fair and equitable economy.[20] Another way of wording Song Maocheng's conclusion to his story is that the Way of Heaven leaves nothing over.

The *huaben* version pays much closer attention still to making sure that every single character is paid back perfectly in kind. The opening to the vernacular story introduces us immediately to its moral terrain, which itself exemplifies the logic of the story:

> If I do not seduce anyone else's wife,
> No one will seduce mine.[21]

The saying explicitly foreshadows Jiang Xingge's unwitting revenge on Chen Dalang, whose punishment for taking someone else's wife is to have his own wife taken away. Later, in describing Xingge's marriage to Sanqiao, the narrator cites a proverb that connects marriage and mercantile transfers of property: "If a business deal goes awry, that's just a moment; if choosing a wife goes awry, that's a lifetime."[22] From Jiang Xingge's perspective, his marriage to Ms Ping pays Chen Dalang back for his dalliance with his beloved wife Sanqiao, but from Ms Ping's perspective, another sort of payback takes place. She sells herself to Xingge to raise money for Chen Dalang's burial: "If I sell myself to bury my husband, nobody will have any grounds to mock me."[23] In paying for his burial, she has discharged her wifely obligations to him. A single action—the marriage of Ms Ping and Xingge—clears both sets of accounts, simultaneously punishing and rewarding Dalang, stripping him of his wife and ensuring his burial. The exceedingly rare surname of Ms Ping—who is otherwise only a bit player—points to the weight of this action; it means "balance," since it is her remarriage to Jiang Xingge that rebalances the karmic scales.[24]

To a remarkable extent, the narrative in this story has to jump back and forth between events taking place in different localities. A single coherent narrative can be told only by incorporating seemingly unrelated actions taking place elsewhere. Simultaneity across space is difficult to convey, and the narrator must repeatedly skip from location to location, each transition prefaced with *huafen liang-*

tou 話分兩頭—"meanwhile." At the same time, the story problematizes the notion of "meanwhile." After Chen Dalang inadvertently tells the cuckolded husband the whole story of the love affair, Jiang Xingge, who by this time has been lingering on the road for two years and three months, hurries off for home on a boat. But first he endures an unpleasant night: "When he thought about it, he fretted; when he fretted, he thought. He wished he could learn some magic means to shrink the road (*suodi fa* 縮地法), so that he could get home in an instant."[25] But if such a *suodi fa* existed, there would be no story. In fact, it is not just simultaneity that is at stake in this story—but precisely the delays and difficulties created by the road.

Consider, for example, the complicated moment in time after Chen Dalang arrives in Zaoyang. He has just been robbed, and he needs to borrow some money from the go-between who brought him and Sanqiao together. When his landlord, Mr. Lü, tells him that Sanqiao is long gone—divorced because of some mess regarding a pearl-sewn shirt—the news so distresses Chen Dalang that he falls ill. After two months of languishing in an inn, he decides to send word home: "It happened that Lü knew an official courier, who, bearing official documents, was going to be on the route between Anhui and Ningbo [Anning]. Going by official water and land routes it would be very quick."[26] Ms Ping receives the letter and then sets off for Zaoyang, accompanied by her father and a pair of servants; her father makes it only part of the way before he returns home ill, and by the time Ms Ping makes it to Zaoyang, Chen Dalang has been dead for ten days. If the order of events in the rest of the story maps out easily, this part defies sequence: does Chen Dalang's death take place before or after Mr. Ping's illness? How long was Chen Dalang ill before his death? We know only that two sets of events are taking place simultaneously—Chen Dalang's final illness and Ms Ping's frantic journey to reach him in Zaoyang.

The road is still a figure for profit, as Jiang Xingge muses ruefully to himself after he finds out about his wife's infidelity: "Back then the two of us as husband and wife were so deeply in love, and it was just because of my greed for a fly's head worth of profit that I abandoned her in her youth to live like a widow, and created this whole mess. How I regret it!"[27] But in addition the road also approaches something like an epistemologically altered state, in which normal knowledge of and relationships to others are suspended. When Sanqiao and Jiang Xingge are in the same place, they understand each other; distance makes for misunderstanding, as when Sanqiao misreads the love tokens from Chen Dalang that Jiang Xingge passes on to her. At any rate, normal time and understanding contrast powerfully with the moment when Chen Dalang sends for Ms Ping: so many characters on the road, all ignorant of where the others are and all acting at cross-purposes, all minds in isolation, each in uncertain relationship to the others. Xu Aji concedes only in the end that the road marks risk and instability; in "The Pearl-Sewn Shirt," that aspect of the road is central.

In the stories we have examined so far, characters travel in circles. Even in "The Pearl-Sewn Shirt," we are meant to feel that, other than Wu Jie, whose travels on government business are different, all the other characters go back to where they belong (Ms Ping's marriage to Xingge is a kind of *guisu* 歸宿, a refuge). Even the unfortunate Chen Dalang is returned, albeit as an encoffined corpse, to his hometown of Xin'an. "The Pearl-Sewn Shirt" introduces us to a world that is immeasurably more complicated than Aji's or Wen Shi's, with not one but five characters, all of them carrying around goods and trading them or exchanging them all over the empire. Even the two characters who are not traders—Ms Ping and Sanqiao, themselves objects of exchange—transport objects in ways that are critical to the story's functioning. Each character proceeds at a distinct pace; their paths intersect in unpredictable ways.

But whereas Xu Aji equates journeying with profit, in "The Pearl-Sewn Shirt," we are never given a sense of how the two traders Chen Dalang and Jiang Xingge have done as businessmen. Moreover, there are losses along the way; when Chen Dalang ventures forth to make money, the rigors of travel (and of his affair with Sanqiao) bring on a fatal illness.[28] The real profits in "The Pearl-Sewn Shirt" are not monetary but intangible; what is earned on the road is the resolution of this complex plot such that every character receives perfect just deserts.

Consequently, the story ends not with profit but with the return of property that is beyond value—the pearl-sewn shirt and Sanqiao—to its rightful owner. What characters exchange with one another are karmic connections of debt and credit, not the goods and silver of the earlier maps. In a world in which fornicators are subject to severe penalty (according to the Ming Code, subject to 100 strokes of the heavy bamboo, a punishment that easily could turn into a grisly and miserable death), how can Sanqiao be divorced, remarried, and then magically returned to her first husband? These circuits of transaction involve much more than simply travel, and they—and the magical gains that are a part of them—are central to conceiving of the community as an organic whole, even at the same time that travel in all these stories is inherently destabilizing. It is partially Jiang Xingge's fault that Sanqiao succumbs to adultery since his absence and his devotion to profit open the door to her fall, but unlike Xu Aji, Jiang Xingge continues as a trader. In fact, when Sanqiao encounters him again, he is on his longest journey yet, and we have no reason to believe that he will give up his career once he and Sanqiao return home.

It is clear that this story, with its many characters and its need to demonstrate perfect reciprocity and perfect retribution for one's sins (*yinguo baoying* 因果報應), has reached almost the limits of what a *huaben* can do. Although the karmic balance between two parties (take, for example, Xu Aji and his mistress and her family) can be dispatched quite readily, "The Pearl-Sewn Shirt" introduces more and more complexities, which in turn make the final judgment—where everyone must be paid back in kind—ever more difficult to achieve. What, for example, does Wu Jie gain from giving up Sanqiao? He has not debauched anyone's wife, and yet in behaving honorably he gives up his concubine. The reward is deferred but must exist: the next concubine the childless Wu Jie takes bears him three sons, all of whom will become successful examination candidates.

Hanan suggests that the vernacular rewriting of Song Maocheng's source story is at its heart an attempt to fix what the redactor (almost certainly Feng Menglong himself) sees as a moral imbalance: how can the couple remarry if all the fault is Sanqiao's and all the forebearance Jiang Xingge's?[29] The *huaben* ameliorates her misdeeds and also allows her to become his benefactor. Song Maocheng's version lacks the fortuneteller, the detailed seduction set in play by

Granny Xue, and Sanqiao's attempted suicide. In both versions, Jiang Xingge generously refrains from publicly humiliating Sanqiao, and to the amazement of all, he even returns her dowry. In turn, she feels profound remorse, and in the *huaben*, when Jiang Xingge finds himself in trouble, she begs her new husband to help him.

My experience teaching this story leads me to believe that most readers in summarizing the *huaben* misremember the circumstances of their reunion, believing that Sanqiao does in fact save Jiang Xingge's life. Readers are responding to a profound need for reciprocity; we want to read her behavior as a perfect recompense to Xingge's. But does she pay him back this way? And is he a criminal to begin with? In fact, the story is uncommonly evasive on the question of whether Jiang Xingge is guilty of murder or not.

> Jiang Xingge had arrived in Hepu to buy pearls. He'd already settled on a price, when the old seller took one of his big pearls and then refused to admit it. Xingge was so angry that he grabbed the old man's sleeve with his hand in an attempt to go through it. How could he have known that the force with which he did it would make the old man fall over? And then when he fell, he was entirely silent. When Xingge hurried to lift him up, the old man was no longer breathing.[30]

Has Xingge killed the old man or not? Ming law would suggest some degree of guilt, perhaps homicide, but at the very least *wusha* 誤殺, or manslaughter, the punishment for which was strangulation. (That sentence would then almost certainly have been mitigated upon review after the assizes.)[31]

In the earlier Song Maocheng version, in marked contrast, the Jiang Xingge character, identified only as a man from Chu, is convincingly innocent of any serious crime; there it is the seller who strikes Xingge, not the other way around. In the course of attacking the Xingge character, the old man collapses and dies, without the younger man's ever laying a finger on him. The redactor of "The Pearl-Sewn Shirt" has gone to some lengths to make Jiang Xingge much more guilty (if ambiguously so); consequently Sanqiao's good deed seems all the weightier—and the ultimate balance between them more equitable. The narrative, Feng Menglong seems to imply, does not work unless Sanqiao has done Xingge a good turn.

Why, then, has the redactor not simply gone ahead to make Xingge a murderer whom Wu Jie reprieves? If Xingge *were* a murderer, Wu Jie could not possibly intervene, and we would have left far behind us the realm of localized good and bad deeds. We cannot have Xingge and Sanqiao's good fortune built out of a murder or out of Wu Jie's corruption. In fact, it is vital that Wu Jie say to Sanqiao that in fact he cannot take charge of the law for her sake: "If a man's life was indeed lost, then it would be impossible for me to pardon him."[32]

Strangely enough, the story leaves open the possibility that Jiang Xingge and Sanqiao are reunited through a murder. Wu Jie admits he cannot tell whether Xingge is guilty or not; in fact, that ambiguity is absolutely necessary. If Xingge is guilty, then Wu Jie is a corrupt official, willing to bend the law for his beautiful young concubine (in which case the equity and reciprocity on which the state itself rests have been violated); if Xingge is innocent, then Sanqiao has not really helped Xingge at all. If Jiang Xingge has committed murder, then Sanqiao's intercession is important, but then the wrong has been passed on, to the Song family. If he has not committed murder, then her intercession was useless, and he would have been freed anyway. Literary critics have traditionally read this story as a valorization of the special bond between husband and wife. Nonetheless, to tie our husband and wife together with bonds of mutual obligation and gratitude turns out to be harder than it appears. Either the tie is weaker than it first appears, or it binds together the wrong people entirely.

Even in a group of only five people, rights and wrongs seem inexorably to spill outward. Have the two sons of the unfortunate pearl salesman been adequately recompensed for the death of their father? To cover that exigency, the last pages of the story linger over the details of Wu Jie's decision, on which much more ink is spilled than Xingge and Sanqiao's reunion. Again, the balance must be perfect: too lenient a sentence for Xingge, and Wu Jie is corrupt; too harsh a judgment on Xingge, and Sanqiao has done nothing for her first husband. The judgment Wu Jie renders is aimed, not at establishing the nature of the crime and rectifying the wrong, nor at seeking legal redress and forwarding the case on to the capital, but instead at re-establishing balance among interested parties and satisfying the two Song brothers.

After the brothers refuse to allow their father's corpse to be examined publicly, Wu Jie proposes the following solution:

> Now I will instruct him [Jiang Xingge] to wear the hempen clothes of a son in mourning and to perform all the rituals exactly as if he were a son of the deceased. All the funeral and burial expenses shall be borne entirely by him. Do you accept this judgment?[33]

Many scholars have observed that Chinese law is set up around the principle of reciprocity—first that a criminal will have some version of the crime he committed visited upon himself as punishment, and also that at the same time he will compensate those whom he injured. In that case, Jiang Xingge's is a strikingly odd punishment (for which the legal historian Matthew Sommer assures me there is no obvious legal precedent).[34] After all, Wu Jie might have decided that Xingge simply shoulder the sizable financial burden for the funeral. An anthropologist might guess that Wu Jie has decided on this punishment so that Xingge will share in the Song brothers' contamination by death.

Wu Jie has interceded by keeping this case local; however, under Ming law, all cases involving the death penalty (or all cases involving homicide, whether intentional or not) were supposed to be forwarded to the throne for review. Sanqiao can help Jiang Xingge only because they are in Hepu, practically a border outpost. At home in Zaoyang, Jiang Xingge's brush with the law would necessarily have involved the central government, as well as a host of other social relations. Lifted out of that normal context in remote Hepu, he can seek help only from Sanqiao and Wu Jie, whose decision draws on another way to conceive of crime, as a disturbance that can be redressed locally.

But how is it that Jiang Xingge can pay back the brothers by taking his place among them in mourning? Wu Jie's decision is supposed to end matters; through his punishment, what Jiang Xingge owes the brothers will be settled once and for all. By killing the Song brothers' father, he has oddly transformed himself into one of them, dressed in mourning. How has recompense—which can end—been transformed into this peculiar form of role-play? That moment of imagining a simple dyadic tie—the bond between husband and wife, strengthened forever by mutual obligation—also involves its breakdown. To become again Sanqiao's husband, Jiang Xingge must first be transformed into the brother of Song Fu and Song Shou. It seems that ties between two always leave something over. We can never limit ourselves to imagining two or even five journeys; these inevitably, it seems, tie into an infinity of other journeys, all crisscrossing one another, with ties of obligation and exchange binding them all together.

Let me pry into Xingge's peculiar punishment a little further. In the course of remarrying Sanqiao, Jiang Xingge is forced to join another family. In some sense, in its bare bones, it almost appears as if Xingge is being married off, as a woman might be, in the course of his own family's being established (or re-established, as it is here), another family (that of the Songs) is changed. Reciprocity here demands that only through a counter-marriage—the mirror image of a marriage, as it were—can Xingge and Sanqiao themselves be married once more.

Within a society, conventional marriages abide by a certain economy; as Claude Lévi-Strauss puts it: "Restricted families are only permitted to live for a limited period of time, either long or short according to case, but under the strict condition that their component parts be ceaselessly displaced, loaned, borrowed, given away, or returned, so that new restricted families may be endlessly created or made to vanish."[35] Families survive only by constantly destroying themselves. A girl marries a boy so that his family can be continued—but, at the same time, that marriage marks a change, a death even, of the two original families from which boy and girl were born. For families to survive, their individual members must constantly change and die.

Men are not supposed to marry when they are in mourning for their parents, as our story points out at the very beginning, when Xingge postpones his first marriage to Sanqiao after his father's death. And yet, with Wu Jie's punishment, this is how he ends, a living paradox: a bridegroom, in mourning, *pima daixiao* 披麻戴孝, for the man he has killed. This last image of Xingge makes something of the same point as Lévi-Strauss. In binding together husband

and wife through ties of mutual obligation, those dyadic ties of exchange have drawn in a family from an almost unimaginably distant locale, all the way on the other side of the empire. And those families themselves are constantly in flux, merging into one another and dissolving, in perfect balance and economy.

—

But that image—whichever way we choose to see it, as an absolutely perfect narrative structure or as a vision of how society holds together—was not sustained for long. The heyday of the *huaben* lasted only two generations, from around 1620 to 1670 or so. After the fall of the Ming, one way in which the genre declined was by replacing with irony the old assertion of organic coherence.

In the fourth story of Li Yu's *Wusheng xi*, "After Losing a Thousand Pieces of Gold, Good Fortune Arrives Through Ill Fortune" (1654), familiar elements, namely, profit through travel and simultaneous action across distance, figure prominently. In the final story considered in this chapter, narrative and economy once again parallel each other in form. But here, the questions take on a decidedly belated feel, as if almost in self-conscious recognition that the form was past its prime. Rather than making assertions about moral economy and social bonds, the questions have turned into literary criticism, reflections on the essence of the short narrative as a genre: When do stories end? Do they end at an arbitrary point, or is their ending predetermined?

"Good Fortune Through Ill" opens in Guangzhou with a moneylender named Millionaire Yang, who was once taught the arts of physiognomy reading and has mastered them to a preternatural extent. Yang uses his abilities to adjust the quantities he loans out: men with lucky faces get more; those with unlucky faces get less. A poor man named Qin Shiliang approaches Yang for a loan; while waiting, Qin Shiliang sees a man who is practically his own double, "in face and figure, just like him, as if printed from the same woodblock."[36] Strangely enough, although Millionaire Yang rejects the double's loan, he meets Qin Shiliang's humble request for 5 taels of silver with an offer of 500. Qin Shiliang is reluctant to accept the silver, but after repeated assurances from the millionaire that a face such as his own can only mean riches and good fortune, he decides to make a go at sea. He thinks to himself, "I'll do business with those merchants who are traveling to foreign places. I'll tell them I'll buy some merchandise, and along the way I'll get to see some foreign sights."[37] He is taken along on a voyage as a scribe, and in the copious spare time of a sea voyage, he labels everything, including the bolts of silk he has bought to trade with. The ship runs into a storm; the crew takes refuge near an island; and then a band of pirates robs them all, sending them homeward on an empty ship.

Instead of demanding the return of his money, Millionaire Yang insists that Qin Shiliang take another 500 taels of silver. This time, Qin Shiliang decides to split the money up, just in case. After hiding 200 taels in a hole, he travels to Huguang to trade grain with the rest. On the road, he befriends the retainer of an honest official, who has been accused of pocketing an official shipment of grain. His master needs 300 taels to pay for legal expenses. One morning, Qin Shiliang wakes up to discover that his bag of silver is gone; a search of the inn reveals that his companion, the old retainer, has disappeared too, without a trace.

Qin Shiliang digs up the remaining 200 taels he had hidden earlier and heads back to Huguang to trade in grain. Once again, he befriends a fellow traveler, this time the double whom he had first encountered at Millionaire Yang's. It turns out this man not only shares Shiliang's appearance, but is also a native of Guangdong, and what is more, the two even share a surname and one character of their given names. In Qin Shifang's case, Millionaire Yang's physiognomic reading seems to have been correct; since his loan was rejected by Yang, Shifang's money has become tied up in a lawsuit, and now he is on the road after raising 200 taels of silver from the sale of what remains of his property. After Shiliang and Shifang swear blood brotherhood, they room together in Huguang, waiting for a shipment of grain to come in. Finally, their landlord announces the grain's arrival, but when Qin Shifang goes to fetch his silver, he discovers that it is gone. The landlord proposes that Shiliang and Shifang share Shiliang's silver. Shiliang quite accurately reads the solomonic solution as an implicit accusation. He insists that he is innocent and would sooner give up all the silver rather than share. Once again penniless, he leaves in a huff, while Shifang takes the capital and proceeds to trade with it.

Up until this point, Qin Shiliang has been anything but the embodiment of good fortune that Millionaire Yang sees in him. Instead, the money Yang gives Qin Shiliang seems to have evaporated. *Huaben* cannot end here; the narrative's closure depends on the enclosed nature of exchange.

After he parts from Qin Shiliang, Shifang's fortunes take a dramatic upswing. The delay caused by the missing silver means that all the husked rice has been bought and Qin Shifang can only buy unhusked rice. Fortunately for him, the city of Yangzhou is experiencing famine, and the cheaper, unhusked rice sells out immediately. Shifang is able to realize a tenfold profit. While in Yangzhou, he buys herbal tea leaves to sell in the capital—where there happens to be an outbreak of malaria, whose debilitating fevers and thirst can be somewhat alleviated by the tea. Once again, Shifang is able to realize a tenfold profit. In Beijing, he buys some more goods and returns south to sell them. The 200 taels with which he began has now become 30,000 taels, and he returns home a rich man.

However, his wife's response when he returns is not delight, but surprise: how was he able to amass such a fortune when he had left all his money at home? She explains that the evening after his departure she discovered his silver wrapped neatly by the pillow. Since then she has been expecting him home any day, knowing that he was lacking even basic travel expenses. With a start, Shifang realizes that he had absentmindedly left his money at home, and that the landlord must have given him Shiliang's money. An honest man, he sets off immediately to return his ill-gotten gains. He discovers his blood brother living in a ramshackle thatched hut, making a living by tutoring schoolboys. Each man insists the other is the rightful owner of the 30,000 taels, and finally Millionaire Yang intercedes and insists that they share the wealth evenly.

Why doesn't the story end at this point? After all, with Yang's explanation to Shifang that only his good deed has been able to counter the effects of his own poor physiognomy, the plot with which the narrator began has come to a natural conclusion. Nonetheless, the story cannot come to an end until all the rest of Millionaire Yang's loans have been accounted for; somehow we must know how restitution will be made for the two times Shiliang was robbed.

A magistrate newly stationed in Qin Shiliang's home of Xinzhi prefecture sends a messenger to look for him and to invite him for a meeting. Shiliang is surprised—and then even more flummoxed when the generosity comes to extend to more than simply hospitality. Before the year is out, the official has given more than 5,000 gold pieces to Shiliang. It turns out that this is the wronged official, now exonerated, whose manservant long ago robbed Shiliang of the silver borrowed from Millionaire Yang. Finally, the debt is discharged, and interest paid back to Qin Shiliang.

In the meantime, hoping to make some advantageous trades, Shifang takes a month-long journey from Guangdong to Korea. He is welcomed on the shores by those eager to buy Chinese goods. One princess has sent her steward, a noble-looking fellow who speaks Chinese and asks Shifang his name and place of origin. Upon hearing Shifang's name, the steward immediately asks him whether he is the brother of a certain Qin Shiliang. This Korean official, originally from China, turns out to have been the ringleader of the pirates who stole all the goods from Qin Shiliang's ship, on his first trading journey. Since Shiliang's silk was bundled together and labeled, the Korean official remembers his name and is able to make restitution—which he does handsomely, returning both the original sum and ten times that sum, as interest. The next morning he gives Qin Shifang two big bundles of silver, one as repayment and restitution and the other to buy all the goods he brought with him to Korea. The silver is used to buy rare Korean goods, and Shifang sails back to Guangdong, prepared to sell them at a magnificent profit. After his return, the two blood brothers live happily ever after.

Partly the story hearkens back to patterns we have seen earlier. For example, one thing that obviously sets Qin Shiliang and Qin Shifang apart is that one travels, and the other is stationary. Qin Shifang covers a great deal of ground, traveling from Guangzhou to Huguang (present-day Hubei and Hunan provinces), from there to Yangzhou, then to Beijing, back to Guangzhou, to Korea, and back. (See Map 6.) The circuit Shifang travels foregrounds the problem of containment. In contrast, although Shiliang travels—to Huguang and on the sea—his journeys are abortive and earn him no money. Mostly he stays close to home, while journeying takes place all

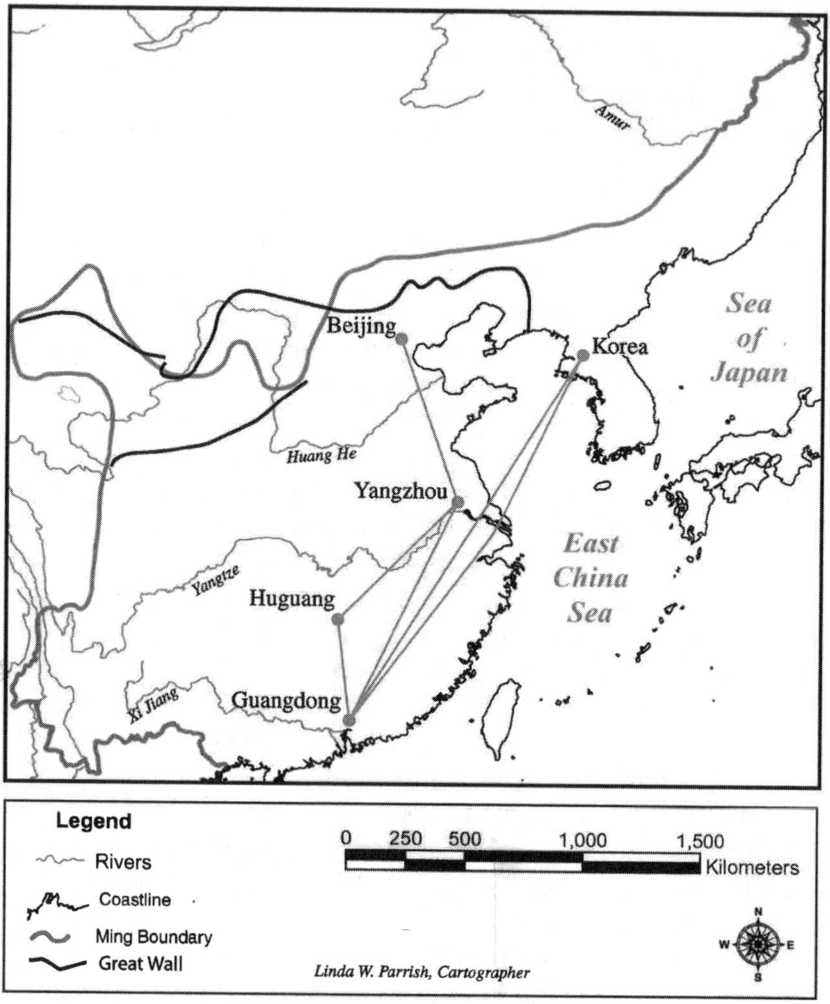

Map 6 Qin Shifang's travels in *Wusheng xi* 4

around him, whether Shifang's or that of the official newly stationed in Xinzhi. As Millionaire Yang says of Shiliang, "He would not expend a hair's worth of energy, nor suffer a hair's worth of hard work, and it would all come to him, that he'd become a rich man with leisure. Now, someone else traveled for him through a thousand mountains and ten thousand waters, earned him silver and brought it to his door. Isn't that a rich man of leisure?"[38] Millionaire Yang's comment suggests two things: first, that traveling is one well-established way to accumulate money, and second, that what makes Shiliang almost miraculously lucky is his exemption from having to travel. That he is a stationary merchant who grows rich seems a great part of his marvel. But it is only with irony that Li Yu can inscribe the enclosures that keep money within Shifang's circuits.

All of Millionaire Yang's predictions have come to pass. The silver originally borrowed from him has been accounted for and repaid with interest, and, with seemingly incontrovertible proof that the world is a finite system, the story can now come to an end. After all, only through a journey to Korea is a debt to a Cantonese merchant to be paid off.

But how can a story about circulation ever truly come to an end? The silver's story does not end, and the silver can never fully be accounted for. After Qin Shifang's return from his first trip, when the accounts are still relatively clear, the 30,000 taels he earns—less 1,300 taels after Yang's loan is paid off, with interest—themselves must be divided and used to establish the two households. And, then, what of the profits from the trip to Korea? We cannot know the precise sum. And naturally even that does not spell the end of the silver's life as an exchange object. What about money spent on household needs? How will the silver be used to make more silver? Money will flow in and out of Qin Shiliang's and Qin Shifang's lives forever.

And karma works similarly. The end to that narrative, too, is postponed indefinitely into the future: whether Qin Shiliang truly is possessed of good fortune cannot be determined until his death—or perhaps not even then, since it has to await scrutiny of his descendants' fates. The money earned by Shifang can be spent or not; the family's descendants might turn out to be frugal or wasteful—who can tell? Neither money nor karma nor family comes to an end.

In fact, the period's widespread anxiety over the diminution of family fortunes and over the impact that a person might have on far-off, as yet unborn descendants certainly has an impact on literary form, undermining and putting off endings. Qin Shiliang's part of the story concludes:

> Millionaire Yang truly liked Qin Shiliang. He had a daughter recently widowed whom he gave Shiliang in marriage. She came with a rich dowry, which was like compounding his good fortune. Shiliang lived with Shifang until their old age, without separating mine from yours, and later on Shiliang's family was wealthy for three more generations.[39]

A story about predictions for the future cannot have a thoroughly satisfactory ending since the future must in some sense extend beyond the story, but this one does not even try. What happens after those "three more generations"? Was it something that Qin Shiliang did that caused the good fortune only to last until then? Reincarnation muddies the waters even further. When Shiliang ponders why the new official would so eagerly befriend him—"Could it be that he was my father in a previous life?"[40]—he throws another wrench into the system.

The narrative itself foregrounds the fragility of an ending point. The story cannot end before Yang's predictions come to pass; the story cannot end before debts are resolved; in fact, it cannot end even after the two good men are rewarded. After Shifang offers all the silver to Shiliang, he returns home a few days later to find the doors smashed with an axe and his wife lying weeping on the bed. She explains that after a gang of bandits had learned of Shifang's good fortune, they broke into his house and beat her in an effort to find out where he had hidden his silver. Shifang's response to this event is not outrage but a delighted respect for Yang's abilities to read physiognomy. He says:

> Millionaire Yang's abilities are truly miraculous. He said that if I didn't do a good deed, then my silver would eventually leave me. And now it has come to pass! If I hadn't taken the silver to return to [Shiliang] and had left it instead at home, then it would certainly have been stolen.[41]

Shifang reads the attempted robbery not as a separate incident of misfortune (contrast his perspective to that of his long-suffering wife, for example) but as part of Millionaire Yang's predictions and thus of an overarching pattern of meaning.

If the beating of his wife and the invasion of his home might be read as markers of good fortune, what sort of event could ever defy Millionaire Yang's predictions? When Shifang and Shiliang go to

Millionaire Yang to pay off the debt, Shifang questions Yang's abilities. After all, he became rich despite Millionaire Yang's predictions that his features promised penury. How could his supposedly doomed physiognomy have led to such fabulous riches? After all, one's face is a constant, or is it? Shifang asks, "Could it be that I grew out another set of ears or a new nose?"[42] Millionaire Yang explains that Shifang's appearance before had been marked by a blockage of *qi*. Now, however, not only has the blockage been cleared, but the new wrinkles he has grown under his eyes predict good fortune: "You must have done some great good deed to have this kind of appearance, and you certainly will strike it rich in the future."[43] In other words, Shifang is said not to have shown the limits of physiognomic theory but instead, with a face transformed by good behavior, to have confirmed it.

Somehow the fact that Shifang's life has gone wholly against Millionaire Yang's earlier predictions is simply pushed under the carpet, and his life, too, comes to illustrate the accuracy of Yang's predictive abilities. Wouldn't a truly predictive physiognomic reading have been able to account for the transformation of Shifang's features? And, of course, no one in the story sees fit to point out that Millionaire Yang does not so much predict Qin Shiliang's good fortune as—by lending him 1,000 taels of silver—create it.

Can anything take place *outside* Yang's predictive framework? Can silver ever leave the network of transactions? Like Hume's black swan, enclosure seems to belong to a category that can never be proved, but only disproved, with the first counterexample collapsing the entire structure. But in Li Yu's story, there is no room for disproof; each piece of silver, each act that generates its own karma, each face that defies prediction, is ultimately placed within a seemingly infinitely capacious framework. In fact, as is Li Yu's point, humor is precisely the only challenge that can be mounted to this sort of unfalsifiable thinking.[44] Ironic distance provides the only exit.

Are all events so connected that no narrative can truly come to an end? By the end of the story, it is evident that narrative, geography, and economics are actually all one. In some ways, the demand for an event that takes place outside and that cannot be incorporated into a predetermined space, a network of transactions, or a story is a demand for arbitrariness. Our two main characters, so we are told repeatedly, resemble each other so closely as to be doppelgängers (doubles who, as the narrator suggests at the opening of the story, test the prognostic powers of physiognomy reading just as people who share the exact same moment of birth test the limits of horoscopes). At their first meeting, Shiliang is amazed that his own physiognomy would promise riches, whereas that of his near twin would not.

Within a physiognomic framework, surely some profound meaning is to be attributed to the identical appearance of these two men. Similarly, within a story about the scope of the human community, surely some profound meaning is to be attributed to the two names that seem to mark these men as brothers. As Shiliang says when they first meet: "That's strange—we look alike; we've got the same surname; our given names make us seem like brothers. We must have some connection from a former life."[45] The problem of doubles (which I address at much greater length with regard to *Hongloumeng* and *Rouputuan*) turns on the dimensions of the human community: if it is indeed infinite, we should not be surprised that there are many men who look exactly alike, or who possess the same name. Qin Shiliang himself brings this matter up. When the new official in town expresses great interest in Shiliang, he first suspects that the official has him confused with some other Qin Shiliang: "There are many men in the world with the same name. He can't be looking for me."[46]

Nonetheless, on the surface the convergence of Qin Shiliang and Qin Shifang's names and appearance seems to be pure, unresolved coincidence of the sort that is practically unthinkable in Feng Menglong's *Sanyan* or Ling Mengchu's *Erpai.* Although they are natives of the same area, look the same, share a surname and one character in their given names, they are not relatives. The commentator writes: "Everyone admires Qin Shiliang, but I'm the only one who admires Qin Shifang. Shiliang's wealth came from heaven, while Shifang's was of his own making."[47] Yet in the context of the story, the distinction is false, for obviously the wealth of the two men is connected. Is it that Shifang's industry piggybacks on Shiliang's destiny, or is it the other way around?

The two are more than a control and a test case, for traveling as opposed to staying put or for hard work as opposed to destiny; their fates are too closely intertwined for that. Instead, their unexplained resemblance opens up a little fissure in the seamless unity of existence. When Wittgenstein wrote, "Die Welt ist alles, was der Fall ist," meaning "the world is everything that is the case," he meant that we have only the world in which we live—we forever lack true counterfactuals and any means to know what might have been otherwise. Here, in these two men who look the same, is such a miraculous (albeit imaginary) counterfactual.

The case of Qin Shiliang and Qin Shifang forces us to confront the fact that we cannot tell what is foreordained from what is coincidental. The question of whether anyone or anything can escape the connected network of economics, geography, and narrative is left deliberately open-ended. Or perhaps it is the case that Li Yu, writing at the end of the great age of *huaben*, a decade after the cataclysmic collapse of the Ming dynasty, has simply conceded that all these forms of cosmic coherence—embodied in his chosen literary form—are equally fictive; only this mockery of order makes sense of what is at its heart random and arbitrary.

THREE
Reunions and Dynastic Fall

This chapter restages and picks up on themes Li Yu treats obliquely in his story about Qin Shiliang and Qin Shifan; here, my central concern is how ties between people change in the course of a dynastic fall. If we can speak of a single archetypal narrative in Chinese, it would be that of the family reunion. Reunion's reach into Chinese culture extends far beyond literature. In *Separation and Reunion in Modern China*, the anthropologist Charles Stafford shows how even in contemporary social life the fantasy of family reunion remains singularly powerful. Within literature, reunion provides the framework for the final act to a *chuanqi* drama—in which everyone is restored to his proper place—the *tuanyuan*, or "reunion."

Any proper investigation of reunions in general would have to tackle these powerful norms of reunion. But I am concerned with the reunions in fiction, in which plots unfold so much less rigidly than in drama, and the generic forces pushing a narrative toward a perfect reunion are much weaker. In fact, all the reunions in this chapter manifest flaws in one way or another.

—

In the short narrative that opens the twelfth *huaben* in Feng Menglong's 1624 collection *Jingshi tongyan* (Common words to warn the world), "Fan Jiuer's Double Mirror Is Reunited," Xu Xin and his wife, Ms Cui, are forced to flee their home when the Jurchens invade. Unfortunately, they encounter Song deserters, who are marauding, robbing, and raping their way through the populace. In the chaos, Xu Xin loses track of his wife, and the two are separated. After a fruitless search, he is forced to continue on his journey. When he stops for something to eat and drink, he hears a woman crying. He steps out to investigate and sees a woman sitting on the ground, with disheveled hair and wearing only a shift. Wang Jinnu is about his wife's age and not too dissimilar from her in appearance. She explains that she became separated from her husband, and after a few days of walking, her bound feet grew so swollen that she could not move. The deserters robbed her of all her clothing and abandoned her. Xu Xin feels sympathy for her, and since he has some money on him, he stays with her for a few days at the inn until her feet heal. In a few days, they set off again, now as husband and wife.

Three years later, with the Song having long since reclaimed control, the couple are at a teashop, where Xu Xin notices a stranger staring intently at his wife (Wang Jinnu is too modest to notice). Eventually, Xu Xin takes the man aside. It turns out that this is Wang Jinnu's husband, who says that he, too, has married again but would like to see his old wife for one last time. Xu Xin invites him and his new wife to come over the next day. Who should that new wife turn out to be but Xu Xin's own former wife, Ms Cui? She explains her story. The couples embrace, and Xu Xin and his wife's new husband, Lie Junqing, swear eternal friendship. That night, each husband reclaims his old wife, and from then on, the two couples are the best of friends, constantly visiting each other.

In this narrative, the wife exchange takes place with extraordinary ease, leaving no trace whatsoever. There are no new parties involved, other than the four; no children are born of either new marriage. Nor was there issue from either original union, whose existence might have challenged the new marriages. In fact, what happened to Ms Wang before her rescue by Xu Xin is carefully left out—all we are told is that she has been "abandoned" by the deserting soldiers, with no comment as to what those soldiers might have done to her before the abandonment. At the end, whatever has happened can be erased entirely (or perhaps, one might argue, both couples even gain a little, with their new close friends). Had his new wife not turned out to be Xu Xin's old wife, Lie Junqing would have regarded his ties with his old wife severed; only the coincidence of the perfect exchange allows for the restoration of the old marriage.

Narrative can resolve at least partly what ultimately cannot be assimilated, the dissolved marriage. To Wang Jinnu's husband, the act of recounting his story to his erstwhile wife could almost take the place of a permanent reunion. He tells Xu Xin: "If I could meet her briefly just once to tell her of all of my sufferings, then I could die without regret."[1] That family members might simply separate and drift apart is a terrible Confucian nightmare, somehow assuaged by the telling.

Suggestively, despite the fact that the two couples were originally separated because of the Northern Song's fall, the ultimate dénouement of the family drama is largely unconnected to any dynastic happenings. This particular sort of reunion ultimately does not make any comment on the dynastic transition. Some of the stories discussed below speculate on what would happen if, when Lie Junqing and his wife had come calling on Xu Xin, it had turned out that the women were actually true strangers. What happens when no exchange can be made that returns everything to just as it was before?

Since *huaben* often consist of two narratives that echo each other, the longer narrative that follows, "Fan Jiuer's Double Mirror," is also a fantasy of a reunion achieved with perfect ease: like its companion set during the fall of the Northern Song, the story tells of an official's daughter, kidnapped by bandits, who ends up marrying the scion of a bandit ringleader's family. Her husband, though, does not agree with his family's politics. When the bandits are ultimately defeated, husband and wife are separated. But miraculously they are reunited—and her husband is (with the simple trick of changing his name) able to serve the empire and be promoted and have his past history simply forgotten. No one's chastity is besmirched; no one's loyalty is impugned; and the polity heals itself seamlessly. But all this was written before the fall of the Ming dynasty.

Well before the dynasty's fall, the separation of family members had become a trope of Chinese literature, strongly associated with dynastic transitions since the dynastic collapse both causes and mirrors the family's separation. But whereas the dynasty can be and must be replaced, the family—whose existence both legitimizes and is legitimized by the dynasty—brooks no substitutions. Unlike the dynasty, the family has to be reconstituted as much as possible with the exact same components;[2] ultimately, a profound disjuncture arises between two structures in whose parallelism so much has been invested. The state is new, but the family is old. I will be skipping from writer to writer, treating the connections between these two problems, one of narrative and one of political philosophy: how can a family once fractured come together again?

In a few stories, the notion of families separated—of people wandering through the polity—is explicitly connected to the fear of incest. In "On His Way Home, Master Dugu Has a Nightmare," the twenty-fifth story of *Xingshi hengyan* (another of the stories Hanan attributes to Langxian), a husband and wife are separated for three years, as the husband, Dugu Xiashu, travels into Shu to find a patron. The story follows the dreams of both husband and wife; until the end of the narrative, the dream frame is presented as reality itself (and this is what most scholars have found most interesting about this story).

The two characters are husband and wife, and any sexual contact between them would be entirely proper, yet they are reintroduced to each other in a peculiar fashion. In the wife's dream, after three years of waiting, she decides to follow her husband into Shu. On her journey, she encounters a gang of young ruffians who drag her to a temple. In her husband's corresponding dream, he finds himself in a temple not far from home. Soon, a group of young men come into the temple, accompanied by a woman. Dugu Xiashu hides and tries to figure out what is going on:

> I was guessing that it's got to be some rich young men out to enjoy the spring, and that's what they are. If this woman is an official entertainer, or a top courtesan, why do they have to keep urging her? Could it be that she is a woman of good family who came here willingly to carouse with them? Might it be that they have kidnapped her and brought her here by force? Or tricked her into coming here?[3]

Only upon closer inspection does he realize that the woman is his very own wife, Bai Juanjuan.

Clearly, he is witnessing a rape of some form—of his own wife, no less—and yet he does *not* do the obvious thing, namely, rush out from hiding to rescue her or call out to her (he reckons that he is far outnumbered, but he also does not seem to entertain any serious thoughts of rescue). Instead, in a scene with a transgressive and illicit sexual charge, he takes on the role of a voyeur while the ruffians' torment of the wife continues for pages. Still in hiding and increasingly filled with rage, he watches as the men compel her to sing song after song and then to drink. Finally he reaches his breaking point, and picking up two bricks, he flings one at the ringleader and then one at his wife's forehead. In a flash, the whole scene vanishes—clearly a figment of the imagination—but in his mind at least he has killed not only her chief attacker but his wife as well, after witnessing the spectacle of her violation.

Dugu Xiashu's morally troubling response to his wife's virtual rape leaves open the question of what his involvement would have been if the woman had been a stranger: would he have joined in? Is there something almost incestuous about raping your own wife in the guise of being a stranger? The gross impropriety of such an act is suggested by one of the biographies in Liu Xiang's *Lienü zhuan* (Biographies of exemplary women; first century BCE). Qiu Huzi, on his way back from government service, attempts to seduce a woman picking mulberries. She rebuffs him, and only when he gets home does he realize to his shame that the woman was his own wife. Dugu Xiashu's virtual participation in a gang rape seems comparable.

In such an encounter, before they are fully restored as husband and wife, he would be both family and stranger. If we think of incest as *luanlun* 亂倫, or confusing the normative relations, the encounter smacks of incest; an unknowing participant in an attack on his wife, Dugu Xiashu would have been a husband taking on the guise of a stranger assuming the role of Bai Juanjuan's husband. An encounter that is similarly licit and illicit takes place in "Shan Falang's Happy Marriage in Quanzhou," the seventeenth story in *Gujin xiaoshuo*, in which the daughter of an official is kidnapped and sold into prostitution. Her fiancé happens to be stationed where she is working, and they meet when he takes a liking to her at a banquet. Later in the story, the two have sex—and only then identify themselves as a formerly affianced couple. (Later still, the two marry and live happily ever after.)

The reunion between family members seems fraught with a very specific kind of danger: it takes place only through narrowly averted acts of inappropriate sexual congress. Although nothing improper takes place between Dugu Xiashu and his wife, it is avoided only by having him recognize his wife and then, with even more finality, by staging this entire transgressive encounter in two simultaneous, intersecting dreams.

Still in the late Ming, Ling Mengchu tells two stories of the dangers of reunion in which once again sexual transgression is the only way for the family order to be restored. Notably, both of the short introductory narratives of these two *huaben* tell, not of ordinary people, but of aristocrats. As I have written elsewhere, how various members of the Ming imperial family were separated from and reunited with one another is a subject of great interest in *yeshi* literature of the early Qing; this is, it seems, a very minor subgenre, whose focus is precisely the breakdown of the parallelism between family and state. Ling Mengchu's aristocrats are torn from their families following the collapse of the Northern Song. One story tells of a commoner who infiltrates her way into the royal family, and the other relates the fate of a young noblewoman sunk into prostitution. When the Emperor Qinzong encounters this young woman, his queries into her identity appear to be sexual approaches—and just as with Dugu Xiashu, a sexual encounter in these circumstances straddles the line between what is acceptable and what is not.

As Ling Mengchu tells it, the moment when families are separated and then reunited is fraught with a very specific sexual danger. In the seventh story of the *Erke Paian jingqi* (Slapping the table in amazement, second collection; 1632), a young girl finds herself separated from her family: first, her father dies on his way to his official posting, and then her stepmother begins an illicit affair with another official. After her stepmother and the man (identified only by his surname Lü) elope, the young girl loses contact with her own family.

Years later, her cousin Zhu Donglao, a son of her mother's brother, himself makes a journey to his new office. On the way, he is fêted by a local magistrate. At the banquet, Zhu Donglao notices one courtesan who seems out of place. The head of the troupe of courtesans naturally assumes that he is soliciting the girl's services. She laughs and asks, "Do you like her?" Donglao replies, "It's not that I like her. It's that she looks different from the rest of you, and I wondered about her, so I asked."[4] To the other characters, Donglao's interest in the young prostitute has a simple explanation, despite his continued protests: "From what I can see, she doesn't look like the rest of you. I was curious, so I asked her boss. Could I have any other intention?" Nonetheless, his host rearranges the seating so that Donglao can have maximum access to the woman and she can serve him during the banquet.

He ends up confirming that she is his cousin, but only after giving the impression to all around him that his interest in her might be sexual. As cousins of different surnames, they might in fact marry (indeed, we are told that for generations the Zhus and the Dongs *have* intermarried); nonetheless, the prospect of one cousin taking another as a prostitute is disturbing. Certainly by allowing her to pour him wine and entertain him, he has accepted something of her services. Why should the only way to identify his cousin be to approach her sexually? Once familial moorings are untethered, the argument seems to go, the door to all sorts of sexual deviancy—whether knowing or unknowing—has been opened. A related problem also seems to be of interest to traditional writers from Mencius on: how society was originally formed out of groups of people who did not understand the relations between father and son or husband and wife. What existed prior to those relations? Were all matches between people acceptable? (Or was something like the transgressive sexual contact we witness here omnipresent?)

In the second story of Ling Mengchu's *Paian jingqi*, this sexual danger is all the more explicit; a young bride named Yao Dizhu runs away from her stern in-laws back to her natal home. On the way, she is kidnapped and eventually sold as a concubine to a rich man. Meanwhile, neither her in-laws nor her parents can figure out where she has gone, and each side blames the other, bringing suit against each other and ruination to the Yaos. Years later, a friend of the family tells Dizhu's brother that he has found his sister. The brother goes to see the young woman, standing in a doorway and beckoning passersby, but she does not respond at all to him. Could it be, he wonders, that she so enjoys her life as a prostitute that she has entirely written off her old family? The friend explains her lack of response: "You don't know. Those pimps are harsh! Since she comes to them dishonestly, they must guard her really tightly—so she's afraid to let anyone know and won't show face to face that she recognizes you."[5] The friend then makes a most peculiar suggestion, that the brother solicit the apparent Dizhu's services, so that he can take her elsewhere. There, he can decide definitively on her identity: "Look her over carefully. If it is your sister, then you can privately have a reunion and figure out what you'll do. If it's not your sister, spend the night with her and let her go."[6]

Yao acts on this plan. Even after closely examining the woman, he remains convinced that she is his sister; only when she speaks does her regional accent give her away as a stranger. The instant he makes that determination: the two have sex. Zheng Yue'e is, after all, a prostitute on the job, and he has paid for her services. Afterward, Yao confesses the whole story to her, including the fact that she is an exact double for his sister. The two devise a plan: the prostitute will pass as his sister, and the family's legal problems will come to an end.

And so, even as he continues to sleep with Yue'e, Yao brings her back home and convinces everyone that she is his long-lost sister. Eventually, the truth comes out; the real Dizhu rejoins her family, and her brother is punished with military exile. Yue'e offers to accompany him, and the two of them marry. Actual incest is neatly averted, but sexual transgression that hints strongly at incest is certainly the order of the day. The quasi-incest here is the reverse of that in *Xingshi hengyan*'s "Master Dugu Has a Nightmare": there Dugu Xiashu approaches his wife in the guise of a stranger; here, young Yao approaches a stranger who then passes as his sister.

In both these stories by Ling Mengchu, once a woman has left the embrace of her family, she becomes a target for a sexual free-for-all, vulnerable to approaches from any and all, including relatives; in fact, the only way such a woman can return to her family is through some form of proxy incest, whether it actually takes place or not. A cousin seemingly invites everyone around him to mistake his interest for desire; a couple who are deemed to be brother and sister by all around them furtively have sex with each other. In the latter narrative, the brother cannot approach his potential sister except through the possibility of sexual relations, and once Yue'e proves herself not to be his sister, Yao immediately hops into bed with her, as if sex cements their unrelated status. Moreover, that odd union with its persistent hint of incest is ultimately legitimized and integrated into the family, with a sister and sister-in-law, doubles for each other who are destined to be members of the same family for life.

All the stories I have discussed so far were written in the late Ming; after an actual dynastic fall, these issues—the separation of families and the threat of rape—become invested with an altogether different weight. Two of the most famous early Qing collections of *huaben*, *Zuixing shi* (The sobering stone; from the late 1640s) and *Doupeng xianhua* (Idle talk under the bean arbor; ca. 1668), contain no narratives about separated families finding their way back together, partly because, I suppose, in the wake of an actual dynastic fall, the possibility of a fractured polity reassembled imperfectly was far too real. Instead, there are plenty of narratives that assert that nothing has happened, choosing not to emphasize the fracture that separated families always represent and valorizing instead claims of seamlessness: chastity and loyalty. Perhaps for similar reasons, the few narratives of separation in *Xihu erji* (Second collection of West Lake stories; from the mid-1640s) are noteworthy only for their blandness.

Reunions in genres more deeply committed to historical fidelity are nothing like the ones we have seen. In various accounts in *biji* (or collections of anecdotes), reunions are shown to be so flawed as to be questionable. In "A Short Biography of Prince Baihong's Concubine Ms Hu," for example, the scholar and poet Shi Runzhang (1618–83) writes of a young woman whose life closely resembles a *huaben* narrative: a native of Jiangxi province, she is kidnapped at the age of eight *sui* and passed along until she ends up as the concubine of a Manchu prince, who dotes on her. Nonetheless, she mourns the fact that she was separated from her parents at such an early age, and she remembers enough from her childhood that her husband is able to track down her mother. Compare this supposedly nonfictional reunion scene with those in other accounts:

> When she got there, mother and child did not recognize each other. Lord Xing'an [her husband, the magistrate of Xing'an] pointed at them and said, "How can you be suspicious about this? Your appearance and your air resemble each other so much! So how can you suspect otherwise?" At this they embraced each other and wept.[7]

This reunion—possibly engineered by a husband to appease a depressed concubine—seems subject to question in a way that probably tainted many a real-life reunion, but none of the fictional ones treated in this chapter.

Two of the stories in Li Yu's collection of short stories *Shier lou* (Twelve towers; 1657) deal with the reunion of a fractured family in the wake of the Ming dynasty's fall. In the eleventh story (a version of which Li Yu later transformed into the *chuanqi* play *Qiao tuanyuan, The Miraculous Reunion*), a family is paradoxically not separated but reunited because of the Mongol invasion, giving the lie to the conventional description of political chaos, that even "fathers and sons will not watch out for each other" (*fuzi bugu* 父子不顧).

The plot unfolds over decades; after their only son vanishes, Yin Xiaolou and his wife, Ms Pang, suppose that he has been taken by a tiger. They fail to conceive another child and begin to consider adoption. Wealthy people who live frugally, they are wary. Even under the best of circumstances, they think, an adopted son cannot be compared to a natural one in his feelings for his parents. And given their reputation for wealth, they are especially afraid that someone mercenary will take advantage of them.

So Yin Xiaolou comes up with a plan. Dressing himself in rags, he wanders from town to town seeking not to sell himself into servitude as a servant but to find a well-to-do orphan interested in adopting a concerned parent. He hangs a placard around his neck announcing his intent, but instead of taking him up on his offer, strangers jeer at him until finally a young man, Yao Ji, comes to his rescue and actually buys him. The two live in perfect harmony for a while, although Yin Xiaolou carefully continues to keep his real name and wealth a secret. But then the Mongols invade, and the Song troops rebel. The new father and son duo prepare to flee, but the son insists first on finding the young woman he regards as his fiancée. She isn't technically so, as even Yao Ji acknowledges; she is the daughter of his former patron, and engagement negotiations between the two parties fell through.

Nonetheless, after the two men hear that rebelling soldiers have gone through the countryside abducting women, Yao Ji determines that he must rescue Miss Cao. Once they reach their destination, the two men are separated, before Yin Xiaolou has a chance to divulge his real name to his now-beloved adopted son. After losing his father, Yao Ji continues on his pursuit to find his fiancée. The rebelling troops have set up a market to sell the captured women, and, with a few taels of silver in hand, Yao Ji decides that he will buy back Miss Cao.

But things do not turn out quite so smoothly. The rebels foresee that all the buyers will want the young and pretty women, leaving them with a surfeit of the old and unattractive that they cannot sell. So instead of auctioning off the women, they decide to sell them by weight. Each woman will be bound and wrapped in a bag, so that no buyer can possibly know anything about her, whether her name, her age, or her appearance.

Yao Ji finds himself in surreal circumstances, somehow redolent with significance; surrounded by the bags of women, all faceless, to be measured and purchased only according to their weight, transformed from individuals into a pure form of commodity. Only after he enters this marketplace, does he read a notice informing him that:

> In this marketplace of people, passersby are not permitted to come in and peek. Anyone who does not buy and leaves empty-handed will be investigated for fraud and will be executed for the crime of smuggling. There will be no lenience. By special directive.[8]

In other words, now that he has entered, he is stuck. He cannot leave without making a purchase. Not only must the choice be random, but it must also be made. Yet from this assortment of unidentifiable bags, he is to find in the next few pages first his mother and then his wife. How does that happen?

Partly it happens because Yao Ji is openly undiscriminating. Obviously he sets off for this marketplace in the hopes of finding a specific woman, Miss Cao, but he also admits to himself that so long as he manages to pick a reasonably attractive young woman, he will be happy to make her his wife. And when the woman who emerges from the bag turns out to be, not white-skinned and young, but white-haired and old, he makes do. He has had such a good experience with his adopted father that perhaps, he thinks, this woman inappropriate to be his own wife can serve him as an adopted mother and even be married to his new father.

The old lady takes to him, too. After Yao Ji confesses his original goal in buying her, she tells him that she and Miss Cao became friends during their captivity, and then she gives him the clue to finding his fiancée: she always carries in her sleeve a thin jade slab, and so by poking around in the bags and feeling for the hard slab he should be able to find her. The old woman's suggestion works, and Yao Ji finds Miss Cao, carrying what turns out to be the jade ruler that Yao Ji himself had given her as a keepsake.

The three of them—new mother, son, and daughter-in-law—head for the old woman's home. Once there, Yao Ji is shocked to find his beloved adopted father. To him, it is coincidence, but of course Yin Xiaolou has simply returned to the house he shares with his wife, Ms Pang—who happens to be the old lady Yao Ji has adopted as his mother. Yin Xiaolou and his wife are thrilled that each has adopted the same son, whom they then proceed to show around their house. Yao Ji is surprised, because the room he is shown comes straight out of his dreams of childhood. Aloud, he recollects all the toys he associates with the room—and the two old people are stunned. This, then, must be their own son, who disappeared in early childhood. Then Yao Ji proves his identity by pulling his pants down and revealing that he, like the boy they lost so many years ago, has only a single testicle. All four celebrate their miraculous reunion and live happily ever after, generation following generation in prosperity and fruitfulness, and with all the sons and grandsons marked by a single testicle.

The joke is fairly obvious: everything normal both about family relations and about literary conventions has been inverted. A family has been put together in backwards order: the son adopts the father and finds a wife for him; the mother has chosen a grown daughter-in-law before she has a son. In another inversion, a family reunion is described precisely as if it were a romance. By the middle of the seventeenth century, one sort of romantic comedy was already a cliché: two young people betrothed to each other in childhood fall in love through coincidence in early adulthood only to find out at the end that they were engaged all along, so that a union created through choice turns out to be sanctioned by orthodoxy. Similarly, Yao Ji treats the old man and old woman with filiality and respect before he discovers that they are his true parents. And finally, the reunion takes place in the midst of the Mongol invasion of China; paradoxically, without the intercession of the Mongols and total political chaos, there would be no family reunion.

—

I want to return to the image of Yao Ji standing in the midst of all the bags of women. The story undoes the power of that image, as if it is too disturbing to be allowed to rest: in fact, he does not draw his wife randomly from a lot of women, and the circumstances in which Yao Ji finds himself are partly defused by the fact that there is nothing at all random in who ends up part of the family. The first day, despite his high hopes, he stands no chance at all of finding his intended, since all the bags are filled with old women. And when he returns the second day, knowing the secret to identifying Miss Cao, he can single her out even though she is covered by a bag, foiling the rules of the rebelling troops who would insist that every choice must be random.

In other words, Yao Ji both cheats and plays fair: he is lucky enough to pick the single woman among all those bags who will enable him to be reunited with his family. But consider his circumstances if he had not been so blessed with outrageous luck and if he hadn't cheated. Are they simply those in which every man finds himself? Certainly there is a way of seeing the dynastic transition as precisely the moment when men are surrounded by bags of women—

when the polity has been fragmented so thoroughly that reassembling the family is an act more of assigning fixed roles to randomly procured women than of finding the right women to assign those titles to. Each bagged woman possessed an identity beforehand—as someone's daughter, certainly, but also perhaps as someone's wife or someone's mother. In wartime all that is taken away, and people are simply commodities, bodies stripped of personhood, capable of sexual union with anybody who will buy them. For a brief moment, we have returned to the world before the sages, before fathers and sons and before husbands and wives. In some sense, the scene in which Yao Ji is faced with these bags of women is a staging of the sort of sexual danger that Langxian and Ling Mengchu describe as being central to the family reunion: here, too, the women can be identified only after they have been purchased for sexual consumption.

Of course, there is even the possibility that these circumstances are not limited to moments of dynastic collapse, but that every man in society is ultimately surrounded by faceless bags, forced to choose unknowingly. Obviously it is true when a man marries; having no idea what she looks like, a groom might as well purchase his bride in a bag, albeit one labeled with her family's name. Is this every man's relationship with every woman? Like Yao Ji, once a man ventures forward, he must make a decision. Or perhaps we are to understand this moment in the story as symbolic of the relation between men and women in some greater sense: men with names and identities choose (or buy, according to the story) women lacking any such markers. Personal identity is an attribute of men—passed on only indirectly to women. Primarily these women are to be regarded as bodies, bought and sold specifically without regard for the contents. After he picks a bagged woman, her primary identity would be through him.

But this theory does not quite work either, since Yao Ji's fixedness of identity turns out to be an illusion. Our ideas about his identity turn out to be false: he thinks that he is an orphan by the name of Yao Ji, and he turns out instead to possess living parents by the surname of Yin. The woman he purchases ultimately does not derive her identity from Yao Ji's but instead as his true mother confers a real identity on him. For, of course, Yao Ji is not who he thinks he is, a fact known even by his erstwhile fiancée (at the very end of the story, she explains that the engagement originally fell through because of her family's uncertainty about Yao Ji's origins). Each immediate member of the family is somehow entirely free-floating, unmoored from any familial fixity, and yet, untethered from any firm identity, each roots the others.

At any rate, the image of Yao Ji, armed with funds enough to buy only one woman, forced to make a selection from among the bags of anonymous women, seems to have a symbolic reach that the story's specifics attempt to undo. Before his troubles, those of Yao Dizhu's brother and Zhu Donglao pale; in both those narratives, the mechanics of determining who belongs to a family—and who does not—take over almost immediately. In contrast, for Yao Ji, only a miracle saves him from perhaps never knowing if he has committed incest. But what of all the other men shopping for women at the same market? They must live without the assurance Yao Ji is almost magically granted. The image of the man standing before the bags of women is a powerful symbol of how a patriarchy's means of maintaining the mechanics of exogamy can be thoroughly and perhaps permanently disabled. Aside from the miracle of Yao Ji's family, we cannot feel particularly sanguine about the future of this polity as a whole. New dynastic structures might be imposed, but new familial ones cannot. How that patriarchy—and not just Yao Ji's family—can be put back together out of such random components is left unclear.

—

The tenth story in the *Shier lou* collection features another family with an unusual history. For seven generations, the line of succession among this branch of the Shu clan has been preserved only by the tenuous thread of a single son. Lacking brothers, "of the *wulun* they were missing one."[9] The only son of the seventh generation, a learned scholar, marries a beautiful and virtuous woman, but they do not have a child together until they are both thirty. Nonetheless, the birth of this much-awaited son, so necessary to the continuation of the family, shocks the rest of the community, since the story takes place precisely at the moment of the Ming's fall when bandits and rebels are rampaging through the south.

The narrator relates that at this time the bodies of pregnant women were rendered for fat and babies were used for target practice. Nine out of ten pregnant women aborted their fetuses, and nine out of ten babies born were killed by their own parents hoping to spare their child from suffering. In deciding to give birth to this baby, Mrs. Shu appears to the community not as virtuous, but as sly and conniving. In such times, so pretty a woman with a baby must surely sacrifice either her chastity or her child's life, and her seemingly natural desire to have a child must have some licentious ulterior motive. We are meant to understand that dynastic crisis has undone all norms of behavior.

Immediately after the boy's birth, Scholar Shu begins to fret over what will become of his family. His wife asks him what he wants her to do, since it seems clear that she will be faced with an impossible choice between two different moral imperatives, each, it would seem, equally absolute: should she sacrifice her life to preserve her chastity, consequently leaving her helpless nursling to starve without her? Or should she do whatever she must to save the baby's life? Mrs. Shu points out that chastity is the ultimate virtue a woman can show; Scholar Shu responds that although that might be so in times of peace, it certainly is not now. Mrs. Shu objects that if she were to accommodate herself, they could certainly never reunite in a time of peace. In other words, even before they are separated, husband and wife worry about how their relation is to be reconstituted.

A cold-blooded decision to submit herself to the bandits would be too radical even for Li Yu's sensibilities, so Mrs. Shu's ultimate surrender must be shown to be involuntary (similarly, Ming and Qing law made it the responsibility of the victim to prove rape). This part of the story is perhaps the grimmest version imaginable of that late Ming debate over which of the Five Normative Relations—marriage or filiality—ought to be given primacy (and also gives some indication of the high stakes of those abstract discussions). Since nothing short of her chastity and the future of the Shu bloodline hang in the balance, the discussions cannot remain private. The decision to trade her chastity for the life of her infant son must be public and involuntary. Scholar Shu calls a meeting of his whole clan and relates the series of discussions between husband and wife. His wife is then brought into the clan temple, and all the clansmen urge her to do whatever is necessary to keep the baby safe, while Mrs. Shu continues to protest: what, for example, if she loses her virtue and yet the baby still dies? Still resistant to their urgings, she insists on asking the ancestors their opinion. To that end, two slips are made up, one reading "Preserve Chastity" and the other "Save the Child"; "Save the Child" is drawn.

Shortly thereafter, she is indeed captured, along with her baby son. Months later, after the establishment of the new dynasty, there is an announcement that the captives, who by this time have mostly found their way into the Qing armies, have begun to be ransomed and returned to their families. Scholar Shu liquidates everything he owns and sets off to find his family, but even as all the families around him reunite, he fails to find his wife and child. Gradually he sinks into total destitution and is taken captive by soldiers.

His wailing disturbs a general's lady, who (separated from him by a curtain) interrogates him as to his identity and his mission. Then she orders him shackled outside until the general arrives to decide his fate. The lady who issues this command turns out to be none other than Mrs. Shu, now attached to the general. For four days of rain, Scholar Shu suffers horribly in his shackles. By the time the general returns and orders the shackles removed, they have rusted and grown stuck to his ankles. At first it seems they will not come off, and when they finally do, they tear off his flesh. Mrs. Shu has masterminded this whole torture to demonstrate to the general that in his absence there was not even the possibility of impropriety. In fact, the severity of Scholar Shu's wounds even precisely dates the length of his confinement, proving that there was no time for any hanky-panky to have taken place. Without such proof, the suspicious general would have killed Scholar Shu. In other words, she tortures her husband to save his life. Virtues are turned on their heads.

Mrs. Shu finds herself in a position where expressing any residual feeling for her husband would show her lack of chastity to another man, who would then kill her husband; paradoxically, showing him any loyalty would be a supremely disloyal act. At this moment, only by treating him as a perfect stranger can she be a dutiful wife. If they had shown any feeling for each other, her behavior would have been licentious fornication, and her husband would have been killed for being an adulterer. (Strangely enough, they, too, are reunited through a barely averted sexual encounter, once again with a twist; this time, a wife avoids even the appearance of adultery with her husband.)

Earlier, Mrs. Shu had told the general that her son was the last of a long line of only sons. Should her husband ever return, the general had promised, the child would be returned to his family; so the child's fate has been decided already. But what of the woman? She responds to the general's query by repeating what she had much earlier told her husband: "It goes without saying that I cannot return to him, but even if I did want to go with him, how would I be able to face him?"[10] Explaining the incredible lengths to which Mrs. Shu went to keep the child alive, the general hands him over to Scholar Shu, who is immensely grateful: "I count getting this boy back as immeasurable good fortune. How could I even hope to get my wife back? With this, I will bid farewell."[11]

On the journey home he weeps, thinking of his wife, now lost to him; and as they sail off, a messenger from the general catches up to them to tell them that the instant they had departed, his wife had hanged herself. When they cut her down, she was already dead, but the general was able to force medicine down her throat and revive her. Afterwards, the general asks her why she has attempted suicide when he already offered to return her to her husband. She explains that she had promised earlier that if she was forced to lose her chastity, she would kill herself after saving the child. The general says, "Now you have already died once, so it can be said that you have not gone back on your word."[12]

And this is indeed what happens. The general sends word to Scholar Shu that Mrs. Shu's return is the general's own intent and has nothing to do with her own desires. Once again, the story stages the internal; what transpires must be *proved* beyond a shadow of a doubt to be against her will. The general concludes with a suggestion to Scholar Shu for how the couple might make things right:

> "When you get back, say that your first wife died, and that you've married another beauty. Set up a memorial arch to that virtuous woman, so that you can commemorate her name to future generations." With that, the

general set up a boat and filled it with all the things that Mrs. Shu used in her daily life—her clothes, her jewelry, household goods—and gave it to them as a dowry. Then the newlyweds along with their boy set off for the return home.[13]

The texts I have discussed so far suggest that for the family to be joined together again something heterodox *must* take place. The moment of neatly skirted transgression lies embedded in this story as well.

But here Li Yu poses an additional question, which in the latter half of the seventeenth century was necessarily a charged political one: whether families that are recreated are the same as the ones that existed before. This is the world of that field of bagged women, where recovering true families seems to depend on a miracle. Li Yu concludes by explaining:

> This act of righteousness is the first notable act since the founding of the dynasty; I only regret that the name of the general could not be established and not daring to give him one without authorization, I have referred to him here simply as "the general."[14]

Li Yu has left the general nameless, but he is clearly not a bandit (unlike the hooligans who capture Mrs. Shu and run everyone out of their homes and with whom the general contrasts so radically). Instead, he seems to be a victorious Manchu, or a Ming general who has turned to the Manchu side. The "act of righteousness" to which Li Yu refers is obviously part Mrs. Shu's and part the general's.

The general says he can have any woman and certainly does not need despoil virtuous ones (*jiefu* 節婦). But that explanation does not account for the extremes of his change of mind. First a rabidly jealous husband, the kind of man who would tally the days Scholar Shu had been shackled by measuring the severity of his wounds, he undergoes a strange transformation over the course of the story and ends as a makeshift father, in charge of preparing a dowry for her and giving advice to Scholar Shu. Without the general, Mrs. Shu could not have returned. Not only would she have died if he had not resurrected her, but her return runs counter to her stated wishes. Instead, just as her sacrifice of chastity was up to her husband's clansmen (and the fates that chose the right chit), her return must be at the general's command.

We can read this reunion as a slightly imperfect metaphor for dynastic change. Reunion and dynastic change beg for comparison with each other, whether one is metaphor for the other, or whether what occurs at the familial scale is simply at the mercy of the imperial. Of course, the comparison between loyalty to one's husband and loyalty to the state is one of the oldest in Chinese literature. Does the general somehow stand in for the new regime? If Mrs. Shu has her dowry made up the first time by her father, the second time the union is sealed with a dowry made up by the general. Long before their separation, Mrs. Shu asks rhetorically how she and her husband could ever reunite if she lost her chastity. The answer turns out to be through the general or, rather, the new order he represents.

Take, for example, Mrs. Shu's behavior when she encounters her first husband again. I have already mentioned how peculiar it is that chastity to her old husband forces her to have him tortured and to treat him as a perfect stranger. It is also notable, though, that chastity to her new husband and chastity to her old husband demand precisely the same behavior—and that initially at least it is impossible to determine whether she behaves as she does because of loyalty to the first or to the second husband. In fact, this sort of loyalty is quite unusual. It is hard to come up with other examples of behavior of exemplary loyalty whose object is unclear, but it seems very close to that encouraged by the Qing dynasts a few generations later, when they valorized Ming loyalists like Shi Kefa who had died opposing their own Manchu ancestors. Loyalty is loyalty, so went the argument, its object relatively unimportant.

The story may appear to end just as it begins, with a husband, his chaste wife, and their son. But it is made excruciatingly clear that Mrs. Shu's return is far from seamless and has exacted a great cost. The dynastic transition cannot be shown to be too easy. A choice had to be made: either rejoin her husband or die for chastity. In other words, the marriage with which we began needs to become two marriages, one concluded by death, just as the order that has fragmented and yet remains the same must be marked by the two dynasties.

There is another effect as well: the general who gives her a dowry and forces the couple back together has been permanently rewritten into their union. This new marriage has no legitimacy without him. And what does that general who represents the new order get for all his troubles? He earns Li Yu's praise, for "the first act of righteousness" in the new dynasty. In relinquishing the woman, he earns his own legitimacy.

Or perhaps rather than two marriages, we might see the story as involving two women, both of whom are called Mrs. Shu (which might explain Li Yu's reticence about her name, in such a long and involved story in which her subjectivity and volition are so important). The name Mrs. Shu refers both to the virtuous woman whose death is commemorated by the arch and, as the general says, to the bride with the new dowry. Scholar Shu is married to both women. What takes place between the general and Scholar Shu is in some senses a wife swap: beneath everything else, some sort of complicated exchange takes place between the men. The general emerges with legitimacy (and divests himself of blame for the wife's suicide, even though, of course, he is her rapist), and Scholar Shu returns home accompanied by a brand-new wife, with no blemish on her reputation. Each has given away something to receive something else; in some sense, *two* women are necessary for this particular act of legitimation to occur, as the narratives with which I conclude this chapter make clear. In the decades to come, when the new dynasty had become well established, it is the specifics of that exchange that would be of interest.

A few decades into the Qing dynasty, the problem looked quite different. Li Yu's concerns in the immediate aftermath of the Ming fall—when only a miracle grants Yao Ji's family names and when Mrs. Shu is faced with such a gutwrenching decision—seemed a thing of the distant past. I conclude this chapter with a discussion of two short classical narratives that pick up where some of the themes from the *Shier lou* stories leave off. Both narratives make some claim, no matter how tenuous, to veracity, even as the events related strain credibility. Where Li Yu's *huaben* treat even the grimmest of themes with humor, these two classical narratives have stripped the same themes down to political philosophy.

In "Biography of the young scholar from Baowu" in the *biji* collection *Beishu xuyan*, Lu Ciyun (whose exact dates are unknown, but who lived through the fall of the Ming to serve the Qing as an official) cites Shi Runzhang's account of another reunion.[15] A man of Shangshan lost his wife in the chaos, only to have her become the wife of a Manchu soldier. That same Manchu soldier also lost his wife—who then married the man of Shangshan. Running into each other, the two men swap wives. Both of the old marriages are restored, and each couple proceeds on its way. Precisely how this could have happened defies the imagination. Surely opportunities for two such peculiar couples to present themselves and then examine each other in public must have been few indeed, but for the swap to have been made it would have been necessary for all four to have been present simultaneously.

As in the tenth story from the *Shier lou*, there is a Manchu here who has been emptied of all content: no longer culturally different, seemingly not responsible for the fall of the Ming, just a marker for a new order that has been recreated and that claims some continuity with the old. The loss of his wife makes his position equal to that of the man from Shangshan, and his marriage is just as necessary to the restoration of order as the man of Shangshan's. Once again, a wife swap edges into allegory for a smooth dynastic transition. After a momentary lapse in which a central Confucian norm is violated (just like Mrs. Shu, these wives are not even widows when they take up with the other men), all is restored as if nothing had happened. Similarly, loyalty to a new dynasty can be restored after a moment of supreme disloyalty. One effect of such an exchange—one wife for another—is to naturalize the Manchu conquest and integrate it fully into the very unions out of which the Chinese polity is created.

Shier lou 10 concludes with a wife swap between the general and Scholar Shu, miraculously effected with a single wife. Here, there is a much more explicit wife swap. Like many *huaben*, this *biji* account breaks into two, the second of which is a straightforward narrative of a wife exchange. The first half is a longer and more complicated meditation on the sexual politics of dynastic fall. Lu Ciyun describes how an unnamed couple who are natives of the Jiangnan region barely survive the conquest: the man is forced to hide himself among a stack of corpses, and in the course of her flight, the woman is captured by Manchu soldiers. After hurrying to the place she was last seen, her husband slumps down in despair at a nearby inn when he discovers that she and her captors have disappeared. After asking him a few questions, the innkeeper hires him on the spot to keep the books.

The young man is so clever and organized that after he begins working for the inn, its profits soar, and the innkeeper even offers him his own daughter in marriage (an offer the young man deflects without really explaining why). One day, a patron hurries in for a quick meal at the crack of dawn and leaves a mysterious package behind. Opening it up, the young man finds fifty *liang* of gold that he keeps in a safe place until the customer returns. When the forgetful customer returns in a panic, he explains that the money is for his wedding. Taking his money, he hurries off again.

In a few days, the young man and the innkeeper receive an invitation to the wedding. Without the brideprice, the wedding could not have taken place, or as the invitation says, "This wedding you gave to me."[16] The innkeeper declines but sends his employee, the young man, in his stead. Once there, he catches a glimpse of the bride, in a boat, dressed in wedding finery. She so resembles his missing wife that he collapses in shock on the riverbank. She, too, collapses. After the boat reaches its destination, the woman explains that she saw a man who looked just like her former husband, and she describes his appearance and his attire.

The prospective groom—the young man whose money had been lost and then found again—quickly goes to find the man singled out by the woman. The would-be groom tells him, "I know. This woman is your wife. Since you found the gold, it's your gold. By returning the gold, you ransomed your wife, and this is heaven's command to me that I took your place to restore your match. Do not be sad! I've been moved by your righteousness. Could I dare not to recompense you?"[17] We finally get some sense of what makes this wedding such an unusual one; the brideprice of fifty *liang* of gold that the prospective groom almost lost turns out not to have gone to the woman's parents as would usually be the case in a match, but, we presume, to her captors. The fortuitous discovery and return of the gold allows the prospective groom to assume a position like that of the bride's parents and give the bride away, this time back to her husband. The original husband is reluctant to accept such generosity, and his employer the innkeeper is brought in to decide what to do. The innkeeper agrees that each prospective man has done the other a good turn: "He who returns money is a righteous man; the act of returning a wife is no less righteous than returning money." Their good turns are equal—which might leave them even, except that the prospective groom has spent fifty *liang* of gold for a bride that he now has renounced any claim to.

But the innkeeper has a way to make it all work out: he offers up his own daughter, the very one he had been offering to his bookkeeper. Now the original husband and wife can be reunited without depriving the prospective groom of a wife. The original husband is rewarded for his good deed by the return of his wife, and the prospective groom is rewarded for his generosity in giving up the wife he bought with the substitution of another, equally suitable one. Now the innkeeper seems to have taken a loss, by giving his daughter away with no brideprice—but he is simply paying back the original husband for having earned the business so much money through his accounting skills and business acumen. In other words, the original husband owes the gift of his wife both to the prospective groom and to his boss. (Unfortunately, though, the fifty *liang* of gold still ends up with the wife's captors.) It all works out perfectly—but not in such a way that these ties can ever be severed. The two marriages that are constituted seal those ties for good.

This account is filled with details that beg for some explanation. Obviously, real-life women who were spoils of war were not commonly disposed of in bags as Yao Ji's fiancée and mother are, nor in the elaborate wedding ceremony described in this narrative. Fifty *liang* of gold seems to have been the going rate for a good-looking woman (or at least so one gathers from one of the narratives I discuss at the end of this chapter).[18] However, one would be quite surprised to find a bride acquired in such a heterodox fashion bedecked in wedding finery since the sellers were not obligated to provide a dowry. After all, these are not family to whom she is bringing pride through an elaborate wedding. Or are they? Is she being married off by her captors or by surrogate parents? The prosperous innkeeper seems an unlikely figure to be selling his daughter into concubinage. He clearly means for his daughter to become the wife of the prospective groom, which leads one to imagine that the prospective groom had been aiming to acquire a wife.

Consequently, the story revolves around a lacuna: how the wife manages to go from a captive of Manchu soldiers to a legitimate bride commanding a lofty price. Wife-selling was illegal throughout the late imperial period, punished with special harshness during the eighteenth century, but really always a practice of people so poor as to have no other options, as Matthew Sommer has shown.[19] The prosperous small business owner here and the original groom with his talent for bookkeeping would be unlikely participants in such a practice.

Everything looks very much like a legitimate wedding, but the story never explicitly explains who ends up getting that gold. Just as she has too many husbands, the unnamed wife also has too many parents. Her Manchu captors seem rather miscast in that role, but like the general with whom Mrs. Shu takes up, somehow they are implicated in this marriage, which is, if anything, *more* right than the marriage between the same two partners which existed before. Once again, I think we are virtually bound to read this—if not precisely as allegory—then as microcosm of what is to happen after the conquest. Just as Li Yu does, Lu Ciyun employs the venerable trope of reunion to articulate a political anxiety connected to dynastic transition.

What happens to families when the mandate changes hands, if the legitimacy of the emperor both formally resembles and is intimately tied to the legitimacy of families? In that light, it is absolutely essential that these separated family members happen to be husband and wife, rather than parent and child or siblings, precisely because the relation between husband and wife *does* allow for interlopers and substitutes in a way that those other familial relations do not. The marital relation resembles that between liege and vassal in a way the other relations do not. Marriage is the one tie among the *wulun* whose moment of origin can be easily pinpointed.

This woman now reunited with her husband has had her chastity violated (we cannot begin to guess what might have happened to her during the period of her captivity, but even the suspicion of such doings led many a late imperial woman to suicide). Nonetheless, her marriage to her original husband is restored seamlessly, except for one detail. Through the transaction and exchange of dowry and brideprice, marriages in general tie together two families. In this narrative of the innkeeper, no less than four parties are involved and necessary—the original husband and wife, the prospective groom, and the innkeeper, father of the other bride.

Reunion that takes place through transgression creates something new. Normatively, gift exchange and continued contact through marriage forges ties between two families, creating one out of two. To an anthropologist, such a marriage is founded on a dyadic, or closed, exchange network. In other words, the tie that binds the bride's and the groom's families together excludes all others. Writing about the Gawa of New Guinea, the anthropologist Nancy Munn speculates as to what would happen if all exchanges took place simply between two parties:

> If partners formed relationships with each other only in terms of *skwayobwa* [a simple exchange], each dyad in which a man participated would constitute an isolated intersubjective spacetime of repeated reciprocities with its own internal timing of transactions relative to his other hospitality relations; but there would be no formal connection (or potential for connection) between these separate spacetimes.[20]

Dyadic exchanges, in other words, can easily become isolated. Marriages work the same way as the Gawans' *skwayobwa*, creating binary connections. One marriage bears no particular connection to another, since each one marks a connection between two parties. So how is one to imagine a polity constructed of marriages, if each is independent of all others?

The trick in imagining a polity constructed out of such marriages is to imagine an infinity of different binary connections, existing at the same time with other connections such as parenthood and siblinghood, linking all together in a complex web. But what of moments—like that of dynastic transition—when that imagined simultaneity has been disrupted, and when, as character after character would tell us, parenthood and sibling relations have also been disabled? Clearly a dyadic exchange would seem insufficient in imagining the regeneration of such a complex network; two tied together is hardly better than one. A tie that binds just two—but that can be imagined in parallel over infinity—loses its imaginative grip at a time of dynastic fall.

When, however, husband and wife are reunited with the help of the innkeeper and the prospective bridegroom, the ties created by marriage function very differently, binding all four together. Just as they would have with only two, financial obligations and new familial ties make these bonds impossible to tear asunder. The old narrative trope of reunion turns out to recapitulate all the complexities of the political transition. Perhaps the four can even stand in for the healing polity as a whole.

—

These exchanges are complicated all the more in Zhou Lianggong's "A Record of the Qi Sanlang Affair," another classical tale of a man whose wife is captured during the fall of the dynasty but who eventually comes to be reunited with her. Posthumously defamed as an *erchen*, or official who served both dynasties, Zhou Lianggong (1612–72) probably wrote this piece while in prison under suspicion of corruption; nonetheless, it breathes not a hint of loyalism or nostalgia for the old order. Instead, this tale shows in miniature how the polity might be woven back together sounder than ever, partly through the restoration of old normative ties like marriage and partly through the creation of a new web of relations.

The first half of this complicated narrative tells, not of separation and reunion, but of miraculous survival in the wake of dynastic fall. After Qi Sanlang is captured and separated from his wife, he is attacked by soldiers and left for dead. Two old neighbors bring him home to care for him. Only when he wakes from his coma does he realize that all along the old couple have been dead; other than his young son, he is alone with the two corpses. He goes to find workmen to help him make coffins for his ghostly benefactors, and they, too, turn out to be ghosts who end up making coffins not just for the two who nursed Qi Sanlang back to life but also for themselves. This narrative foreshadows what is to come. One debt—in this case, Qi Sanlang's to the old neighbors who rescue him—is discharged in a way that defies simple dyadic exchange. He owes just two old people, but in paying them back, others find their final resting places, too.

Qi Sanlang then sets off to find his kidnapped wife. Before the war, Qi Sanlang, his wife, and son had made their home near a temple to the god Guan Yu, so Qi Sanlang is not too surprised when Guan Yu appears in a dream to tell him where to find a boat, among the willows at a nearby ford. But there is a man waiting inside the boat: like Qi Sanlang, Cheng San is also on a mission to find his wife, also captured and taken to the south. Cheng San is looking for a companion and takes Qi Sanlang on immediately because he is so impressed by his tale of magical survival.

Together they proceed to Shengzhou, where at a crossroads Qi Sanlang puts up a public notice identifying himself and promising a reward in gold to anyone who can help him find his wife. A Mr. X comes forward—at which point, Qi Sanlang is forced to confess that he has lied about the reward money. Instead, Qi Sanlang and Cheng San tell Mr. X how Qi Sanlang has made it thus far: how divine protection has manifested itself first in his salvation and then in his dream. The story takes the place of the reward, and Mr. X even helps Qi Sanlang earn some money, by copying sutras for a certain lord.

Mr. X takes Qi Sanlang to the household of a Mr. He, and Qi immediately goes to the women's quarters to ask Mrs. He whether she knows anything about his missing wife. Mrs. He proposes a straightforward trade: "Give me the gold, and I will give you your wife."[21] After Qi Sanlang gives Mrs. He all of his hard-earned gold, she simply disappears within the house, only to emerge pretending that she had never received any gold. Qi Sanlang and Mr. X protest, but she accuses them of lying.

Qi Sanlang returns to Cheng San with neither gold nor wife. Next morning, Cheng goes to call on Mr. He. With nothing left to trade, Cheng bargains with the only thing he has left, his life. Whipping out a dagger from his shoe, he says: "If you do not give Qi his wife, you will be splattered with blood as I slit my throat."[22]

Mr. He goes into the house, and as Cheng San and Qi Sanlang kneel outside begging him to stop, Mr. He scolds and beats his wife. He returns with the ten gold pieces, which he then throws on the ground. Cheng speaks for both: the gold is not important, but the return of the woman is, and Mr. He should keep the gold. Mr. He is moved by Cheng's righteousness and his willingness to lay his life on the line for his friend's wife, and so he has the woman in question come out.

When Ms Wang emerges, she does not look familiar to Qi. Instead, Cheng rushes forward to embrace her, and the two weep with joy: she is his wife, and not his friend's. Mr. X has misidentified this woman: after she was kidnapped, she managed to leave a message on a wall identifying herself, her husband, and her kidnapper, Mr. He. Over time, pen strokes faded from the character Cheng (成), leaving only the character Wu (戊), which Mr. X had misread as Qi (戚).

Everyone knows that Cheng San's efforts on behalf of his friend were sincere and that the mix-up was an honest one. If the woman had indeed been Mrs. Qi, the tale would be at an end, but the ransoming of Cheng San's wife means that there are still some complicated debts outstanding. Cheng San explains why he is now even more embroiled in this situation: "But the gold came from Qi, and the woman is coming to me. How can I go? If I leave, then Qi's gold will not be returned, and I will truly have fought just for myself."[23] Mr. He takes the ten pieces of gold in exchange for the woman, leaving Cheng San and Qi Sanlang once again entirely penniless. This time, Mr. He recommends Cheng to a General Zhang, and Cheng indentures himself and his wife to Zhang for twenty gold pieces. With that sum, Cheng San intends for his friend to find his wife, but instead of taking the gold and buying his wife back in a straightforward way, Qi Sanlang insists that General Zhang keep the money and instead help him search for Ms Wang. Cheng San has not sold himself at all, but instead—Mauss-like—bestowed himself as a gift to General Zhang.

Relegated to cleaning the latrines for his new master, Cheng happens to hear women speaking in his native dialect. He walks over to the wall and, hoping that the women will overhear, mentions his friend Qi Sanlang, who is looking for his wife, née Wang. That night, a woman walks over to the latrines and leaves a note; she is indeed Qi's wife, Ms Wang. Mr. He, Cheng San, Qi Sanlang, and Qi's young son all go to General Zhang to tell him that Qi's wife is on his premises. Zhang checks their report with his harem of captured women—and sees at their head none other than Ms Wang, Qi Sanlang's wife.

When she emerges, both she and Qi Sanlang are so paralyzed by the depth of their feelings that neither approaches the other. But General Zhang, unlike everyone else Qi Sanlang has met on his journey, does not cooperate. Everyone else has refused to accept payment or participate in a simple exchange, thus freeing Qi Sanlang to continue on his way. We are almost expecting General Zhang to be so impressed by all that Cheng San and Qi Sanlang have gone through that he will return Qi's wife free of charge.

Instead, although the general agrees that Ms Wang is indeed Qi's wife, he points out, "But this person has some beauty. Therefore, I made her the head of my harem. She is worth approximately fifty pieces of gold. Half of that would still be insufficient. Do you expect to get your wife back?"[24] Qi Sanlang repeats the plea that he has used before: with "cities fallen and families ruined," he has no way to earn any money. General Zhang refuses, countering with the logic of the market. If he should release one woman so far beneath her market value, what will he do when others approach him for their wives?

At this point, General Zhang has both the twenty gold pieces and Qi Sanlang's wife. Qi Sanlang has nothing else to give, and he points out once again that General Zhang's is no ordinary sum of gold. These twenty pieces are what his friend Cheng and his wife have exchanged themselves for. Qi Sanlang beseeches heaven and weeps, which sets off a chain reaction: pretty soon, everybody—his wife, their child, Mr. He, all of Zhang's retainers, all the women, and finally even hard-hearted General Zhang himself—are weeping.

Finally, General Zhang agrees to participate in what is almost a version of a pyramid scheme: he concedes that Qi's story indicates divine intervention; he sees that unless he is willing to be generous, Qi Sanlang and Cheng San will be stuck in a cycle of mutual debt, with neither man able to pay the other back; and so he will return

Qi Sanlang's wife to her husband without any payment. He tells Qi Sanlang before the assembled crowd: "Because of you, Cheng sold himself to me. If you, husband and wife, are to return and Cheng remains and Cheng does not resent you, how will you pay him back?"[25] He had possessed the twenty gold pieces, Ms Wang, Cheng San, and his wife. Rather than participating in a trade and keeping some of these gains, he is now prepared to give everything back, leaving Qi Sanlang, Cheng San, and their wives to use the money for traveling expenses.

But there is one thing that Qi Sanlang has that General Zhang wants. Even with all the women in his harem, he has no son, and he would like to adopt Qi Sanlang's as his own. Qi Sanlang and his wife agree to the arrangement; the general fêtes them as relatives and sends them on their way. Over the next few years, the general stays in touch with Qi Sanlang, often showering him and his wife with presents. Later still, the general dies, and his clansmen seize his estate—forcing his adopted son, Qi Sanlang's biological son, to return to his own parents. The harem of women insist that young Qi return with many gifts and goods, and for generations thereafter, the Qis are a prosperous clan who make a point of continuing to serve the god Guan Yu faithfully.

—

In premodern China, buying a concubine to bear children was common, and of course money and the exchange of gifts were central to all premodern Chinese marriage practices, at all levels of society. In other words, under normal circumstances, money played an important, necessary, and entirely legitimate role in the construction of family. To buy a person—and specifically, a woman—with money was simply to participate in the market economy of the times, but each of these men, the husband of whom Lu Ciyun writes, Qi Sanlang, Cheng San, steadfastly avoids doing just that. Why not construct a tale around a husband's repurchase of his wife? Perhaps the husbands eschew using money partly because that sort of straightforward redemption of loved ones touches too closely on what actually happened, the random, haphazard buying back and replacing of the missing. (Recall Yao Ji's situation again—in real life, such a person would simply have had to resort to buying a new woman, as Yao Ji himself admits he is perfectly willing to do.) If the missing are to be replaced by the randomly selected, the reconstructed society hardly seems continuous at all with the old. Indeed, we are told over and over, society is not simply rebuilt through the buying back and replacing of women into their old positions.

All the moments that might turn into a purchase—the exchange of money for a person—are instead deferred and transformed. Sometimes, these deferrals appear highly formulaic, as when Cheng San threatens to kill himself with a dagger that he whips out from his shoe and so convinces Mr. He to return the woman he believes to be Qi Sanlang's wife. That moment, in which someone in the position of a liege is coerced through a demonstration of virtue, recalls earlier texts like Sima Qian's "Biographies of the Assassin-Retainers" ("Cike liezhuan"). In this story, however, the motivation for this moment is quite different: if the Hes keep both the money and the woman, the story comes to an end. Ostensibly Cheng San is hoping for the return of either the woman *or* the money, as would be fair in a market economy, but in reality, he demands the return of both. As he puts it, "Without our families, we die. Without our wives, we die. Without this gold, we also die."[26]

With so little to trade, Qi Sanlang verges dangerously close to existence as a stripped-down body. He begins with only two things of value, his person and his story of miraculous survival (the little boy is mentioned so rarely it comes almost as a surprise that he has been along for the entire journey). Cheng San and Qi Sanlang are penniless, with no means whatsoever to earn money other than selling themselves—which of course is a zero-sum proposition that defeats the entire purpose of reuniting both couples. Qi Sanlang even acquires his friend Cheng San only through his story. After all, Cheng San is the one with the boat—although the value of that object is never mentioned again (logically, we would assume that a boat should be worth quite a bit, perhaps even as much as a woman, but *that* trade cannot enter into the calculus of this tale, and so the boat is abandoned without explanation).

Qi Sanlang and Cheng San are engaged in a kind of shell game, in which each will trade himself for the other, but that kind of cycle of trading leaves the pair always short. By offering up his own life,

Cheng San demands that Mr. He participate in this cycle—Mr. He essentially makes a gift of Cheng San and his wife to the next patron down the line—which would not be the case if Mr. He had kept either the woman or the gold. Someone will always be in bondage for someone else's freedom; in fact, by the time they reach General Zhang's, all the pair's work has accomplished is the bondage of both Cheng San and his wife, instead of just his wife. If General Zhang had agreed to their proposal and accepted twenty pieces of gold for Ms Wang, the story would still not be at an end until Qi Sanlang and his wife had figured out how to bail Cheng San and his wife out. And simply selling themselves to free Cheng San and his wife would leave the foursome in the same bind. How to redeem all four, if they themselves are their only possessions of value?

Qi Sanlang's two articles of value (himself and his story) defeat the rules of commercial transaction; neither can be sold cleanly, in such a way that they cannot be sold again or so that the relationship between buyer and seller is concluded with the purchase. (For example, when Qi Sanlang shares his story of miraculous survival, it serves to bind him more strongly with the listener; unlike his money, the story can be duplicated infinitely without weakening its effect.) Purchase after purchase is deferred. Sometimes, Qi Sanlang manages to make unnecessary his own sale or Cheng San's by managing to convince people with his story of divine intervention; at other times Cheng San or Qi Sanlang simply refuse to participate in a purchase, as when Cheng indentures himself but then refuses to accept the price.

These deferrals continue all the way to the young boy, who is hardly mentioned until the very end of this story. One person is traded for another, even though we are told that all are indispensable to a true reunion, until we make our way to the little boy, who is somehow coded as dispensable (in contrast, Scholar Shu ranks his son above his wife, and both parents regard the boy as the single indispensable in their family). Nonetheless, the story ends happily only because even this final trade—Ms Wang for the little boy—is ultimately a failed one, and young Qi returns to his biological parents to continue a line of prosperous and successful Qis. In other words, down to the last one, none of the trades go through, and the story resolves the problem of trading only by deferring it.

To me, that suggests we are in a world of ritualized exchange and gift-giving, whose rules are articulated specifically in contrast to those of the market. Despite their complaints about the impossibility of earning money, twice Cheng and Qi actually refuse gold: instead of having money in hand, they prefer that the powerful men Mr. He and General Zhang should owe them indeterminate favors. General Zhang's attempt to bring up the logic of the market, namely what would happen to the value of all the women he holds should he sell one woman below market value, falls on deaf ears. Instead, all the men and women who weep when Qi Sanlang beseeches heaven for help—and whose response eventually badgers General Zhang into submission—proudly declare themselves bound by another brand of logic. They shame General Zhang into abandoning market logic, and he is essentially coerced into giving Qi Sanlang his wife as a handsome gift, worth fifty *liang* of gold. The self-consciousness with which characters ally themselves with the gift system on one hand—in full recognition of the market system on the other—suggests something of the sophistication with which people approached such matters.

If marriage is usually based on closed, dyadic exchange, here the circulation of men and women takes on a very different form. Li Yu makes the reunion between Scholar Shu and Mrs. Shu work out by introducing two more parties (even though one woman plays two roles, sacrificial victim and new bride); Lu Ciyun describes a marriage with four parties; but what takes place here is even more complicated. In this tale, both men and women approach the status not of gifts that bind together a single giver and a single recipient but of Munn's *kula* shells. Although they speak of being bought and sold, in fact these people are passed along not as commodities but as gifts.

Munn describes some closed exchanges, of the model that Marcel Mauss most famously described and explained—like the hospitality that is offered to a traveler who will reciprocate when his hosts visit his island later. However, her main focus is a very different kind of exchange, that of *kula* shells, ceremonial items of great symbolic value that circulate around a ring of islands. The giving of *kula* shells confers great honor on the giver—but unlike gestures of hospitality (like food) the gift of *kula* shells *cannot* be reciprocated by the recipient, because *kula* shells circulate only in a single direction around the large archipelago. No one who gives a specific *kula* shell (and these shells are so prized and individual that they even have names) can ever expect a return from the specific individual to whom he has given the shell. The goal is not to bind giver and recipient together but to forge a much wider network, which may not come to fruition until years after the giving of the *kula* shell:

> Although *kula* shell transactions also entail dyadic exchange units, in that a man and an immediate partner exchange shells of opposite categories, these transactions are not restricted exchanges or closed spacetimes. The shells that the two men transact travel beyond them, and these travels may be sequentially followed and defined in any given instance as the path (*keda*) of a shell.[27]

In other words, the giver participates in this cycle of giving and receiving only because he can imagine a finite circuit of space and time in which these shells circulate. Without this imagined "spacetime," gifts like *kula* shells make no sense. Why else give to an individual who will never return your present?

As I have discussed elsewhere, anxieties associated with reciprocity are a literary commonplace in this period—whether, for example, it is ever possible adequately to requite a gift of righteous behavior.[28] Here, however, the gifts—or the debts and credits—create a chain of people, all bound to one another. Each man is obligated to continue this cycle of generosity. One by one, each of the patrons, Mr. X, Mr. He, and General Zhang, is placed in a position in which he owns either Qi Sanlang or Cheng San but cannot assume control over his property; in each case, unspoken rules of society demand that the property be passed on as a gift.

According to this logic, one sacrifice almost inexorably leads to another: Cheng San offers his life up for the woman he thinks is Qi Sanlang's wife; Qi Sanlang offers up all he has for Cheng San's wife; Cheng San offers up himself and his wife for Qi Sanlang's wife; and finally, Qi Sanlang's little son is offered up for both Cheng San and his wife. By the end, we have a complicated series of debts and credits involving not two men, nor two men and their wives, but a whole series of benefactors and *their* wives as well. Does Qi Sanlang owe

Cheng San a debt of gratitude, or vice versa? Whom has Mr. He saved, or General Zhang? To whom do Qi Sanlang and Cheng San owe their good fortune? If the trope of a man and wife separated during a dynastic fall is a way of indicating the primal fear of society torn to its fundaments, with all manner of sexual horror now possible, it also—in this narrative from the 1660s—becomes a way of imagining how those links that have been destroyed might be restored, or a way of imagining the empire rendered whole again in the wake of dynastic tragedy.

—

Let me conclude this chapter by moving two centuries back to a very different reunion narrative, set during an earlier dynastic fall. In the early Ming collection of classical tales *Jiandeng xinhua* (New tales to trim the lamp by), Qu You (1347–1433) writes of Liu Cuicui, a young matron in the city of Huaian who is kidnapped by troops rebelling against the Yuan. Her husband, Jin Ding, "swears that he will not return home without seeing her."[29] He then embarks on a long journey. From their home in Huaian, he goes to Pingjiang; following a tip there, he heads on to Shaoxing; thence to Anfeng, and then to Huzhou. Although the story does not give specifics, much of this journey would have been taken by water; however, in the context of the tale, the journey is meant to be a very difficult one. Finally, he finds his wife, now the wife of a general.

But this hard-won reunion with his wife is an abortive one, since Jin Ding must pretend to the general that he is Cuicui's brother. Eventually, both die and are buried together, far from home, in mislabeled graves that pronounce them brother and sister. After a stranger encounters their ghosts and after a magical letter is sent home to her parents, her parents find the burial mound where their daughter and son-in-law are buried and bring the two bodies back home for proper interment.

At a dynasty's fall, the round-trip journey for the sake of a reunion bodes no good. Reunion and round-trip journey, seemingly so similar, cannot both take place. A family with live members might reunite anywhere, as the experiences of Qi Sanlang and others seem to show; live family members might build up networks and set down roots in a new location. In contrast, the family with dead members—beyond the ability to forge new ties—can reunite only in their own proper ancestral home. Whether by moving or by dying, someone in the separated family must pay the price for the fall of the dynasty.

FOUR
Exchange Across Borders

This chapter concerns a single text, the third of the four stories in *Zhaoshi bei* (The cup that reflects the world), "On a Journey to Vietnam a Jade Horse Miniature Is Exchanged for Crimson Velvet" (hereafter "Journey to Annam").[1] Written in the 1660s by an author who identifies himself only as Zhuoyuan ting zhu, or the Master of the Zhuoyuan Pavilion, the story begins with a poem that suggests the subject of the story. The final couplet reads:

> As dusk approaches, the cry of the cuckoo grows
> ever more plaintive,
> And in my leisure, I edit an unofficial history (*yeshi*),
> adding to my incomplete collection.[2]

The text opens with reference to another genre, an unofficial history. In reflecting on its own form, that of the *huaben*, the story that follows concerns itself precisely with what can and cannot be enclosed within the bounds of Chinese writing. By the end of this story, *huaben*'s characteristic move of enclosure is shown to be impossible when the subject lies outside the borders of the empire.

As I argued in Chapter 2, short narrative in general and vernacular short narratives in particular at once enact enclosure and foreground how difficult it can be. Keith McMahon has written of self-containment as an internal, subjective state of equilibrium mirrored by certain external manifestations, among them the boundaries between country and city and between the world of men and that of women.[3] Those external boundaries are an especial concern of this particular collection. In *Zhaoshi bei*'s final and best-known story, "The Miser Makes a Fortune from New Pits," a dealer in night soil lives in a valley so perfectly enclosed that no fertilizer can be imported, making excrement a precious commodity, as much the desired end product as rice itself. The dealer becomes a miser, obsessed with accumulating both money and night soil, but working on altogether different economic assumptions, his son becomes a successful gambler. The other stories, too, concern failures of enclosure—those things that are ultimately impossible to explain in a theory, conceive in a plan, or contain within borders. In the first story, a young man is the victim of two hoaxes, both of which end up coming true; he is duped into believing that a beautiful courtesan loves him, but the hoax itself leads to her falling in love. In the second, a professional freeloader attempts to inveigle himself into the household of a wealthy widow. In all three cases, the stories' twists and turns question the powers of containment and borders.

Among tributary states, Annam's position is special, partly because of its location, right outside Guangxi. As the writer and scholar Wang Shizhen notes in *Chibei outan* (Random notes from north of the pond; 1700), "As far as the reputation of our dynasty reaches, with those who come to us over land and sea reaching many tens of countries, of those who have received titles and send regular emissaries there number only two: Annam and Okinawa."[4] Border locations like Annam have in recent years begun to attract the notice of many scholars, as part of work on the greater empire. Laura Hostetler's recent work on Qing efforts to enclose the minority Miao cartographically comes to mind.[5]

These regions took on a special meaning during the 1660s, the decade when this story was written, as Ming loyalists retreated southward. In her treatment of Chen Chen's *Shuihu houzhuan* (*The Water Margin*, a sequel; 1664), Ellen Widmer discusses the implications of the outlaws' choice of far-off Siam as the location for their utopian society.[6] Like *Shuihu houzhuan*, in some ways "Journey to Annam" treats Annam not as a real-life location but as an idea—or, more precisely, as a set of problems in political philosophy that can be addressed only through the prism of a vernacular short story. At the same time, the story seems genuinely concerned with Annam as an autonomous world with its own customs and history. And unlike *Jinghua yuan* (Flowers in the mirror; 1828), in which infinite distances only remind the reader of the finitude of the world and every far-flung encounter only emphasizes the narrowness of Chang'an court circles, in "Journey to Annam," travel puts one face to face with what is incontrovertibly and permanently alien.

In its discussions of various circulations—specifically what happens to a jade horse and some bolts of fabric, and what happens to women who make their presence public—the story uses Annam's liminal position to ask whether the empire is a closed system or an open one, and the extent to which the outside plays a part in the empire's internal circulations. In so doing, this story challenges the very form of late imperial narrative. One of the imperium's claims was that it could erase borders entirely and be *wuwai*, literally "without an outside." The story wonders whether this is so: can what is "other" be written and absorbed wholly into the totalizing imperium (whether a map, or a history, or tax records, or the narrative form of a *huaben* story)?

—

Chapters 2 and 3 concerned some ways in which short narrative formally conceives of the empire as a spontaneous human community and how those ideas were shaken by the fall of the dynasty. The expansionist policies of the early Qing posed a different challenge to narrative. "Journey to Annam" posits various ways in which what lies outside the empire is to be related to what lies within. Along the way, the story includes many elaborate descriptions of Annamese customs, with specific attention paid to the contrast between them and Chinese ones. The story, with ethnography embedded within, inevitably comments on the rhetoric of ethnography.

During the Kangxi reign, an album of woodblock illustrations was prepared for the emperor depicting all the tribute-offering subjects of the empire, with each picture accompanied by a brief description. With some peoples, the sheer act of description seems to form the substance of the relationship. In China as elsewhere, inscribing, mapping, and cataloguing were central to the imperial enterprise.

Take, for example, this description of the Dutch, accompanied by a woodblock illustration by an artist whose exposure to the Dutch was probably no closer than second- or thirdhand:

> These barbarians wear hats of black velvet. When they meet people, their custom is to take the hat off and clasp it under the arm. They wear brocaded and embroidered wool, and they grasp a whip and a sword hung at the side. The barbarian women use green veils to wrap their heads, and their necks are encircled with pearls and precious stones, while their shoulders are draped with plain silk, and they wear open-necked clothes that reveal their bosoms, and are attached to long skirts. Their shoes are made of red leather.[7]

Since there is no mention of what tribute they submit to the court, nor of where their land is geographically in relation to China, one can only gather that the description stands in for these political details and affirms by its very existence the tributary relationship; to some extent, ethnography was a speech act.

Other descriptions carefully interlace ethnographic details with details of how various groups fit within the greater polity, as if to naturalize the political. In a description of one of the aboriginal tribes of Taiwan, for example, there is hardly any separating the people's customs from the details of their political submission.[8] The literary act of being folded into the empire, to be written into the maps and records—and ethnographic descriptions such as this one—efface the military force involved in the conquest of Taiwan.

> The men and women take great pleasure in each other and have undomesticated unions. The *Local Registrar* says that the men live all their lives in their wives' homes, and that son-in-laws are brought in as male descendants. Every year each submits more than seventy taels of silver as tribute. Two communities, Xin'gang and Zhuohou, were formerly called Zhulo, and now the whole region has been named the Taiwan administrative district.[9]

Ethnography and political geography blur into each other here, one hardly to be separated from the other. Simply by juxtaposing the customs of the aborigines and the political details of their colonial status, the *Local Registrar* makes their precise degree of subordination as intrinsic a part of them as their clothing and their sexual customs.

Parts of "Journey to Annam" come very close to the ethnographic descriptions I have quoted above. The story features descriptions of Annamese habits that differ from Chinese ones, along with a veritable catalogue of exotica (including a description of wine brewed out of pineapple that makes that fruit seem well-nigh magical). Here, ethnographic description has been embedded in *huaben* narrative. But is the end goal the same—to encapsulate, to render the political natural? At stake in this story is a certain universalism—which here hinges upon the question of whether a *huaben* can be told from outside the Chinese heartland.

—

The Annamese in the story themselves bring up the issue of what is universal and who determines it. Fairly early on, the two visitors from Guangxi watch a Buddhist procession pass by, with hundreds of men bearing aloft flaming tree trunks. The hero's friend Zhu Chunhui explains that the tree trunks are actually sandalwood and that the women standing on the side of the road, clasping large pieces of coral, are well-born ladies of official houses. Part of the marvel is simply the exotic. In the midst of all the strange sights and sounds, Zhu Chunhui also comments on the smells; before burning, the trees have been coated with pine pitch and lard. Part of it is the old fantasy that what is worthless in one place might be priceless in another: the protagonist Du Jingshan marvels that expensive sandalwood is being burnt in such a prodigal manner and that the sticks carried around by the women are of so precious a substance as coral. Du Jingshan's wonder recalls the first set of transactions that enrich the hero of "The Tangerines and the Tortoiseshell" when tangerines are exchanged for heavy coins of silver. (In both texts, the promise of cross-cultural understanding and the possibility of a fair transaction are closely related.)

This peculiar religious rite—on the surface a sign of the profound alienness of the Annamese—turns out to be a reflection on how this place, on the far outskirts of Chinese civilization, claims for itself a place within a universalist ideology. A Confucian polity has the potential to be imagined as a universal one, with the possibility of encompassing all peoples—but only in the absence of other, equal polities. Nonetheless, even a universal polity singular in its legitimacy retains a center and a periphery. All obey the lord and master, but within this equality some are closer to him than others; and—eventually, with distance—do those ties not attenuate to nothingness? Forget the greater matter of the Confucian polity. Can even a narrative built out of Confucian principles—consisting of interlocking personalities and relations—truly live up to the description of *wuwai*, "without an outside"?

This scene, however, highlights a contrasting *credo*, whose claims to universality are much less fraught. This peculiar rite, Zhu Chunhui explains, is called "Venerating the Buddha"; behind those burning trees is a carriage, carved of sandalwood and surrounded by icon boxes encrusted with jewels, in which a saintly monk sits. The narrator then concludes this section with a poem, with mention first of the richness of the adornments and then of the monk's spiritual attainments, and concludes:

> The Kingdom of Fo was once in command of the
> Buddha Nature;
> Annam will once again be the forefront of the
> Southern school.[10]

The Kingdom of Fo refers to Sanfoqi, a real-life place within present-day Indonesia. But it might also mean literally "the realm of Buddhism." Like Confucianism, Buddhism promises universalism, inasmuch as one might imagine a world where everyone was Buddhist. But unlike Confucianism, Buddhism does not depend on the presence of a single center, or even of any center at all. Or perhaps one might imagine a center not in Beijing or in Tibet, Qing lamaists to the contrary, but rather—according to this poem at least—in Sanfoqi, or even in remote Annam.

—

By the late seventeenth century, one of the story's early scenes was a cliché: a pretty young wife stands on the balcony of her house or its doorway or at a window, attracting the sexual notice of an onlooker. In fact, as early as the *Zuozhuan* (The Zuo commentary), the earliest work of narrative history, dating from the fourth century BCE, the woman standing at the *limen*, visible to passersby, marks a moment of danger. Such an encounter between Sanqiao and Chen Dalang in "The Pearl-Sewn Shirt" takes many journeys, involving numerous characters and thousands of *li*, to resolve. But in more sinister fashion, a similar meeting between a man and a woman also starts the action in *Jinpingmei* (The plum in the golden vase; ~1590) when the licentious Pan Jinlian attracts Ximen Qing's attention as she stands in her doorway.

Chapter 3 discusses the dangers implicit when husbands and wives are separated. More broadly, danger seems to be present simply when women in general are—even temporarily—unenclosed. Consider the novel *Suishi yiwen* (1633, which Robert Hegel renders *Forgotten Tales of the Sui*), which includes a grueling rape scene. A young woman is violated first by a young lordling and then by all his pages until she is at the point of death. All the while, her mother, who had been abducted with her, wails for her daughter and is brutally beaten. The narrator tells us that the blame is partially their own: "A lone widow and a young virgin, even from a poor house, ought not to go out into the crowds to view lanterns by themselves."[11] All their troubles turn out to be the fault of the permissive atmosphere of the Lantern Festival.

Numerous plays begin at precisely this moment in the calendar year. Action is initiated through the Lantern Festival's sanctioned license when for one evening women might leave their homes to look at the lights. These plays can come to an end only when all has returned to normal, and the women have been securely matched up to husbands and shut up in their houses again.

Women who violate norms by appearing in public recur in "Journey to Annam": one opens the story, and others end it; one appears in China, and others appear in Annam. In this story, the clichéd image of a wife on a balcony is seemingly framed, a commentary on a narrative convention whose limitations are thus shown. Does a woman who exposes herself in public mean the same thing, regardless of whether she is in Annam or Guangxi? The question is not simply one of whether morals are relative but also whether the empire and the political ideology that grounds it are universal or local, closed or open, finite or potentially infinite.

When Du Jingshan's pretty young wife, Fenggu, inadvertently attracts the attention of a local official's son, he throws to her his handkerchief with a little jade horse attached to it. It accidentally strikes Fenggu in the face, and she cries out. When Du Jingshan hears the noise, he sees the voyeur and grabs at him, ripping off the stranger's hat, so that he has no choice but to flee, hair in disarray.

What happens next? The narrator introduces us to the happy young couple, the capable importer Du Jingshan and his loving wife Fenggu, and then explains what a monumental stroke of bad luck the encounter was:

> Fenggu had just happened to go upstairs to take a look into the street. How could she have known that she would run into that source of trouble, Mr. Hu from inside the *yamen*? See, if they'd messed with anyone else, it would have been all right, but this Mr. Hu was a VIP. If you threw dirt on his head, at worst you'd lose your life, and at best you'd get away with financial ruin.[12]

At this point a late imperial reader would have certain expectations, shared by Fenggu herself. She scolds her husband for his rashness when they look at the hat and discover a pearl on it that marks her unwelcome admirer as a powerful rich man: "And for you to hit someone without having figured out the situation first! I hope you haven't struck some root of disaster!"[13] She—and we—presume that the narrative will cleverly tie together the domestic and political realms, since the little jade horse once owned by the adopted son of the local pacification commissioner and now given illicitly to a married lady seems to have mixed these two worlds together.

Has the wife's carelessness ruined the young couple? On the basis of hundreds of other narratives, the reader thinks a certain chain of events likely. Perhaps the powerful official's son will use his connections to kill the husband and seize the pretty wife. Or the official's son might use the jade horse as false evidence of some wrongdoing on the part of the husband. Eventually, though, the jade horse might form a critical piece of evidence to absolve Du Jingshan, who at this point would be on the verge of execution. Some sort of dramatic outcome involving the jade horse seems overdetermined, and all the expected outcomes revolve around the jade horse, as an emblem of how the people of Guangxi—and of the polity as a whole—are bound together. The horse might change hands, but ultimately its return to where it belongs will right other wrongs too, whether personal or political, but perhaps not before Fenggu and Du Jingshan suffer unduly. All that would be true, except that this story takes place, not in Jiangnan (where, we are told, our storyteller actually lives), but on the remote southern borders of the empire between Guangxi and Annam.

—

The narrator begins by describing the location, the central condition of the story: "Merchants from China who want to buy cinnabar, or *suhe xiang*, or aloeswood don't go to Annam, but gather these goods in Guangxi. They don't know that these items are all products of Annam, and Guangxi is nothing but a place where they are gathered."[14] In other words, the border is so carefully mediated that even those who travel to the edges of the empire do not themselves pass through the border; instead, goods seem to appear spontaneously, so that even traders might imagine that there are no borders (or at least be freed of the bother of having to deal with them).

But of course the border does exist, and a complex explanation follows of how it is sustained, at once policed and permeable. Only open on certain days, the market is staffed by government soldiers who monitor all transactions. Maintaining this border is a great deal of work:

> This area was near the coast, so the fear of privateering was always present. There was also an appraiser, stationed there by the local *yamen*; so that if there was any private transaction taking place, those involved could be detained and their goods confiscated by the official, and even the managers and merchants would also be punished.[15]

The narrator goes on to explain that the appraiser takes a cut from the transactions. For the pacification commissioner himself, a corrupt representative of the central government whose distance from it gives him virtually unlimited power, the border forms an almost limitless source of wealth: "Because heaven is distant and its powers of hearing distant, he was practically half an emperor."[16] With no child of his own, the pacification commissioner and his wife have adopted her nephew, a lecherous ne'er-do-well in his twenties named Hu. This young man has been kept out of trouble by being locked up studying with a tutor.

He begs his adoptive mother for the chance to go out to explore the town. She intercedes on his behalf with her husband, arguing that their son's rigorous schedule of studying might impair his health. The pacification commissioner allows him a visit to the marketplace the next day, but only on the condition that he disguise himself. Before any actual misbehavior, the reader is on alert, knowing that this family has violated a whole slew of norms: an adopted son, official corruption, an uxorious husband persuaded to offend his own instincts. Once again, a late imperial reader has all sorts of guesses as to how this family will fall, all predicated on the enclosed nature of moral payback.

At the very beginning of his holiday, the young man sneaks out from the custody of the appraiser. After throwing the jade horse at the pretty matron and incurring the husband's angry attack, young Hu continues his run of bad luck; as he stands in a narrow street, another young woman accidentally empties a latrine on his head. Then having stripped off the soiled top layer of his clothes, he decides to hop on a saddled horse, so as to make a quick getaway. Unfortunately for him, the instant he climbs on, he is chased by the horse's owner, who accuses him of being a horse thief. After the horse charges into the crowded marketplace, the young man is quickly captured, identified, and returned to the *yamen*. In a story about the possibility of escape—from narrative convention and from the borders of the empire—his break from the confines of the *yamen* is only a brief one. The next day, various employees of the *yamen* come by to see how the young master is doing—which arouses the father's suspicions. The son explains that he was waylaid, and the jade horse and his cap with the pearl were snatched. Remembering the sign on the storefront, he names Du Jingshan as the perpetrator.

The pacification commissioner considers behaving like a run-of-the-mill corrupt official. He thinks about bringing in Du Jingshan for punishment. Just as expected, the accidental encounter has led to a run-in with the powers of the state. But he decides on another course of action, thus instantly differentiating this tale from many other narratives about corrupt officials: "If I bring in Du Jingshan for a good beating, then the public will think that I'm taking vengeance for a private wrong."[17] Like the story as a whole, the pacification commissioner is acutely aware of generic pressures; and like the story, he does not simply succumb to them, but instead reflects on them.

Hu thinks he has come up with the perfect solution: he drafts a command for Du Jingshan to submit thirty spans of scarlet velvet, a precious substance available only in Annam. That way, Hu reasons, he himself will get a little bonus, his son's wrong will be avenged, and it will not even be such a hardship for Du Jingshan (Hu thinks Du's family is rich and due for a minor shakedown anyway). Du Jingshan panics; since scarlet velvet is contraband, he cannot think how to get a single yard of it, much less thirty. He immediately goes to the *yamen*, where the pacification commissioner tells him a barefaced lie: that the velvet is meant not for him but instead as tribute to be sent to the court in Beijing. Du Jingshan is then given three months and thirty taels of silver to go to Annam and bring back the velvet. A sleepless night and a tearful farewell to Fenggu later, he sets off.

After a few days' journey, he enters the territory of Annam. Du Jingshan crosses a moat, and then:

> When he entered the gate, his papers were checked over, and his luggage was examined. When it was established that he was from Guangxi, he was requested, "Go to Dolo Lodge to rest. It's all you people from Guangxi there." All the way there Du Jingshan asked where it was, and it turned out there was a great lodge, with three barbarian [*fan* 番] words before the gate, of which he could not recognize even a single one.[18]

These words that are allowed to remain untranslated and illegible mark an entrance into a world where Du Jingshan is decidedly the foreigner. As I argued in Chapter 2, *huaben* obsessively account for all goods and karma; within this generic context, these words, left over, untranslated, unknowable, bear an enormous weight, as that which must remain forever unassimilated and outside the ken of the text.

Du Jingshan goes to the lodge, where he is delighted to find the company of other men from Guangxi, including a newfound friend, Zhu Chunhui. Any confidence that we may have had in how people are related no longer holds. Du Jingshan is the barbarian now: when his new friend Zhu Chunhui asks why Du Jingshan did not turn down this difficult commission, he responds, "I couldn't say no to that barbarian cow of a pacification commissioner, with nary an ounce of human nature, so I didn't even bother trying."[19] He calls the official *manniu* 蠻牛, where *man* refers to southern barbarians, although it is used repeatedly as an insult emptied of any meaning. In another instance, an Annamese refers to the pacification commissioner's son as a *manzi* 蠻子. Once one is among those whom one formerly called *man* and is the *man* oneself, who is *man* and who is not *man* becomes a much trickier question. And the same turns out to be true about human status, as well.

In this part of the world, barbarian status is not simply an incidental characteristic, subject to being turned into metaphor. Order is sustained in this region by keeping people where they belong and deciding who might be accorded human and civilized status. In this *huaben*, once relatedness is unsettled by movement across borders, so, too, are the narratives dependent on it. Du Jingshan wants to know why somebody he has only just met, Zhu Chunhui, should go to such lengths to help him. His new friend responds: "In a foreign land, we're like the closest of flesh and blood."[20] The old ties of flesh and blood—with their uncontestable claims to absolute truth—are suddenly weakened such that they admit acquaintances who have known each other for a few minutes, whose only claim to relatedness is that they both come from Guangxi.

The two friends then go through a series of adventures in Annam, all to acquire the thirty spans of cloth. Zhu Chunhui introduces Du Jingshan to Master Li, a native informant who explains to the two men from Guangxi the exact nature of the velvet, which turns out to be cloth dyed from the blood of apes. Shortly thereafter, Du Jingshan returns to the inn to discover that his silver is missing. Zhu Chunhui explains that a master of the magical arts on Mount Nituo tests his students by challenging them to relieve Chinese merchants of their money. All Du Jingshan has to do, his friend explains, is to go to Mount Nituo to ask for his money back. Unfortunately, on his way there, he is chased by a monster into a river, where he espies a group of women bathing. The women take him into a mansion, where he is asked to change from his own soiled and wet clothes into a set of dry ones. A little child standing nearby sees the jade horse that Du Jingshan still has tied around him and joyfully insists on taking it, claiming that it is a match to his own jade horse.

The jade horse that had originally been thrown up in a handkerchief turns out to be much more than what Du Jingshan thought it was. The woman who has welcomed Du Jingshan into the mansion explains that they are the victims of a political vendetta. The only heir left of Grand Councilor Zhuzhu is the little boy who has just taken Du Jingshan's jade horse; he was given one just like it by the king of Annam, in recognition of his family's contributions. There had originally been a pair of horses, the king explains to the little boy, but one was given to the pacification commissioner of Guangxi as tribute.

And finally this is how Du Jingshan's troubles are ended. The woman who relates the history of the jade horse then offers our hero forty-odd spans of scarlet velvet in return for it. Du Jingshan journeys home, ready to turn over most of his ape-dyed cloth to the pacification commissioner, but he is in no state to collect the fruits of his mission. His lecherous adopted son has involved the whole family in a sexual scandal, and the pacification commissioner himself has fallen ill. With his treasures from Annam, Du Jingshan becomes a very rich man, and he and Fenggu live happily ever after.

As readers of traditional narrative, we have very powerful expectations of the little jade horse; it is clearly an inalienable object whose ownership cannot be permanently transferred to another. Yet to whom does it really belong? The ne'er-do-well, who flings it away in an abuse of official power, or the young wife, who presses it on her husband as a sign of conjugal love? Compare it to another inalienable object, the pearl-sewn shirt, whose ownership is always clear, even as it repeatedly changes hands. According to the model of the pearl-sewn shirt, the horse ought to lead us back to the pacification commissioner and his family; as an emblem of their willingness to undo other families, it—and not some other crisis entirely—ought to become the instrument of their downfall. In other words, the jade horse *ought* to gesture toward enclosure. Instead, the jade horse turns out to be something else entirely, pointing us to another world with its own separate concerns and its own separate dynastic politics and history. The jade horse is indeed an inalienable object, but its proper matrix is the politics and history of Annam, and thence it must return. Each figure for enclosure turns out to be something very different: the young wife's presence on the balcony does not affirm connectedness but is instead the first step in a chain of events that ends up sending her husband outside the borders of the empire. What lies outside the borders turns out to be necessary to resolve conflicts within, and vice versa: the fates of the two official families—those of the Grand Councilor Zhuzhu and the Pacification Commissioner Hu—turn out to be closely connected, but not in such a way that either narrative entirely assimilates the other.

And what of the cloth, upon whose perfect trade for the jade horse is predicated so much? After Du Jingshan tells the lady of the noble house his mission, she replies, "I thought that you wanted some extraordinarily rare treasure, but if you want thirty spans of ape-dyed cloth, that's easy enough. Why didn't you say something earlier?"[21] Both horse and cloth are of indeterminate value, neither convertible into silver: the one, a priceless heirloom; the other, valuable, but only within the borders of Guangxi. This magical trade also serves as one way to imagine equality between different regions. The perfectness of the exchange—precisely this jade horse for the velvet, two things otherwise entirely unattainable—makes promises about the possibility of transparent translation, exchanges, and equivalences.

—

Although the markers themselves are clear, the exact nature of the difference between Guangxi and Annam is very deliberately kept opaque. Throughout the story, the author refuses to pin down a single grounds for difference, whether language, or culture, or ethnicity. Naturally, no seventeenth-century author would rely on one of these categories, with their own nineteenth-century European lineages, or to use Chinese translations of these concepts, one of the Japanese-language-derived neologisms. But the words that the author *does* choose are categorically fraught.

Even though on the outside the lodge is labeled with barbarian (*fan*) words he cannot read, inside Du Jingshan is overjoyed to hear the familiar *shengqi* 聲氣 of men of Guangxi. Those words on the sign remain, as I have said, alien and unknowable, but exactly what makes the men of Guangxi familiar and knowable remains just as unclear. *Shengqi* has something to do with spoken language, since Du Jingshan has just been confronted with evidence of linguistic difference, and in fact one of its modern meanings is "accent."

But it also turns out to be an extremely rich word, with a history extending far back to the *Yijing* (Book of changes). The author has chosen a highly resonant, well-nigh untranslatable binome, whose closest English approximation would be something like "spirit" or "air." But the binome's usage in classical texts suggests that the term resists reduction. In a common saying, *shengqi* is what ties together people of a single kind. As the *Yijing* puts it, "One note will resonate with the same (*sheng* 聲); one air will connect with the same (*qi* 氣)." *Shengqi* suggests a cosmic resonance arising out of a profound similarity. But similarity of what? Its context in the story suggests something obviously acquired and extrinsic like a regional accent, but the word gives a hint that the men of Guangxi are intrinsically of the same kind, while at the same time suggesting that whatever makes them similar might be something that cannot quite be pinned down.

Just a few lines later, when Du Jingshan and Zhu Chunhui leave the lodge, they see Annamese walking around with "hammer-shaped topknots and shorn hair."[22] The narrator comments on their hair, concluding that these people have no Chinese (*zhonghua* 中華) *titong* 體統. *Titong* is no easier a word to wrap one's mind around than *shengqi*; once again the author has chosen a complicated word with a rich history of usage, this one quite frequently used in philosophical texts. It spans a range of meanings, extending from something like "style" to "form" and finally to "system." On one end, "style" would suggest that their hairstyle is merely an external difference, subject to modification and choice; on the other end, "system" suggests something considerably more deep-seated and resistant to understanding. Perhaps the hairstyle is merely the external manifestation of a consistent internal difference. Are the differences between people of Annam and Guangxi such that they could be fully accounted for simply by enumeration? Does one internal difference account for all these external manifestations? Or are all the differences vague, by nature impossible to explain? For *shengqi* and *titong* seem mutually exclusive: if *titong* implies the structural, *shengqi* is whatever amorphous substance fills it. We are given no easy answers for what makes the merchants of Guangxi like each other and unlike the people of Annam, and all the focus on surface—hairstyle, clothing, accent, and cuisine—does not answer the question of whether these things constitute the sum total of difference or are only surface manifestations of what is truly different.

The *fan* words on the lodge are actually an exception. Elsewhere, a whole range of cultural practices—naked women, bratty children, strange foods, bizarre religious customs, drinks that ought to be consumed hot but are instead served cold—are translated and accounted for, so that nothing remains left over to elude understanding. The most striking example of how the opaque is rendered transparent is Du Jingshan's initial meeting with Master Li, who gives them advice on the scarlet velvet. Zhu Chunhui gives his friend a quick description of Master Li, a descendant of the Grand Councilor Li Jili and a member of an extremely powerful clan. With a name that sounds superficially Chinese and an ancestor in official service, he seems like someone Du Jingshan might be able to picture back home in Guangxi.

But in fact Du Jingshan cannot make sense of the old man before him. His behavior seems inexplicable: this old man with a curly white beard does not bow; he laughingly says things that Du Jingshan can make neither head nor tail of; he drags Zhu Chunhui inside; and he does not respond when Du Jingshan bows to him. But once Zhu Chunhui explains who Master Li is—accounting for him—then Master Li becomes entirely understandable, and what he says requires no translation. A successful narrative can take the place of translation, or it so subsumes its object that nothing alien is left over. Zhu Chunhui's explanation of Master Li's identity serves a function similar to the description of the Dutch in the *Tribute Pictures*; like those captions, a description can stand in the place of a relationship. Zhu Chunhui includes as part of Master Li's introduction the reason that Du Jingshan should not take offense at the old man's strange behavior: "In their country, they are not held to proprieties. Just take a seat. This is Master Li."[23] To be understood, Master Li needs to be properly placed, but once fully accounted for, he requires no other mediation to be understood.

Fully accounting for matters, or enclosing them within narrative, is an act of central importance in this story. Surely it is not coincidental that the same Du Jingshan who is so satisfied with this account of Master Li finds himself in Annam as a trader; he arrives hoping to exchange silver for textiles, and he leaves after swapping the jade horse for textiles. Along the way he discovers that no amount of silver can be traded for scarlet velvet, whereas the jade horse happens to convert perfectly—not into thirty—but into forty spans of scarlet velvet. Other than that jade horse, nothing would convert into scarlet velvet. In other words, Du Jingshan's whole enterprise in Annam turns out to have been about finding perfect equivalents, *les mots justes*, as it were. He seems to have been just as much translator as trader.

Marc Shell points out that in a number of Indo-European languages, translation and transaction are related; in German, for example, "*Übertragung* means both 'economic transference of property' and 'linguistic transfer of meaning,'" and in Latin, "*translatio* refers both to intra- and interlinguistic translation and to propertal transfer."[24] Translation poses one of the central literary-theoretical problems in the Western tradition, but its presence in the Chinese tradition is much less overt. In this *huaben* (as in the European texts like Goethe's *Faust* discussed by Shell), translation serves as a figure for economic transaction and vice versa. And yet Du Jingshan's experiences suggest something more far-reaching. One important trade—the horse for the cloth—takes place across borders, but equally important transactions take place *within* borders. Du Jingshan's experiences suggest a recognition not only of translation's difficulties but also of its ubiquity, that its presence, as Stanley Cavell puts it, is internal to all cultural enterprises.[25]

Near the end of the story, when Du Jingshan discovers that his jade horse is one of a pair, he also learns a little about the history of the family in whose mansion he finds himself. They are an official family who has been targeted and maligned by the same Li Jili who was the illustrious ancestor of our own Master Li, our hero's friend and native informant. In fact, Master Li's ancestor so persecuted the family that the little boy is the only heir left. The narrator does not add any explanation, nor does he remind the reader that this is the Li Jili mentioned elsewhere.

Complicated equations concerning the history of Annam suggest themselves. A pair of descendants, Master Li and the little boy, serve as proxies for their two families, and in a stroke of karmic retribution, the adventure abetted by Master Li returns the jade horse to the very family from whom his own had taken it. In other words, Du Jingshan's mission has succeeded partly because of the separateness of Annam's political economy. But at the same time, the horse shows the complicated connections—karmic, economic, and political—between the economies of Guangxi and Annam. That exchange of jade horse for scarlet velvet at once resolves two separate political injustices: the persecution of the little boy's family and the unfair punishment of Du Jingshan himself by Pacification Commissioner Hu.

The *huaben* is all about trades. Du Jingshan's primary task, to complete the trade for the precious velvet, is mysteriously connected to and dependent on another task, that of understanding the Annamese setting in which he finds himself. Consequently, questions of commensurateness and exchange become burdened with the problem of translation, and vice versa. Is the trade of jade horse for scarlet velvet perfectly even, or does one side of the trade gain advantage? Or similarly, when someone translates something from one language to another, is the conversion perfect—each side equivalent to the other—or is something always left over?

This is what is at stake in the story's meditations on cultural relativism, which itself—as a conversion between two equivalents—resembles a sort of trade. Twice in the story, the Annamese are accused of lacking in *liyi* 禮義, "propriety and righteousness." The first time, the two men of Guangxi watch as some Annamese women, evidently of good family, participate in a Buddhist ceremony. Surprised by their presence in public, Du Jingshan listens to Zhu Chunhui's explanation: "In this land they never did know 'propriety and righteousness.'"[26] A few pages later, he makes the same comment, to explain the disappearance of Du Jingshan's silver, which was not theft but instead a test set to his disciples by a religious leader on

Mount Nituo: "Don't you know that even though the Annamese don't know about 'propriety and righteousness,' they've never had thieves?"[27]

In both cases, the criticism differs from the simple, absolute condemnation it would be back in Guangxi. In my translation, I have placed "propriety and righteousness" (*liyi*) in quotation marks because it is difficult to understand Zhu Chunhui's comment otherwise. I considered translating *liyi* as "Confucianism" (whose ubiquity in the intellectual landscape of premodern China makes it notoriously difficult to translate) because here *liyi* is revealed as a manifestly provincial value, a cultural artifact with no claim to the universal. As he uses it, *liyi* must refer not to virtue itself but to a particular, culturally limited code, with its own geographically limited sphere. In wealthy Annam, where nobody bothers to steal the possessions of others, other forces must be at work to prevent thievery (of course, the classical standard for a moral society—governed by *liyi*—is one in which objects left by the side of the road lie undisturbed). Zhu Chunhui's seemingly paradoxical statement suggests that any understanding of Annam—if the theft of one's personal possessions is not robbery, and the presence of women in public isn't licentiousness—must be constantly mediated by translation.

The two Chinese men accuse the Annamese of offending moral norms, but then the same complaint is directed at Du Jingshan himself. When Master Li begins his explanation of why apes' blood is so difficult to collect, Du Jingshan interrupts him with a question, addressing him as *dianguan* (店官), something along the lines of "manager." Offended by Du Jingshan's rudeness, Master Li responds, "This gentleman isn't worthy of interaction, since his words hold me in such slight regard."[28] I have translated *buzhong xiangyu* (不中相與) as "not worthy of interaction," but *xiangyu* (相與) implies a whole range of reciprocal relations, probably suggesting in this case conversation, information, and of course trade. If Du Jingshan shows himself unworthy of this sort of reciprocation, any hope of success in any other transaction must surely be dashed.

Zhu Chunhui makes a quick apology on his friend's behalf: "Do not take offense, sir; my compatriot is a good fellow who doesn't mean to slight you; it's only that he doesn't know how one refers to people (*chenghu* 稱呼) in your country."[29] Classifying people according to one's relationship to them and properly referring to them is of singular importance in Chinese culture, so that Du Jingshan's sin against Master Li is a uniquely Chinese one. But the Chinese system of *chenghu* is predicated on the notion that every person has a place and a name within a closed system; Du Jingshan is rightly stymied by a man who is an aristocrat and an official in a system that is alien to Du Jingshan. It is not clear at all what role Master Li ought to occupy vis-à-vis Du Jingshan.

An exchange has been transacted here. Du Jingshan and Master Li commit the same offense against each other, and Zhu Chunhui mediates both acts of misunderstanding. This is a rare moment of explicit, realistic relativism in Chinese literature. Master Li accepts the apology: "Those who are ignorant aren't subject to judgment. It's all right."[30] It is after this exchange—which renders their offenses against each other even—that Master Li launches into an explanation of how the velvet is produced.

—

Du Jingshan spends much of this story grappling with the strangeness of the Annamese. But the story's central commodity is in fact produced by another, much more alien group. Master Li explains the source of this mysterious scarlet velvet. *Xingrong* 猩絨, which means literally "ape velvet," usually refers simply to a color of cloth, based on the legendary belief in the deep redness of ape's blood. Elsewhere in Chinese, *xinghong* 猩紅 means simply "scarlet," with no more direct relationship to an ape than any blue-green object has to a kingfisher. In this story, though, *xingrong* is no metaphor, but literally dyed with ape's blood.

This time, as Master Li explains how the apes' blood is harvested, the power of ethnography and description is in the hands of the Annamese Master Li. First he describes the apes, attributing to them a liminal appearance, precisely between human and beast: they have human faces, but bodies like pigs, or like gibbons. To catch them as they travel in their packs of three or four, local hunters (who are called exorcists, or *bunuo* 卜儺) strew the paths they are known to frequent with liquor and high-heeled wooden clogs.

The apes immediately recognize the trap for what it is, and yell out angrily, "You have set a trap to ensnare us! You wish to take our lives, but we will refuse to drink this liquor—and see what you can do."[31] They rush off, but then return, unable to resist the fragrant liquor. They say to one another, "Let's just take a little taste, but not get drunk."[32] But the instant they taste the alcohol, they cannot help but drink to intoxication. Then they prance about in the wooden clogs that have been strewn about until they are captured, still protesting: "You wish to harm us by pumping us full of liquor, but we are restrained and won't get drunk, and what will you do then?"[33]

The exorcists tell the apes that they are acting on the king's orders and entreat them to give up their blood voluntarily. The apes can prevent their blood from being taken, even as they are being killed, so if they refuse, they will simply be killed in vain. Only their consent makes their murder useful. Because the apes crave recognition, they agree to give a few spoons of their blood; the exorcists are able to tap precisely that amount, not a drop more, not a drop less. With a very stubborn ape, the exorcists get nothing at all.

Master Li concludes by explaining that the blood goes first to the monarch's household and then to highly placed ministers of court. What is left dyes fabrics for merchants from Guangxi, although lately, since ape-dyed cloth is banned in Guangxi, its use is restricted to officials' families in Annam.

Although it is never questioned by the characters and not elaborated on after this point, Master Li's description has resonances that beg to be unpacked. At first glance, the apes are simply an inversion, standing in identical relation to the Annamese as the Annamese themselves do to the Chinese. If the Chinese have their imperial subjects (among them the Annamese, who are obligated to render tribute to the monarch in the Chinese capital), then so, too, do the Annamese themselves have such subjects—the apes whose blood is used to dye the velvet that will be presented to the King of Annam.

A humorist like Li Yu might assign yet another subject for the apes themselves. But the point here seems to be precisely that relativism—as a way of envisioning how different cultures relate to one another—has its limits. Other than the language that allows them to narrate their own plight, the only power that these apes have is the ability to withhold their own blood. Since their quasi-colonial relationship with the Annamese subjugators involves the loss of their lives, clearly the buck stops here. The apes can have no colonial subjects of their own. With hierarchical relationships like these, relativism simply cannot exist.

The apes' encounter with colonialists sounds very much like that of natives all over the world; in fact, it reads almost as allegory for the entire colonial experience, with ape-natives who knowingly trade their freedom for liquor, and with exorcists/colonialists who are not content with power over their lives but actually demand their subjects' permission to exploit them. What finally dooms the apes in Master Li's story is their desire to emulate their subjugators, namely, their wearing of human shoes; in the high clogs, they stumble about until they are caught.

When the exorcists approach the apes for their blood, they cite the king's commands; only because of these orders, they explain, do they dare to approach the apes for blood. When the apes' murder and tribute are explicitly compared, tribute itself cannot help but appear sinister. In describing the relationship between apes and hunters, the story casts doubt on the relationship between China and its tributary states. The apes inhabit a region between human and bestial; they speak and have free will, yet their bodies are a composite of various animal parts. Just as between the men of Guangxi and the Annamese, here, too, the degree and quality of difference between man and ape can never be made clear.

William Shakespeare's *The Tempest* (1611) transposes the dynamics of a colonial outpost to a fantastic island. Two very different natives, the submissive Ariel and the angry Caliban, possess some claim to the island. Neither seems wholly human, but between them they divide up the traits of the subaltern, Ariel the docile and Caliban the rebellious. Prospero is both teacher and master to Caliban, but after having been civilized by him, Caliban betrayed Prospero by making overtures to his daughter, Miranda. Caliban summarizes his complex relationship to Prospero by invoking language:

> You taught me language; and my profit on't
> Is, I know how to curse. The red plague rid you
> For learning me your language! (I.ii.363–65)

Like Caliban, the apes in this *huaben* seem almost painfully aware of the contrast between their command of language and their subordinate position; like him, their only power lies in the ability to articulate their powerless positions.

Parallels with *The Tempest* continue. The apes' conversations with the exorcists—their soon-to-be murderers—echo Caliban's dealings with Sebastian and Trinculo, except that the apes do Caliban one step better and are tricked by drink not just out of their birthright but out of their lives. Although he will not recognize Prospero's legitimacy, insisting instead that the island is his own inheritance through his mother, Sycorax, Caliban is all too willing to recognize the buffoons Sebastian and Trinculo in return for alcohol.

"Journey to Annam" is marked throughout by a savviness about the intelligibility of language. His adventures in Annam confront Du Jingshan with evidence of foreignness everywhere he turns, whether the obscurity of other cultural practices or the opacity of another language, embodied in those *fan* words he cannot understand. In Master Li's account of the apes, by contrast, linguistic difference is no issue at all, and the apes are masters of human language. While the apes narrate what is happening to them, curiously it is the exorcists who are mostly silent. Like Caliban, the apes confront their adversaries in the adversaries' own language, so that Master Li praises the apes' morals by drawing attention again to the matter of language and understandability: "The apes' word is good, and they can be relied on."[34]

Master Li's praise for them also foregrounds their power to choose, but his precise terms invite a closer look. With the apes, *yanyu xiangfu* 言語相符: "*yan* and *yu* accord." *Yan* 言 and *yu* 語 are usually close to synonyms, both signifying language.[35] What Master Li means is that what the apes say and what they do accord. But how does it happen that the apes enjoy a perfect transparency denied to everyone else, in a story that so foregrounds difference and misunderstanding? The problem returns us to foreignness in general: Du

Jingshan is faced over and over again with language, culture, and even food that cannot be understood without mediation. These human-faced, linguistic apes complicate matters by introducing an entire new layer of difference, and of course their murder lies at the heart of this *huaben*. On their blood depends exchange—and the possibility of commensurateness—between Du Jingshan and the people of Annam (not to mention the happy ending that makes the story coherent).

The apes speak, but the exorcists remain quiet until the apes are seized: at that point, the balance changes. One might almost read all of the apes' speech as efforts to provoke the exorcists into interaction. Certainly the apes' commentary and their constant affirmations of their own agency seem calculated to demand response. They speak only to one another but clearly invite interruption; twice they say, as their would-be killers overhear, "Let's see what means they have to deal with us!"[36] All they demand is conversation, its own form of commerce and intercourse. As they are captured, they finally succeed. For only then do the formerly silent exorcists, now in the position of petitioners, speak to their captives as if they were perfect equals, first explaining that they act under orders and then urging them to give up a few spoonfuls of their own blood: "It will be used to dye goods and serve to spread your reputation. And we will be grateful for your great virtue, so that in dying you will be famous."[37] From prey they transform themselves into martyrs, and finally, their subjectivity is acknowledged.

Of course throughout the story, other than this brief, secondhand interlude, we are shown how the border between Annam and Guangxi can be negotiated; *Übertragung*—some combination of transaction and translation—is, we are shown over and over again, possible over this permeable membrane. And yet the apes play a critical part in these relations: Du Jingshan comes to Annam precisely to get their blood. How, then, are we to understand the apes in the midst of all this commensurateness? Can they be drawn into this network of transactions? The apes suggest the finitude of this network's range. For all their agency and their linguistic ability, they cannot be assimilated into any position of equality.

It seems that understanding between the traders of Guangxi and the people of Annam necessarily rests on the exclusion of somebody else. If the Annamese are basically human, then someone else must be opaque and bestial. It may be that understanding one alien always demands that another is demonized. Are the apes some kind of scapegoat, either for the Annamese, or for the traders from Guangxi? Perhaps what is excluded has simply been displaced: no longer the Annamese, now the apes.

The precision of the exchange—this jade horse for thirty spans of velvet—makes promises about the possibility of transparent translation, of exchanges, of equivalences. Moreover, the final transaction takes place only near the end of the story, after we have learned something of the apes' interaction with the exorcists, and our knowledge of the apes' role cannot help but color our understanding of the story's conclusion. The exchange of the jade horse for the cloth—which on the surface seems like a happy ending for all, each trading the unprized for the otherwise unattainable—turns out to be grounded in blood money. At its simplest level, the apes stand in the way of the mercantile fantasy in which differing scales of value and meaning allow for an infinity of profit. In this story, that miraculous profit is actually grounded on one infinitely unfair transaction.

For behind the exchange of velvet for jade horse lie other exchanges, that of liquor for the chance to wear clogs and that of ostensibly voluntary death for a chance to be remembered. These transactions between the apes and the exorcists strain any definition of equity. Nonetheless, from beginning to end, this trade is coded as voluntary. The apes recognize (perhaps falsely) that whether they resist or succumb to the temptation of the alcohol is a choice. After they are captured, they have the choice to withhold their blood, even when keeping their lives is no longer an option. Maybe this trade parallels the story's other major trade, of horse for fabric. Or—perhaps the apes are the real proof that Annam and Guangxi are parts of the same world. In this fiscal sense at least, the world is wholly of a piece. If someone is to make a profit, someone else has experienced a loss. For both the House of Zhuzhu *and* Du Jingshan to benefit, the apes must sacrifice their lives.

Can one trade away one's own life? The apes' trade does not resemble the sort that we will see in the next chapter, the sacrifice of a filial child for a parent. Suggestively, although Master Li reports the offer given to the captured apes, he does not record the apes' answer to the exorcists' pleas (although it is implied, since a refusal would have meant no velvet). These voluble apes are silenced; or, perhaps, we might read the bloodstained velvet itself as a last statement of free will. Notably, Master Li never mentions the actual death of the apes. After they volunteer their blood, their deaths are not important enough to relate. Like the *fan* words on the lodge, the apes' blood remains irreducible, an emblem for the untranslatable, for which no equivalence can be found. Their final silence makes it impossible for us to judge how the apes themselves view their relationship to their Annamese captors.

Like a political border, the line between the animal and the human is not easily sustained but must be constantly negotiated. For example, in the minor Qing subgenre of the righteous animal, a tiger or ox or dog displays loyalty or filiality, seemingly the most human of virtues. Chen Ding (fl. mid-seventeenth century) writes of a righteous ox who has assumed a position in a human family not unlike that of a loyal human retainer. First, the ox saves its young master from a tiger's attack, and then it intercedes in a feud that has consumed the lives of both of the ox's masters and involved a lawsuit as well. After trampling the family's mortal enemy and his two sons, the ox also frightens to death the corrupt official who has contributed to its family's downfall.[38] The ox has become a part not merely of the human world but of this particular Chinese family and even of the Chinese state. The ox's righteousness lies not just in its protecting its master's family but also in cleansing the local government of corruption. In this narrative, there seems to be no space outside the Chinese human order, not even for animals. By contrast, our *huaben* consistently leaves space outside the purview of both the Chinese and the human realms. Unlike the righteous ox, the speaking apes cannot be perfectly assimilated into the human world.

McMahon writes of how the story juggles multiple "plays of simian semantics."[39] Sorting the various people and apes by degrees of humanity is no easy task when, as McMahon points out, homophonous versions of *xingxing* appear and reappear with different radicals—meaning both "ape" (猩猩) and "lucid" (惺惺). Earlier, in describing the rake's desire to leave the walls of the *yamen* in search of a good time, the narrator invokes a rhetorical figure very important to the rest of the story, that of the animal whose existence cannot be integrated into the human order. The narrator compares the official's son to a beast: "Just think if you have a monkey in the wilds, can you tie him up with a rope? And then if you want him to study—why, it's like forcing that monkey to dress up in costume and sing opera like *Tertia Fetches Water* or *Old Man Bao Sends off the Baby*."[40] The later image of the doomed apes, stumbling around in their human clogs, echoes this earlier characterization of the animal-like man, a failed simulacrum of a human being. This passage, so early in the story, long before we have encountered the apes, foreshadows them, and it even intimates the possibility—in the midst of Chinese civilization, in the person of no less than an official's son—of something unassimilable, an echo of what we eventually find in the wilds of Annam.

McMahon also comments on the sexual element of Du Jingshan's visit to Annam, specifically the voyeurism involved in his encounter with the bathing Annamese women. Oddly though, it is the encounter between the exorcists and the apes that seems to me to be more replete with sexual tension. The apes know that to succumb to the liquor is death, and yet their efforts to resist temptation, accompanied by taunts at those who tempt them, are ultimately futile. All the elements of a seduction are here. First, they make a show of spurning the exorcists' advances, and then even after they are ensnared, the captors insist that the apes make the capitulation voluntary. To get the precious blood, the apes must consent to their own murder.

The dynamic resembles nothing if not the model of a late imperial rape (or seduction, depending on who is asked); according to the law, any semblance of consent on the part of the woman reduced the charges from rape to fornication, which meant punishment for both participants. Imperial statutes on rape made it the woman's burden to prove that sexual contact had been involuntary, and usually only her death or serious injury constituted sufficient proof. The apes are ensnared in the same predicament; even at the last moment, when they know that they have lost their freedom and their lives, it is still their responsibility either to resist or to grant their own blood.

Like late imperial sexual aggressors, the exorcists carefully plan and set up this scene of seduction. After placing themselves in a position of power, the final indignity is the demand that the victims give up the prize willingly. Of course in the courts, proving consent *ex post facto* was difficult and often marked only by an absence of evidence—a woman, for example, whose injuries looked suspiciously minor to a magistrate. Armed with the proof that all sexual aggressors lack, the exorcists have it easier than a late imperial rapist; the dyed velvet carries something of the charge of hymeneal blood, proof—not of virginity—but of consent. The ape-dyed cloth, elsewhere a token of perfect exchange, also recapitulates the execution of two varieties of power: that of men over women and the colonial relationship (whether that of the Chinese to the Annamese, or the Annamese to the apes).

On his way to recover his funds on Mount Nituo, Du Jingshan sees some women blithely bathing nude in a stream. The narrator explains that they are simply following the customs of Annam, where children begin swimming from the age of eight or so. When Du Jingshan first sees the bathing women, he does not know what to make of them. This *could* be an intensely sexual scene: "Some were wrestling; some teasing each other; some rubbing each other's backs; some in tight embraces as if they were men and women making love; some singing."[41] Nonetheless, confronted with this scene, Du Jingshan responds not with arousal but fear: "This early in the morning, how could there be women bathing in a spring? It's clear that these must be demons (*yaonü* 妖女). What ill luck I, Du Jingshan, have met with!"[42] Having just been attacked by something he considered a yeti-like monster, he is convinced that these women, too, are supernatural, but then he figures that it is better to be witched to death by sirens than eaten by a monster. He heads for the water.

By this point, Du Jingshan's experience in a foreign land has eliminated any trust he might have had for his own first instincts; in

Annam, he knows he cannot rely on his senses and intuitive judgment. Even erotic response must be questioned. Du Jingshan is educated into becoming a very different sort of observer, one who recognizes his own limitations in understanding his surroundings—and who in fact has been convinced that beneath the surface might lie an infinity of different, implicit meanings. The lesson he has learned, in other words, seems awash with literary implications.

But then the narrator switches us to the women's perspective. Startled by a big splash, they rush up to the bank; mirroring Du Jingshan's own misplaced guesses, they speculate among themselves that what they heard was a big fish. Du Jingshan steps forward to identify himself as a man; the women look him over and comment on his foreign accent. One old woman then says, "Where does this barbarian with his outlandish accent come from, that he's peeping on us like that? Tell him to get up."[43] Du Jingshan identifies himself, adding that he had been on his way to Mount Nituo when he had been attacked by a monster. The women titter at what a stupid barbarian he is. His monster, they explain, was actually a *feifei* 狒狒, or baboon, yet another anthropoid of indeterminate relation to Du Jingshan's own kind. At this point, the presence of yet another anthropoid suggests a world so filled with varieties of human and almost human that the conventional model of the Confucian polity—humans linked to one another through clear relations—is strained beyond the breaking point.

The women take pity on Du Jingshan. When they offer him some wine to calm him down and prepare to take him to the manor house, Du Jingshan finally stands up from the water. As he does so, "He looked at himself: his top half looked like a rain-soaked chicken; looking at his bottom half, since he had been kneeling on the soil, he saw it was muddied, like a monkey in ashes."[44] In his quest for cloth dyed in the blood of apes, he discovers that he himself is the monkey (*husun* 猢猻).

We have experienced something like this before, when Master Li accuses Du Jingshan of insufferable rudeness, but now all by himself Du Jingshan experiences a moment of mirroring. All along he has been marveling at the oddness of all that lies around him, how peculiar these people's habits are, how lacking in propriety. But this dialogue with the bathing women stands out: when the ladies call him *man*, or barbarian, it is his foreignness and not theirs that is foregrounded. Moreover, he does not dismiss their perspective. In a story filled with observations of Annamese oddities, in this moment he chooses to look—not at them, naked bathing beauties—but at himself. Is there anywhere else in Chinese literature that a man, confronted with a band of naked women, chooses instead to gaze at himself, through their eyes, as they must see him?

And this moment is entirely necessary. If we are to believe in the equitable nature of the trade that grants Du Jingshan the ape-dyed cloth, then we must have an equivalent to all the looking to which Du Jingshan has subjected the Annamese—even if it is, for him, merely a gaze into an imaginary mirror.

After he concludes the trade with the lady of the mansion, Du Jingshan hurries back to the lodge, where his friend Zhu Chunhui awaits him, having found the silver that had been presumed stolen. As Du Jingshan packs everything up to take home, Zhu Chunhui suggests that he buy some goods to sell back in China. Du Jingshan, far too impatient to return home to his wife, decides he would rather not. In response, Zhu Chunhui offers to sell him some of the Annamese incense Zhu has been gathering. Du Jingshan hands over everything but the travel expenses he needs for the journey home, and he returns with nothing but goods from Annam, the forty spans of velvet and an indeterminate quantity of fragrance.

After Du Jingshan's joyous reunion with his wife, he has to tear himself away to submit the cloth to the pacification commissioner. The final transaction in this story about transactions is a highly peculiar one. An assistant submits the velvet and then emerges to relate the reaction of the pacification commissioner, whose grudge against Du Jingshan remains as powerful as ever. Nonetheless, an official fee is prepared for Du Jingshan, who insists that the assistant keep it. Du Jingshan ends up with neither silver nor velvet, both disappearing into an anonymous official maw. For all his trouble in procuring that velvet—and for all the many apes we presume died to create it—its ultimate fate is something of an anticlimax, and Du Jingshan has gained nothing.

Like Mauss's gift, it is impossible to pin any value on the velvet (or on the apes' sacrifice); all we know is that the velvet can be traded for the jade horse, whose value is equally indeterminate. Indeed, the velvet cannot be drawn into any further webs of transaction. It does not become integrated into Chinese trades and transactions. The ten extra spans that remain at home are never mentioned again; the goods that make Du Jingshan a rich man are instead the fragrances he bought from his friend Zhu Chunhui, with his officially bankrolled travel allowance. Whether in Du Jingshan's or the pacification commissioner's possession, the cloth seems simply to disappear.

The assistant then shares gossip about his boss with Du Jingshan. In the two months that Du Jingshan has been away, that ne'er-do-well adopted son became enamored of two of his mother's serving girls. Attempting to seduce them with his usual ineptitude, he hid himself under his mother's bed and grabbed at the girls in the darkness. Naturally, they screamed, and he ran off, only to be caught by other servant women, who beat him black and blue before they discovered his identity. After his mother learned of these events, she took her vengeance on the two young servant girls, having the two of them beaten to death. The girls' spirits tormented the young man until he slipped into a fatal illness. The family is in no position to pursue any further grudge with Du Jingshan.

A story all about what lies beyond the borders makes the peculiar choice to conclude with an entirely enclosed narrative about the connection between the state sphere and the domestic sphere: no outside forces contribute to the death of the young lecher or to the fall of his father. Everything necessary to their destruction lies within their own four walls.

The ending is peculiar. Of course, on one hand, the assistant's gossip serves an important function in filling in the gaps in our protagonist's knowledge, since only then does Du Jingshan finally piece together the full story of what happened—that it must have been the commissioner's adopted son who ogled Fenggu, which explains the commissioner's grudge against himself. But, on the other hand, the submission of the velvet—and Du Jingshan's whole complicated adventure—then is rendered practically irrelevant: if the corruption of the pacification commissioner and his family can be punished without Du Jingshan's travels to Annam, then why did those travels have to take place at all? If the punishment of this corrupt official and the ruin of his family are the true focus of this story, then Du Jingshan himself seems almost an afterthought. Is all that we have come to learn about the world outside the borders ultimately unimportant?

At the beginning of the story, Fenggu's presence in public suggests to us a narrative powered by the drive to enclose; her presence outside must be punished, and she must be returned safely inside. The story's conclusion returns to her, but by this point, the figure of the public woman is no longer what it was at the beginning of the story, instead bearing the weight of an implicit comparison to those naked but innocent beauties in Annam. If, at the beginning, her appearance elicited speculation as to how family and state were to be bound together, at the end, a return cannot fail to suggest those women in Annam, who though publicly bathing are anything but harlots. Is a single full accounting of both Annam and Guangxi—something like that *yeshi* in the opening couplet—possible?

The story concludes with a rare comment by the narrator, in which he harshly judges Chinese women who expose themselves in public—despite the fact that Du Jingshan's mission succeeds only because of public nudity in Annam. To concede the value of certain Annamese mores—their foods, their religious practices, even their attitudes toward social hierarchy—is very different from accepting different sexual values; to a late imperial writer, the segregation of men from women must have been close to an ethical absolute. The question of whether a naked woman in Guangxi is the same as a naked woman in Annam restages the story's other musings on translation and transaction.

The narrator expresses contempt toward those women from his own region of Wu and Yue (classical names for the Jiangnan region) who carelessly reveal their feet and bosoms—and then even worse, those who claim modesty and insist on bathing only in the privacy of their own homes, yet hypocritically mingle with men in society. Such women naturally remind the narrator of another woman who exposes herself by appearing in public, Fenggu herself: "That Du Jingshan had to bear all this trouble and undergo all this danger was because his wife caused these problems."[45] The narrator continues:

> I urge everyone to keep the women's quarters pure and maintain strict control over your wives, daughters, and sisters—that they should not leave the home is the first priority. If they're going to lose their decency, then they might as well be like the Annamese, with women mixed up with men, exposing their nude bodies, with customs like these.[46]

The naked beauties might have led another observer—someone who wanted to use foreigners to cast light on his own people, like Montesquieu and his Persians—to very different conclusions, for example, that Chinese women might mingle with men in relative freedom, so long as they preserved chaste hearts (as Fenggu herself does). Instead, to the narrator, the behavior of women demands the mediation of translation; between the virtuous naked bathers and the immodest women of Wu and Yue, there is an insurmountable gulf, a border that cannot be traversed.

At this long story's conclusion, the narrator returns again to the problem of the exposed woman: "So you can see that women should never leave their quarters to invite mischief; all of this happened because a stranger espied her beauty and that unblocked his depraved inclinations. 'Beauty is the beginning of debauchery'—this saying is truly worthy of careful consideration."[47] This ending seems curiously incommensurate with the story we have just read. Carlitz has pointed out that such a disparity—between the action and the narrator's comments—is a commonplace in Chinese short fiction. Even though *huaben* themselves reveal "tightly constructed chains of causality whose unified vision is quite clear,"[48] the narrator's comments are often curiously unworthy of the stories, as if that commentarial voice is incapable of treating the story's moral complexities. Of course, in "Journey to Annam," that lack of fit is precisely the point. The narrator's conclusion *cannot* address this particular story; his final words would have applied perfectly well to a story that does not exist, in which no one leaves the empire to travel to Annam and in which Fenggu and Du Jingshan are brought to disaster through their encounter with the evil official's family. The conclusion emerges perfectly out of its genre, that of the *huaben*. In tying up narrative threads perfectly, *huaben* as a genre make the point that the whole polity is ultimately tied together in a web of relations, enclosed within narrative.

But this story concerns the borders, with what is left out by those other narratives. For once in Chinese literature, when we read the word about women in the comments at the end, we must internally transpose "Chinese women." We have seen women in public whose presence was not the beginning of debauchery. We have seen a culture and a politics independent from the Confucian mainstream.

I suppose one way to phrase the final question is whether those naked beauties are successfully absorbed within the narrative arc. Are they fully accounted for by the narrator's intrusion? Our narrator straddles both positions, on one hand suggesting that the naked women in the stream are not licentious (and instead demand translation to be understood), but on the other hand drawing equivalences between them and the women of Wu and Yue who parade around publicly. The return to Fenggu and a rebuke of her forwardness fails to enclose the narrative that has taken place.

It seems fitting to conclude my discussion of the *huaben* form with the happy couple and the story's own recognition of the form's limitations. Fenggu is not punished—she is rewarded with riches: Du Jingshan's journey has not been particularly arduous; he returns with goods he sells at an enormous profit; and the two of them live in comfort happily ever after. Their happiness rests on the existence of a world outside, on histories and politics that are not encompassed by the empire, on narratives whose closedness is challenged and defied.

FIVE
The Arithmetic of Filial Piety

This chapter forms a necessary transition from the themes of the first half of the book to those of the second. The first half of this book examines a variety of relationships between two parties—whether trade or marriage—and how such dyadic relations might function as building blocks for society as a whole. The second half of this book concerns itself more specifically with the structure of families, as seen through the prism of the long novel (*zhanghui xiaoshuo*). The bonds in the preceding chapters are centrifugal, tending to spin outward. But the same is not true for the relationship between parent and child. The relations discussed above—trading partners, even marriage—are always in some sense subject to a dissolution and substitution that traditional writers were noticeably reluctant to apply to the parent-child relationship. The filial relationship, unlike, say, that between lovers, cannot be so easily externalized with a token because father and son should not need anything to mark them as bound. (Yao Ji's lone testicle, which marks him as Yin Xiaolou's true son, is notably inalienable from his person.)

—

"Yang Balao's Miraculous Reunion," the eighteenth story in Feng Menglong's *Gujin xiaoshuo*, tells of a merchant from Xi'an who is held captive by Japanese pirates for nineteen years. Finally, Yang is released in Shaoxing, where he is reunited first with one son—born of his first wife and now an official stationed in Shaoxing—and then with his second son—who was born of a second wife in Guangdong, grew up with his mother's surname, and is, of all things, also an official stationed in Shaoxing. The story concludes with the emperor's praises of this family. But where will this blended family live after the sons' service in Shaoxing is concluded? One can only assume that the second wife and her son will need to pick up and move to Xi'an.

Reunions between parents and children are fundamentally different from those between husbands and wives. A husband and wife may set down roots anywhere. No matter how solid, a marriage can always admit interlopers: a husband may remarry if his wife is dead or truly not to be found; and, although discouraged, widow remarriage was quite widespread in late imperial China. So narratives of reunion between husband and wife tend not to concern themselves with space and distance; but, across various genres, reunions between parents and children seem always to situate themselves in specific geography. This is nowhere more apparent than when a son sets out to find his parents against all odds.[1]

Such journeys must begin where they end. Unlike Qi Sanlang's family, which can restart at any location, these travelers (who are all of scholarly families) must return home with their parents, dead or alive. This chapter begins with a filial son's compulsion to return home. What does a round-trip journey mean in the context, not of profiteering or of marriage, but of filial piety? The round-trip journey poses an important question of filial piety. Marriages, particularly when they take place in clusters, as we saw in Chapter, 3 are one way to imagine the reconstruction of a society. But the filial relation—although like marriage considered a building block for society as a whole—is not only profoundly unsocial, limited to two people (or three, if we count both parents), but also, as these round-trip journeys indicate, much more bound to location.

In "Biography of Filial Son Zhao," the eighteenth-century writer Hu Tianyou describes a young man whose father, a poor scholar, goes wandering before his son's first birthday. Many years later, as a young adult, the son goes off to find the father, covering enormous distances in the process of his search: "The filial son, in his search for his father, meandered north and south of the Huai River, inspected Qi and Lu, covered Ji and surrounded Yan, penetrated Chu and Yu, left footprints in Qin and Long."[2] There is no path to trace here, since what Filial Son Zhao produces is not a map that links one point to another and to another (like the route books, or like Jiang Xingge's journey), but instead a static map. The archaic place-names—timeless, unbound by Qing renamings—evoke a connection to something greater than immediate concerns.

The suggestion—that the space carved out by the filial son is timeless and apolitical—is made all the more explicit in other records. The Ming loyalist writer and painter Gui Zhuang (1613–73) writes of a family friend, Huang Xiangjian, who inscribed a phenomenal loop in search of his parents, traveling all the way from his home near Suzhou to Dayao in the far reaches of Yunnan province. Huang covered almost precisely the same territory as the longest, final journey of the celebrated diarist, traveler, and geographer Xu Hongzu—better known as Xu Xiake—but his account postdates Xu's by a few years (Xu's travels from Jiangyin to Yunnan took place between 1636 and 1640).

In 1644, the very last year of the Chongzhen reign (and thus of the Ming dynasty itself), Huang Xiangjian's father was posted to Dayao, but the chaos of the dynastic transition made it impossible for him and his wife to return to their home in Suzhou. Years later, the son set out on an arduous journey to find his parents. After finding them, he made the journey back, parents in tow. Written for the most part in a deliberately plain style, Gui Zhuang's biography relates Huang's sufferings at considerable length. His journey begins:

> The filial son in the year *xinmao* [1651], the first day of twelfth month, set out on his journey, carrying one bag, one umbrella, and grass shoes. From Wujiang he entered Jiaxing. Thence he went to Hangzhou. He crossed the Qiantang River. He moved through Yanzhou and Quzhou. He entered the Yushan Range of Guangxing. He passed through the Lin River of Fuzhou. He crossed the Zhang River. He passed through Yuanzhou.[3]

And so on in the same vein. These ten place-names move the filial son only eight hundred kilometers, of the easier and less described half of the journey; the rest, with side journeys along the way, is described in even more meticulous geographic detail. A pointilist's map of the known world emerges by plotting out all the hundreds of locations to which Gui Zhuang refers.

The journey is marked in distance (more than 25,000 *li*), in time (more than nineteen months of actual travel, but three years away from home), and in difficulty (the modes of transport Huang took and the weather). Finally, the journey is also written on his very body:

> Constantly holding the umbrella up, his arms grew so sore he could scarcely raise them. Sometimes his feet were so painful he could not bear it, and sometimes bloody blisters were red and swollen until he popped them and then blood flowed out. Then he would continue again on his path. He was so exhausted that he often collapsed by the side of the road.[4]

However, ultimately, the real danger of the journey lies in its taking place precisely at the moment of dynastic transition, so that compounding Huang's physical miseries are the hardships of war.

As Huang travels further and further away from the heartland, he notices an enormous change: "From here on out, the landscapes he passed and the officials and citizens he saw were something else. In Jiangnan, the customs had changed six or seven years ago. To see these people suddenly was as if they were from another country."[5] One suspects that in this case the past is the other country; just as he is shocked by their appearance, those he encounters are equally surprised by his (Huang's own short hair—*duanfa* 短髮—is mentioned specifically, an elliptical reference to the Manchu queue and shaved pate he sports, in contrast to the Ming garb they do). When he gets to Yunnan, those separated from the heartland by war gather around him: "It was like the people of the Peach Blossom Spring encountering the fishermen."[6] Like the fishermen in Tao Qian's "Taohua yuan ji" (Record of Peach Blossom Spring), Huang Xiangjian has found his way outside imperial time and space.

The return trip is an almost cinematic representation of the dynasty's fall. On the way back, the family discovers fighting still going on in Guizhou, and in the first month of *kuiyi* (1653), they are finally able to leave Yunnan. Later, in Pingba, they encounter a group of cavalrymen, accompanied by several hundred female captives from Guangxi. Further down the same road, they find several thousand defeated troops from Sichuan, fleeing—or rather staggering away—with an elephant. The dynasty's fall puts the family on the road amid thousands of others—losers, victors, and captives—converging from all directions, Guangxi in the southwest, Sichuan in the west, the Manchurian northeast, and the Huangs themselves, making their way from Yunnan back home to Suzhou. Huang's story—given its combination of imperial scope and familial focus—was particularly open to transformation into a *chuanqi* play, Li Xuanyu's *Wanli yuan* (Union across ten thousand miles; mid-eighteenth century). But the biography differs from all drama in that the filial relation does not compete or compare with loyalty to the old dynasty; nor does it even replace loyalty to the old dynasty. Instead, filiality completely obscures loyalty.

Gui Zhuang's greatest fame derived from leading the resistance against the Manchus in his hometown of Kunshan. Afterward, disguised as a Buddhist monk, he fled in the company of his friend, the polymath man of letters Gu Yanwu. But the author, who was himself prepared to die to defend the Ming dynasty from Manchu invaders, writes a biography in which the outcome of that fighting is largely irrelevant. Instead, the filial son's response to these massive troop movements, the pathetic female captives, and the material traces of imperial collapse—all converging on a single road—focuses entirely on his parents: "From Baiyan jing all the way to Pingba, that was all the original road taken by the filial son on his way out. But now that he was returning with his family, it wasn't at all like going out on his own."[7] He spares not a thought for the tragedy befalling the empire. To keep his parents safe, the filial son quickly takes to side roads, with no more mention of geopolitics.

Gui Zhuang enumerates the length of the journey in terms of provinces traversed, rivers crossed, and mountains climbed. But at the same time he points out that, like the unprecedented geopolitical turmoil of the times, the sights of the journey go entirely unnoticed by the filial son: "Of unusual, deep, magical mountains and rivers, famous ancient ruins, strange birds and beasts, variations in climate and custom, there can be no exhaustive account. But everything that the filial son passed, he did so quickly."[8] In other circumstances, the well-born Suzhou *literatus* Huang Xiangjian might have been a pleasure traveler or an explorer like Xu Xiake, focused precisely on those aspects of the journey that hardly register now.

On one hand, the biography's comprehensiveness and post-apocalyptic qualities make it seem a prose version of Gui Zhuang's long narrative poem *Wanchou qu* (Song of myriad sorrows), which relates the entire span of history from Pan Gu's creation of the world to Nanjing's fall at the hands of the Manchus. In painting a picture at this scale, the biography transposes geography for *Wanchou qu*'s march through time. On the other hand, the geographical specificity of the biography is also strangely reminiscent of writings circulating in the late 1640s that speculate on how the Southern Ming might overturn the Manchu presence in the north.[9]

And yet it is neither of these. Gui Zhuang concludes the biography with a note that makes it clear that even as he is recording an individual journey, he is also creating a very specific kind of geography. He appends a detailed philological note explaining the language with which he has described Huang's journey:

> There is order to how I have written the place-names in this piece. . . . The places where he arrived, if he passed through their borders, I called it *guo* 過, "to pass." If he went through to another province, I called it *ru* 入, "to enter." If he entered, I would definitely record the county, and sometimes the garrison, the way station, or the detailed path. When he arrived through shortcuts, I called it *da* 達, "to reach." When he got to provincial seats, I called it *zhi* 至, "to arrive." Only in the case of Wugang county did I also call it *zhi*, "to arrive."[10]

After having painted a map in words, Gui Zhuang self-consciously explains the means by which he has represented an enormous swathe of space through the prism of a single family's experiences, as if inscribing the Huang family onto a map, or the map onto the family. The prodigious filial feat (or Gui Zhuang's representation of it) supersedes every other way of making sense of space, as if transforming the empire itself into a vast terrain whose function is the reunion of these three people. Gui Zhuang paints a landscape literally constructed out of filiality, but lacking any mention of the state. In an age of martyr-suicides, Huang Xiangjian and his family (who are officials, yet) hardly seem to notice that the dynasty has fallen. Gui Zhuang's filial son suggests that family concerns can eclipse political ones.

During the turmoil of dynastic transition, some made heroic efforts to write filiality and loyalty on the body or to combine these two virtues in a single gesture. For example, in 1674, the imprisoned general Fan Chengmo (a Qing loyalist who refused to ally himself with the Rebellion of the Three Feudatories) awaited his own execution costumed in a veritable uniform of virtue: he ceremonially garbed himself in the hat given to him by the Kangxi emperor and in the garment he wore the last time he saw his mother.[11] Even more seamlessly than Fan Chengmo, the mother of Gui Zhuang's good friend Gu Yanwu was able fully and literally to embody virtue. She was noteworthy for three acts of spectacular virtue: as a teenager, she joined the household of her deceased fiancé, thus condemning herself to life as a widow without ever having enjoyed the pleasures of marriage; a few years after that, she cut off her little finger to prepare a medicine for her mother-in-law; and finally as an older woman she starved herself when the Ming dynasty fell.[12] Her body—forever virginal, less a finger, starved to death—fuses the three political and familial virtues: chastity, filiality, and loyalty.

In contrast, Gui Zhuang imagines not only the possibility of filial piety in the absence of a state but also a filial piety that has taken over the purview of the state—prefectures, provinces, way stations featuring in a landscape only insofar as they structure a filial son's journey. It is hard to imagine that anyone in the immediate aftermath of the cataclysmic dynastic fall should not comment on what is happening all around him, but that is indeed what happens here. Instead of geopolitics, Huang Xiangjian's father makes mention of a literary text when he compares his son's journey to Wang Yuan's, as related by the Ming writer Li Zhi. Although the Huangs are displaced by the forces of history, the journey itself takes place on a literary, abstract, and seemingly ahistorical plane. Gui Zhuang could not be clearer on this matter.

Gui Zhuang touches on something central to filial piety; somehow this relation *does* precede all other ties. In the previous chapters, writers responded to political theory or to contemporary political problems. The fall of the Ming dynasty challenged notions of coherence, whether of justice, of familial structure, or even of narrative. Here, in contrast, a text that comprises many of the same elements, written at the same time, makes an altogether different argument: that some ties so thoroughly precede political ones that they obscure politics altogether. To Gui Zhuang, even the fall of the Ming can have no impact on the filial relation. In reassembling a central problem—how it is that the quintessentially dyadic, apolitical relationship between parent and child can be regarded as fundamental to society as a whole—I have allowed this one chapter to be organized with no particular historical focus. Nor is this chapter, unlike the others, an implicit work of genre criticism. Instead, I have attempted to reconstruct a set of issues as an ongoing discussion that spans about a century and a half as it appears not just in short narrative but also in imperial edicts and essayistic writing.

—

In "Da'nan," a tale in the late seventeenth-century collection *Liaozhai zhiyi*, Pu Songling relates another cross-country journey undertaken by a son to reunite with his father. The story suggests one way that filial piety might turn from a limited relation involving just parent and child to one that organizes relations with other people as well. Natives of Chengdu, Da'nan's family is possessed of some wealth. Da'nan is born of a concubine, Ms He, some months after his father Xi Chenglie runs away from home, driven away by his shrewish wife Ms Shen. As a young boy, Da'nan himself runs away from home in search of his missing father.

He joins a man named Qian who is going to Kuizhou; once there, Qian drugs Da'nan and sells him to some monks. The monks take pity on him and put him back on the road, where he joins a scholar named Jiang who is headed home to Luzhou. All along the way, Da'nan has been inquiring after his father, and in Luzhou, he hears about a man named Xi whose companions are traders from Fujian. Da'nan tags along with merchants on their way to Fuqing, in Fujian, but unfortunately, they betray him. After he is beaten and robbed, a Mr. Chen from Yongfu takes a liking to the boy and brings him home. His new benefactor is a wealthy man, and, while Da'nan himself is encouraged to study with Mr. Chen's sons, merchants from all over travel to his establishment, and all are told to keep an eye out for a Mr. Xi.

Meanwhile, Da'nan's mother Ms He is sold to a merchant who takes her to Chongqing, but she attempts suicide rather than submit to him. She is passed on to a merchant from Yanting. When she is sold yet again, to a merchant said to be looking for a housekeeper, the buyer turns out to be her own husband Xi Chenglie now making a living as a merchant. When Xi Chenglie learns of his son's existence, he is overjoyed and immediately sends his people out to look for Da'nan. Ms He's suicide attempt has taken a toll on her health, and she needs help with the housework. She urges her husband to take a concubine. Reluctantly, he agrees. Amazingly, it turns out to be none other than his erstwhile wife Ms Shen, who had been remarried to a merchant from Baoning. After learning that this merchant was impotent, she attempts suicide; since he was on his way to Kuizhou anyway, he sells her on the road.

Husband, wife, and concubine are reunited, only now the wife and the concubine have exchanged positions. A neighbor reports Xi Chenglie to the *yamen* for forcing his wife to be a concubine, but surprisingly the couple is not brought in for questioning. Instead, the magistrate himself comes to visit them, and he is none other than their son, Da'nan himself. In the intervening years, Da'nan had found success in the examinations; on his way home from the capital, he stopped by Chengdu, where he learned that both of his mothers had been remarried. He reclaims his family estate and then heads to his posting at Yanting, where all four members of the family reunite. Eventually, of course, all four will return to live in their ancestral home in Chengdu.

Mapping this story out reveals a pattern of travels not too dissimilar from that in "The Pearl-Sewn Shirt"—an imagined world of many simultaneous journeys, totaling many thousands of *li* and revolving around two poles, western Sichuan and the southeast coast of Fujian—all in the service of a single family reunion. In fact, the geographical specificity of the tale is such that the anonymous Juqizi's vernacular rewriting in *Xingmeng pianyan* (Refined words to awaken one from dreams; from the last years of the eighteenth century), although longer and more detailed in almost every other respect, hardly touches the place-names of its predecessor (a striking fact, since most classical tales possess a much vaguer geography than their vernacular counterparts). Instead of only involving three people, the filial relation in "Da'nan" draws in scores, a veritable cross-section of late seventeenth-century life: at its core a well-off farming family, but also scholars, traders, monks, traveling merchants, representatives of the state, and the neighbors in Chengdu.

And the whole elaborate production has had but one obvious end, the reassignment of family roles, or the switch between Xi Chenglie's wife and concubine. At the end, Da'nan can express filiality to his birth mother, the former concubine. In fact, the sloughing off and reassignment of familial roles seems to be one of the central ways in which filial piety—at its heart a relation between two—can extend to others and be transformed into a more capacious and flexible version of kinship.

—

Almost a century earlier, Song Maocheng's "Filial Son from Wu" (published in 1612) strips this shell game down to its bare essentials. The filial son's mother and wife do not get along, and while he is away on a business trip, his wife sells his mother into domestic servitude. Ominously telling her that she needn't bring along any baggage, the younger woman takes her mother-in-law on a trip, supposedly to visit the older woman's daughter. Only after setting sail does the mother-in-law recognize that she has been tricked and has been sold to become a nanny. (Fortunately, the family to whom she is sold treats her well.)

When the son returns home, the wife tells him that his mother has run away. He is dubious but has no choice but to believe his wife. Years later, again on business, he happens to see a familiar-looking woman doing laundry on the bank of the river. It is his mother, and the two enjoy a tearful reunion. Later, he tricks his wife into accompanying him on a trip, where he explains to his mother's masters that his mother had been tricked. He offers them his wife in exchange and returns home with his mother.

In an age of dramatic filial gestures, this one is on the surface unimpressive, except in that it represents a kind of exchange stripped down to its core—the filial son's choice of his mother over his wife, or the exchange of family members of one generation for those of another. Nonetheless, the specifics of this particular trade are commercial enough to be troubling. The son offers his mother's employers a deal: "Sir, the old woman from Gusu whom you bought is actually my mother who met with an unfilial daughter-in-law. If you would give her back, I would be willing to exchange her for a young and beautiful one."[13] Unlike most gestures of filiality, the son's can be condensed to a specific monetary value, as if the filial debt itself had a discrete value, specifically the difference in market value between the two women.

Moreover, even if the family that purchased his mother was happy to employ her solely as a babysitter, no such guarantee holds for the younger and better-looking daughter-in-law, thus potentially grounding a son's filiality in his wife's loss of chastity. (Wife-selling was a crime in both the Ming and the Qing precisely so that men could not profit from their wives' loss of chastity.) In fact, Song Maocheng's account does its best to skirt the mother's sexuality. She is, as we are told when she is introduced in the beginning, only forty, undiminished by age, and neat and clean in appearance—and yet strikingly she is sold not to serve as a concubine (as would certainly be likelier and more remunerative) but to act as a nanny. The switch between mother and daughter-in-law is made as cleanly as possible, but it cannot entirely skirt certain uncomfortable questions.

—

Studied extensively by modern-day critics for its reversals of gender, "A Male Mencius' Mother Raises Her Son Properly By Moving Three Times," the sixth tale in Li Yu's *Wusheng xi* concerns a much less tidy role shift, which poses questions about the nature of the filial debt. Ostensibly, the story simply substitutes the transgendered You Ruilang/Ruiniang for Mencius' mother, a paragon of womanly virtue who in moving three times demonstrated an absolute commitment to her son's moral education. But the hero You Ruilang undergoes more than a mere sex change, as the change from male to female is overshadowed by the transformation first from friend (or homosexual lover—at any rate, some sort of relation of equals) into wife and then into mother.

A beautiful youth, You Ruilang is forced to sell himself sexually because his father needs to raise the money to pay for his wives' funerals. Xu Jifang, a handsome widower with a young son, sells all his property to secure exclusive sexual rights to the boy. Ruilang and his father live with Xu Jifang until the father's death, and then Ruilang castrates himself when he enters puberty (to prevent his boyish beauty from being ruined). Afterward, Ruilang dresses as a woman, practices embroidery, and even changes his name to Ruiniang (*niang* 娘 means "lass," as opposed to the "lad" of *lang* 郎). When news of his illegal castration circulates, both he and his lover are taken to court, where Xu Jifang is subjected to a beating. Later, as a result of the humiliation, Xu Jifang dies, but not before asking Ruilang to assume the role of virtuous widow, by preserving his chastity and taking care of Xu's little boy. Ruilang manages both and brings up the boy to be a successful official.

Back when Ruilang and Jifang are dragged to court, the official in charge of the case wants to know why anyone would castrate himself. Ruilang explains to the magistrate that he castrated himself because he owes Jifang everything, for having paid for the funerals of his mother, stepmother, and father. Furious that Ruilang attributes his castration to filial piety, the magistrate derides the younger man:

> What nonsense! Was there no other way for you to return his favor other than by doing this? Your body, your skin, and your hair you received from your parents. How could you for the sake of this shameful liaison get rid of your organ? Haven't you heard "the most unfilial act of all is to die without issue"? First I will beat you for unfiliality![14]

What enrages the magistrate is that Ruilang has chosen the single behavior—castration—that most defeats the ultimate end of filial piety, leaving descendants for the next generation. Out of filial piety, Ruilang has sold himself, so that his buyer Jifang assumes the filial debts of caring for Ruilang's father and burying Ruilang's mothers. When Ruilang anticipates Jifang's desire for him to remain forever smooth and boyish, his only choice is to castrate himself to pay back Jifang for everything he has done for Ruilang's parents. Can the obligations of filial piety be transferred to another party, even when they then involve a son's castration? In this story, once Jifang assumes Ruilang's filial obligations, it follows quite logically that Ruilang should serve his parents by rendering himself forever childless.

As in "Da'nan," part of the story concerns the shuffling around of family roles, or how to make a family come out right without the addition of any more people. In Da'nan's family, wife and concubine, each properly requited, switch places; the family covers thousands of kilometers before all returning to Chengdu. Nonetheless, the switch in roles parallels the difference between making a round-trip journey and staying put: on the surface, nothing has changed, but in reality everything has. In "A Male Mencius' Mother," the act of castration turns the male lover into a female widow, although only one body, that of Ruilang (or Ruiniang) is involved.

Unlike other obligations, the filial one can never be paid off, nor can it ever be transferred to another. But if one figures it specifically as a debt in an economic matrix, then it seems as if what Ruilang owes his parents can be transferred to Jifang, who has bought him and assumed his debts. The implication is that whatever Ruilang had owed his father, he now owes to Xu Jifang. And if that is the case, then the act of castration—seemingly self-defeating to filiality—could be an act of filial piety.

Xu Jifang turns into a proxy son for Ruilang's parents, and the older male lover himself becomes a strange kind of proxy father to the younger man. After the humiliation at the *yamen*, Jifang grows sick, and the castrated Ruilang does everything he can to nurse his lover. Finally, Ruilang presents Jifang a meal of his own flesh: "Ruilang burnt incense and prayed and even cut out a piece of flesh from his own thigh (*gegu*) in an attempt to save [Jifang], all to no avail."[15] Cutting a piece of one's flesh and serving it as food to a sick person is a filial trope, not a treatment I have ever heard applied to husband and wife (the relation that Ruiniang and Jifang seem to enter into). And between friends—the reciprocal relation of *pengyou* 朋友, as the two are referred to early on in the story—this sort of cannibalism seems unthinkable. In other words, Ruilang, in feeding Jifang bits from his own body, fully enacts the transfer of obligation, treating Jifang as if he were his own father.

Ruilang has marred his body not just by castration but by cutting off his flesh to feed Jifang. Why does his filial piety need to be marked on his flesh? In the late imperial period, filiality and cannibalism are inextricably linked, as is suggested by Qing local histories in which the filial act mentioned above all others is the act of cannibalism, or *gegu* 割股 (literally, "the slicing of a limb"): filial sons and daughters who prepare curative soups for their parents out of pieces of their own arms or legs. We do not know how common in actual, lived life this practice was, but in imagination at least it was a central component of filial behavior, mentioned far more often than more quotidian expressions of devotion. Perhaps, as we moderns are inclined to think, these cases represent a perverted extreme of filial devotion, but it seems more likely that, as their centrality within written records of the late imperial period indicates, they are at the very heart of filiality.

Gegu does not appear in the classical canon, one reason some late imperial observers were somewhat uncomfortable about the morality of these extreme acts. In writing about a filial son named Yang who practiced *gegu*, the early Qing philologist and official Mao Qiling treats it as an exotic act, claiming that he had not known of it until his travels (suggesting that the practice was geographically limited). Even as he disavows this behavior as counter to the canon's prescriptions for filial behavior, Mao graphically describes how Yang slices his arm to cure his mother, after which he is honored by a ceremonial gate on which is inscribed, "With his body, he increased the longevity of his mother." Mao makes the arithmetic even more explicit, explaining that the son "reduced his own years so as to increase his mother's,"[16] as if longevity existed in a fixed and limited amount, to be distributed between mother and son.

Perhaps it is not just longevity that functions in this way, but bodies themselves. In an earlier act of filial piety, Yang tastes his elderly father's feces and laments that their sweetness indicates his father's final decline. His two filial acts parallel each other, and not just in their embrace of the bodily (and the disgusting): in the first, he eats of his father's body; in the second, his mother eats of his body.

Parenthood's essence is to create new bodies; when Yang chooses coprophagy and cannibalism to express devotion to his parents, he seems to suggest that filiality's point is to defy—or at least undo—the heart of parenthood. If biology makes three where there were two, this filial son, through both eating and feeding, attempts to make one of three.

—

Inheritance squabbles between brothers are a commonplace in late imperial literature and culture, but, in fact, the relationship of parent and child is just as inherently vulnerable to anxieties about division. In literature, this anxiety often appears in the metaphorical comparison between the circulation of people and the circulation of silver (in the late sixteenth-century novel *Jinpingmei* a related comparison is made between semen and silver).[17] For example, people might save up silver for a rainy day, just as they might engender sons to care for them in old age. In other words, children and money are comparable investments in the future.

"The Tangerines and the Tortoiseshell" begins with a short narrative that concerns itself precisely with the problem of whether there is any difference between these two forms of planning for the future. The elderly Mr. Jin lovingly rubs the ingots he has accumulated over a lifetime every night before he goes to sleep. On his seventieth birthday, he promises, he will divide the eight giant ingots among his four sons. But the night before his birthday, just as he is falling asleep, he hears some suspicious sounds, which at first he thinks must be thieves. Instead, he sees something peculiar: eight big men, each dressed in white, with a red sash tied around the waist. These men then speak to the old man:

> We brothers, according to our foreordained destiny, ought to obey your command. But your too fond love has elevated us to human status. By not having us labor and for cherishing us for so many years, our days before reincarnation have just about been filled. Originally we were going to find our own direction after your return to heaven. Now we've heard that you are going to split us up to serve your sons. But we have no previous karma with your sons, so we have come to bid you goodbye. We are going to join a certain Mr. Wang in X village of Y county. But since our karmic

connection to you has not yet been exhausted, we were able to come and bid you goodbye.[18]

Upon waking, Mr. Jin discovers that his precious silver has vanished.

Later, to corroborate the dream, Mr. Jin pays a visit to X village, where there is indeed a Mr. Wang, who reports an odd dream he recently had, in which eight men dressed in white robes with red sashes announced they were joining his household. When Mr. Wang moves his bed, he finds the eight silver ingots, each tied with a red ribbon. Even when Mr. Wang gives Mr. Jin a little silver to take back with him, it manages to slip out of his sleeve.

The value created by sons and that invested in silver somehow parallel each other: old Mr. Jin has accumulated two categories of value for the future, eight ingots of silver and four human sons, and he is punished for doing a poor job "rearing" his silver: as a miser, he keeps it too close by and never allows it to work. ("Gold," the surname shared by him and his sons, is of course more valuable than silver.) But if Mr. Jin does a better job with his sons than his silver, in another *huaben* it is the very ownership of sons that is questioned.

The opening anecdote in "A Son and Grandson Abandon a Body, While a Servant Mourns" (*Wusheng xi* 11) also sets up a comparison between silver and sons. Li Yu writes of two men—one with no sons, the other with two—who are good friends. The man with sons divides his estate between them, but these two turn out to be so unfilial that their father is reduced to penury. The childless man takes his friend in, explaining that he himself has adopted two foster sons who vie with each other in filiality. He invites his friend to stay for a few days, to enjoy the hospitality of these two sons. On the first day, the elder foster son provides a delicious banquet; on the second day, the second foster son serves up an equally delicious and lavish banquet. For some days, the two foster sons take turns offering generous hospitality.

The guest expresses admiration for the filiality of his host's adopted sons, especially compared to the ungrateful behavior of his own natural-born sons. But after a few days he asks why he has not caught a glimpse of either of these two paragons of filial piety. The host answers:

"It won't be hard to meet them. Just wait for me to call them out." So he turned to the left and called out, "First Master, please come out." He stretched his left hand into his pocket and pulled out a bag of silver and put it on the table. He then called to the right, "Second Master, please come out." He stretched his hand into his pocket and pulled out a bag of silver and put it on the table. He then turned to the man with sons and pointing said, "These are my two sons. Please take a good look."[19]

The man with sons is flummoxed: how can his friend call these bags of silver children, when they patently are not? His friend in turn wonders in what way this silver can be compared unfavorably to sons: they are more filial; they unfailingly do his bidding; he never need worry about them, nor show any concern.

He even contends that they are as much of his substance as any natural-born son. The filial son Yang tastes his father's feces and feeds his mother his own flesh; here, the man with no offspring makes the same claims about his silver, that he and they—human and bullion—are actually of the same substance. He tells his friend that this silver has been "wrested out of my sweat and blood" (*gutou shang zheng chulai* 骨頭上掙出來)—an odd metaphor for paternity, fully as violent and carnal as Yang's version of the filial relation—and so naturally he "regards it as his own flesh and blood" (*dang zijia gu rou* 當自家骨肉). His frugality (like Mr. Jin's) blurs into familial feeling: "From the beginning," he explains, "I told them [these bags of silver] to abide with me, not bearing to live apart."[20] In the end, the man without sons takes care of his friend with the undutiful sons, making sure that he does not starve to death. Silver takes care of both of them, when sons do not, and the man with no sons boasts: "Aren't they the most dutiful filial sons ever? My hard-won struggle to get them in the first place was not in vain."[21]

—

In other words, anxieties about money are bound up closely with anxieties about paternity—not in the sense that a failure of paternity is what is at stake (the identity of these characters is not questioned)—but in that paternity itself seems uncomfortably comparable to earning silver. In both texts, engendering sons and earning more money mirror each other in turning one body into many. In "The Tangerines and the Tortoiseshell," it is the accumulation of silver—not sons—that is shown to be precarious; in "A Son and Grandson Abandon a Body," silver is reliable, and sons are not. Whichever the case, these two acts of projecting value into the future parallel each other. Any control of value is lost once either the sons are born, or the silver appears and begins to accumulate; there is also the suggestion that both more sons and more silver imply increasing dilution. Perhaps, with fewer sons and less silver, Mr. Jin could have kept track of both, but an increase in sons and money makes him vulnerable to uncontrollable centripetal forces. Consequently, stories about filiality always focus, so far as I can tell, on only children (whether sons or daughters or daughters-in-law). In such a context, Filial Son Yang's insistence on one body, shared by the three, does not seem so illogical. The focus is on a tie of singular intensity that excludes others from its sphere.

Nonetheless, as discomfiting as it might be, division is biologically and culturally inevitable, sons from their fathers' bodies, and brothers from brothers. A father dies, and sons succeed to his property. Brothers will eventually inherit their father's estate and then decide whether or not it ought to be divided. Numerous late imperial narratives treat the division of estates. Perhaps most famous among these is "Three Filial and Incorruptible Paragons Relinquish Their Property and Establish High Reputations," the third story from Feng Menglong's third collection *Xingshi hengyan*, which tells of three virtuous brothers whose refusal to divide the estate allows for almost infinite gain and profit. But even when brothers stave off division for a generation, it only postpones the inevitable. Their sons, or their sons' sons, will inevitably split the estate. If the patrilineage is to continue, it must divide and dilute itself.

—

Why does Filial Son Yang stop after he gives his mother a portion of his health and lifespan? Wouldn't giving her all of it be an even more profound statement of devotion? Yang's wound takes 120 days to heal. But what if it had killed him? Would the act still have been a filial one? Or would it have been transformed into a profoundly unfilial one? By its nature, *gegu*—and its even more dangerous close cousin, *gegan* (割肝), cutting a slice off the liver—is always a flirtation with suicide. The seventeenth-century Qiu Weiping writes of a young scholar named Zhao Xiqian, whose mother suffers from malaria. A shaman tells the son that his mother can be saved only by eating a slice of his heart. Recognizing the finality of such a sacrifice, Zhao Xiqian performs ablutions and prepares a will before he opens up his chest and places the flesh on a table. Unable to get to his heart, he settles for a few inches of intestine, which he presents to his mother, together with the flesh on the table.

His mother recovers, and miraculously Zhao Xiqian himself survives (a piece of bamboo piping replaces the missing intestine). In other words, the central problem is averted. Would he still have been a filial son if he had been able to get to his heart and died? Cannibalism poses certain questions: if self-sacrifice is at the heart of filial piety, does that self-sacrifice at some point (say, when it involves total consumption and sacrifice) turn into something self-destructive and consequently entirely unfilial? Ruilang's two gestures of devotion—castration to pay off his father's debt and *gegu* in an attempt to save Jifang's life—are figuratively identical; in both acts, in the name of filiality, a family consumes itself. Can one declare a point at which self-consumption ceases to be filiality? Or is it instead the case that the very essence of filial piety is self-consumption? Perhaps filial piety is a virtue that stands always at the brink of self-erasure, since the total consumption of children by their parents at once seems to represent both the highest pinnacle of filiality and its undoing.

The problem echoes one of the obsessions of this money-minded age: the point at which spending turns into earning, and vice versa. Giving charitable donations—out of an uncalculating spirit of compassion—to earn karmic rewards for the future is one example of this paradoxical arithmetic. In "A Young Lordling Goes Bankrupt and Revives the Family Fortunes," the fourth story in *Doupeng xianhua*, the pseudonymous Aina tells of a profligate rich man who makes it his project to run through his inheritance like water, spending enormous sums on hospitality, including a show for the Qingming Festival to which he invites ten thousand guests to watch twenty opera troupes. He also helps out a young scholar fallen on hard times. Later, when all of the rich man's money is gone, the young scholar, who has since found examination success, helps his former benefactor out. Later still, when the White Lotus rebels rise up, the only area they spare is the spendthrift's home area; those rebels answer to yet another man helped by him. So were his wild spending sprees spending or earning? In retrospect, they turn out to have been savvy investments for the future. Only by spending all his silver in the past has he come to earn rewards in the present; now he owns much more than those who carefully scrimped and saved. If other virtues work this way, why should not filial piety?

—

In an effort to bureaucratize and popularize what had earlier been *literati* norms, the Yongzheng emperor instituted various awards and punishments to encourage orthodox behavior. In 1728, the emperor addressed the case of the Fujian native Li Shengshan, who made for his mother a curative soup of his own liver. Li Shengshan's mother recovered from her illness, but not surprisingly the resulting wound killed Li Shengshan himself, who as a result forces the emperor to confront the dilemma that Zhao Xiqian miraculously skirts. Did Li Shengshan merit an honorary plaque (as the governor of Fujian believed) or not (as the Board of Rites argued)? After all, although the state promoted Confucian virtues, it could not encourage sui-cide, which would be harmful to the fabric of society.

The Yongzheng emperor granted the honors, but only after some internal conflict. After asserting that a spontaneous act of devotion deserved recognition, he still cites practically the full range of the orthodox canon—the *Analects*, Mencius, the Tang thinker Han Yu, and the most influential neo-Confucian of them all, the Song dynasty Zhu Xi—on the primacy of preserving life. Ultimately the emperor departed not just from canonical precedent, but even from that established by his ancestor the Shunzhi emperor, who refused to grant any honors to those who injured themselves.[22]

Decades later, however, when it came to another case—that of a young woman who did not save her father's life through sacrifice, but merely followed him to his death (*xunfu*)—the ruling was different: Yongzheng's son the Qianlong emperor refused to grant posthumous honors, pointing out that the ritually specified form for mourning is not suicide, but sacrifices at the grave.

The distinction between the two cases adjudicated by imperial father and son hinges on the efficacy of *gegu*. If one believes, as Yongzheng and his contemporaries seem to have, that *gegu* possesses actual medicinal value, then it is almost impossible not to concede some legitimate merit to its practice. (As with Filial Son Yang, a zero-sum game is in operation here, with Li Shengshan's giving his life up so that his mother might live.) Once we have conceded that *gegu* works, we find ourselves forced to decide whose life matters more, that of the parent or that of the child. In the other hierarchical relations, the determination is much easier: the lord's life outweighs that of his vassal; the husband's life is more important to the family than the wife's, but in the case of filiality, we cannot tell.

Any emperor finds himself in a unique position: to be emperor is to imagine universality, to conceive of what is moral in itself and then imagine its effects on the polity as a whole—in short, to ask of every action, what would happen if everyone behaved so? What would happen if everyone practiced *gegan*? It does not bear thinking of. After comparing *gegan* to widow suicide, which all Qing emperors opposed adamantly and which had been outlawed by the emperor's father, the Kangxi emperor, Yongzheng's focus wanders to the family as a whole and even more broadly to the network of relations out of which emerges the state:

> Through the course of his life, a man carries on from his ancestors and starts his descendants off. This responsibility is an enormous one. Now if one were to abandon one's life in a moment of haste and forget the weightiness of ritual and of continuing the family, I daresay that would not be what is filial piety.[23]

He is moved by the individual act, but conflicted as to its significance. Instead, the emperor can only emphasize the continuation of the family, and each individual's position between two generations. His discussion of *gegan*, in other words, focuses on everything but the relationship between parent and child, which suggests to me that *gegu* and *gegan* are central to thinking about filial piety, precisely because their focus is not all the ways in which the interests of parent and child merge, but instead the single moment at which their interests are most incontrovertibly opposed.

Along with the round-trip journey and *gegu*, there is another important literary expression of filial piety: arranging for a parent's burial—whether in buying a coffin, or selling oneself to provide a funeral (hence, the filial exemplars who sell themselves into bondage to pay for a parent's burial). The dead parent awaiting burial no longer can punish or reward the child; anything done for such a parent takes place fully outside the ties of reciprocity, obligation, and exchange. Compare these acts to the Yongzheng emperor's description of the filial network—the ancestors before and the descendants after—and we can see that what might constitute filiality from the state's perspective contrasts dramatically with filiality in the popular imagination. Instead of a network of generations, each of these three supremely filial acts contracts the whole universe to the bond between parent and child, and all resist being placed within the context of other virtues and other relations.

Human communities always find themselves caught between two ends: contraction to nothingness or infinite expansion to a dilution that is another kind of nothingness. The two filial gestures this chapter treats—the round-trip journey and *gegu*—reflect the two ends of this anxiety, in the son who paints the entire landscape of the empire in filiality and the child whose devotion to his parents literally consumes him.

—

To the Enlightenment thinker Jean-Jacques Rousseau, these two poles can become balanced only after language arises. Rousseau imagines a prehistory before language and society when people "had the concept of a father, a son, a brother, but not that of a man. Their hut contained all of their fellow men. Stranger, beast, monster: these were all one to them. Apart from themselves and their family, the whole universe would count as nothing to them."[24] Before language, he argues, the human community could not exist because communication between strangers could not take place: "There were families, but there were no nations."[25] Moreover, Rousseau asserts, even these impromptu prelinguistic families are nothing we would consider families, but instead were simply gatherings of genetically related people who could not even properly conceive of their own relations. Before language and any notion of a community, there could be—in Rousseau's imagined prehistory—no concept of incest either. (Rousseau puts it, "They become husband and wife without ceasing to be brother and sister.") In place of a human community capable of expansion and growth, groups of humans contract to a single point, with the perpetuation of the species possible only with the union of brother and sister (who themselves are descendants of earlier brother-sister unions, *ad infinitum*).

There are interesting parallels between Rousseau's concern with language, as a means by which families are to be organized and exogamy to arise, and a Chinese concern with filial piety. If for Rousseau it is language that gives rise to families and to social order and that makes the human community distinctive, for most Chinese thinkers since the time of Confucius it is filial piety that creates families, and by extension society. Since filiality is a defining feature of human society, it is significant that Ming and Qing writers were as fascinated by animals who exhibited filiality as their European counterparts were by talking beasts.[26]

In pondering the origins of the human community, Mencius contemplates Rousseau's problem. Here is Mencius' version of how human society originated:

> The Sage [Yao] felt concern for the people and ordered Xue to serve as minister of education and to teach them about the normative relations (*renlun*), so that between father and son there would be familiarity; between lord and liege, righteousness; between husband and wife, difference; between senior and junior, hierarchy; between friends, righteousness.[27]

Mencius is primarily concerned with the content of Xue's teachings, rather than the seemingly separate issue of how they were to be effected. But what exactly did Xue do to teach this primal human community about proper relations? At first glance, instituting the bonds of matrimony between husband and wife might simply involve Xue's presiding over a wedding ceremony, in which he pronounced two people husband and wife in a performative utterance that rooted the legitimacy of that union in Yao's own legitimacy. For the other relations, we assume Xue presided over a similar sort of declaration that could establish, say, the roles of lord and liege.

But what of father and son? No ceremony would serve to establish such a relation, since it cannot be arbitrary, nor can it be established *ex post facto*. Did Xue first preside over marriages and then just sit and wait for children to emerge whom he could declare to be legitimate issue? And what about brothers? The wait would have been even longer. Mencius' concern is with the Three Bonds and not the Five Relations, but even more than paternity, brotherhood must follow on marriage.

For that matter, how could Xue even join in matrimony men and women whose relationship he was necessarily unclear about? He might after all have been sanctioning the union of brothers with biological sisters, or of mothers with their sons, or any number of other unacceptable matches. If he had been in Xue's place, putting together a human society, the late Ming polemicist Li Zhi would have begun by marrying couples together: "The relationship between man and wife lies at the beginning of humanity. Only after man and wife can there be the relationship between father and son; only after father and son can there be the relationship between brothers; only after brothers can there be a relationship between senior and junior."[28] But Li Zhi ranks values within a society in which such relations are already well established. What about Xue, hoping to establish these relations *ex nihilo*? Whom would he have tied together thus, and how could he have ensured that they were not already related?

In other words, the beginnings of the family almost defy imagination. Unanswerable questions present themselves. First, how can that primal family have been born out of nothing? And yet it must somehow have arisen. Second, how can a world of separate families all practicing exogamy and incest avoidance have arisen, and (of necessity) simultaneously? (Otherwise, whom would the sons and daughters of the first legitimate union have married?) In those first generations, before siblings were established, how could any non-incestuous marriage have been entered into? And who were the parents to have decided on those first matches?

Perhaps that is why a mythological version of humanity's origins begins with incest as well; Fu Xi, the progenitor of civilization (and specifically the institution of marriage), begets all of humankind through a union with his sister Nü Wa. As Nü Wa and Fu Xi's experience makes clear, before the first marriage—their own, as it happens—there could have been no true brothers and sisters.[29] Fu Xi and Nü Wa happen to be born of the same parents, but they make themselves husband and wife. Or, rather, as Rousseau points out too, marriage and knowledge of incest are born at the same moment, and the first marriage—unlike all that follow—is one that might be (or must be) between brother and sister.

At least one eighteenth-century Chinese writer saw the human condition *sans* civilization as something quite like Rousseau's imagined prelinguistic world. In one of Ji Yun's anecdotes from *Yuewei caotang biji*, a fellow magistrate oversees a complicated case. A boy and girl, each around fifteen or sixteen, approach the magistrate to resolve a dispute. Ji Yun writes of how each insists the other is lying:

> The young boy said, "This is my fiancée who was brought up in our home. After my parents died, she now wants to leave me and marry someone else." The girl said, "We are really blood siblings. Now that our parents have died, he wants to take me as his wife."[30]

How could such confusion arise? Under normal circumstances, it cannot. These two young people, raised by vagrants who are now dead, are so entirely cut off from the community of other human beings that they are unsure even of their own surname. Nor have they any native place, so there are no neighbors or family members to consult. The two waifs are human beings stripped of everything that keeps us straight and exogamous—name, status, and place. Ultimately, it is impossible to determine whether relations between them even constitute incest.

The clerk recommends to the magistrate that the two be separated. With no way to determine their proper relationship, the clerk reasons, the danger of incest far overrides the injustice of a voided marriage contract. However, the clerk fails to point out that by being separated and sent forth, the two young people are also stripped of the only bond they possess. Without identifying them properly, the magistrate allows these two nameless souls to commit other acts of potential incest. Who can guarantee that their next liaisons will be any more exogamous? If one way an empire can collapse is when incest avoidance is disabled—as we have seen in the reunions between husband and wife, and the narrowly averted mis-reunions between other relations—exogamy is also at the heart of civilization's beginnings and survival.

And what does this have to do with the self-consumption of cannibalism? Rousseau's community seems in danger of contracting to a single hut incapable of expansion outward, to the union of brother and sister unable to understand any stranger, with procreation the result only of incest and not of marriage. Similarly, filial piety is about a tendency to self-consumption, sometimes explicitly so, a human community that has lost the wherewithal to expand outward. It is no coincidence that the filial relation is strongly and repeatedly associated with cannibalism. Why, as is recorded in fictional and nonfictional accounts of many genres, should daughters, daughters-in-law, and sons feed ill parents with their own flesh to cure them? Why does devotion to parents (and perhaps more frequently to parents-in-law) express itself as consumption of the body of the daughter or daughter-in-law?[31]

The three years of mourning for a parent is often explicitly compared to the three years of intense, life-sustaining care that parents must provide their infants. Confucius makes one of the central filial acts, the ritually correct mourning of one's parents, seem almost a simple act of reciprocation: "Only when a child is three years old does it leave its parents' arms. The three years' mourning is the universal observance in the world" (17.21). Of course, there is a difference between care of one's offspring and respect for one's parents: that parents should care for their offspring is seen as natural, whereas the disciplined reciprocation offered by their children is both the very essence of civilization and the aim of all education. However, if only parents are supported at the expense of children, the human community—though civilized—will come to an end. How, then, to have a human community that manages both to perpetuate itself and to remain civilized? In some sense, grandparents and grandchildren are involved in a competition for the attention of that middle generation, and sustaining this balance is at the heart of the problem of filial piety. Keith Knapp suggests that the contrast between the care that parents give to their children (*yang* 養) and the reverent care (*gongyang* 恭養) they offer to their own parents has been central to conceptions of filial piety since the end of the Warring States period.[32] Carlitz writes of the Han paragon Filial Daughter-in-Law Dou (Dou *xiaofu*), much venerated by the people of Yangzhou, whose mother-in-law committed suicide precisely to avoid competing for resources with younger generations.[33]

Song Maocheng's filial son has pared down one version of the problem by simply substituting his mother for his wife. "Lord Yao's Supreme Filial Piety Receives Great Glory," the sixth story in *Xihu erji* (Second collection of stories from West Lake, which dates from the late seventeenth century) begins with a short narrative about Cao Baoer, who dotes on his toddler son. One day, his wife accidentally drops the little boy, hurting his head. When her mother-in-law sees how terrified the young wife is of her husband's possible reaction, the older woman tells the younger woman: "Just say that I dropped him. He won't touch my old life."[34] Unfortunately, she has overestimated her son. When Cao Baoer sees his son hurt, he goes into a homicidal rage and grabs his wife, who tells him that it was his mother who hurt the boy. The next day, Cao Baoer lures his mother out to where he has hidden a knife. He reaches for the knife to kill her, and as he does so, he sees a big snake rearing up to strike. And then, orifices spouting blood, he begins to sink into the earth. The earth swallows him slowly, while his mother makes futile attempts to save him: "She hurried home and told her daughter-in-law to bring a shovel to dig him out. As they dug, he sank. When they dug one foot, he sank two feet, and there was nothing they could do but feed him. Their cries pierced the heavens, and after three days he died."[35]

The main story that follows in the same *huaben* tells of a filial son who goes to extreme lengths to bury his parents. The introductory narrative of Cao Baoer the failed matricide—whose crime is to choose his son above his mother—parodies that exemplum perfectly. Instead of burying his mother, Cao Baoer is buried alive while his mother looks on helplessly, frantically digging him out, all her efforts ultimately in vain. The role reversal begins with his crime, which is to invert the filial dictate to treat one's parents as nature would have one nurture one's children.

With limited resources, how should a division between parents and children be decided upon? If absolute priority is given to the children, then one finds oneself in a world like that of Cao Baoer's, with no filiality at all. Children would no longer bury their parents, and the only burial one could expect would be a self-burial where the earth sucks a person in of its own accord. But what if one does the opposite and assigns total priority to the parents' needs? In that case, children are consumed to prolong their grandparents' lives, and there is no family left.

In choosing his son's life over that of his mother, Cao Baoer does precisely the opposite of Guo Ju (known in some accounts as Guo Xiang). One of the virtuous models in *Twenty-Four Paragons of Filial Piety*, the impoverished Guo Ju prepares to kill his son. Because his mother dotes on her only grandson and shares with him their meager food supplies, Guo Ju and his wife hope that by killing the baby, they will save enough food that his mother can be sustained. Guo Ju does "Lord Yao's Supreme Filial Piety" one better; rather than going to any length to bury his mother, Guo Ju plans to bury his son alive to avoid having to bury his mother at all.

What can the husband and wife do if the grandmother continues to give her share of food to her beloved grandson? Their decision to murder the boy is made after Guo Ju argues to his wife that, although they can have another son, they can never have another mother. What is unsaid is that if they go on killing their sons to support the mother, they will have no sons—or for that matter any family at all. But their problems are solved magically: as Guo Ju digs his child's grave, he unearths a gold ingot, which not only relieves the family of financial worries but also miraculously mentions Guo Ju by name and praises him for his superlative filial piety (and also exculpates him from the moral taint of what is, after all, a highly questionable choice).

The scholar-official Fang Xiaoru (1357–1402), later famous for his principled, fatal resistance to the Yongle emperor, is outraged that anyone could regard Guo Ju as filial. Serving one's parents cannot be an end to itself, he argues: "If it is not according to propriety, then even if the parents are offered all three meats daily, it would still not be filial piety. That's not to mention someone who causes his parent to harm an innocent child through his parent's personal needs!"[36] Fang Xiaoru considers the problem from the perspective of Guo Ju's mother as a moral agent; even if he had saved his mother's life through infanticide, he would have implicated the grandmother in the murder of her own grandchild: "Guo Ju has sunk his own mother into unrighteousness, and there is no crime greater than that."[37] By so fully concentrating on his bond to his mother, Guo Ju loses sight of the grandmother's bond to her grandson and also her life as a moral human being. Even the ingot of gold, which to others seemingly confirms Guo Ju's righteousness, becomes in Fang Xiaoru's thinking merely a means of saving the little boy's life. Ultimately, though, Fang Xiaoru plays his trump card by asking: "To commit the great sin of being without issue, how can [Guo Ju] be filial?"

In other words, Confucius' declaration that the greatest of all unfilial acts is to leave no issue (*buxiao you san wuhou weida* 不孝有三無後爲大) is the only thing that allows a family both to continue and to practice filial piety. Otherwise, truly filial families would leave no heirs, turning everything over instead to their parents. We can read Guo Ju's story as a negotiation of this dictum. Guo Ju and his wife decide on their course of action after he points out that his mother is singular and irreplaceable, whereas a child is important only for being a child—therefore, any child of his will do. He and his wife have pushed *wuhou weida* to its logical conclusion: irreplaceable parents are important as individuals, but children only as members of a group, each son fully substitutable for another. Note that Fang Xiaoru's condemnation is still grounded on what Guo Ju's plan does, not to his child, but to his mother as a moral agent. Guo Ju's plan to murder one child, with the expectation of replacing him in the future, is fully compatible with Confucius' injunction to leave descendants.

—

In "In a Jiangdu Marketplace, a Filial Daughter-in-Law Sells Her Body to Be Butchered," the eleventh story of *Shi diantou* (The rocks nod their heads; 1635), this tension between generations is at the center. The story—written by the same Langxian who was probably responsible for many of the stories in *Xingshi hengyan*, the third of the *Sanyan*—begins by retelling another of the *Twenty-Four Paragons of Filial Piety*: the younger Mrs. Cui serves her elderly mother-in-law by breastfeeding her. As a result, the old woman is brought back from the brink of death and enjoys a hale and hearty old age. To the narrator, this is the very essence of filial piety: "This was the number one filial woman from ancient times on."[38]

In fact, her filiality—like that of Song Maocheng's filial son—consists solely of replacing one family member with a parent. In her case, she does for her mother-in-law what it is assumed mothers do for their children, so that the parent sucking at the daughter-in-law's breast quite literally supplants the grandchild. Like Guo Ju's mother, grandmother and grandchild vie for the same food. Substituting his mother for his wife, Song Maocheng's filial son leaves his wife and returns home with his mother in a topsy-turvy version of a marriage, except that the new match leaves no prospect of perpetuating the family. Transferring his filial obligations to Xu Jifang, You Ruilang castrates himself. In all these cases, substitution very explicitly stands in the way of the family's continuation, as if that in its heart is the filial impulse.

The daughter-in-law's breastmilk is a not uncommon medicine in narratives of filial piety, although seemingly not so common as soup made out of the child or daughter-in-law's flesh. A grandparent's consumption of breastmilk is in some sense no less a cannibalistic gesture than *gegu*, since here, too, the family literally consumes itself, as the old take what the young need to survive. Carlitz writes of other Ming women who fed their mothers-in-law not with breastmilk but with the flesh of the breasts themselves.[39] Such a sacrifice not only deprives the grandchildren who are already born, but starves those yet to come. (Caroline Walker Bynum writes of lactation offered up to a father or other senior adult male as a gesture of filial piety in both ancient and medieval European literature and art. Such cross-cultural examples suggest that this kind of substitution and self-consumption might be central to any concept of filial love.)[40]

If the three-year mourning period is equated to the three years of nursing, then the story of Mrs. Cui makes the competition between grandchildren and grandparents all the clearer, so that filial piety lies precisely in the substitution of the mother-in-law for the baby at the breast. Filial piety is at its height—and yet unsustainable, as Guo Ju's case shows—when parents fully usurp the grandchildren causing the family literally to erase itself, as the old woman drinks the milk meant for her descendants. And so the author conveys important information by stressing the family's ongoing fruitfulness: "Later the Cui family had all filial sons and daughters; for ten generations they had success in the examinations, and for three generations they served high at court."[41] Their fertility and long-standing hold on success demonstrate that the daughter-in-law has perfectly balanced the competing needs of old and young and properly marshaled the family resources. In supporting the old, she has earned karmic benefits for the young.

But such a woman might be less filial than the one who assigned even more priority to the older generation: "Now that filial daughter-in-law of the Cuis still retained her own body, so that she could breastfeed her mother-in-law. There's nothing too extraordinary about her actions. I will now tell of a daughter-in-law who sold her own body to a butcher for money to feed her mother-in-law."[42] We have seen a number of examples of the family shell game, not just centered around the filial relation. In "A Record of the Qi Sanlang Affair," for example, Zhou Lianggong writes of the two husbands' pooling their resources to try to buy back their two wives. Lacking enough money to redeem all four people at the same time, each takes turns being sold into bondage and then trading himself in for another. So in some sense this is the same plot: what to do when there are insufficient resources to support all the members of a family? Literature of this period abounds with families that dissolve when some members are forced to sell others: children either sell themselves or are sold to support parents or to finance a parent's burial; husbands sell their wives to raise enough money to survive. Elsewhere the anxiety of dividing up resources, among brothers, usually, is expressed as a fear of diminution, that the sum of what is divided is less than the whole was before. Narratives in which one family member is sold for another represent an apotheosis of the anxieties associated with family division. Like an incestuous family, these families have set themselves up in such a way that continuation is impossible. In consuming themselves, they allow for no perpetuation; this kind of economics is figured as cannibalism. One member eats another until there is no one left.

In "Liu xing" from *Liaozhai zhiyi*, Pu Songling tells of the stingy Mr. Liu, who is redeemed for a single good deed committed years earlier, when he allowed a husband and wife to stay together. In the eleventh year of the Chongzhen period (1640), during a time of famine, Mr. Liu encounters a married couple weeping by the side of the road. The couple explains to Mr. Liu, "We cannot both survive, so we are grieving."[43] They have been living on the leavings from sesame seeds pressed for their oil, and the husband attempts to sell his wife to the oil seller. The oil seller—who has already bought a number of women—will not pay them enough, and so the husband beseeches Mr. Liu:

> These days grain is as precious as pearls. I reckon that if I do not get 300 cash I won't have enough to escape from here. Of course we want to both survive. If I sell my wife and still cannot escape death, then why would I do it? I daren't give you a price; I only ask that you do something to accrue a good deed.[44]

Mr. Liu tries to work out a deal with the oil seller, so that each will pay half, but the oil seller refuses to pay more than 100 cash. Finally, Liu makes a present of the whole sum, sending the couple off with his best wishes that both survive. (Later on, as in the case of *Doupeng xianhua*'s "A Young Lordling," what looks like a gift turns out to be something closer to an investment; because of this single act of generosity, Liu's tightfistedness in later life is forgiven.)

All the husband and wife have to sell is themselves, but ownership even of their bodies is tenuous, since the cost of keeping them fed exceeds what they can earn by selling the bodies. Because the two depend on loans from the same oil seller to whom they plan to sell the wife, each day of survival drives them deeper into debt, and further away from clear ownership of even their own bodies. Even before the actual transaction, this family of two is being eroded into nothingness. Without Mr. Liu's intercession, the husband will have sold his wife, eaten the proceeds, and then starved on his own; the couple will have come close to literally eating themselves. To what end has the oil seller accumulated more than ten women? We suspect he has something worse in mind than simply selling them into prostitution; significantly, the story's description of the famine explains that people are resorting to cannibalism to keep themselves alive. Under these circumstances, cannibalism is much more than simply a figure for one kind of family economics or a gesture of devotion. Instead, it has turned into a universal condition.

After the story of the Cuis, "A Filial Daughter-in-Law Is Butchered" turns to its main narrative, which like "Liu xing," is set during a time of terrible instability. But neither of these stories is really concerned with the effect of political unrest on the social fabric. Instead, the setting of almost unimaginable deprivation gives Pu Songling and Langxian a chance to pose theoretical problems about how a family might prioritize its different members. (The fact that the narratives' conclusions do not introduce any new political order or any new relations forged by the characters reveals how unimportant the political setting actually is.)

The protagonist of "A Filial Daughter-in-Law Is Butchered," Zhou Di, is a merchant of limited means, stuck at home because of political turmoil. He plans to set out alone to collect some outstanding debts, but his elderly mother insists on a change of plan. Zhou Di and his wife are nearing forty and childless. As one variant of the grandmother who contests for space with a (potential) grandchild, Mrs. Zhou recognizes that if her daughter-in-law stays home to care for her, then there will be no chance of a grandchild. The elderly mother insists that husband and wife travel together, on the chance that they will be able to conceive a baby.

Taking the sum of money earmarked for the care and burial of the older Mrs. Zhou, the couple set out to earn more. Unfortunately, they encounter disaster after disaster. In Xiangyang, they are unable to collect any of the debts owed to them; when they ask their landlady what sorts of goods they might purchase, they are overheard—and before they know it, the ne'er-do-well son of the family has robbed them blind. Far away from home and penniless, they no longer have the means to return. When they are evicted from their lodgings, a merchant from their hometown happens to hear their familiar accent and takes them in to do his accounts.

They follow him to Yangzhou, where the merchant means to collect some debts. But this safe refuge does not last for long. The city is about to fall, and after handing the couple some money, their benefactor abandons them. Ms Zong's bound feet slow her down, and they find themselves trapped when the general in charge of the city, horrified by the flight of all the city's residents, closes the gates an instant before the couple can leave. Locked into the city, their former lodgings now sealed to them, they have no choice but to eat through their savings, even as the rest of the city starves along with them. People are driven to eat everything they can, bark from trees, horses, rats and sparrows they manage to catch, and even the corpses of those who have died before them of hunger. Finally, the rich begin paying people for their own flesh, and family members begin to sell each other to be eaten.

Eight months later, their money used up entirely, the husband bemoans their fate. His mother sent them out on two parallel projects of gain, he recalls regretfully: to earn profit on their capital and to beget a son. Instead, now they have nothing but their own bodies. The wife proposes that one of them sell himself or herself, so that the other might live to care for the older Mrs. Zhou. In a conversation whose psychological subtlety rivals the best of any in premodern fiction, each offers to make the sacrifice, but ultimately the husband breaks down, revealing himself to be the weaker one. As he weeps, she scolds:

> If you cry until tomorrow, and then until the day after, we still won't be able both to get home. . . . Now there are sellers of human flesh, and no matter what we're going to be able to get two strings of cash. Maybe you'll sell me and use the money for travel expenses and go home and take care of your mother; maybe I'll sell you and use the money for travel expenses and go home and take care of her.[45]

According to Zong Erniang's intractable economic logic, husband and wife are practical equivalents. This is the family shell game in another form; only by selling one can two of the three survive.

He lacks nerve. She will have to sell herself. She negotiates a price with the butcher, forcing him to go up to four strings of cash.

After bidding goodbye to her husband, Zong Erniang then returns to the butcher's where she asks for a bath to honor the body received from her own parents and cared for by her parents-in-law. In her final act, right before she is cut apart, she writes and reads aloud an epitaph for herself. Afterward, Mr. Zhou heads out to the marketplace, and when he sees his wife's dismembered body, he collapses in shock, claiming that he had not thought that she would really go through with her plan. He is handed the epitaph she wrote for herself, and upon reading it the passersby all marvel at her martyrdom.

The landlord forgives him the balance of the rent, and armed with the money from his wife's sale, he begins to trudge home. Exhausted and starved, he makes very slow progress, and one night, he collapses in a dilapidated temple to Qu Yuan. When he wakes in the middle of the night, he confesses his whole story to a stranger who identifies himself as a descendant of Qu Yuan and gives Mr. Zhou a horse that carries him home before dawn. His mother greets him by asking where her daughter-in-law is. Zhou weeps bitterly.

His mother then relates a strange, dream-like vision she had of her daughter-in-law the day before. She says:

> I saw her come in and greet me. She said: "Mother, I have returned. Your son has taken a concubine, neither tall nor short, neither coarse nor fine [thin nor fat], with ground-up bones and broken body, just the same woman as always. Your son now has a child, big and small, real and fake, with messy hair and an ashen face, no different from the young Master Zhou of yesteryear."[46]

Then, in a puff of wind, the vision disappears. After she relates it, the elder Mrs. Zhou beats her breast and bemoans the death of such a virtuous daughter-in-law.

At no point in the story is this vision explained, but here is what I make of it. The concubine is the butchered Zong Erniang, formerly his wife, now transformed into a pile of meat: "ground-up bones and broken body." In her new form, she is his concubine, because only through her body is Mr. Zhou himself able to be given new life, hence the child who looks exactly like Master Zhou himself, messy-haired and ashen-faced from his ordeal. The child born of her body is none other than her husband himself. Mrs. Zhou sends her son and daughter-in-law out together for a very specific reason: she is hoping for a grandchild to continue the family. Instead, the grandson who is given life through her daughter-in-law's body is her own son, and there is nothing left, literally, to engender a new generation. The internal substitutions I have been discussing throughout this chapter have reached an extreme in Mrs. Zhou's vision. The family might have been able to continue itself with some additions—whether that of a concubine for Zhou Di, or a baby born of the couple—but the substitutions that have taken place allow only for Zhou Di's survival.

At this point, neighbors rush in to ask about the clay horse on the steps of the house: how did it arrive here, and did Zhou Di steal it from a temple? Only when Zhou goes out to inspect the horse does he realize that it was of course magic, and that the stranger in the temple was the god himself. Zhou decides that the horse must be moved inside, so that he can provide it offerings, but no matter how many men try, the horse remains rooted to the ground.

One person in the crowd says, "This must be the divinity's desire to spread the reputation of this filial woman. That's why he doesn't want the earthenware horse to be moved into the house."[47] Zhou Di proposes a temporary hut to cover the horse that eventually he will replace with a pavilion to commemorate his wife's spirit. The next morning, the horse mysteriously disappears, but a poem commemorating Zong Erniang's outstanding filiality has appeared in its stead.

The story's ending is unusual; if all their troubles began with the elder Mrs. Zhou's wish for grandchildren, how can the story never take that up again? After he reads the poem commemorating his wife's filiality, the husband has statues built of the magical horse and of Qu Yuan, and then: "He dedicated himself totally to taking care of his mother and never married again."[48] Zong Erniang herself is turned into a goddess whose special purview is rewarding filial behavior and punishing disobedience. In fact, she "gave her [mother-in-law] years numbering 130. Zhou Di himself lived to be 110. Both mother and son died without illness. Right before they died, the five stars shone brightly; an auspicious cloud filled their house; and an unusual smell filled the city."[49]

This story concerns investments, both successful and failed. At the end, Zhou Di returns less a wife, but with four strings of cash realized from her sale, too little to buy a concubine or arrange for an adoption—but then those possibilities are never even mentioned. Zhou never tries to continue the family; instead of working to earn enough money to buy another woman, he chooses to commemorate his deceased wife, and the family comes to an end. Or rather, the family expends its positive karma in long life and miracles rather than descendants. Mother and son die at the same time, and only the timing of his own death allows the son to be remembered as a filial paragon. What if she had been the only one to enjoy such extraordinary longevity? What is the use of living to 130 in the absence of any family?

And what an odd paragon of filial piety the consumed Zong Erniang is. She sacrifices so that Zhou Di can return home to support his mother, but also, one presumes, so that he can find some way to continue their family. Her death does not buy that return. The god grants the Zhous a miracle—the magic horse that turns to flesh and then to earthenware, the poem that appears out of nowhere—but somehow that miracle takes the place of Zong Erniang's ostensible objective, the family's continuation. At the same time that it publicizes her sacrifice, the miracle also renders it meaningless. (In fact, if Qu Yuan had seen fit to provide the Zhous with even a modest windfall with which to buy a concubine, instead of an earthenware horse and a poem, the family's future would not be a problem at all.)

The story of the Zhou family's fate can be read as that of a failed investment. The money earmarked for the old woman's burial is instead invested in their travels, with the hope that the return will be a grandson. Instead of being miraculously increased through trade, as they all hope, that money is whittled away even more inexorably than if they had stayed home, turned first into twenty taels and then into just four, at the same time that three people—who embody the possibility of creating many more—are turned into two and then one, and then after Zhou Di's own eventual death, into none.

Partly, the fate of the Zhous represents a kind of punishment for certain economic practices; very early on in the story we are told that since they have no farmland the Zhous cannot stay put and earn. As the mother puts it, "We have just relied on trade. If we just stupidly stay here at home, we'll sit and eat our coffers empty. We can't do that for long."[50] Trade, we are meant to conclude, is barren; for these tradesmen, no earnings and no baby can be produced at home. But even more significantly, trade opens the Zhous to a kind of cannibalism, in which every day they sink a little more deeply into debt, according to the sort of self-consumptive economics practiced by the husband and wife whom Pu Songling's Mr. Liu saves. (Clearly, if the Zhous were farmers, they would be able somehow to create value and produce the family's next generation even by staying put.)

Instead, they are forced to rely on debt collection and on trade, both of which backfire to the point that the husband must trade the wife for food. In a grotesque parody of Confucian notions of commerce, according to which more and more is accumulated out of nothing, the family suffers a pattern of constant loss; their experience is the opposite of Xu Aji's, as each trade leaves them incrementally with a little less.

How does the long narrative in *Shi diantou* 11 (the story of Zong Erniang, that is) mirror the shorter one that introduces it? In the opening narrative, when the old woman feeds at the young woman's breasts, she takes the place of grandchildren who, as we need to be told, are plentiful nonetheless. In the longer narrative, however, the self-consuming nature of filial piety shows its destructive side. When the mother-in-law consumes the body of the daughter-in-law, the family loses any hope of continuing.

After Zong Erniang sells herself, she goes back to the couple's lodgings. She sets the proceeds down and says to her husband, "This is the money from your old lady's selling herself. You ought to come down to the marketplace to take a look. I've given you this money for travel expenses, so that you can go back and take care of your mother."[51] Curiously, when she refers to selling herself, she says, *laoniang mai erzi* 老娘賣兒子, which can just as easily be read as "your old lady's selling her son"—which her mother-in-law would certainly understand to mean not that there is a son but that Zong Erniang's selling herself eliminates that possibility. She stands in for her own, never-to-be-born son. Or rather, by feeding the grandmother, that grandson starves, before he ever comes into existence. As surely as Guo Ju, this family has chosen older generation over younger generation.

Or consider the contorted, almost incestuous nature of the elder Mrs. Zhou's dream, in which the young wife is transformed into a concubine of meat, and Mr. Zhou has become his own son. All the complex substitutions here are propelled by the conflict between caring for the parent and trying to give rise to a new generation. When the elder Mrs. Cui nurses at her daughter-in-law's breast, the old woman is practically transformed into the child of her own son and daughter-in-law. In Mrs. Zhou's vision, Zong Erniang is turned into another person, a concubine of minced flesh, whose sole purpose is to feed her mother-in-law and out of her flesh give life to a son—who is not her own, but her mother-in-law's. The son given life literally out of her flesh is her own husband.

Finally, the old woman—after ineffectual self-destructive gestures of her own, banging her head against the wall, beating her own chest—addresses the dead woman, "Oh, daughter-in-law, the one who harmed you was I!"[52] She apostrophizes *xifu de er* 媳婦的兒: does she mean her daughter-in-law, or the son of her daughter-in-law, whom she has harmed in causing him never to be born? Significantly, even without producing an heir, Zong Erniang manages to transform herself into an ancestor to be worshipped, except in this case, those doing the worshipping are not her descendants, but her husband and mother-in-law. Mother to her husband and even to her mother-in-law, she can mother no one else.

Room for the young—for the babies that according to nature ought to be suckling at their mother's breast—has been erased in the interests of filial piety. With Zong Erniang serving as wife, concubine, and mother to Mr. Zhou, having fed her mother-in-law until there is nothing left of her flesh, there simply is nothing with which to engender the child whose absence seems glaring at the story's conclusion. Let me return to this chapter's beginning: why the compulsion for a round-trip? Mr. Zhou's return journey leads to a family that doubles back, erasing itself entirely. The forces that spin outward, whose participants might be anyone—marriage, trade—have no power over a relationship at whose very heart is to sacrifice, to return, to reduce. Rousseau writes of a beginning in which "they become husband and wife without ceasing to be brother and sister." In the ending to the eleventh story of *Shi diantou*, everyone is a parent, and yet there are no children.

SIX

Jinpingmei and the Bounds of Community

This book began with some thoughts on the genre of the *chuanqi* drama; for the most part, the four chapters that followed concerned short narrative; the final three chapters focus on long novels. My discussion of short narrative focuses on relations between two parties—sometimes branching outward and sometimes subject to centripetal forces that push them inward—and how one might embed these relations in a broader society. In considering how novels address the problem of the human community, let me return momentarily to the *chuanqi* drama, the dominant literary genre of the age, to examine some of the ways in which the long novel contrasts so strongly with the *chuanqi*. The mechanics of exposition in *chuanqi* are so powerful as to admit no surprises: we are generally given a plot summary in the first act, from which the rest of the play does not diverge. At no moment in a *chuanqi* play are there open-ended actions.

Moreover, characters, even when depicted with tremendous psychological realism, always fall into different role types. From the moment they set foot onstage, we can tell from makeup and costuming whether characters are romantic heroes, villains, or clowns. Although these types might be challenged (as they are throughout the corpus) when girls pose as boys or servants pose as masters or characters muse self-reflexively on the nature of their roles, role types nonetheless render identity into incontrovertible matter of fact. Because of role types, even a conclusive change of status in a play—whether success in the examinations, marriage, or even death—does not have the effect of creating a new self, but instead exposes what was there all along. Personal and familial ties are shown to be foreordained; no matter how unlikely a union between the lead female (*dan*) and the lead male (*sheng*) might be at the beginning of a play, no matter how many obstacles stand between them, we know in advance that such a union will take place.

These generic forces inextricably tie together romance and drama. Role types, the power of the final reunion, the inevitability of outcome—all of these legitimate romantic choice, which in prose often permanently taints the union of lovers. Consider the pull over the centuries exerted by a text like Tang Xianzu's *Mudan ting*, and compare it to the many *caizi jiaren* (scholar and beauty) novels that first became popular at the end of the seventeenth century. These novels never escaped a certain louche reputation in the culture. In prose rewritings of *Mudan ting*, whether as novel or as short story, the two young lovers seem not to succumb to a death-transcending passion so much as actively choose a licentious path.

In drama, it is almost as if choice has been displaced to a lexical level. Since the Tang dynasty, poets have used dense and allusive verse to represent desire, a device that reached its apotheosis in the radical indeterminacy of Tang Xianzu and other members of the Linchuan School. There the reader is asked to decide between multiple readings, sometimes several times a line; quite often, there is no single correct reading, but rather multiple coexisting ones.

At any rate, whatever their other strengths, *chuanqi* dramas cannot accommodate a full range of political opinion, even within the confines of what a thoughtful late imperial person might have conceived. *Chuanqi* provide no way of examining state orthodoxy by standing outside it. Instead, the very form, with its buildup to a reunion where all return to their proper places, produces a certain way of thinking of how the polity hangs together. Class identities—so much more important in drama than in fiction—are reinforced; characters who begin as maids end as maids. Family ties are immutable; no matter how prodigal, family members return to the fold. These biases extend to the material world as well; when it comes to ownership of the signature objects so important in *chuanqi*, transfer through purchase is usually trumped by inheritance, as if birthright were more legitimate than any mercantile force. Of course, certain features of how that polity ought to hang together are still to be contested within each drama. But if the correlations at the heart of lyric poetry speak to some uncontestable tie that binds man, the cosmos, and political institutions, something of that persists in drama, especially *chuanqi*. The cosmic and the personal are set side by side, linked by the state. (Over the course of the nineteenth century, as *chuanqi* lost its cachet and became ever more associated with a kind of literati decadence, it was largely replaced at the imperial court by another dramatic genre—*pihuang*—more moralistic than *chuanqi*. What was permanently lost when *chuanqi* faded was not the culture's love of the theater, but instead the genre's promise of integrating the full dimensions of a person's internal life with the external trappings of imperial orthodoxy.)

In contrast, short narratives both in the vernacular and in the classical allow for considerable flexibility in these matters of political theory, but they are subject to other pressures. Miniatures inscribing the movements of a handful of characters on a tiny canvas, *huaben* always conclude with the reintegration of the few into the many: one character (or two or perhaps a nuclear family) somehow rejoins the greater polity, whose values and behavior as a whole are assumed to be orthodox. The powerful narrative abacus Idema describes holds far truer for these short narratives than for any other texts of the period. The impersonal calculations of reward and punishment are unnecessary in the overdetermined *chuanqi* plot, and long novels err in the other direction, toward the open-ended and underdetermined.

In Chapter 2, I discussed Idema's abacus with regard to forms of accounting, since it and narrative are closely related. However stories in Feng Menglong's three collections might differ from Ling Mengchu's or from later examples, or however much *huaben*'s concerns might diverge from those of the classical tale, short narratives as a whole share an interest in working out in detail the mathematics of Confucian ideology, particularly in cases where a fair accounting would seem on the surface impossible. How to punish the unwise Zhou Di in "A Filial Daughter-in-Law Is Butchered" without at the same time rendering his wife's sacrifice of her own life in vain? How to reward Jiang Xingge in "The Pearl-Sewn Shirt" for his kind-hearted treatment of his wife without rewarding her adultery?

At their best, the solutions are wonderfully clever. Nonetheless, even if sometimes mocked with humor (as by Li Yu), the math (or the map, or however we envision these enclosures and equations) is unchallenged. Ultimately, these narratives are politically conservative—punitive even—in the way that their characters are reintegrated into the community at large. Within the context of these imperatives, it is a foregone conclusion that individual desire will be subsumed by the demands of the community as a whole. Consider Zhou Lianggong's Qi Sanlang again: that the new polity works according to the old rules of reciprocity and recompense is never in doubt. No matter how devastated Qi Sanlang and Cheng San are by the loss of their wives, they have become subjects of new rulers and must submit themselves to a new order. Reunion with their wives, even the very survival of all of the characters, can take place only according to those greater political truths. So when Li Yu chooses to write about his experiences during the dynastic transition in a short narrative, the genre makes clear at the onset the author's primary political point; he has already accommodated himself to Manchu rule. No one can write a revolutionary or even seditious *huaben*. Yearning for the lost dynasty has to take another form.

So the long novel, sometimes with hundreds of characters followed over a period of years, finds itself in a uniquely privileged position. It can take on the project of conceiving of the human community in more inconclusive ways, with a much fuller range of possibility than other genres. Critics have noticed the ways in which these long narratives can stand slightly outside orthodoxy. Robert Hegel has suggested that novels are allowed to ask what in the late imperial period can only be regarded as subversive questions of mainstream histories: Are traditional heroes always good? Are Confucian socialization and sincere self-expression fundamentally at war with each other? Do histories really possess the capacity to tell the whole truth, or are they by their nature limited?[1]

Even though no novel, and perhaps no text written in the period, can fully abandon the orthodoxy of the Five Normative Relations, long novels can still imagine other ways in which people might be connected and might form a community. In part, this fluidity has to do with how the novel—as opposed to dramatic forms—copes with class differences. Instead of an immutable part of a person's identity, social position in novels is subject to constant negotiation and reinvention.

In novels, connections between people often cannot be classified according to normative categories and are instead open-ended. The mid-eighteenth-century novel *Hongloumeng* involves a boy who has special bonds with a number of girls. Which girl is Baoyu's destiny in *Hongloumeng*? His beloved maids Xiren and Qingwen claim a place in his feelings that the novel's mythology legitimates and exalts, even if actual marriage with them lies outside the realm of possibility. But that indeterminacy is not simply a matter of class; even when it comes to his two cousins Lin Daiyu and Xue Baochai, two hundred years of experts and admirers of the novels cannot agree on which his predestined lover is. Does Jia Baoyu—a reincarnated stone, as we know from his name 賈寶玉—find his karmic match in the metal of Xue Baochai (寶釵 "Precious Hairpin") or in the wood of Lin Daiyu (林黛玉, whose surname means "forest")? As their names reveal, both girls possess competing and seemingly equal claims on him that even death cannot resolve.

The characteristic open-endedness that makes novels difficult to wrap up also invites the possibility of sequels or continuations, the *xushu* that are so important in late imperial literature. Dozens of late Qing writers, for example, sought to solve once and for all the conundrum of Lin Daiyu's relationship with Jia Baoyu. And just as much as figuring out ambiguities in relationships, *xushu* often aim to pin down any political indeterminacy in the parent novel. The outlaws of the novel *Shuihuzhuan* seem genuinely transgressive of social norms, not only because they engage in rebellion against local officials but also because of their freedom as bachelors from familial constraints. In *Shuihu houzhuan*, Chen Chen moves the same characters to underpopulated Siam, where they marry local women and create a new society.

Not bound as tightly to the political form of the imperium, long novels—which did not dominate the mainstream imagination of the sixteenth and seventeenth centuries in the way that drama did—

continued to flourish even as the Qing dynasty itself collapsed slowly over the course of the nineteenth century. A number of nineteenth-century long novels treat intrusions by foreign powers and the faltering of the very concept of the old empire. Hanan has written of the complicated negotiations between the traditional novel and the West—in the form of translators, translations, and foreign influence in general. But even before the nineteenth century and entirely aside from its superficial formal resemblance to the European novel, the genre itself had a long history of accommodating and expressing a range of political ideas, some of them challenges to the very core of late imperial orthodoxy. It is impossible to imagine a *huaben* or a *chuanqi* that interrogated imperial power in such a way. Beyond other factors in the decline of the *chuanqi*, the collapse of Jiangnan culture in the wake of the Taiping Rebellion, the prolonged economic depression of the nineteenth century that made private troupes of actors simply too expensive,[2] surely it was *chuanqi*'s fundamental inseparability from the imperial model that was its true death knell.

This chapter and the next two concern precisely the novel's ability to distance itself and reflect on the imperial model. I treat three novels, each with an unusual take on what comprises the human community. Even if the novels posit theories that take into account everyone, my readings themselves are far from comprehensive. These chapters have a relatively narrow focus: how these three novels describe the world as a network of relations, some rooted in kinship, others in voluntary associations.

—

By the end of the *Jinpingmei* (written sometime toward the end of the sixteenth century and of still undetermined authorship; translated by David Roy as *The Plum in the Golden Vase*), the cast of characters is sadly diminished. *Jinpingmei*, not only the tradition's most important sexually explicit novel, but also revolutionary in its careful treatment of family and society, features hundreds of characters, but as the novel draws to a close, this number is pruned dramatically. Most readers know the novel as the story of the prosperous merchant Ximen Qing and his feuding gaggle of wives. But Ximen Qing himself dies with more than one-fifth of the novel to go, and one by one the primary female characters (each of whom contributes one character in her name to the novel's title) dies—first his favorite, the sixth wife, Li Ping'er; then his fifth wife, Pan Jinlian; and finally, her maid and partner in crime, Pang Chunmei.

Still, as each death takes place, nothing fundamental to the universe they inhabit changes. And in fact, as many critics and readers have noted, other characters step into their places. After her marriage to General Zhou, the erstwhile maidservant Chunmei takes on characteristics of both Li Ping'er and Pan Jinlian, and Chen Jingji (Ximen Qing's son-in-law) comes to serve as a poor man's Ximen Qing. As Chunmei earlier says to her mistress, when she is busily arranging an assignation with their shared lover, Chen Jingji, "You and I are really the same person."[3]

In other words, Li Ping'er, Ximen Qing, and Pan Jinlian experience a sort of literary reincarnation, not entirely inappropriate in a novel infused so thoroughly with Buddhist thought. The names change, but the actions—a combination of sexual and political corruption—stay the same. Chunmei's marriage to the conspicuously loyal and righteous General Zhou might seem to allow her a fresh start, but instead she returns to the old web of sexual deceit, eventually dying of her own excesses.

—

With *Jinpingmei*, unlike most of the other texts I draw on, we simply cannot sustain the illusion of a single definitive version, based on the earliest printed version. The novel was initially circulated in manuscript among a circle of elite readers who passed chapters among themselves; first mentioned in the 1590s, the novel's earliest complete manuscript dates to 1606. That complicated textual history means that the novel now exists in two main recensions, neither definitive, but each clearly marked by the same distinctive hand. (Some scholars suggest that there might well have been other versions, now lost.)

In late imperial times, the shorter, illustrated version (*xiuxiang*) circulated much more widely, and Zhang Zhupo (1670–98) based his own version of the novel (*diyi qishu* 第一奇書, or "most marvelous book") on it. To take advantage of Zhang's commentary, by far the most important critical work on the text from late imperial times, this chapter is based on his version, which differs in important ways from the *cihua* recension. Because most modern scholars use the *cihua*, I have drawn on their work only where the *cihua* and the *xiuxiang* versions are the same, or where their conclusions apply to both recensions.

Readers have long noticed that *Jinpingmei* is constructed out of repetitions, or patterns of figural recurrence. Separated by three hundred years, Zhang Zhupo and Andrew Plaks point out the parallels between Pan Jinlian's and Li Ping'er's entrances into the Ximen household; both young women are widows who have managed to divest themselves of inconvenient husbands.[4] Of course, these patterns and repetitions also form part of the novel's theme, demonstrating in the case of Pan Jinlian and Li Ping'er, for example, that Ximen Qing's desires can never be slaked and are simply to be whetted again and again, *ad infinitum*. Elsewhere, the repetition of character types suggests questions about the nature of society and the nature of individuality: would the Ximen household of Qinghe be just as debauched in the absence of a Pan Jinlian? Of a Ximen Qing? How much does each of these characters count? The long novel, built out of recurrences, is a medium for posing questions about the nature of the human community and what it is beyond the specific individuals that constitute it at any given moment.

Perhaps figural recurrence suggests that we ought to read the characters not as unique individuals but as types. If characters are at once different from one another and composed of the same elements, the events of the novel might be taking place elsewhere, with only slight variation, whether in Xuzhou or in the Eastern Capital or in any of a thousand other locales. In effect, figural recurrence would suggest a kind of universality to the events and people depicted in the novel.

On the other hand, reading the characters as types also invites an allegorical reading. Rather than standing in for a corrupt patriarch who might be living anywhere, Ximen Qing might represent (as readers have been suggesting since the seventeenth century) the Wanli emperor, guilty of causing turmoil at court for favoring a concubine over his legitimate wife. Or perhaps Ximen Qing stands in for the human consciousness, led astray by the senses, each one embodied by one of the wives. When we choose among readings, we are essentially deciding the extent to which Ximen Qing is unique, and if not how many of him there might be.

—

How does one end a novel if one character's death leads only to another's stepping into her tiny shoes? In the penultimate chapter, Chunmei's husband General Zhou embarks on a campaign to beat the invading Jurchen army back. In his farewell to his family, he uses the very words inscribed on his real-life contemporary Yue Fei's back. Yue Fei's mother is said to have tattooed *jinzhong baoguo* 盡忠報國 on him before sending the Southern Song patriot into doomed battle with the same Jurchens General Zhou goes forth to fight. General Zhou uses these words in his valediction:

> Those of you at home, be pure in heart and without desire. Take good care of the child, and do not worry on my behalf. Since I have received this commission from the court, I will exert all loyalty in service of the state (*jinzhong baoguo*). Whether I live or die, flourish or wither, that is up to heaven.[5]

Not only does he cite Yue Fei, but General Zhou also restages the archetypal Confucian moment, when the demands of the greater good are set against those of the family.

Of course, this is not quite the Sage-King Yu walking past his home three times on his way to save the people from floods. Well-connected and impeccably loyal to the Song state though he might be, General Zhou has utterly failed to manage his home life. Moreover, nowhere in the preceding ninety-nine chapters has anyone actually behaved according to the ideals of filiality and loyalty to the state. As a result, the reader hardly knows how to deal with these worthy sentiments. Perhaps we are to pity General Zhou's blindness about the corruption in his own family, even as he demonstrates loyalty to the state. Perhaps this is a joke, meant to elicit a bitter smile. Orthodoxy—in the cultural hero Yue Fei's *cri de guerre*, even—cannot escape being thoroughly tinged by the ironic.

By the novel's end, one longs for a world outside this sordid one, in which people behave according to normative demands, where *jinzhong baoguo* might mean simply that. We seek, in other words, borders and limits to the world we have been shown—to know how the world of the novel relates to the world outside the novel. How are we to situate the events we have just experienced? Is the whole world like the disgustingly muddled one of the novel, or do there remain places where wives sleep only with their husbands, where children know who their fathers are, where in short people live according to their normative roles?

Practically every member of the Ximen household is guilty in some way of *luanlun*, the muddling of proper relations that is the Confucian form of incest. Although some characters engage in this *luanlun* out of depravity, others like the well-intentioned General Zhou find themselves in situations beyond their control. The reader knows that these problems cannot be limited to the immediate circle of characters in Qinghe since Ximen Qing has ties to a centrally placed patron, Cai Jing, a historical figure in the Huizong emperor's court. When Ximen Qing visits the capital, we realize the extent to which it, too, is subject to the most extreme corruption. In other words, what we observe must be much more than an extended family in crisis.

But even the ramifications of a single dysfunctional family could be extremely far-reaching, as the opening of *The Great Learning (Daxue)* makes evident:

> Through the investigation of things, one's knowledge is extended; once one's knowledge is extended, one's will can be stabilized; once one's will has been stabilized, one's mind can be rectified; once one's mind has been rectified, one's self can be cultivated; once one's self has been cultivated, one's family can be ordered; once one's family has been ordered, the state can be properly ruled; once the state is properly ruled, the entire world can be kept in harmony. (1.5)

Every literate person in late imperial China knew by heart this passage, one of the most famous in the Four Books, while its argument, that subjectivity, the family, and the state are all linked together in a single web, even more thoroughly pervaded the culture. One might say that General Zhou's farewell to his family echoes the *Daxue*'s assertions. Still, even if we all know that the family and the state are bound together, the precise mechanics of these bonds are left unspoken. It is as if the whole of the novel poses a question of the *Daxue*: if we are all bound together, does not a single misdeed pollute the whole?

—

Critics for the last four hundred years have marveled at the skill and intricacy with which *Jinpingmei*, beginning with just a few characters from the world of *Shuihuzhuan*, first draws in their families and then follows those characters, drawing in their families, and their acquaintances, and so on—building to a cast of hundreds of characters, a simulacrum of a society in its entirety that includes all echelons of society and walks of life. But partly because of the way the novel is constructed, there are no strangers in this world. Even as the world of the novel expands, we can never be introduced to true strangers, only to an ever more complicated web of connections that grows denser and more corrupt with each passing chapter. There are, it seems, no new people with whom to forge innocent ties, only old ones with ties that seem to become ever more involuted and incestuous. In a world such as this, once relations between people have become disordered, it is hard to imagine how any sexual union might perfectly avoid the taint of incest.

For example, Lin Taitai (Madame Lin) makes her first appearance in the novel only in Chapter 69, a few chapters after the death of Li Ping'er. A go-between whets her curiosity, and ostensibly seeking guidance for her own son, she makes Ximen Qing's acquaintance. They begin an entirely loveless affair, and Ximen Qing takes as a godson her son, Wang Sanguan. As Plaks points out, the circle of incest is completed when Wang Sanguan himself has sex with the courtesan Li Guijie, who much earlier was deflowered by Ximen Qing.[6] Guijie in turn has earlier been adopted by Ximen Qing's senior wife, Wu Yueniang. It goes without saying that the Five Normative Relations are grossly inadequate to describe how any two of these people are related. Ximen Qing, for example, is simultaneously father, father-in-law, and husband to Li Guijie.[7]

The fact that characters stand in multiple relations to one another has far-reaching implications. Zhang Zhupo points out that this particular net of relations is even more complicated than it first appears: Lin Taitai also happens to be the widow of the imperial commissioner to whom Pan Jinlian had been sold as a little girl (this relation, never explicitly explained, is left for the careful reader to uncover on his own). Consequently, in his *dufa* ("How to Read the *Jinpingmei*"), Zhang Zhupo suggests that it is Lin Taitai herself and the household she led that are responsible for having made Pan Jinlian into a monster.[8] Decades later, Pan Jinlian is one of the prime sources of discord in the Ximen household. Not only does she sow the seeds of conflict among the various wives, but she also encourages her husband in continued promiscuity outside the home. She would much prefer for her husband to engage in meaningless, short-term liaisons than to have him express favor to any of the other wives. (A good wife, of whom we have no examples in the novel, would have fostered sisterhood and harmony among the other wives.)

Chaos in normative relations means that karmic causality becomes impossible to establish. Lin Taitai comes to have sex with Ximen Qing partly because his wife Pan Jinlian encourages his debaucheries. But Pan Jinlian is a jealous shrew lacking any sense of morals partly because she spent her childhood in Lin Taitai's dissolute establishment. Each degenerate relation has contributed to the other. Do Lin Taitai's depravities cause Pan Jinlian's? Or do Pan Jinlian's cause Lin Taitai's? We will never know, but purging this moral cesspool of its sources of corruption will obviously require more than the death of any single individual. How are we to disentangle these complex relations, so that they can be understood in normative terms? How can we position this world according to Confucian orthodoxy? Perhaps ultimately we can only situate the novel's world by understanding that it is nothing more or less than our own—and that both in the novel and outside it purely normative relations simply cannot exist.

Hanan has argued that one text with a clear influence on *Jinpingmei* is the vernacular short story, "The Lovers' Rendezvous" (the fourteenth story from *Qingping shantang huaben*, also known as *Sixty Stories*, which dates from around 1550),[9] a representative of the subgenre he refers to as "folly and consequences." According to Hanan, *Jinpingmei*'s opening is drawn directly from the earlier text. But folly and consequences work themselves out very differently in a *huaben*—

with its handful of characters—than in a novel of a hundred chapters, whose characters total a fair percentage of the population of a good-sized town. Revenge plots in short stories almost always highlight the interconnectedness and hermetic nature of society, culminating with the evildoer's eventually finding himself face to face with some relation or connection of the party he has wronged. The moral implicitly hangs on the finitude of the world, which makes it impossible to escape the consequences of one's crimes. With so many characters and so much plot, *Jinpingmei* cannot help but make a very different argument.

Although some characters are tied together by sex, others are bound just as firmly by enmity. Pan Jinlian's brother-in-law Wu Song waits eighty-two chapters to exact his revenge on her for the murder by poison of his brother Wu Da. Once Wu Song kills his sister-in-law, he can leave. No ties keep him; so after he viciously disembowels her, Wu Song flees to join the bandits of *Shuihuzhuan*. But the relationship between Wu Song and Pan Jinlian is practically anomalous in the novel. The constancy with which Wu Song hates Pan Jinlian is in some ways the closest thing the novel has to an orthodox marriage, writ in hatred rather than in devotion.

Wu Song can exact such pure vengeance precisely because his only relation to Pan Jinlian is as wronged brother-in-law, for enmity is practically another of the *wulun*—or at least a corollary of *wulun* thinking—in that it also implies a world in which a person has only a single relation to another. Pan Jinlian and Wu Song's relationship possesses this purity only because of his righteousness. Before killing Wu Da, Pan Jinlian does all she can to seduce her brother-in-law. And even in this case, as Xiaofei Tian points out, Wu Song's killing of Pan Jinlian actually involves another tie, too; when he leaves for the bandit hideout of Liangshan, he abandons his niece, Wu Da's daughter from a previous marriage, Ying'er.[10] Her fate reminds the reader that even in the relation between Pan Jinlian and Wu Song something is still left over at the end.

In no other case in the novel is vengeance so clean. Consider, as a contrast, the enmity between Ximen Qing's son-in-law Chen Jingji and the gangster Zhang Sheng. By the time of Chen Jingji's death at Zhang Sheng's hands in the penultimate chapter, a complicated karmic web drawing in scores of other characters has been woven around these two. Chapter 99 both resolves their enmity and begins to weave the individual lives we have observed in Qinghe together with what is transpiring in the empire at large.

Much earlier, when Chen Jingji is kicked out of the Ximen household for his incestuous relationship with Pan Jinlian, he becomes a monk and is beaten up by a local tough named Liu the Second. Years later, after his fortunes improve, Chen Jingji lives in General Zhou's household, while sleeping with his wife Chunmei and at the same time conducting a passionate affair with Han Aijie, daughter of the prostitute Wang Liu'er and Han Daoguo. Because Chunmei claims him as her cousin, General Zhou has helped Chen Jingji find a wife of his own and has also set up a business for him. Conveniently enough, he can check the books and visit his lover Han Aijie at the same time.

During one daytime assignation, the gangster Liu the Second comes to intimidate and collect on a debt from one of Wang Liu'er's customers (she is still entertaining guests, although she lives with her husband in a perfectly harmonious relationship). Chen Jingji and Liu the Second narrowly miss running into each other, but Chen Jingji seethes with anger, recollecting the beating he suffered years ago at Liu the Second's hands. He vows vengeance against both local toughs, Liu the Second and Zhang Sheng (Liu's brother-in-law and colleague).

Then war breaks out, and General Zhou leaves his affairs to be managed by Li An and Zhang Sheng. While at General Zhou's establishment, Zhang Sheng overhears Chunmei and Chen Jingji's illicit lovemaking. The two lovers chat, and Chen Jingji tells Chunmei how much he hates Zhang Sheng. Chen Jingji also tells Chunmei that Sun Xue'e—formerly Ximen Qing's fourth wife and Chunmei's longtime nemesis—has become Zhang Sheng's kept woman. Chunmei is furious because earlier she had been responsible for selling Xue'e into prostitution, and she is disgusted to hear that her enemy has found a safe haven.

As he listens, Zhang Sheng realizes that to survive, he will have to kill Chen Jingji before he himself is killed. So Zhang Sheng storms in with a knife. (In the moments it takes him to arm himself,

Chunmei has left to go attend to her baby.) After Zhang Sheng kills Chen Jingji, he sets out to kill Chunmei too but is quickly apprehended. Upon General Zhou's return, he has Zhang Sheng killed for his crime. Then General Zhou orders the capture and execution of Liu the Second. Zhang Sheng's lover Xue'e so despairs at Liu's capture that she kills herself.

If at this point the reader is confused, who can blame him? So many plot threads are integrated into this climactic moment that it can hardly be summarized. Even a cursory summary, though, reveals how different this sort of vengeance plot is from Wu Song's. Most importantly, I think we are right to wonder whether any resolution has been achieved by the deaths one after another of Chen Jingji, Zhang Sheng, Liu the Second, and Xue'e. Pan Jinlian's death at least provides a certain narrative satisfaction. Finally she receives her just reward, at the hands of someone whom she has grossly wronged and who himself is more or less an innocent. All her debts to Wu Song are discharged (although his—with regard to his niece—are ongoing).

But whose folly is being punished in this busy penultimate chapter? Whose vengeance is even being exacted? No chain of events leads inexorably to this conclusion. Since Chunmei hates Xue'e fully as much as Chen Jingji hates Zhang Sheng, it is impossible to determine which of the lovers sets things into motion. Finally, none of these deaths changes anything, much less effects any sort of moral improvement. In life, Zhang Sheng and Liu the Second went about demanding protection money from prostitutes and singing girls; the instant they are dead, we presume, someone else will occupy this economic niche. To somebody like the prostitute Wang Liu'er, Han Aijie's mother, their deaths alter absolutely nothing.

Another way to approach this question is to wonder why Chunmei fortuitously leaves the room and thus escapes death until the next chapter, when she dies in an entirely unrelated incident. If she *had* died in this episode, then all the main parties would have been eliminated together; instead, she survives for one more sexual escapade. Her lover killed, Chunmei's behavior continues in precisely the same vein. Folly is unquestionably punished, but not everyone's folly, and the roots of further misdoing are not eliminated. This open-ended model of punishment is the rule in the novel; Wu Song's, the exception. As the novel ends, various plots do come to a close, and Chen Jingji's violent death marks one of the most important of these resolutions. But this bloody act of vengeance seems only to touch the surface of the kind of corruption present. Chen Jingji, Liu the Second, and Zhang Sheng are obviously the main actors in a subplot that draws in scores of others, but whether they are important as individuals remains indeterminate.

Critics since the seventeenth century have been interested in a paradox. On one hand, among traditional Chinese works of fiction, only *Hongloumeng* rivals *Jinpingmei* in the care with which an imagined world has been described. Details of everyday life abound: foods eaten, goods bought, clothing worn. On the other hand, the novel obviously depicts an elaborately constructed world, whose details resonate with figural significance (we might consider, for example, the way in which hair and hairnets are treated, as they pass from one set of hands to another). We emerge with a picture of a family that is unrivaled among sixteenth-century sources in its detail and its seeming verisimilitude; nowhere else do we get such a precise sense of how secondary wives might have jockeyed for status with one another, and how they saw themselves next to the primary wife and to maidservants. Nonetheless, the extent to which we can regard these characters as individuals is never clear. Perhaps their significance is simply as exemplars or as part of an elaborate pattern whose algorithm lies slightly beyond reach.

The problems that these complicated acts of revenge bring into focus—who these actors are, whether redress is possible—are repeated when it comes to the fall of the dynasty. Whereas the action earlier has been mostly limited to the town of Qinghe, in this final chapter of the novel, the perspective of the novel changes, encompassing events that shake the empire itself. Before the last two chapters of the novel, imperial politics has been treated solely from the perspective of our characters based in Qinghe. Even though Ximen Qing journeys to the imperial court and is the direct beneficiary of its corruption, the novel shares his very limited, self-interested perspective. The implicit joke is that the point of view of a semi-literate provincial merchant—a tunnel vision focused narrowly on personal gain—might serve him quite well in dealing with court politics. We learn very little about the imperial tutor, who is Ximen Qing's benefactor, and almost nothing about the workings of the court. In the last two chapters, however, suddenly the doings of Emperor Huizong and his son come into sharp focus.

In the course of this shift in perspective, it is as if we have returned to a world like that of a *chuanqi* drama, where we are presented with a history organized around the concerns of the state and then shown how a single family fits within it:

> Unexpectedly, the Jurchen troops seized the Eastern Capital. Both the senior emperor [Huizong] and the Jingkang emperor were captured and taken to the north. The central plains were left without a master, and everything was in a state of chaos. Armed troops were everywhere, and the populace fled. The multitudes wept out of distress; the commoners suffered from these vicissitudes of fortune. The armored troops had already made their way into the territory of Shandong, and among the people, husbands and wives were separated from each other; ghosts cried, and spirits howled; and even fathers and sons could not keep track of each other.[11]

This version of dynastic collapse—whose essence is the dissolution of the family, as wives, husbands, fathers, and sons are separated from each other—is familiar to us. It comes right out of the concerns I discuss in Chapter 3, in which any restoration of imperial order must necessarily also involve the reassembling of these families.

But these concerns are actually quite alien to the first ninety-nine chapters of *Jinpingmei* since this version of imperial fall demands a particular understanding of families' relationship to one another and to a greater collective. The passage above is followed immediately by Han Aijie's quest to find her parents, a trope that as we have seen again and again highlights precisely this tension, as when Huang Xiangjian's rescue of his parents in a time of dynastic collapse forces us to juxtapose and compare political and familial ties. In short, the ending forces the reader first to confront a set of questions posed by multiple texts of the period and also to resolve the ambiguity between archetype and individual that has been part of this novel from its beginning. How are we to localize the corruption in Qinghe? Is it singular or emblematic of a more widespread problem?

—

In the final chapter of the novel, Ximen Qing's widow, Wu Yueniang, accompanied by her son and the few other remaining members of the Ximen household, flees the approach of the Jurchen troops. The party is stopped on the road by a monk, who mysteriously knows her name and shouts at her: "Mistress Wu! Where are you going? Give me back my disciple!"[12] The monk Pujing wants Ximen Qing's sole surviving son, Xiaoge, to join religious orders, a request Wu Yueniang naturally refuses, but the family still stays the night in Pujing's temple, the Yongfu si. While the others sleep, the maidservant Xiaoyu peeks in on the monk and witnesses something amazing. One by one, the spirits of the deceased characters appear before the monk, identify themselves, and then announce their next reincarnation. One of these is Ximen Qing, who explains his rebirth to a family named Shen in Dongjing, the Eastern Capital (Kaifeng).

Xiaoyu rushes to tell her mistress what she has seen, but she fails to wake Wu Yueniang, who is dreaming of what will happen after they leave the temple. Wu Yueniang had been planning to seek refuge with Yun Lishou, an acquaintance to whose daughter Xiaoge is betrothed. In the dream, Yun Lishou proposes marriage to Wu Yueniang herself; he claims that the two matches will be completed simultaneously, but of course what he has in mind offends all norms. Xiaoge's mother would in one moment be transformed into his mother-in-law, and his prospective bride into a sister. (In some ways, this double marriage is almost the mirror opposite of Fu Xi's marriage with his sister Nü Wa, which in a single speech act turns what is transgressive into what is normative; here, a double speech act would turn a few conventional relations into a nightmare of incest.)

Still dreaming, Wu Yueniang resists, and Yun Lishou kills her brother, her faithful servant Daian, and then finally her son. At this, she wakes with a start and goes to the monk, who confirms that her dream would become reality if she were to continue on the road to Yun Lishou. Pujing explains why this fate has befallen the sole heir of the Ximen house: Xiaoge, born at the exact moment of his father's death, is actually his reincarnation. To prove Pujing's point, with one touch of his staff, the sleeping Xiaoge metamorphoses into

Ximen Qing and then back again. In a novel filled with incestuous acts, this must be the capstone moment, and perhaps the most disturbing. After fifteen years of chaste widowhood, Wu Yueniang, who throughout the novel has done her best to steer clear of untoward behavior, is caught up anyway in the web of *luanlun*, first in her dream and now in this terrifying vision. Her husband and her son are one.

Zhang Zhupo suggests a similar confusion in the case of the first Ximen son, the sickly Guan'ge, born of Li Ping'er and later the victim of Pan Jinlian's machinations. That boy, Zhang Zhupo writes, is a reincarnation of Li Ping'er's first husband, Hua Zixu,[13] so that Li Ping'er too somehow ends up as mother to her husband.

Within the space of a few moments, Ximen Qing's karmic destiny has been assigned to two different locations: first, the spirit who joins the Shen family as a baby boy, and second, the essence of his own living son. How can Ximen Qing be both? Zhang Zhupo says nothing of this contradiction, perhaps because it is ultimately unimportant: either way, it is clear Ximen Qing's soul remains just as enmeshed and entrapped. (It is freed only later when Xiaoge—now given the Buddhist clerical name of Mingwu—evaporates in a puff of smoke.)

Similarly, whichever path the well-meaning Wu Yueniang chooses, whether she takes her son to be married, or she accepts the monk's identification of him as her deceased husband, she is ensnared in *luanlun*. Go one way, and she is forced to marry her son's father-in-law. Go the other, and she has taken her husband as son. In this world, neither path truly takes her out of Qinghe's moral cesspool since neither way allows her to avoid incest.

Zhang Zhupo reads the novel's geographical terrain symbolically. Pujing detains the family at a crossroads that Zhang Zhupo reads as a choice "between filiality and misconduct."[14] But neither road, just like neither possible destination for Ximen Qing's soul, really promises moral reform. Right before the disappearance of Pujing and Xiaoge (now the new monk Mingwu), the older monk says to Wu Yueniang: "You all need not continue further on the road. Before long, the Jurchen troops will retreat; the north and the south will split up; and the central plains will once again have an emperor. In ten days or so, the troops will leave. Things will calm down. You all can go back and live out your days."[15] From Wu Yueniang's perspective, the monk's pronouncements about the future mean that she is trapped in Qinghe. For her and her family, there is no leaving.

In the previous chapter, I discuss an important problem as it recurs in both the Chinese and the European traditions: the birth of civilization—whether the focus is on language (as Rousseau's was) or family structure (as Mencius' was)—forces us to speculate on how social ties could be established *ex nihilo*. However, almost always in the Chinese tradition, it is not the moment of origin that invites these questions, but dynastic collapse that reveals the nature of social ties and whether they are arbitrary or fixed. In *Jinpingmei*, the Jurchen invasion serves this function. As the various characters flee, our narrator tells us, family ties collapse—*futao qisan* 夫逃妻散, *fuzi bugu* 父子不顧—husbands and wives are separated; fathers and sons can no longer care for each other. But in this novel, those familial ties were not strong in the first place and are perhaps invulnerable to further attenuation.

After a hundred chapters that are almost a catalogue of *luanlun*, the real trick is how we are to emerge from that to forge a society wherein people stand only in a singular relation to one another. But such relations seem not to exist. How is one to reform the *wulun* in a world without strangers? As one progresses through the novel, even as the mind reels at the number of characters, it becomes increasingly clear that strangers do not exist: even when people do not turn out to be related in increasingly baroque ways to members of the Ximen family, figural recurrence suggests familiarity.

In the last chapter, what remains of Chen Jingji's household dissolves after his death. His wife returns to her parents, and his lover Han Aijie is forced out of seclusion and pathetically, on bound feet, goes off in search of her parents, planning to support herself by singing. At this point, dispossessed of everything familiar, one would think her surrounded by strangers. And yet when she finds herself in an inn, she runs into her long-lost uncle, Han the Second. A singing girl, an inn, a dynastic crisis—all the elements are here for a reunion that takes place through the narrowly averted incestuous encounter. A world in which families have dissolved is one in which anyone might be a family member, and even the most well-meaning might commit a horrible act of *luanlun*.

Zhang Zhupo would have us believe that the society depicted by the novel simply self-destructs and that what remains is the foundation for a new, purged, and cleansed society. Accordingly, he makes much of the survival of two characters in particular, Li An and Han Aijie. "If there were no Li An, the sole example of a filial son," he asks, "would this not be tantamount to the extinction of men of conscience?"[16] The manservant Li An's survival comes about after Chunmei's attempted seduction. After Li An reports his mistress's suspicious behavior to his mother, she persuades him to return to their ancestral home. Zhang Zhupo's commentary sighs in admiration at Li An and his mother's exemplary behavior, setting the two up as paragons, but Zhang Zhupo's admiration seems incommensurate with Li An's actions, especially since, as we have seen, filiality is usually measured by the degree to which personal self-interest is violated. In contrast, all Li An and his mother have done is ensure his survival, by extricating him from a potentially disastrous situation. Only in this particular novel's context can these actions be read as exemplary and not simply as expedient.

Or take the case of Han Aijie, Zhang Zhupo's symbol of chastity. After Chen Jingji's death, Han Aijie lives the sequestered life of the loyal widow (later becoming a Buddhist nun). In another novel, the same character might be the furthest thing from a model of chastity, the very picture of depravity: the widowed daughter of a prostitute who herself has taken on a lover. When she encounters Chen Jingji's family at his grave, Han Aijie introduces herself to them, abandoning her parents and joining his family. The whole scene smacks of parody. Han Aijie's actions are an inversion of the highest form of chastity, the fiancée whose betrothed dies before the marriage but who joins her intended's household regardless, becoming a widow without ever having been a wife. But in Han Aijie's case, never having been married to him, she cannot be chaste for Chen Jingji either.

Zhang Zhupo's reassurances notwithstanding, the embodiments of these virtues—the chaste Han Aijie and the filial Li An—seem flimsy pediments on which to rest our hopes for a cleansed society. Out of single examples of chastity and loyalty a society is not made—and not just because two out of hundreds is such a woefully small percentage. The greater reason that a single chaste woman and a single loyal man cannot create a new virtuous society is that Confucian virtues are societal ones. Any Chinese reader knows that such single examples of virtue are precisely what characterize the extensive literature of dynastic fall. Practiced by single individuals, chastity, loyalty, and filiality are not the cornerstones of society but the essence of pathos.

Zhang Zhupo argues that the transfiguration of Xiaoge speaks for the survival of filial piety, since his name itself refers to that virtue—as Roy translates, the ending signifies that "filiality has the power to transform all evils."[17] But filiality's manifestations here are hardly promising. Born at the moment of his father's death, Xiaoge has no chance to serve Ximen Qing; nor can he ever serve the spirit of his father since he *is* that very spirit. As a posthumous child, the only way in which Xiaoge can ever exercise filiality is by perpetuating the family line. And yet ultimately, in a reflection on filial piety that ought by now to seem familiar to us, Ximen Qing's line can be redeemed only by being terminated. Xiaoge saves the family by going off with Pujing and never having children of his own, a filial paradox the equal of those in the previous chapter. His name represents not a noble survival but a sad joke.

—

In the very last paragraph of the novel, both the empire and the Ximen family are restored, each in an attenuated form that mirrors the other. The events of the world stage that had driven the family to flee from Qinghe are neatly tied up in a few lines; a balance is struck with the Jurchen, and the Southern Song is able to maintain a state of relative peace (or at least an equilibrium with the northern invaders) that would persist for several centuries. The empire is diminished, its new form perhaps slightly questionable in its legitimacy, but unvanquished.

Similarly, Wu Yueniang adopts the servant Daian, who assumes the Ximen surname and takes care of Yueniang until her death of old age. Zhang Zhupo comments on this conclusion: "The conclusion turns to Daian. Now 'Daian' signifies '*da an*' ('great peace'), and with this, injustice is righted, and evil is dispersed. Only after this can the house of Ximen achieve peace. Is this final conclusion not grand?"[18] Still, though they parallel each other, the relationship between the household in Qinghe and the empire at large remains ambiguous. After Wu Yueniang gives Pujing her son, both monk and young boy vanish. Our novel ends by juxtaposing the two resolutions of crisis, one local and the other imperial:

> Wu Yueniang, Uncle Wu the Second, and the others stayed at Yongfu Temple for ten days' time. It turned out that the Jurchens crowned Zhang Bangchang as emperor in the Eastern Capital and installed a full array of both civil and military officials. Both Huizong and Qinzong were still in captivity in the north. Prince Kang, fleeing on a horse as reluctant to ford the river as if it had been made of mud, crossed the river. He ascended to the throne in Jiankang, therewith becoming Emperor Gaozong. After entreating Zong Ze to serve him as general, Shandong and Hebei were recaptured. The two dynasties were established. The world was at peace, and the citizenry was able to take up their livelihood again. Later, Yueniang returned home; opening up the compound, she discovered that none of the property had been touched. Later, she had Daian change his name to Ximen An, and take up the family business.[19]

The goings-on of the empire are sandwiched between the two references to Wu Yueniang and the family. The central problem of how we position the family and Qinghe with regard to the doings of the empire at large is foregrounded but remains unresolved.

Wu Yueniang's dream has already shown us one narrowly averted turn of events; Pujing explains that what she dreamed would have come to pass if she had insisted on keeping her son with her. When the conclusion so oddly juxtaposes the domestic and the imperial, another counterfactual is intimated, that something isn't allowed to happen because Wu Yueniang returns home to Qinghe. Are we to understand that when Wu Yueniang gives up her son she also somehow allows the Southern Song to remain in power? No explanations of causality bridge these two levels of narrative. One can see how Zhang Zhupo derives his reading of the novel, according to which Daian comes to signify much more than simply an individual's name, taking on symbolic weight, perhaps even as the reign name which it resembles.

Xiaoyu's vision at the temple includes many of the important characters who have died. After introducing themselves, the various characters' spirits then disclose their new place of rebirth. Virtually all the characters are to be reincarnated in a single location, the Eastern Capital. Why should they have all moved together from one place to another? All their souls born again in close proximity, one guesses that they will have simply shifted their activities from Qinghe to the capital, engaging once more in the avarice, lust, jealousy, adultery, incest, and homicide that dominated their existences in Qinghe. In that sense, the fact that fifteen years have elapsed between Ximen Qing's death and this scene seems quite significant. Not only does the elapsed time mean that Xiaoge is ready for marriage, but the reborn Ximen Qing—now fifteen—and the reborn Pan Jinlian—who dies a year or so after Ximen Qing, which would make the reborn girl around fourteen—are at an appropriate age to resume their old exploits.

Now that we know what happens to the main characters after their deaths, we also suspect that what we have understood to be an orgy of *luanlun* is only the tip of the iceberg; taking place over lifetimes, the degree to which these lives are interwoven is hardly to be imagined. One novelistic theme addressed by the following chapters is whether the human population is finite or infinite. Here, we can see how even a finite population can sustain infinite drama. Pan Jinlian's first husband, Wu Da, is the only exception, slated for rebirth instead to a farmer's family in Xuzhou, spared perhaps because he truly existed only in one relation to the other characters, nothing but Pan Jinlian's husband (and later of course the victim of her lust). In his next life, he is granted the privilege of being a stranger to the other characters.

In much of Chinese culture, the change of identity effected by reincarnation is permanent and of a different order from all other changes of identity. Once a person has been reincarnated, she no longer possesses claim to the specifics of her previous identity, and in consequence, there would be nothing incestuous about liaisons between these various unrelated teenagers in the Eastern Capital. This way of thinking about reincarnation is absolutely necessary, first if we are to consider that death a true end, but also, and perhaps more important, if we are to preserve any belief in the sanctity of patrilineal identity, since otherwise, after generations of reincarnation, any liaisons would be rife with *luanlun*, and anyone—no matter how careful—might be inadvertently marrying the soul of his mother or father, for example. In other words, a reader's first instinct is to regard reincarnation and death as the clean slate they are elsewhere in the culture.

But this novel operates by different rules, as Ding Yaokang recognizes in his 1690 *Xu Jinpingmei*. In this famous sequel to the novel, there are two main plot lines: one that traces the fates of the surviving characters in the original novel and another that follows the souls of dead characters reincarnated in the Eastern Capital. Both plots focus on how characters are paid back for their misdeeds in *Jinpingmei*. Although they sometimes operate in parallel, characters from these two different plots interact with one another. Ding Yaokang, in other words, shares my basic take on his sequel's parent novel: that within *Jinpingmei*'s context, reincarnation cannot allow characters to start afresh, and that it instead provides yet another way for relationships to be further involuted and interconnected.

—

Zhang Zhupo notes that *Jinpingmei* begins by setting up a territory bounded by the two temples,[20] and that this sealed-off geographic space either mirrors or generates another kind of closedness. An unprecedented percentage of this long novel takes place within the walls of a single household, and almost all the rest of it takes place in the small city of Qinghe. In other words, it is entirely appropriate that the novel ends when the remnants of the Ximen household find themselves literally at a crossroads.[21] Turn one way, and they end up at the temple. Turn the other, and they might pass into the world beyond. Of course, ultimately they are stuck in Qinghe, where caught within this matrix of relations, as all the members of the Ximen household are, theirs is a world of inevitable *luanlun*, whether deliberate or inadvertent.

In Qinghe—and soon, in the Eastern Capital—there seem to be no true strangers. Zhang Zhupo suggests that when Li An flees Chunmei's clutches to his ancestral home, he will have found himself in a place where he can begin entirely anew.[22] Of course, Zhang Zhupo must entertain this hope, to sustain the possibility of virtuous behavior. But we certainly recognize that if Li An were to encounter any old acquaintance, it would spell the doom of his efforts to reform. Wu Yueniang's flight reveals an empire that is truly *wuwai*, lacking in borders, making any true escape from this time and space an impossibility.

Deeply indebted to *Jinpingmei* in terms of character development and keen social observation, *Hongloumeng* is obviously different in that a precise moment of imperial time is replaced in the later novel by an absence. Nevertheless, even with so specific a temporal setting, *Jinpingmei*'s story and form prevent us from attributing singularity to any character, with implicit suggestions that what takes place in this wealthy merchant's household in Qinghe might also be taking place all over the empire, with different names and slightly different actions—but in its essence the same. Where is Qinghe? We do not know where this fictional location is, and there is the hint that it is no single location, as if the novel itself ought to be read as a perverse sociological study. What happens in the novel is significant not because of the uniqueness of the Ximen household and of Qinghe—but for the impossibility of containing the characters' doings and for the possibility of these misdeeds' taking place elsewhere, in other places and other times. At the end of *Jinpingmei*, imperial history and family history become one. But that does not in any way help us determine exactly *who* the individuals of the novel are, whether exempla or allegorical figures. And this vagueness—displaced in its epigone *Hongloumeng*—has far-reaching effects.

SEVEN

Hongloumeng and the Borders of Family

Even though there are plenty of hints that the Jia family whose fortunes are at the heart of *Hongloumeng* resides either in Nanjing or in Beijing, the novel steadfastly refuses to say which it is. And if we only knew which city contained the Jias' home, we might know *when* the novel's events took place. An eighteenth-century reader would have been exquisitely sensitized to subtle clues that tied geography to a historical moment: for example, if the capital city in which the Jias live were Nanjing, then the novel would have to be set in the early Ming. But although the Jias' home city shares the decadent elegance of Nanjing and the imperial grandeur of Beijing, the novel takes place in neither but in some fantastical amalgam of both.

Similarly, the novel is at once clear and vague on the matter of its dates. The middle chapters carefully chart the progress of time, so that it is perfectly easy to reckon, for example, that chapters 27 to 53 span precisely 257 days. But markers of time blur at both the novel's beginning and its end, and all the philological energy in the world would not help us determine which year of whose reign the novel begins in, or the dynasty the Jia ancestors have served with such distinction, or the name of the emperor whose favor the imperial concubine Yuanchun, our protagonist Baoyu's elder sister, has won.

Some readers suggest that the author Cao Xueqin (or his redactors) skirted a precise date and location to avoid political trouble.[1] Cao belonged to a family of Han Bannermen whose access to fabulous wealth was the product of the Kangxi emperor's personal patronage and of a specific historical moment, when the Qing monarchs had to rely heavily on the cultural know-how of Han Bannermen. One of the Cao women, perhaps the inspiration for Grandmother Jia, was the emperor's own nanny, but when the emperor died and his son the Yongzheng emperor succeeded to the throne, the Jias' source of power and influence also disappeared. Cao Xueqin, whose childhood must have been filled with reminders of vanished wealth, lived his life in poverty and obscurity. Ever since he was identified as the author, much of the criticism on *Hongloumeng* (of the *suoyin* variety, "seeking out the hidden" clues in the novel) has attempted to uncover a historical biography, supposedly encoded within the novel.

But setting aside autobiography, the novel's indeterminate setting leads to a cascade of consequences. If we do not know the name of this empire, we cannot tell what room there is outside, whether outside the imperium or outside the Jia mansion. Do outsides and insides as such even exist? In late imperial China, space is constructed, as I have argued elsewhere in this book, not just by buildings, roads, and cities (or in this novel by a mansion and a garden we come to know in intimate detail) but also by kinship structures and the relationships among separate patrilineages. That way of considering space is the focus of this chapter.

Just as with *Jinpingmei*, some traditional readers interpret the novel's peculiar treatment of space allegorically: the commentator Zhang Xinzhi (fl. 1828–50), for example, uses the *Yijing* to understand directional markings and relations, both within and outside the garden. Zhang Xinzhi is only one of a long line of critics to interpret the novel's cosmological intimations allegorically (whether through the lens of *Yijing* numerology, Buddhist theology, or *yinyang* correspondences). Readers both traditional and modern have made much of the novel's geography and particularly the layout of the Great Prospect Garden, the magical green world built originally for the visit of Baoyu's sister Yuanchun and where the young people of the household grow up. Spaces and enclosures have been widely recognized as important to the novel, the only premodern text whose modern editions often include a map.

But these allegorical resonances rest on a presumption of singularity that is repeatedly undermined. Are people, even the Jias, fantastically wealthy and powerful as they are, unique or not? On one hand, the novel asks whether coincidence is possible in an imagined world where all details (as critics like Zhang Xinzhi and Plaks suggest) seem redolent with cosmological significance. On the other, the novel poses a companion question, whether singularity is even possible in an imagined world of seemingly infinite size.

—

Late imperial literature operates on a knife's edge, on the delicate balance between the political and the domestic, or the global and the parochial. Private events make sense only as they are understood through shared global events and vice versa. In a way, neither set of events exists without the other. This book began by examining *chuanqi* plays, whose very form is grounded on a balance that in *Hongloumeng* is constantly and repeatedly unsettled.

The novel makes occasional reference to a bigger picture that spans the empire. There are a few updates on Yuanchun's health (and concern over what the imperial concubine's decline might mean to the family), some reports on problems defending the coast against pirates, an account of Jia Zheng's brief and unhappy official appointment in the south supervising grain distribution. Again and again, it is clear that what happens on an imperial scale has immediate bearing on the family's well-being: Yuanchun's death in the palace presages the family's ruin; after she is married, Tanchun longs for a visit home, but cannot return until the pirates are pacified.

Still, these references to the outside world are significant only in their effects on the individual members of the family. In contrast to other texts, we are never shown the family as one among many others, all commensurate and equal in standing, all suffering from the same global events beyond their control. In the absence of a dynastic context within which to situate the novel, the balance between domestic and global has become so unhinged that events taking place outside the compound are significant only for their consequences within.

In chapter 96, Lady Wang cannot help but weep to herself. A number of tragedies have simultaneously befallen the family, each with a significance that extends beyond the immediate family: her daughter Yuanchun has died in the imperial palace; her brother Wang Ziteng has also passed away, on his way to assume a lofty official position; and finally, her son Baoyu seems to be losing his mind. Each blow is bad enough on its own merits, but as one commentator observes, all of them seem to be connected.[2] Instead of painting a picture of the world consisting of different families suffering simultaneously, this convergence of misfortune—some public, like the deaths of the imperial concubine or of the official Wang Ziteng, some as private as the unraveling of her son's mind—still makes it appear as if the Jias themselves were the nexus for all occurrences.

One of the most important influences on *Hongloumeng*, the late Ming *chuanqi* play *Jiaohong ji*, features young lovers who are cousins and who closely parallel *Hongloumeng*'s Jia Baoyu and Lin Daiyu in temperament, the sociable and affectionate young man Shen Chun and the sensitive and jealous Wang Jiaoniang. Literary historians have long observed that Cao Xueqin was much influenced by Meng Chengshun's play in depicting the relationship between Lin Daiyu and Jia Baoyu (who, like the earlier pair of cousins, veer wildly between perfect sympathy and tempestuous misunderstanding).

But whereas young Shen travels back and forth between his family's home in Chengdu and hers in Meizhou, Baoyu's life is almost as circumscribed within the family's walls as those of his sisters and girl cousins. Beginning in Act 8 of *Jiaohong ji*, a barbarian tribe threatens to invade, seemingly for no purpose other than to gesture toward the concerns of the world at large (and to drag our hero back to his besieged hometown and away from the heroine just as their flirtation starts to heat up). Another act finds him in the capital taking examinations.

Cao Xueqin flirted with the notion of writing *Hongloumeng* as a *chuanqi* drama, but that play is almost impossible to imagine. Where are the traces of those particularly *chuanqi* concerns in the novel as it stands? Where in the novel are the journeys and the exchanges that establish the borders of the political community and our awareness of other families, counterparts to our main characters? In the never-written play, the Jia mansion would have a location; Yuanchun's imperial husband, a name; and Jia Baoyu, the experience of far-reaching travel. And yet we do know something about that unwritten *chuanqi*. Its token object would have been the stone that is born with Baoyu and after which the text—in good *chuanqi* fashion—is named. (*Shitouji*, *The Story of the Stone*, circulated under the title *Hongloumeng* only with its first imprints, the authenticity of whose last forty chapters has been impugned, especially by modern scholars.)

Daiyu has nothing to fear from the harum-scarum Shi Xiangyun, Grandmother Jia's grandniece, whose interactions with Baoyu seem utterly free of flirtation and whose old-fashioned guardians are later to marry her off to a young man she has never seen. Nonetheless, Daiyu jealously frets, based not on what she sees between the two cousins, but on what she has read. Xiangyun possesses a gold *qilin*, whose double Baoyu is eager to acquire:

> The stories (*waizhuan yeshi* 外傳野史) that Baoyu had smuggled in mostly featured scholars and beauties (*caizi jiaren*) who came together because of some small clever object, whether a mandarin duck, or a phoenix, or a jade bracelet or gold ornament, or a silk handkerchief or an embroidered sash, and it was always through these little objects that they were able to find their true loves. Now having seen Baoyu with his *qilin*, she [Daiyu] was afraid that he would take this as an opportunity to start such an affair with Xiangyun.[3]

Throughout the novel, and most especially in the dynamics between Daiyu and Baoyu, the literary conventions of romance intrude—not so much that the characters are unwittingly subject to them—but insofar as they self-consciously imagine they are. Here Daiyu invests objects with all the importance they would have in a play.

Nonetheless, those trinkets or ornaments that in other texts mark the bonds of exchange here function quite differently. Why does Baoyu's jade not travel from his possession into the hands of another and so make its way across the empire? In *Hongloumeng*'s imaginary *chuanqi* twin, it would have, inviting us to follow its history not just as an object but as a commodity, alternately gaining and losing value, separating from and merging with people. In contrast, here in *Hongloumeng*, each token of exchange, and not just Baoyu's jade, has been transformed into what is fundamentally immobile, a badge of identity. Xue Baochai's golden locket, given to her by a mysterious monk when she was a small child, reveals her metallic nature, a counterpart to Baoyu's essential stone-like qualities, and perhaps augurs Baochai's destiny as Baoyu's wife.

Like Baoyu's stone, the locket can never switch hands. With no set boundaries to the world of *Hongloumeng*, there is no way for the stone to travel to the edges and then journey back into Baoyu's hands. When toward the end of the novel Baoyu's jade vanishes, it does not pass from character to character, strengthening bonds as it goes, carving out its own biography, which cannot be encapsulated by that of any single human character. Instead, its existence incompletely autonomous from Baoyu's, the jade's disappearance marks the loss of Baoyu's very essence. Giving the jade away or discarding it, as Baoyu threatens to do at his first meeting with Daiyu, is not an option.

—

We do not know the name of this age or of its emperor, but we are constantly reassured of the sageliness of both. In chapter 78, Baoyu's father, Jia Zheng, tells his entourage about one of the emperor's projects, to seek out and praise all the worthies in history, even those as lowly as monks, nuns, beggars, or women. Jia Zheng explains that even a single praiseworthy deed should be reported immediately to the Ministry of Rites. The entourage responds: "This is as it should be. What is most admirable is that this dynasty is acting in ways unparalleled in history. It can truly be called 'a sagely dynasty with nothing left unrecorded.'"[4] Many historians, Janet Theiss and Matthew Sommer among them, have explored the various means by which the eighteenth-century state attempted to popularize Confucian morals previously associated primarily with the elite. Theiss writes of how chaste behavior came first to be extolled, and then expected when it came to women from social categories "previously considered unworthy of canonization, like Daoist nuns, wives of yamen runners and criminals, freed bondservants, and women from prostitute families."[5] The imperial project Jia Zheng describes seems an outgrowth of the real-life attitudes of the eighteenth-century state. Only the project's total comprehensiveness is fantastic.

This sort of totalizing project characterized other empires as well. In *The Imperial Archive*, Thomas Richards discusses the importance to the British empire of three models: the library, the museum, and something else that claims to encompass both of the others in its promise of comprehensive knowledge, "a unified archive, an imperial archive holding together the vast and various parts of the Empire."[6] The archive of worthy deeds and individuals to which Jia Zheng refers covers the same territory as the novel itself, which focuses precisely on those people—the young, the female, and in some cases, the mean of birth—who are easily omitted by other texts. We might even see the two, imperial record and novel, both purporting to record the merits of a group of otherwise insignificant girls, as replicating the competitive oedipal relationship between Baoyu and Jia Zheng: the one, a novel, giving priority to the aesthetic and the imaginative—and to girls like the tragic maid Qingwen (Skybright), beautiful, spirited, and doomed; the other, a historical project, recording precisely the sort of conventional moral behavior for which Baoyu has nothing but disdain. With our sympathy for Baoyu, we are conditioned already to regard this imperial project with some trepidation.

But the unnamed emperor is not just interested in every *deed* of his subjects. He also wants to know how they are related to one another. Several times, he inquires into the genealogy of the Jias. The Qing dynasty sponsored a number of totalizing projects, like the Kangxi Dictionary and the *Siku quanshu*, but it was another ambitious project that had the most immediate impact on Cao Xueqin's family. After the first generations of Qing rule, during which Han Bannermen served in vital capacities as translators, interpreters, and cultural middlemen, all Bannermen had to present elaborate genealogies to court to prove their descent and so entitle them to their stipends and other privileges. The Banner population had grown so large—and Qing rule so stable—that it had become impractical to support so many people. Mark Elliott marvels at the comprehensiveness of Banner genealogies: "The consistent, precise documentation of births, deaths, marriages, and adoptions among the people of the Eight Banners surely qualifies them as one of the most intensely inventoried and monitored populations in history."[7] These genealogies were intended to separate "real" Bannermen (of Manchu descent from time immemorial) from "false" ones (people like the Caos, who had joined the Banners in recorded history).

In real life, imperial genealogical interests must have been met with by fear among people like the Caos, since the intent of these queries was precisely to deprive families of the privileges that they had enjoyed for generations. In the context of the novel, in the absence of any other way to map this fictional world and within this historical context, an extra burden falls on the ability to construct almost fantastically complicated genealogies, as if they might permit total inclusiveness. Where other narratives treat marriage or death as an end point, plots come to a conclusion in *Hongloumeng* when the precise relations between people in a family are established. This interest is reflected in the presence of family trees in many modern editions of the novel to help a reader figure out how, for example, a more distant cousin like Xing Xiuyan is related to other members of the family. But these family trees do not help us when it comes to the surfeit of Jias who appear in the last part of the novel.

Ominously, Jias keep cropping up everywhere. The surname Jia is a homophone for "false," and its frequency in the novel is a sort of running joke (since in the real world Jia is a relatively rare surname, not among the hundred most common that account for well over 95 percent of the population). In chapter 104, after a number of Jias appear in criminal cases of varying degrees of seriousness, the novel's emperor makes inquiries about the Jia lineage, and even though Jia Zheng earlier praised the emperor's recordkeeping capabilities, it is clear that this confidence is at least partially misplaced. The emperor might aspire to encompass all knowledge of his subjects both past and present, yet he fails to know something so obvious as Jia Zheng's identity as the father of his recently deceased favorite concubine, Jia Yuanchun. We cannot fault the emperor too much, though; even to the careful reader, there remains something impenetrable about how the novel's various Jias are related. Are there many unrelated Jias, or are all Jias filiated? Is it possible to emerge with a single genealogy that includes all Jias?

That uncertainty centers on Jia Yucun, the first Jia to whom the reader is introduced, and whose name (really his *zi*, or style) is a pun, a homophone for *jiayu cunhua* 假語村話: "false talk and nonsense." His degree of distance or propinquity to our Jias is the heart of the problem because Jia Yucun—surnamed Jia and yet not quite one of our family—not only connects our Jias to the rest of the world but also connects the novel's cosmological plot to its domestic one. The inscription on the stone in chapter 1 introduces the reader to Zhen Shiyin, who has befriended an impoverished scholar named Jia Yucun. Later, Jia Yucun finds employment as the tutor of the little girl Lin Daiyu, who is sent to her maternal grandmother under his charge. Later, he appears from time to time throughout the novel, as he rises and falls on the wheel of fortune. Through his association with Lin Daiyu, he manages to intrude himself as part of the outer circle of the Jia clan.

The shared surname is both coincidental and significant. The servants and attendants of the Rongguo and Ningguo houses sneer that Jia Yucun is no relation at all, just a hanger-on who has made a great deal out of his coincidental connection with the noble Jias. Toward the end of the novel, another member of Jia Zheng's entourage, Feng Ziying, asks directly how precisely Jia Yucun is related to our Jias. Are they members of the same clan or distant cousins? Is he within the five degrees of mourning?[8] Jia Zheng explains that Yucun's hometown is Huzhou in Zhejiang province but gives no answer to Feng Ziying's other questions. After the family came to know him as Lin Daiyu's tutor, Jia Zheng continues, "I saw that he was a fine fellow, and we all gathered together frequently. Yucun himself was a bit peculiar: our family's rise, from the generation named 'Tai' onward, both the Ning and Rong households, our numbers and our real estate, and where we live and what we do—he knew it all."[9] In other words, although Jia Yucun himself is the master of the Rongguo and Ningguo genealogies, his own position within them is mysterious.[10]

These genealogies become critically important when Jia Lian and Jia Zheng separately learn of transgressions committed by other Jias that might implicate the family. In fact, the Jias' road to ruination begins with confusion among the different Jias. If as readers we are never precisely able to determine how what happens outside the family's walls is related to what happens inside, or how the domestic world relates to the political and global, or how our Jias are related to other Jias, this indeterminacy is also the origin of the family's downfall. In chapter 101, during a visit to a highly placed eunuch, Jia Lian glances over a court newsletter that covers two unconnected cases: the first, involving a gang of firearms smugglers in the southeast, whose ringleader claims to be the servant of a noble named Jia Hua; the second, concerning a corrupt servant employed by the nobleman Jia Fan. Other than being left with a sense of unease, Jia Lian does not know what to make of these names. In a foul mood, he goes home to instigate an argument with his wife, Wang Xifeng, about her natal family, whose members, after the death of her uncle, have been engaging in all sorts of corruption. Jia Lian had been petitioning the eunuch not on his own behalf but on his in-laws', the Wangs, and now he seems fully entrapped by the actions of relations who aren't relations—Jias of indeterminate relationship and Wangs who are relatives by marriage.

After a disastrous tour of service, Jia Zheng is recalled to the capital. When he is summoned to an audience with the emperor, Jia Zheng is terrified that he is to be punished, but the emperor's attention is on other matters. Jia Lian is not the only person to notice the shared surname of the people involved in those cases. The emperor asks Jia Zheng whether the Jia Hua in the firearms-smuggling scandal is a relation. Jia Zheng hastens to explain that although Jia Daihua was his ancestor, Jia Hua is someone else entirely. But what about, the emperor goes on to ask, the Jia Hua currently serving as the mayor? (The reader knows that this is Jia Yucun's proper name.) Without waiting for the response that would finally answer our questions about Jia Yucun, the emperor turns to the second case, regarding Jia Fan's servant. This Jia Fan is, Jia Zheng admits, a relative, although from a distant clan (*yuanzu* 遠族).[11]

Jia Yucun happens to be among the hangers-on listening when Jia Zheng frets on his return home: "It can't be a good thing for the emperor to have in his mind the name Jia."[12] After the government raid, which initially seems to come unprovoked, the servant Bao Yong overhears a conversation between two strangers that finally explains why it happened. One man says to the other, "I often saw him [Jia Yucun] hanging out in the two mansions. When the censor brought the indictment against the family, the emperor ordered him [Yucun] to establish the facts of the matter. What do you think he did? He'd derived every advantage from the two mansions, and he was afraid that people would say that he was sticking up for the family. So he went ahead and kicked them when they were down. That's why the two mansions were raided."[13] Even if Jia Zheng manages to explain to the emperor that the shared surname is just a coincidence, he cannot prevent Jia Yucun—however he is related to the family—from being so anxious to clear his own name that he turns on the Jias.

Jia Yucun is also at the center of one of the state's most ominous charges. When Officer Zhao raids the household, he is armed with an imperial edict that contains a charge against Jia She (Jia Zheng's elder brother) that was first mentioned much earlier in the novel. An avid collector of antique fans, Jia She finds out about the spectacular collection of a poor man nicknamed Shitou daizi (石頭呆子; Hawkes translates his name as Stony). After considerable effort, Jia Lian manages to catch a glimpse of this collection, but his offer to buy it is turned down; rather than give up his fans, Stony tells him, he would prefer to die of hunger. Jia Lian returns home to his father's disappointment (and a vicious beating). Stony's story would have ended there, except for Jia Yucun's desire to ingratiate himself with Jia She. To get the fans, Jia Yucun falsely accuses Stony of owing the government money. He is arrested—and the precious fans seized and turned over to Jia She, compliments of Jia Yucun. Spooked by the emperor's questions about the Jias, Yucun reports this crime, at whose heart lies his own meddling.

Much later, at the end of the novel, the Jia family tree comes to the emperor's attention once again; this time, the emperor's scrutiny sets up the restoration of their fortunes. At the beginning of the novel, Jia Yucun's friend Leng Zixing explains to him how the two houses are related. That conversation has now taken place many times within the novel, each time between different characters. Each explanation, somehow inconclusive on its own, demands a repeat until the final iteration takes place between a minister of state and the emperor himself. When the examinations are graded, both

Baoyu and his nephew Jia Lan have passed with distinction, Baoyu in seventh place. The recurrence of the Jia surname piques the emperor's curiosity. Both successful candidates are Jias from the capital: could they possibly be relations of his deceased favorite? Baoyu and Jia Lan are summoned to an audience to explain. Because Baoyu has long since disappeared, Jia Lan appears by himself to speak to a high official: "He laid out and explained the three generations of Jias, and the minister presented it to the throne on his behalf."[14]

Even after marriage with Yuanchun, a private audience with Jia Zheng, and the duplicity of Jia Yucun, the same emperor needs to have the Jia family explained to him yet again: yes, the Jia Baoyu who took the seventh place was indeed the beloved younger brother of his own deceased concubine. The emperor is so moved by Baoyu's seemingly magical disappearance he declares a general amnesty that includes a reprieve for Baochai's brother Xue Pan, still awaiting execution for his part in a barroom brawl. Through the amnesty, the Ningguo fortunes are restored as well, when Jia She and Jia Zhen are allowed to return without completing their sentences.

—

How are we to account for the superabundance of Jias that provokes the emperor's suspicions in the first place? Zhang Xinzhi refuses even to entertain the possibility of coincidence.[15] Yao Xie (1805–64) remarks: "Another member of the same family. What misfortune those who are surnamed Jia find themselves in these days!"[16] Traditional commentators make much of other surname repetitions in the novel. To Zhang Xinzhi, for example, it is highly significant that Aunt Zhao, Jia Zheng's fractious concubine and the biological mother of Tanchun and Jia Huan, shares the same common surname with Officer Zhao, who is in charge of the crew who raid the mansion.[17] From the inside, Aunt Zhao makes an attempt on Baoyu's life; from the outside, Officer Zhao is bent on destroying the family. But the novel has so many characters—and Chinese so few surnames—that it would be difficult not to repeat the commonest of family names. And none of the characters make anything of Aunt Zhao's sharing a surname with Officer Zhao. Is the presence of multiple Jias the coincidence that two unrelated characters named Zhao or Zhang might be, or is it something more significant?

When characters wrestle with the surfeit of Jias, the extent of the family, and the relatedness of the characters, the problem hinges on the scope of the empire, which in turn implies the issues of coincidence and necessity. What to the commentators Zhang Xinzhi and Yao Xie is redolent with cosmological significance is merely a statistical probability to the prosaic Jia Zheng: "But it isn't odd. We have so many poor relatives, and it's been so long that there are members of the family everywhere."[18]

Another way to pose this question of coincidence and necessity is to ask whether the proliferation of Jias is random—so that it is simply a matter of time until enough Jias happen to gather together—or whether their appearance does in fact portend ill. By extension, is what appears exceptional actually nothing but the product of probability, or is there something cosmologically unique about this family? As in *Jinpingmei*, singularity is bound up with the question of coincidence and the imagined borders of the human community; in this nameless, borderless empire, the argument for individual distinctiveness becomes increasingly difficult to make.

These efforts to separate what is statistically likely from what must be cosmologically ordained take place throughout the novel in moments as seemingly trivial as the characters' debate over whether shared birthdays are meaningful. As Grandmother Jia's favorite, Baoyu's birthday is naturally celebrated in grand style. But even a day especially set aside as his own turns out not to be his alone. One by one, other members of the household disclose (or have disclosed for them) that they share Baoyu's birthday: the maid in charge of Jia Lian's household, Ping'er; Xue Baochai's cousin Xue Baoqin; and Xing Xiuyan, a niece of Lady Xing currently on a long visit to the Jias. The shared birthday is the source of much hilarity, as the four honorees exchange kowtows (a custom predicated on the exclusive hold that a person has on his birthday, here jokingly undermined since the one day is shared by so many). Before making impromptu arrangements for the other three celebrants, Tanchun comments: "How funny! Each month we've got a number of birthdays. But once you've got enough people, then you get coincidences like this. We've also got days with two and three birthdays."[19] Tanchun then goes through the calendar, listing when family members have their birthdays.

Despite Tanchun's lighthearted (and statistically perspicacious)[20] comments, birthdays *do* hold a mysterious and profound significance in this household. The two members of the household who share the most intimate ties with the emperor also share the same birthday: first, Yuanchun, named after her New Year's birthday, and second, the great-grandfather whose achievements and personal service opened the way to the family's prominence and power. (Tanchun says about her older sister's birthday, "It's no wonder that she's had such good fortune; her birthday comes before anyone else's.")[21] Nor is Yuanchun the only daughter of the family named after her birthday: in her first visit to the Jias, Grannie Liu names Qiaojie after her birthday, one of the least auspicious days of the year, *qiqiao*, the seventh of the seventh month. The best way to deal with unpropitious signs, according to Grannie Liu, is head on.

Qiaojie and Yuanchun mirror each other: one a symbol of the family's zenith, the other of the family's decline, and there is nothing coincidental about these two cousins' birthdays. But what about other birthdays? In the same breath in which she suggests that Yuanchun and the patriarch's birthdays are necessary, Tanchun explains away the convergence of the other four birthdays as coincidence. An offhand conversation—and yet one of many throughout the novel that concerns the place of coincidence and necessity.

If anything does set the Jias apart, it has to do with the way in which they, alone of all families, in a world of exogamous patrilineages, function. In chapter 57, Daiyu's loyal maidservant Zijuan (Hawkes's Nightingale) decides to test Baoyu's feelings for her mistress. Very deliberately telling a lie, she casually refers to Daiyu's imminent return home to Suzhou, and when Baoyu asks her what she means, she explains that Daiyu will soon be leaving the Jias to have her marriage arranged. Baoyu dismisses Zijuan's story, reassuring himself that his beloved cousin—orphaned of both mother and father—has no family left in Suzhou to care for her, which by omission is what the reader has been led to believe. But soon Zijuan does manage to persuade him, with disastrous effects. It is her wording just as much as the possibility of Daiyu's marriage that causes Baoyu to have a nervous breakdown, the first of the attacks that eventually turn him into an invalid and idiot. Zijuan says, sarcastically, "It's only you Jias who are a grand clan, with so many people then! Other than your family, everybody else only has one father and one mother. Could it be that they [the Lins] have no other uncles?"[22]

Most commentators accuse Zijuan of cruelty, but one points out that she is just telling the truth: "It's true and right, and what she says is so. What response could Baoyu possibly have for her?"[23] In the context of Chinese culture (or for that matter, Manchu custom), it makes no sense that Lin Daiyu should have so thoroughly been thrown at the mercy of her mother's family. Despite the Lins' relative poverty, even a distant Lin uncle would be in a more legitimate place to make decisions concerning Daiyu's marital future. In fact, Grandmother Jia's laxity in arranging a match for Daiyu reveals clearly that Zijuan's remarks are grounded in reality: on some level, Daiyu remains an outsider.

Baoyu is driven to a nervous breakdown in confronting what are actually fairly obvious truths about his family—not the least of which is the curious absence of any Lin uncles. But where are other families in the novel, not surnamed Wang, Xue, Shi, or Jia? Or for that matter, why aren't even the Wangs, Xues, and Shis equal to the Jias? Although all four families are extraordinarily rich and powerful, the other three households appear to operate by different rules, which much more closely approximate those that govern the behavior of all families.

How does it come to be that the Jias should be so different, not just in quantity, but in quality from all other families in the novel? Why is it that they alone should have come to accumulate so many relatives of different surnames? Why do the Xues come to live with the Jias? Within the context of the novel it seems reasonable that Aunt Xue should stay at her sister Lady Wang's for a protracted visit, and that the orphaned Xiangyun, whose Shi guardians are dour and stern, should visit her fun-loving cousins rather than the other way around. Still, the cumulative pattern is striking and increasingly improbable, especially when it comes to the slew of ever more distant relations, who are almost all marriageable young girls, among them

Xue Baoqin, Li Wen, Li Qin, and Xing Xiuyan. The real question is how the Jias circumvent the fundamental organizing principle of Chinese kinship: affines who are Jias trump agnates, even though properly it should be the other way around.

By pointing out the obvious inequity among families on which the novel rests, Zijuan also makes a broader point about Baoyu's self-perception. She hints at what Baochai later makes explicit: Baoyu has certain expectations of his immediate family that make sense only if the Jias are exceptional among all others. If the Wangs, Xues, and Shis were truly the Jias' equals, then the idyll he enjoys could no longer exist. Or, even more broadly, his family—in the form it takes for most of the novel—can be sustained only so long as there are no other families like his.

Much later, Baoyu remains convinced of the family's exceptionalism. When his cousin Yingchun returns home for a short visit, she confides to Lady Wang that her new husband mistreats her. Beyond offering some empty, comforting words, neither Lady Wang nor anybody else can do anything for her, and Yingchun herself has fatalistically resigned herself to whatever fate awaits her when she returns to her husband: "If I can just stay in the garden for another few days, I can die at peace."[24] Lady Wang warns the convalescing Baoyu, "Don't drop a hint of this to your grandmother. If she should know anything about it, it'll be because you said it."[25] Grandmother Jia, who herself has been ailing, must be protected from news of her granddaughter's suffering and humiliation.

But Baoyu misunderstands the warning. In the next chapter, he tells his mother that he has come up with a plan to save his cousin: "I thought of something last night: we might as well tell Grandmother, and she'll bring back Yingchun and have her live again at home. And just like before, we'll be brother and sister eating together, playing together—and we won't ever again have to put up with that horrible Sun. When he comes to get her, we just won't let him. If he comes a hundred times, we'll turn him down a hundred times. We'll just say that it's Grandmother's idea."[26] Lady Wang responds to Baoyu's suggestion with a laugh, but it is unclear whether Baoyu himself knows he has told a joke. Instead, it seems he thinks that he can simply explain Yingchun's situation to Grandmother Jia, who will then send for Yingchun to return home.

Partly the point is the searing naïveté of the grown Baoyu about marriage. Less than twenty chapters away from his own wedding, he seems not to understand anything about what marriage implies, namely that Yingchun has permanently joined another family. Just as strikingly, Baoyu fails to recognize Grandmother Jia's limitations. To him, it makes sense that the Suns would be just as awed by a whim of Grandmother Jia's as the Jias themselves are and that simply explaining anything away as her decision would place it beyond argument in another household as much as in their own. The particular circumstances of the family almost make Baoyu's mistake understandable; Grandmother Jia *does* seem all-powerful, and the existence of other, independent, equally powerful, equally self-enclosed entities seems almost unimaginable (there are ways, for example, in which the garden and the household seem to partake of the cultural and political energies of the Qing empire and the imperial court itself).[27]

But in Yingchun's unhappy marriage, Baoyu's belief in his grandmother's power could not be more misplaced. Her groom, Sun Shaozu, humiliates Yingchun precisely by pointing out the decline of her grand family. Jia She, unable to pay back his debts to the Suns, has given them his daughter in marriage—an ugly fact thrown back repeatedly in Yingchun's face: "Don't play the lady with me! Your father owed me 5,000 taels of silver and sold you to me on discount."[28] Having been bought, she is no different in status from that of any bondservant or serving girl.

If Baoyu implicitly believes in the singularity of his grandmother and of his family, Sun Shaozu repeatedly sets the two families up in a comparison. To Jia Zheng and the rest of the family, the Suns are not equals, but parvenu leeches, who have manipulated their connections with the Jias into wealth and power. Sun Shaozu sees the relationship between the two families very differently. To him, it is his bride who has forgotten her station in marrying him. He insults the gentle Yingchun:

> Back when your grandfather was around, he had his eyes on our wealth and power and hurried to make an alliance. So by rights, I should be of the

same generation as your father—and now with him pressing down from above, I've been moved down a generation. We ought not to have made this match. Certainly there's nothing about it that would make it seem as if *we* were the ones ingratiating ourselves for some advantages.[29]

Later on, Yingchun is allowed to return home for a visit (but only after the Jia fortunes are improved slightly). As she leaves for the last time, Grandmother Jia comforts her with a promise of another visit soon. Yingchun knows better; she knows that her grandmother loves her but is powerless even in the smallest ways to help her. One chapter later, both Grandmother Jia and Yingchun are dead.

In this part of the novel, Baoyu never seems entirely clear of mind; nonetheless, his perception of Grandmother Jia's power is a telling blind spot. It is almost as if he cannot understand that she, the matriarch of his family, is not everyone's matriarch. In some sense, what Baoyu fails to understand is not so much marriage or the adult world as the very existence of other families as equals to his own. How could one woman be the grandmother of all? How could a young bride live with her grandmother, who was also the grandmother of her groom? In fact, such things *do* happen, but only through a specific pattern of marriage, where cousins marry; if Daiyu *had* married Baoyu, then Grandmother Jia would have been her grandmother twice over. It is a side effect of cousin marriage and not just in his mind that she is grandmother of all.

Cousin marriage confuses matters. We cannot fully comprehend the family's borders partly because of people like Jia Yucun, whose relationship to our Jias is indeterminate, but also because of a character like Wang Xifeng, whose relationship to the Jias is precisely determined. A teenager at the novel's beginning, her power in the household exceeds considerably what we might expect of a young daughter-in-law. Compare her unusual status to that of another young matron, the virtuous and retiring Li Wan, Baoyu's widowed sister-in-law. In part, Wang Xifeng's standing has to do with her ambition, but it also has to do with her natal family. Unlike a stereotypically powerless daughter-in-law, Wang Xifeng has a powerful ally. Lady Wang, Baoyu's mother, is Wang Xifeng's aunt both by marriage and by blood, so that Xifeng's status in the household emerges not out of a single relationship (her marriage to Jia Lian) but out of multiple ones.

Zhang Xinzhi compares Xifeng to He San, the insider who made the robbery after Grandmother Jia's funeral possible. He even claims that the name He San (何三) is a visual pun for Wang Xifeng's surname, 王 (since He merged with San looks like Wang). The godson of the Jias' steward Zhou Rui, He San and Wang Xifeng obviously parallel each other in that each represents domestic wrongdoing that eventually becomes public: Wang Xifeng's usurious loans and shady legal dealings form part of the charges against the family, and He San divulges to the other thieves the places where Grandmother Jia has hidden her fortune. But He San's corruption also takes another form; to the other robbers, he explains, "It was just out of respect for godmother's feelings that I went and recognized him [Zhou Rui] as my godfather."[30] In the absence of family ties, what kind of relationship could a married woman and an unmarried man share? Evidently, He San and Zhou Rui's wife shared a pre-existing illicit relationship that is cemented when He San signs on as Zhou Rui's godson. Zhou Rui and He San are a twisted incestuous version of father and son, where the son swears allegiance to a father only because he has had sex with the mother.

Wang Xifeng's position resembles He San's in that his overt incest and her marriage into a family stocked with natal relations prevent us from ever establishing *prima facie* relations to individual family members. Like any daughter-in-law, she must seek the approval of older women in the household, but when she approaches Lady Wang, it is not just as the wife of her husband's uncle but also as her father's sister. No doubt this sense of corruption—that the source of her power in the household comes close to the incestuous—contributes to the hatred that so many traditional readers have felt for her.

In the novel, cousin marriage, though perfectly legal and common, never escapes a certain moral taint. Our first explanation of how all four families are related takes place in a moment of high corruption, when justice is being suborned. In one of Jia Yucun's first cases after assuming a position as magistrate, Baochai's brother Xue Pan is accused of murder. Introducing all four families, the Jias, the Wangs, the Xues, and the Shis, in a doggerel verse, an underling warns Jia

Yucun against punishing Xue Pan. With that, Jia Yucun lets Xue Pan off the hook. The relations among these four families do not simply constitute mutual protection, however. With four families so tightly bound, each controlling the fates of all the others, no degree of care can—as Jia Lian and Jia Zheng know too well—keep one from eventually stepping afoul of the law and dragging in the others.

From a sampling of single-surname villages in rural Zhejiang province, the anthropologists Eugene Cooper and Meng Zhang estimate that somewhere between 5 and 30 percent of marriages earlier in the twentieth century took place between *biao* cousins (i.e., those who do not share a surname).[31] The informants of another anthropologist, Francis Hsu, claimed that 70 percent of local marriages in a small town in Yunnan were cross-cousin marriages.[32] Given those figures, it might well be the case that the Jias' marital habits are not at all fantastic. Scholars both of marital practices and of the novel have independently speculated that cousin marriages took place for a number of reasons, among them, to keep property within extended families, to strengthen ties between families, or to maintain political prominence. One informant interviewed by Cooper and Zhang even uses the same justification for cousin marriage that Grandmother Jia makes in chapter 90, *qin shang jia qin* 親上加親; cousin marriage allows for a doubled sense of relatedness.

The native informants interviewed by Cooper and Zhang differentiated among three kinds of *biao* unions: of a man to his mother's brother's daughter (the relation between *Jiaohong ji*'s young lovers), to his mother's sister's daughter (the relation shared by Baoyu and Baochai), and to his father's sister's daughter (which, following Cooper and Zhang's convention, I will refer to as FSD, the relation shared by Baoyu and Daiyu). What Cooper, Hsu,[33] and Daniel Harrison Kulp[34] discovered is that across multiple diverse regions cousin marriages were universally ranked in the order listed above, with Baoyu and Daiyu's proposed union as the least favored form, which might go a little way toward explaining why no one in the Jia family enthusiastically supports the proposed match between Baoyu and Daiyu (and why the opposition of Wang Jiaoniang's father in *Jiaohong ji* is made to seem unreasonable). Nonetheless, despite the apparent stigma attached to FSD, it was by no means entirely shunned and was still practiced not infrequently.

There is, however, no consensus for why cousin matches should be ranked this way, and native informants and anthropologists come up with a variety of different explanations for the widespread aversion to FSD. Hsu suggests that sending a daughter to her mother's *niangjia* 娘家 (natal home) seems uncomfortably close—morphologically speaking, that is—to the mother's having been divorced and sent home in shame.[35] Especially in light of traditional beliefs that a girl inherited her mother's essence and a son, his father's, Daiyu's stay at her maternal grandmother's home might echo her mother Jia Min's return home. (We see in Grandmother Jia's sorrowful welcome to Daiyu that these resonances very much hold in the novel.)

Other observers attribute the stigma attached to FSD to the broadly based Chinese tendency toward hypergamy, in which families seek to marry their daughters to families of higher status than their own. As Hsu points out, in FSD marriages, at some point, someone has married a daughter to someone of lower status. For example, Daiyu's mother marries into the Lin family, who, though perfectly respectable, are of decidedly lower status than the Jias. When girls who are not cousins marry Jia boys, the trend to hypergamy holds: the young daughter-in-law who dies in mysterious circumstances at the beginning of the novel, Qin Keqing, though from humble circumstances, marries Jia Rong, eldest son of the eldest son of the Ningguo house. With hypergamy as the goal, it is almost impossible for the Jia girls to marry well, since there are so few families of higher status (in fact, the only ones mentioned are the imperial family and those of princely status), hence, the implicit assumption that all the girls of the household are doomed to marry poorly.

The sociologist Fei Xiaotong has a more complicated explanation for why a match like that between Daiyu and Baoyu was discouraged.[36] In what seems like the digest of a novel, Fei imagines two such marriages in a row:

> The girl will be the daughter-in-law of her mother's brother's wife, who has suffered from her own mother-in-law who is the girl's mother's mother. An intimate relation of a mother towards her married daughter is usually

jealously resented by her son's wife. When the girl comes under her control, she will take her as a target for revenge.[37]

Fei Xiaotong imagines a drama of almost Jacobean involution: a family—not unlike the Jias—that so habitually inbreeds that all the women are related to one another in multiple ways, culminating in a mother-in-law who cannot wait to exact revenge on her daughter-in-law, who happens to be the granddaughter of her own erstwhile tormenter of a mother-in-law. Other anthropologists have dismissed Fei's explanation as fanciful: for example, there would be no need for the original daughter-in-law to exact revenge a generation later if she had gotten along well originally with her mother-in-law. But more fundamentally, how can a widespread disdain for this form of cousin marriage possibly be built on an emotional dynamic that might take place only after two successive FSD marriages? Nonetheless, Fei Xiaotong's imagined family suggests that cross-cousin marriage makes for complicated, involuted family trees, and that its effects linger across generations. Like a novel that includes characters from different generations, cross-cousin marriage demands a long view.

—

Among the last of the cousins to have her marriage arranged is Baoyu's own half-sister Tanchun, and he finds the prospect of her marriage particularly affecting. Not only is she a special favorite of Baoyu's, but she is also to be married off to an official family stationed far off. Baoyu extravagantly mourns Tanchun's imminent departure, listing all the girls he grew up with—Lin Daiyu, Yuanchun, Yingchun, Tanchun, Shi Xiangyun, Xue Baoqin, all his *jiemei* 姐妹, or "sisters"—and bemoaning that each has now abandoned him, whether through death or marriage. His lament concludes: "Could it be that not a single one is to be left at home? What use is it just to leave me by myself?"[38]

I have translated *jiemei* as "sisters" because the particular girl central to his lament is Baoyu's half-sister Tanchun, but elsewhere Hawkes often translates *jiemei* as "cousin." Baoyu's list includes a whole range of relations: Tanchun, his father's daughter; Daiyu, his father's sister's daughter; Yingchun, his father's brother's daughter;

and even Xue Baoqin, his mother's sister's husband's brother's daughter, who is not a blood relation and can hardly be classified as a cousin. What the commentators find most troubling is the way in which Baoyu lumps together two young women who had been considered possible matches, Daiyu and Baoqin, with his actual sisters, first Tanchun but also his paternal cousin Yingchun, with whom any union would be unthinkable incest. Effectively he equates his relations with all these girls.

Even if he calls them all sister, how can Baoyu possibly think that he bears the same relation to girls so different in consanguinity? Zhang Xinzhi writes that in this list, Baoyu has blurred together different relationships, mixing up lustful and brotherly sentiments. There is also an obvious omission, Baochai herself, once his beloved cousin and now his wife (and whom he always addresses as Bao Jiejie, or Sister Bao, both before and after his marriage). Unlike the others, she has not left, but stayed on in another capacity. If Baochai had married someone else, Baoyu would have included her in the list of *jiemei* whose departure he mourned. Cousinage transforms her from sister into wife, a troubling possibility. Just as Zhang Xinzhi suggests, forms of emotional entanglement that ought to be absolutely separate—sisters, wives, romantic attachments—are jumbled together in unseemly fashion.

To the commentator Hong Qiufan, Baoyu's wishes are not lechery, but the essence of Baoyu's susceptibility to *qing*: "He mourns the dispersal of all the sisters, which is nothing but the crazed sentiment of someone filled with sentiment (*duoqing* 多情). It's not that he wants to keep all the sisters at home to debauch at will!"[39] Hong Qiufan's defense goes without saying; nowhere are we ever led to believe that what Baoyu really longs for is a harem composed of sisters and cousins at his sexual disposal. On the other hand, what he does desire is an inequitable claim to all these girls. Baoyu's feelings for his *jiemei*—authentic and even chaste though they might be—reek of special privilege. And this is the thrust of Baochai's reproach:

> So, according to your feelings, then you want all your sisters (*jiemei*) to keep you company until they grow old, with none of them ever marrying? Maybe some of them have their own ideas. None of your other sisters has had to marry so far away, but now that your father has made up his mind,

what can you do about it? I suppose you're the only person in the world who loves your sisters? If everyone were like you, then even I wouldn't be able to keep you company.[40]

Like Zijuan before her, Baochai has done nothing but point out the obvious; finally, one of the characters makes explicit reference to a striking feature of the Jia household that more than wealth or power sets it aside from all other late imperial households. Through the course of the novel, it has seemed increasingly inexplicable that the household should have accumulated all those girl cousins of many surnames, some of no blood relation to Baoyu at all.

Baochai objects on universal grounds. If all the brothers in the world were Baoyu, then Baochai herself would not have been allowed to marry, lest she have deprived Xue Pan of a sister. If he wishes to be consistent, he has a choice to make: either he may exist in a world where sisters grow up and marry, or he may exist in a world where no one ever marries and he retains all his sisters. This is a matter not simply of a Kantian ethics but of the conservation of population. If all men retain their sisters, then there are no girls left to be wives.

One can see why much earlier in the novel the immortal Jinghuan xiangu (Hawkes' Disenchantment) called Baoyu a paragon of lustfulness: paralleling Ximen Qing's unslakable desire for ever more concubines and sexual partners, Baoyu's fantasy is to be the only brother monopolizing an increasing cohort of sisters and cousins, none of whom is ever to leave him. Since cousin marriage is one mechanism by which this group can grow, Baoyu is clearly not the only member of the family possessed by this particular fantasy. Through cross-cousin matches, the family can be perpetuated (and the losses of patriarchy compensated for) without members ever leaving, precisely through the cousins who arrive and never leave because they become wives. It is not just Baoyu's list that blurs the lines between sister and wife, but the practices of the household that seem suspect in this regard. For example, Daiyu's passage into the Jia household and into the guardianship of her maternal grandmother so morphologically mimics a bride's entry into her new family that we are not surprised to learn that the arrangement is essentially permanent.

Or consider the extremely unusual exchange of presents that accompanies Baochai's marriage to Baoyu. In traditional China, many customs governed the exchange of gifts between the bride's and groom's families, since as much as anything else it was the ritual surrounding these exchanges that legitimated marriages. But here, almost haphazardly shuttled back and forth within the same compound, the presents have shed their ritual weight: they do not welcome a bride into a new home while still acknowledging the continuing importance of her old one. Instead, since the bride has actually lived in the Jia household for years, the movement of the gifts has been emptied of content. Baoyu—now an idiot, kept in the dark as to the identity of his own bride—remarks: "Sending them from here to the garden, and then from the garden to here. Our people giving them, our people receiving them. What's the point?"[41] What is the point indeed? Wang Xifeng makes the situation clear when she gives the order about the delivery of the presents, "Don't bother going through the front door. Just go from that side-gate in the garden that used to be kept open."[42] This is no alliance between two equals where the details of the exchange honor both parties. Aunt Xue and Baochai, who need the Jias' help for Xue Pan's legal troubles, are forced to swallow any sense of resentment.

In certain ways, the Jia family treats Baochai and Daiyu as *tongyang xi* (同養媳), the brides who in the practice of "minor marriage" were brought up in households in expectation of marrying the family's sons (although they were sometimes as young as two years old when they joined the grooms' households, the actual consummation of these marriages was postponed until the girl reached sexual maturity). In Taiwan, where this practice was common and has been an important part of the anthropological literature, these girls were referred to as *simpua*, "little daughters-in-law." But across China as a whole, minor marriage was not the norm and appears to have flourished only in certain places under specific economic pressures, namely where the scarcity of women encouraged families to buy up brides early. Raising these daughters-in-law alongside their sons made sense as a hedge against inflation in a hot marriage market. But the Jias are clearly not motivated by the scarcity of women or financial anxiety.[43] Instead the cousinage that forms so much a part of the texture of the novel allows the whole household to circumvent the normal life cycle. The novel's adults do not seem subject to the universal law to which Baochai refers, the pattern of girls marrying out to join other households.

Naturally Baoyu does not understand the imperative of cousins to grow up and move away from one another; if all the child cousins live together, so, too, do many of the adult ones as well. Wang Xifeng is not an isolated case. How does Grandmother Jia develop such an intimate relationship with her daughter's child, not to mention far more distant blood relations? Shi Xiangyun, for example, is granddaughter to her brother. For Baoyu, no other matrimonial future is given serious consideration. At one point, Jia Zheng halfheartedly proposes a match for his son, one of two times in the novel a potential bride for Baoyu is mentioned who is not one of his own cousins (the first takes place very early in the novel, and Grandmother Jia shrugs that match off because her beloved boy is too young). The girl Jia Zheng mentions is the only daughter of a very wealthy and aristocratic family named Zhang, but this match is immediately dismissed by Grandmother Jia. Since Miss Zhang is an only child, her groom would have to move in with her to take care of her family's business. As Grandmother Jia says, "That won't do. Our Baoyu—we can hardly take care of him, much less that he should go somewhere else to run a household!"[44] For a young man of a family as wealthy as the Jias, joining the bride's family would have been somewhat irregular, although clearly Jia Zheng does not regard it as a mark of shame. What is important, though, is that any suggestion of parity or reciprocity can be dismissed out of hand. People from other families live with Jias, but the Jias themselves never live elsewhere.

In other words, instead of an incidental feature of the family, or a literary conceit, cousin marriage ends up setting the Jia family apart from others, as violators of the fundamental rule of exogamy by which all other families abide. Commentators make much not just of the marital misfortunes of the girl cousins, but also of the ill luck of unrelated brides brought into the household: among them, Qin Keqing, who dies young in mysterious circumstances; Xia Jingui, Xue Pan's licentious and greedy bride who eventually kills herself in her attempt to murder her husband's concubine; and the unlucky You Sanjie, Jia Lian's gentle concubine brought to her death by Wang Xifeng's jealousy. Who can end up truly joining the family other than someone already related?

There is nothing unusual in mourning the loss of a daughter to marriage; we have plenty of record of real-life premodern families responding this way. But the Jias' feelings seem misdirected in their excess. When Grandmother Jia worries about sending Tanchun so far away, Lady Wang comforts her with the example of Yingchun, whose match has turned out so disastrously. Since even being close to home is no guarantee of happiness, Lady Wang suggests, Grandmother Jia should not worry more about a granddaughter married off to a faraway family. Rather than comforting the worried grandmother with reassurances that Tanchun's cleverness and social graces will surely carry her through (as they indeed seem to later on—capable Tanchun is made of sturdier stuff than her tragic cousin), Lady Wang instead presents Grandmother Jia with Yingchun, deprived even of warm clothing and food and soon to die of this abuse (hardly a typical outcome even in the unhappiest of marriages).

Why should she bring up the worst-case scenario, and not somebody whose marital experience was happier? Lady Wang's own experience has been so different from both Yingchun's and Tanchun's. Living in her marital home, she remains surrounded by her natal relatives, her sister, her nieces, and her cousins. No wonder that the commentator Zhang Xinzhi laments: "Yingchun married off for money, and Tanchun married off for prestige—who could have a chance for some happy days!"[45] The target of both Lady Wang's and Zhang Xinzhi's lamentations is not simply the individual cases of Tanchun or Yingchun. Until the end, exogamy itself seems doomed to unhappiness in the novel.

—

Lévi-Strauss cites one of Margaret Mead's Samoan informants who is given Baoyu's choice. Would he like to turn one of his sisters into a wife, if he could? Unlike Baoyu, the informant dismisses that possibility:

> What, you would like to marry your sister! What is the matter with you anyway? Don't you want a brother-in-law? Don't you realize that if you

marry another man's sister and another man marries your sister, you will have at least two brothers-in-law, while if you marry your own sister you will have none? With whom will you hunt, with whom will you garden, whom will you go to visit?[46]

The native informant's response surprises because it hinges not on the taboo qualities of marrying one's sister but on the *necessity* for exogamy. But the Jia family is unlike this informant's family, which is formed by exogamous ties; instead, it is based on marriages that border on the incestuous. Evidently, the Samoan informant knows something that the elders who arrange Baoyu's marriage do not; in the course of maintaining and increasing the circle of *jiemei* Baoyu cherishes so much, the Jias do a dreadful job of finding new brothers-in-law for Baoyu to hunt or garden with. What ends up happening to a family practicing such a pattern of marriage?

Baochai suggests that Baoyu desires a world in which he occupies a singular, central, and ultimately unsustainable position. If everyone treated his sisters as Baoyu does, no girl would ever be allowed to marry; a world full of Baoyus could not exist. Baoyu's emotional and aesthetic world rests on denying others the privileges he enjoys, lest there be no sisters for him to marry. Baochai is quite right to point out the ultimate limitations of an ethics and family structure based on one's own singularity. Lévi-Strauss makes the same point when he writes, "The incredulous exclamation from the informant: 'So you do not want to have a brother-in-law?' provides the veritable golden rule for the state of society."[47]

Exogamy is an inviolable universal, not only the organizing principle behind any community but also the means by which one imagines one's own family as ultimately the same as all others, all subject to the same rule. Recall Lévi-Strauss' description of a family as constantly in flux, surviving only by destroying itself through exogamy. Daughters are married off, so that daughters-in-law might be brought in and new daughters produced. The Jias have been working on a different principle, that a family continues by keeping the same members in it forever. This is Baoyu's hope that he might keep his *jiemei* about him forever, or Lady Wang's life, surrounded by her natal relatives. There are reasons that other families, much as they might love their own daughters, do not act on the same impulses:

when daughters are retained, family members might continue to live together, but only at the expense of the family itself. Who are the other in-laws of equal rank to themselves who might step in to help when the Jias find themselves in trouble? There are none.

—

Jinpingmei concludes when the surviving characters make an attempt to leave their surroundings. Their efforts suggest a struggle with one of the central problems of the novel as a genre: how we position the fictional world vis-à-vis the real one. Is their world ours? And if not, how is it different? *Hongloumeng*, whose penultimate chapter is all about the difficulties of leaving the Jia manor, ends in similar fashion. In the first half of the chapter, Jia Lan and Baoyu go off to take the examinations; in the second half, Qiaojie and Ping'er flee the mansion to join Grannie Liu's family in the country. Is there anywhere for Qiaojie and Baoyu to go? Is it possible for them to break out of their world?[48] By the time Baoyu and Qiaojie attempt to leave in chapter 119, departure from this household is weighed down with significance.

Lady Wang and Baochai's grief indicates their understanding of the departure's finality; otherwise, the emotional farewell would seem wildly incommensurate with such a short journey, especially since even the sheltered Baoyu has left home on multiple occasions in the past. But this time seems different. As he leaves, he explains to his mother that his success in the examinations will not only discharge all of his debts to her but actually erase his very existence: "Once I go into the examinations, work hard on my essay, and emerge as a provincial graduate (*juren*), then you will be pleased, but also, then my life's work will have been concluded, and all of my failings will be effaced."[49] Baoyu's aim is not mere departure but total self-erasure. Just like the jade—which also cannot make a circuit of the empire and whose only movement is disappearance—Baoyu can only leave home by vanishing and entering into a different plane.

Jinpingmei's conclusion seems to argue adamantly for the impossibility of true escape. The novel turns the imperial claim of *wuwai* into something quite terrifying; the idea that there is an outside to the sordid world we have seen turns out to be illusion. (At the same time, the idea that individuals matter—as singular, unique phenomena—is shown to be an equally futile hope.) In contrast, both Baoyu and Qiaojie escape. Baoyu goes off with the scabby-headed monk, never to be seen by any member of the household again, except in a glimpse by his father. Qiaojie flees her uncles' trap to stay with Grannie Liu on her tiny farm; when she returns, she is betrothed at Grannie Liu's suggestion to a wealthy farmer's son, a boy of humble birth but of good education and solid character.

Baoyu leaves the Jia household and the human community; his examination success will never lead to an official position, and he will never again see his wife, Baochai, or meet their unborn son. In marrying the farmer's son, Qiaojie leaves just as permanently, but her departure allows her to rejoin the human community. As the cousin most related to Baoyu, Qiaojie's fate speaks to the future of the family's peculiar marital arrangements. Baoyu's double cousin, she is at once his father's brother's son's daughter and his mother's father's brother's daughter's daughter, the product of generations of cousinage. Her initial flight into the countryside with Ping'er leads to a much more permanent departure from what makes the Jias' sphere so distinctive, namely the incestuousness of cousinage and the fuzziness of the clan's borders.

Earlier, making a similar point, Tanchun sighs longingly, "I say, wouldn't it be nicer to live in a small family? Even if one had to live in a plainer style, mother and children would get to spend all their time together, and everyone would be happy."[50] Caught between the conflicting demands of her legal mother, Lady Wang, and her biological mother, Aunt Zhao, Tanchun means a family without these complexities, but surely she means other peculiarities too. Unlike other Jia girls who marry for official connections or to pay off debts, Yingchun's marriage marks a re-entry into a wholesome, anonymous life.

Qiaojie's fate has attracted a great deal of critical attention, much of it anger at the perceived inferiorities of the Gao E redaction. To the great Yu Pingbo (1900–1990), one of the founding fathers of *Xinhongxue*, the modern study of the novel, Qiaojie's reunion with her father and subsequent marriage to a farmer's son lack proper tragedy, a fault that can be laid at the feet of the 120-chapter version.[51] In place of her fate as it stands, Yu Pingbo draws on Zhen Shiyin's commentary on the "Won-Done Song" from chapter 1 to reconstruct an alternative ending (or, from Yu Pingbo's perspective, the true one, as originally conceived by Cao Xueqin). Yu Pingbo imagines another ending in which Qiaojie barely escapes being sold to a brothel before her miraculous rescue by Grannie Liu, and Qiaojie's name—巧 "fortuitous"—comes to pass.

Other critics elaborate. Many agree that in some earlier draft Qiaojie was intended to have married Grannie Liu's own grandson Ban'er. Even their names bear a connection, as these readers point out: *qiqiao ban* (七巧板) was a game in traditional China. In chapter 41, Qiaojie and Ban'er, both still small children, exchange fruits, an act that Zhiyanzhai (Hawkes' Red Inkstone, whose commentary graces the earliest manuscripts and who clearly not only knew the author but shared a host of childhood memories) invests with enormous significance: "The affections of these small children foreshadow what will happen far off."[52] Some scholars paint Qiaojie's fate before her marriage in even grimmer colors than Yu Pingbo. In these versions of the "real" ending, Grannie Liu rescues Qiaojie only after she has actually sunk into prostitution. Then, in an act of generosity, Grannie Liu marries the disgraced girl to Ban'er. In *Hongloumeng de zhen gushi* (The true story of *Hongloumeng*), the scholar Zhou Ruchang expands on these suggestions, adding a slew of improbable details: a sinister madam, aged 40 or so, who wears too much makeup, Qiaojie's harrowing escape from the merchant to whom she is sold, and a sanctimonious speech by Jia Lan, who refuses to offer Qiaojie any help.

All these "reconstructions" of what Cao Xueqin really planned—had he been solely responsible for the last 40 chapters—share certain problems. For one thing, they build enormous detail out of very scant evidence. Zhen Shiyin's commentary does not specify a character and could easily refer to the gently born, would-be Buddhist novitiate Miaoyu (Hawkes' Adamantina), who was abducted and indeed might have been sold into prostitution. The real crux, though, is that there is no particular reason to privilege hints in the opening chapters over the actual dénouement in the 120-chapter redaction—no version, in essence, more real than the one we have, Yu Pingbo's misgivings notwithstanding. Scholars like Zhou Ruchang have built whole alternative novels based largely on hints in these early poems, but because of rhymes, poems cannot be edited as easily as the plot around them. Those poems that do not square with the novel in its current state—"flies in amber" as Hawkes calls them, evidence of an earlier version—do not reveal what ought to be or what really is, but are instead hints of what might have been but isn't.

There is an additional reason to doubt that Qiaojie could only have been intended for Ban'er. Grannie Liu, though impoverished, is a remote relation of the Wangs, Qiaojie's mother's family. A marriage with Ban'er does nothing but underline the magnitude of the Jias' fall from wealth and power—no longer for them the matches between the interrelated wealthiest families of Nanjing, but still a marriage to a cousin, although one so impoverished his family never seems too far from real deprivation. Marriage with Ban'er does not allow for escape from the enclosed involution of a family tree that recognizes no equal counterparts.

When the novel poses questions about Jia exceptionalism, it sometimes suggests a world in which everyone is Baoyu or one in which all families are Jias. And indeed the novel repeatedly gestures toward Baoyu's undistinctiveness. Emissaries from the Shi family pay a visit to the Jias right after Xiangyun's wedding, and they comment on how very much the new groom resembles Baoyu: "We've seen him a number of times, and he looks just about like Second Master here."[53] Earlier, Xiangyun herself, dressed for fun in Baoyu's clothing, looks so much like him as to confuse Grandmother Jia. And then there are the novel's other gender-bending males—among them, Qin Zhong, Jiang Yuhan, and the Prince of Beijing—all of them closely resembling Baoyu.

Even his externalized token of identity, the jade, is vulnerable to doubling. Baoyu's patron, the Prince of Beijing, who has gone out of his way to take a look at Baoyu's magical jade, later gives him a peculiar present, an exact replica of the jade. (Zhang Xinzhi quite rightly asks: "Whoever heard of the logic of giving a fake jade to the real jade?") In fact, the gift seems strangely pernicious, foreshadowing some of the problems later on; when the real jade *does* disappear and a fake one turns up, the reader cannot help but remember the earlier gift and wonder whether the forgery is the old gift, somehow recirculated.

These two themes—both whether we might imagine everyone as a Jia Baoyu and whether other families exist that are commensurate to the Jias—are most pointedly brought to the fore by the presence of the Zhen family, and specifically of Zhen Baoyu. All along, we have been aware of the Zhens, another official family whose fate curiously mirrors that of the Jias; they too run afoul of the emperor, and later they too are restored to his good graces. Finally, they too have a daughter who is brought to the capital to become the emperor's concubine—and even a coddled boy named Baoyu. Much more than the Wangs, Shis, and Xues, this is one family whose status as equals to the Jias no one questions.

And yet we do not know how the Zhens stand with regard to the Jias: are they simply an equally wealthy and powerful family, whose sons the Jia girls might marry and whose daughters might enter the Jia household? Or is there instead some mysterious relationship between the two houses, so that they are cosmic mirror images of each other and not really two separate and commensurate families at all? The Zhen family—and specifically Zhen Baoyu—are critical to our understanding of the Jias' place in the world. Fundamentally, the questions hinges on whether the Zhens' resemblance to the Jias is random coincidence or cosmic design. Is the world filled with clans like the Jias, overlapping, exchanging women with one another, and so peopling the empire? Or is the Jia family unique, uncopyable, its mysterious echo clan living in Nanjing, much as the northern capital's architecture is mirrored in the southern's?

To some of the characters, the congruence between the two Baoyus is utterly meaningless. Grandmother Jia thinks nothing much of it, and to explain it, she deploys once again the logic of statistics, here as demography: "The children of great houses are brought up so solicitously and tenderly that, unless their faces are scarred or they're terribly ugly, for the most part all share the same good looks. There's nothing too strange about that."[54] Her listeners agree that the matter is one of statistical probability: "Everyone thought as big as the world was with all the noble families in the world, there must be very many with children of the same name; and a grandmother who excessively dotes on her grandson is also a common affair, nothing rare at all, so no one said anything to her."[55] The empire is so vast, in other words, that there is simply insufficient difference to go around. (Difference between individuals seems just as trivial to loyal Zijuan when she catches a glimpse of Zhen Baoyu: she wishes that her mistress Daiyu could have married him, instead of dying for love of Jia Baoyu.)

Much of this chapter has been an implicit defense of the way in which the final forty chapters—whatever their real authorship—tie together at least a few of the themes introduced in the first eighty chapters. But I conclude with a discussion of a chapter indisputably of Cao Xueqin's own hand, where the themes of this chapter converge. Much earlier, before they actually meet, our Baoyu regards his resemblance to Zhen Baoyu as something of an affront. The idea that someone shares his name and his face horrifies him. Xiangyun tries to comfort him with something like Grandmother Jia's logic. Sharing a name with someone else is not really so uncommon, she argues, listing a number of examples from history. But did these people with the same name look alike, her cousin counters? Xiangyun then proceeds to list those in history who shared the same face, Confucius and the Madman from Chu, for example. According to Xiangyun, even Baoyu's unsingularity is not particularly singular. But surely, Baoyu demands, no one who shared the same name could possibly also have shared the same face? Xiangyun then drops off to sleep, leaving Baoyu alone with his thoughts.

Baoyu begins by thinking of the Zhens and of Zhen Baoyu as a counterpart to himself and his own family, whose similarity to himself might not be so remarkable in the unfathomably large human community: "Could one say he certainly did *not* have a double? But it seemed as if he certainly *did*. Even if he certainly did, he still had not seen him with his own eyes."[56] The essence of the matter, as Baoyu recognizes, is necessity: both whether—as Xiangyun and his grandmother suggest—he must have a double, and how anyone could ever prove that he does not have a double.

After he leaves the sleeping Xiangyun and returns to his own rooms, he grows drowsy and falls asleep. In his dream, he finds himself in a garden that seems like his own Great Prospect Garden, greeted by maids who seem like the Jias' own Xiren, Yuanyang, and Ping'er. Other maids deride him as an intruder, but he continues walking toward the equivalent of his own rooms, where to his astonishment he finds a boy who looks like himself talking to the maids about the rumors of *his* double, a boy named Baoyu who lives in the capital. In the presence of this other Baoyu, our Baoyu cannot help but regard himself as the interloper and impostor.

Then our Baoyu—in the midst of a dream—hears the other Baoyu describing the dream from which he himself has just awakened, and that dream is almost exactly the dream in which our Baoyu finds himself: "I dreamt that I went to a garden in the city, and I saw some maids who scolded me and wouldn't pay me any mind. I managed to find his room, but he was asleep. It was just a husk of his body, and I could not tell where his spirit had gone."[57] As Yao Xie points out, this is a dream within a dream; our Baoyu dreams of the other Baoyu dreaming. Only the difference between the husk—literally *pi'nang*, 皮囊, a sack of skin—and the speaking Baoyu stops us from imagining dream within dream *ad infinitum*. In Baoyu's dream, he finds another boy; in that boy, there is another dream—but in that dream, there is no corresponding boy, only an opaque, impenetrable sack of skin.

A chilling image. How do we understand it? The dream works through the problem that Baoyu finds so vexing, namely, whether there is truly one Baoyu or two, whether the Zhens really exist as an independent family, or merely as an echo or reflection of the Jias. The dream rejects statistical explanation—namely, the prosaic possibility the empire is so big that another family just like the Jias must exist (a reflection on the infinitude of the world that has threaded itself through so many of the texts discussed in this book). Instead, Baoyu's dreaming mind wrestles with the second possibility, that this other family, seemingly so equivalent in status and equal in every respect, does not possess the same claim to existence as his own.

For the most part, all the traditional commentators read the additional Baoyu in the context of the novel's play on real and fake: one Baoyu must be real and the other an imitation just as their surnames indicate. After our Baoyu wakes, still confused, his maid Xiren tries to clear things up by pointing to his reflection in the mirror near his bed, as if that duplicated Baoyu were the source of all the confusion. One of the minor maids then passes on Grandmother Jia's warning that young people—with their imperfectly formed souls—should not sleep near mirrors. Hong Qiufan interprets the mirror in the same vein: "Zhen Baoyu is [our] Baoyu's reflection—as a single stroke of the pen makes clear."[58]

But the mirror is a supercharged symbol in *Hongloumeng*, with its alternative title, *Fengyue baojian* 風月寶鑒, or *A Mirror for the Romantic*.[59] The mirror is a figure for the limitations of subjectivity and the mind (unlike other texts, like *Mudan ting*, for example, in which the mind's reality is *more* real than external, shared existence). In chapter 13, Jia Rui, infatuated with his cousin-in-law Wang Xifeng, is given a magical mirror by a mysterious monk, with a warning never to flip it over. When he does and sees therein an image of the beautiful, seductive Xifeng, Jia Rui cannot help but masturbate himself to death; that mirror allows the mind, bent on pursuing illusion, to trap itself. A mirror at the foot of the bed—like the dream itself—is a figure for a dangerous solipsism.

But in this case we cannot even tell wherein illusion lies. Which Baoyu is the reflection and which the gazer? Perhaps—as we would guess from the rest of the novel, in which the Jias are the most real-seeming presences in Chinese literature, and the Zhens only phantom presences—the Zhens are nothing but a figment, and the other Baoyu is nothing more than a sack of skin.

But the dream turns our waking perspective upside-down. For the first and only time, we see what the Jias look like from the Zhens' perspective, and in this duel of subjectivities, it is *our* Baoyu who comes up empty, just as their surnames indicate. The *meipi* puts the question tersely: "Is he the butterfly, or is he Zhuangzi?"[60] At the conclusion of his dream, Zhuangzi is unsure which subjectivity has priority, that of the butterfly or that of the man; the sack of skin—or the lack of reciprocity in the two Baoyus' dreams—means that Zhuangzi's abeyance of judgment cannot apply here. The two Baoyus dream of each other, but where our Baoyu finds his counterpart, that other Baoyu finds in place of our Baoyu only an opaque sack of skin, the very absence of personhood, a frightening facsimile of a boy.

The looking glass seals it. There is a solipsist here, trapped in unreality. The problem of other minds *is* the problem of other families: to Baochai, Baoyu's fantasy of retaining all his sisters implies a world where only his desires count. Here, too, a dream that answers the question of whether the Zhens truly exist, as an equal, commensurate family, also asks whether other *minds* exist. It is not the Zhens' existence that is so vulnerable, but that of the Jias themselves.

Baoyu wakes up, shaken by his dream precisely because he intuits its import, that he is the husk, that he truly is a Jia Baoyu, a fake precious jade. It is not just his singularity but his very reality that is at risk. But what does this have to do with marriage? After all, no one ever proposes a marriage between the Zhens and the Jias. Exogamous marriage in a limited universe, when it is premised on exchange between commensurate families, forces an acceptance not just of other families but of other minds. Insofar as it compels the characters to imagine networks of other commensurate families, normative, exogamous marriage forces a person to confront the problem of other minds and families. At the novel's end, Baoyu liberates himself from the entrapments of the human mind. And in equal measure, his cousin Qiaojie makes a humble marriage that allows for a restoration of equilibrium not just with other families but also with other minds.

EPILOGUE

The Public and the Populace, or Thoughts on Genre

One aspect of the human community thematized by the novel is its very size. *Jinpingmei* and *Hongloumeng* sustain their population of characters by treading a fine line between two opposing forces—on one hand, *luanlun*, whereby the characters grow ever more inbred, and on the other hand, infinitude, in which the sheer abundance of people threatens to water down human connections to nothingness. In the character Zhen Baoyu, our Baoyu's double, both these forces are at work; in general, each force, a necessary counterpoint to the other, is just as important an organizing principle for the novel.

It is no coincidence that the long novel took off in the sixteenth century, just as the Ming empire's population did; the genre as a whole explicitly treats problems associated with large populations. Historians disagree quite a bit as to the population of the Ming at around 1600. Estimates range from 120 million to 231 million, but there is widespread consensus that the population had increased enormously, perhaps even tripling, from the beginning of the dynasty. Moreover, a much larger percentage of this increasingly mobile population lived in cities and towns, no longer in small, interrelated communities, but among strangers.

As a genre, the novel poses questions hardly conceivable in other literary forms but at the heart of making sense of this polity, now encompassing hundreds of millions of souls, the vast majority of them unknown and unknowable. Even when many characters are members of an extended family, others are introduced who are for all intents and purposes strangers. Or, as in *Jinpingmei*, the presence of true strangers stands out in relief. The genre wrestles with questions that hinge on anonymity and populousness. Does largeness in and of itself make an orthodox Confucian society impossible? Do any human relations—even families—make sense in an infinitely diluted empire? Why in a world of such size should we not conceive of ourselves simply as free agents, with no particular obligations to our fellow people? And within such a populous empire, how does one retain any individual distinctiveness?

—

In *Rouputuan* (the erotic novel translated by Hanan as *The Carnal Prayer Mat* and generally attributed to Li Yu, author of the stories discussed in Chapter 3; 1657), a young rake recalls a conversation he held with a monk years ago. The monk Gufeng warns him of the consequences of sexual promiscuity, but the young man (who goes by the sobriquet Weiyang sheng—or Master Before Midnight—rendered by Hanan as Vesperus) is sure that he himself will be an exception: "I daresay it isn't *always* like that, though. The law of the Lord of Heaven might be strict, but the way it's effected isn't always unforgiving. Although those who debauch and besmirch women and are then punished are many, those who do that and are not punished are not necessarily few."[1]

Weiyang sheng believes that his lechery will not come back to haunt him: the world is so big that debauching an individual woman or two will almost certainly have no personal consequences. In other words, the polity's size makes karmic retribution a statistical unlikelihood and hence justifies immorality. How can any single action, or any individual moral agent for that matter, be meaningful within the context of such an enormous polity? In choosing to behave immorally, one is simply playing the odds. Even if not infinite, for him, the empire's scope is so nearly infinite that he might act as if it were.

This line of thought should remind us of other moments in fiction. When in *Hongloumeng* the Jia household tries to understand how it is that Baoyu has a double, every explanation has something to do with the size of the polity, whose enormity weakens everyone's claim to individuality. Similarly we end *Jinpingmei* with no sense as to how we are to understand each character, whether as a negative exemplum or as a random sample. Where the place of the individual with regard to the polity is fixed both in short narrative and in *chuanqi*, part of the project of some long novels is precisely to ask how important any single individual is, or what an individual is, or even whether one *can* exist in a meaningfully distinctive way within the context of a densely populated empire.

One intellectual challenge that *Jinpingmei* presents—how one can keep track of the novel's enormous cast of characters—seems to be a central feature of the human brain. In research on the primate neocortex (the portion of the brain responsible for higher reasoning), the anthropologist Robin Dunbar has concluded that the size of a species' neocortex is closely related to the size of that species' social group. Compared to other mammals, primates in general possess disproportionately large neocortices; within primates, a chimpanzee (with its larger neocortex) also inhabits a proportionally larger social group than a baboon does (with its smaller neocortex). Dunbar even emerges with a ratio that predicts the size of a species' social group on the basis of its neocortical size; applied to human beings, Dunbar's number predicts a natural human social group comprising 147.8 individuals. To Dunbar, this number makes sense: "The figure of 150 seems to represent the maximum number of individuals with whom we can have a genuinely social relationship, the kind of relationship that goes with knowing who they are and how they relate to us."[2] Dunbar lists a wide variety of groups whose natural size hovers around 150 or 200: villages, army troops, subspecializations within academic disciplines, and others. I would argue that the idea of the *wulun*—that society as a whole consists of the five interlocking normative relations—seems fully comprehensible at around this number and mindboggling at any higher numbers.

Two hundred also happens to be just about the number of significant characters in *Hongloumeng* (those known only by name account for a few dozen more). But there is the suggestion of many, many more people, among others, official families briefly glimpsed, Grannie Liu's neighbors in the country, You Erjie's neighbors in the town. Too many more characters, and the mind could not cope (in fact, one can partially account for the novel's radical change in tone after chapter 80 by the imperative to pare down, rather than add, characters).

Imagine another twenty chapters inserted in the middle of *Jinpingmei*, perhaps another wife for Ximen Qing, with her relations and her contacts, and the novel's already fragile coherence would teeter and collapse.

The shorter *Rouputuan* has fewer than a score of characters, but unlike the others, *Rouputuan* explicitly treats one aspect of the problem of "social capacity." Dunbar suggests that two things happen when social groups exceed the point at which we can know all the individuals personally; these groups can split (as neighborhoods frequently do, for example, forming two where there was one), or they can create institutions and rules that take the place of personal knowledge of others. In other words, to borrow the terminology of the sociologist Ferdinand Tönnies, simple, homogeneous *Gemeinschaft* (or community) turns into *Gesellschaft* (or society) with its complicated rules, hierarchies, and external institutions. This—the world beyond one's immediate acquaintance, beyond Dunbar's number—is precisely the turn that *Rouputuan* explores.

—

Lighthearted in tone, erotic in content, *Rouputuan* might seem an odd choice to follow the two monumental masterworks *Jinpingmei* and *Hongloumeng*—and an unlikely political text. Still, the novel ties together a number of this book's concerns—namely, the connection between a population and a public, between individuals and the public sphere. *Rouputuan* is so different from *Jinpingmei* and *Hongloumeng* that we might almost consider it a different kind of novel entirely. Even though all novels of this period were circulated under pseudonyms, the status of these three was clearly quite different. Both *Jinpingmei* and *Hongloumeng* inspired sequels and had an abiding influence on the literary tradition as a whole. *Jinpingmei* created the genre of the domestic novel; *Hongloumeng* is practically singular in the depth of its impact on Chinese culture to this day. Both novels were authored by members of the elite and then passed around in manuscript among privileged circles of acquaintance for decades before being printed; in contrast, *Rouputuan* was written for profit and circulated from the beginning primarily in print. Examples from more than a dozen different editions survive, and the novel was clearly at least something of a commercial success, reaching a relatively broad audience—but its impact on literary culture was much more limited. Compared to the other two novels I discuss, *Rouputuan* is lightweight not just in length and content but also in literary impact and ambitions; hence, it differs from *Jinpingmei* and *Hongloumeng* partly in that there are no great premodern critical voices with whom to grapple. The novel's entertaining and self-congratulatory commentary was almost certainly written by Li Yu himself.

At the conclusion to the second chapter, Li Yu the commentator assigns his characters dramatic role types.[3] Hanan, too, has pointed out that certain features of the novel's structure, most particularly the way in which each chapter forms a perfectly enclosed narrative, reflect an influence from the *chuanqi* drama. Nonetheless, despite these dramatic touches, *Rouputuan*'s concerns are unmistakably novelistic and of a piece with *Jinpingmei*'s and *Hongloumeng*'s; some of these are at the core of what makes a late imperial novel set in the domestic sphere tick. *Rouputuan*'s twenty chapters make clear that a profound concern with comprehensiveness—meaning both with what makes the whole human community hang together and how (and whether) we can understand it in its entirety—is not simply a reflection of a long novel's length but is instead a concern common to the genre that can be central even to a much shorter work.

All three of these novels, even this comic pornographic novel, set up communities of characters that cannot be easily localized to within the novel and so end up suggesting qualities that must pertain to the human community at large outside the novel. It is impossible to conclude upon reading *Jinpingmei* that our own world works the way we have seen in narratives as disparate as "The Record of the Qi Sanlang Affair" and "The Pearl-Sewn Shirt": parallel families whose borders are perfectly demarcated and who perpetuate themselves through exogamy. Instead, as its conclusion hints, the novel's morass of incest and corruption cannot easily be contained within the borders of Qinghe, or the pages of the novel, and instead must leach its way into the world outside. Often almost claustrophobically enclosed within the household walls, the plot of *Jinpingmei* centers around the Ximen household. The same effect is further exaggerated in *Hongloumeng*, in which the confines of the Jia mansion almost seem to stand in for the borders of the empire itself. In contrast, *Rouputuan* concerns a young man's journeys outside the domestic sphere. It follows the adventures of the young rake Weiyang sheng as he sets out to seduce the most beautiful women in the empire. (I refer to him throughout this chapter by this sobriquet; however, after his change of heart and subsequent Buddhist conversion, he renames himself Wanshi, or Stubborn Stone.)

Weiyang sheng's sexual adventures come to an end when he hears about a courtesan who supposedly possesses nonpareil sexual techniques. When he visits her, she turns out to be his own wife, Yuxiang, whom he had earlier abandoned in favor of sexual exploration and who was then seduced and sold into prostitution. When she catches a glimpse of her own husband approaching her as a customer she hangs herself out of shame. The ensuing shock—which concerns not just his wife, but is a realization about the nature of the world—drives Weiyang sheng to repent his misdoings. On the surface so infinitely large and full of innumerable female charms, the world is actually quite the opposite. Not only is every prostitute properly someone's wife, this one happens to be his own. *Rouputuan*'s is the other version of the domestic plot: in *Hongloumeng* and *Jinpingmei* the household somehow contains the whole world. In *Rouputuan* the whole world has become one man's household.

At the same time, *Rouputuan*'s conclusion is also a perverse mirror image of the *tuanyuan*, or reunions, that bring *chuanqi* to a close. As in such a reunion, the encounter with Yuxiang does return everyone to his proper place, but in a fundamentally novelistic way the reunion also stages an encounter between the forces of infinitude and *luanlun*. Travel to parts unknown to sample the exotic leads Weiyang sheng only to a narrowly averted, semi-incestuous encounter with his own wife.

—

Both "The Pearl-Sewn Shirt" and *Rouputuan* treat practically as epigraphs the same old saw—"If I don't seduce other men's wives, my wife won't be seduced by others." The aphorism begins the story, and in the novel, it forms part of the monk's initial warning to the young scholar Weiyang sheng before he embarks on his career of debauchery.

The saying appears on first glance as a way to conceive narrowly of reciprocity (*bao*, or *baoying*) and then to provide more broadly a framework for understanding how the entire human community hangs together. Both "The Pearl-Sewn Shirt" and *Rouputuan* allow for the saying's prophecy to be fulfilled in precisely the same way. Rather than demonstrating as a general principle how ill behavior reaps its own rewards, the two protagonists are cuckolded by the very men whom they themselves had first cuckolded. One might translate this particular enactment of the aphorism as "If I don't seduce somebody's wife, then that particular somebody won't seduce mine." Chen Dalang seduces Jiang Xingge's wife, and later, after Chen Dalang's death, his wife, Ms Ping, remarries Jiang Xingge, so that Chen Dalang's punishment is a perfect mirror of his crime. In the short story, the pleasure of the ending is both mathematical and moral; each character's outcome depends on that of the others, while each is punished or rewarded in perfect reflection of his or her behavior.

Although it involves many more characters, the plot of *Rouputuan* follows a parallel course. Weiyang sheng seduces a number of women, and through a phenomenal set of coincidences, each of their husbands has sex with his wife, Yuxiang, who herself has been seduced by the first man Weiyang sheng cuckolded, Quan Laoshi, and then sold into prostitution. The novelistic trope that Plaks calls "figurative repetition" (closely related to what traditional critics called *fubi*, or foreshadowing) in which images, tropes, and characters are repeated throughout a narrative is deployed heavily here. For example, Yuxiang and Quan Laoshi's wife, Yanfang, mirror each other in multiple ways. Both become pregnant in their illicit unions and are spirited away from their husbands. But in this novel, these echoes do more than integrate and unify a narrative; they also serve as a literary means to enact perfect retribution. Consequently, Weiyang sheng's orgy with Woyun sheng's and Yiyun sheng's wives is repeated in their having sex with Weiyang sheng's own wife. These repetitions, worked into the texture of the novel, have the effect of making Weiyang sheng's ultimate punishment necessary from both a karmic and a narrative perspective.

Both "The Pearl-Sewn Shirt" and *Rouputuan* insist on a misreading of the saying "If I don't seduce other men's wives, my wife won't be seduced by others." In each text, "others" (*ren*, 人) refers to a set of individuals rather than the human community in general. Nonetheless, retribution in the two texts has an altogether different focus. When recompense takes place in the context of a twenty-chapter novel and not a *huaben*, the central problem is not mathematical. For one thing, with so many characters, the punishments stubbornly resist any kind of perfect aptness. We never do find out what happens to Woyun sheng or Yiyun sheng or their wives Ruiyun or Ruizhu, never mind Yuxiang's untold numbers of unnamed customers. The arithmetic of perfect recompense is not the point. Instead, the novel uses Weiyang sheng's punishment to question the nature of the public and how it hangs together.

Toward the end of the novel, when Weiyang sheng repents, he rephrases Gufeng's initial warning in a way that foregrounds the novel's central thematic problems: "I was over here sleeping with those people's wives; and those people were over there sleeping with my wife."[4] When Weiyang sheng makes this comment, he already knows that Woyun sheng and Yiyun sheng (whom he cuckolded) have in turn enjoyed his own wife. The reader has an even more complete picture of the "people" involved. Far from an abstraction, the men constitute a discrete list of individuals: Quan Laoshi and the brothers Woyun sheng and Yiyun sheng. The question of whether *ren* properly refers to a list of individuals or an abstraction shades into equally important matters: Are true strangers—or *ren* fully as abstractions—possible? Or is it instead the case that no real strangers can exist because all people are bound together by a finite set of connections?

—

The connection between a discrete set of individuals and a community—whether we mean a large town like Qinghe in *Jinpingmei*, or something like those gestures toward a universal empire in *Hongloumeng*—points to a question that has absorbed many social thinkers in our own day: at what point do a handful of individual coffeehouses, newspapers, and editors coalesce into a public sphere? What is it that turns individuals into a public?[5]

The general philosophical problem, of the individual's relationship to a collective, maps easily onto a literary or representational one, namely what makes the characters in a novel hang together.

The answer must have something to do with how the novel's characters relate to the social world outside the text. For example, we might consider a novel's characters merely representative, interesting as a random sampling; this seems most often the case for novels about nationhood, in which representation and citizenship are closely related, and characters must stride the line between being unmistakably *of* their nation and yet somehow randomly assigned to it. Or it might be the case that the characters are important because of their place in the cosmos (as we guess is true of Jia Baoyu, Nü Wa's reincarnated extra stone). Or, as was true in scores of historical novels, the characters' claim to significance rests on the basis of their position in the monumental sweep of imperial history. Why characters are important and why they are included in a novel determine what we think both of them and of the world outside the novel.

Honoré de Balzac, in his preface to *La Comédie humaine*, that monumental, interlocking set of ninety-five novels and stories, involving more than 2,000 characters, faces the same set of problems head-on. Balzac describes himself as a historian, attempting to record real life in France under the July Monarchy. What in Balzac's view distinguishes him from other historians is his focus, not on "the public life of nations," but on "acts of individual existence."[6] In other words, the entirety of *La Comédie humaine* emerges out of the point at which the individual and the collective converge, each fully important. Even as we are drawn to care about the pathetic Père Goriot, for example, we must still retain awareness of his relatively insignificant place, as a single individual in a canvas depicting thousands.

Chinese novels often pose questions of the infinite and wrestle with the possibility of covering all of history or all of an empire. *Rouputuan* is far from alone in featuring a long, meandering journey, over the course of which many new characters are introduced; somehow this journey makes a declaration about the state of the empire as a whole. Many novels are witness to the difficulty of ending a text possessed of such aspirations. Some fail to end in any satisfying way at all. The author of *Jinpingmei* decided that only the thorough purging of a dynastic fall could conclude the novel; *Hongloumeng* disappears within itself, returning to an inscription on a stone. In its scope, *Rouputuan* displays nothing like these ambitions, but they are part of the genre itself. One imagines that some of the authors of the very longest premodern novels must have been asking themselves: What is the longest novel that can be written? What novel can represent the greatest part of the cosmos? The short, humble *Rouputuan* treats these themes directly, as the characters seek to know the world around them in its entirety, beyond the limitations of their own birth and experience.

Ambitious narratives and genres end up being partly about human limitations, and in that way, a Chinese long novel, especially from the seventeenth century onward when these became increasingly associated with single authorial voices, can be more like the entirety of *La Comédie humaine* than any one of its component texts. I include among these eighteenth-century works like *Rulin waishi* (The scholars) and the 154-chapter *Yesou puyan* (A country codger's words of exposure). Like *La Comédie humaine*, writing a Chinese novel often consumed decades of its author's life and was the sole work associated with him. In Balzac's case, the two decades of writing culminated with his death, seemingly of exhaustion, at the age of 51, but he still had not come close to finishing the project. Even after completing almost a hundred texts, he had plans for at least forty-eight other works in the cycle. Did he think he had in him another decade or two of round-the-clock coffee consumption and writing at a pace hardly equaled in world literature? If social capacity hovers at around 150 individuals, Balzac hoped to keep track of the characters in 150 narratives. Exceeding what Dunbar judges to be the natural limitation of the human brain by many times, the project as a whole pushes up against the limits of human endurance and concentration and ultimately the human brain and even lifespan.

Balzac's goal might have had some set limits, but it was not arbitrary. His depiction of two or three or even four thousand persons (Balzac vacillates on which precisely it is) "presents a single society" and will provide some future reader a perfect and true history of the France of his time. There is even a suggestion that the *only* way to know the whole of France is to comprehend thoroughly these few thousands; after all, if Balzac planned a three-decade-long project to write a few thousand lives, any more would simply have been beyond human capacity. Human powers would be inadequate to read, never mind to write, a history of every one of the thirty-odd million Frenchmen and women of the 1830s.

But such a history would be unnecessary because, Balzac implies, the millions in France beyond that number are no longer important for their singularity. Instead, they simply repeat the pattern laid out by the thousands; it is Balzac's own few thousands who are "the salient figures of the age," in the sense not that they are the best known or most influential but that these are the types that appear in each generation, with all the variations produced by chance. In the early nineteenth century, the social thinker Charles Fourier imagined a utopian community, called a phalanx and comprising 1,620 individuals, two of each personality type, properly distributed in age, in rank, and in sex. That number closely approximates what Balzac had in mind, in the never completed *La Comédie humaine*. It is almost as if *La Comédie humaine* was meant to trace such a phalanx, an archetype of a community embedded within the larger polity (whose scope means that its full entirety necessarily remains obscure).

Both Balzac's characters and Fourier's phalanx emerge out of nascent social science, or more precisely, out of a sense of the representative and of the statistically accurate. The statistical is an important mode of knowledge in *Rouputuan* as well, related closely to the idea that whereas one person is incapable of fully knowing the whole, he can understand the representative sufficiently to guess at the whole. If we can only know a few thousand (or worse, a couple hundred), perhaps we have no need to know more: Weiyang sheng's travels do not take him far, but if they had, we are led to believe, all he would find would be a repeat of what he has already encountered—perhaps a beauty different in some incidental details from one already met, but not one fundamentally novel. Beyond a certain horizon, there is nothing new, just your own wife, passing as a stranger.

Even the match of the beauty and scholar, usually a matter of foreordained romantic destiny and absolute individuality, is instead here a matter of cold-blooded statistics. Weiyang sheng, pleased with his own looks and talents, wonders how his search for a proper match could possibly fail: "Since heaven made me such a man, then how can it not have made such a woman to be my match?" Later,

Ruizhu and Ruiyun want to know whether a woman with such prodigious sexual skills as the mysterious courtesan in the capital *can* possibly exist. All these characters pose questions—have all the types been represented? how many of certain types coexist at one time?—that Balzac himself would not have found too alien.

—

A novel's list of characters can suggest something broader and more than itself partly by claiming to be representative, but also by claiming to be a spontaneous public assembly, untainted by private interests. We can see Yuxiang's sex partners in one of two ways: a discrete list of individual men tied together through common experience or an anonymous public. *Rouputuan* is quite concerned with how individual men coalesce into something approaching a public and with the spaces where that transformation takes place. At the conclusion, when Yuxiang kills herself rather than deal with the shame of encountering her husband, her customers, enraged that their favorite courtesan is dead, form a mob and beat him up. All of them find themselves in the brothel, but that space is only incidental in bringing together these strangers. Instead it is her vagina that forms a space through which this public can imagine itself. (Jürgen Habermas's word that is usually translated as "public sphere" is *Öffentlichkeit*, which neatly suggests Yuxiang's opening, an *Öffnung* in German.)

The courtesan was one way for late Ming culture to imagine the public, much as her opposite—the chaste widow—was a way to imagine the private. But Yuxiang is not like the real-life Liu Rushi, a demimondaine mingling with high officials, a woman who has somehow transcended mere womanhood. In a world where a wife is also a *neiren* 内人, a person on the inside, Yuxiang—referred to repeatedly as "everyone's wife" (*wanren de qi* 萬人的妻)—is both private and public. She is not merely the public space that connects all these men together but at the same time the most private space, to be occupied by only one man at a time. This public sphere exists not independently of familial ties but as a perversion of them. A place that only one man has any business entering has turned into one where many might meet.

Another passage makes the construction of this particular social space even clearer. The brothers Woyun sheng and Yiyun sheng tacitly assume that even a whore like Yuxiang would still respect some taboos. Surely she would not take on two brothers as customers. They hoped, in other words, that even within the brothel some concern for the Five Normative Relations would prevail. Instead, the law of the market organizes society very differently, literally making for odd bed partners. The narrator explains just how unrealistic Woyun sheng and Yiyun sheng's hopes were:

> How could they know that prostitutes only care about money and not about the normative relations? Forget that brothers and classmates were sharing that thing under her skirt—there were even grandfathers and grandsons, fathers and sons, and it welcomed them all. That little thing turned into an ancestral temple for all three generations, so that young and old, venerable and lowly, all went in and out.[7]

The vagina is not an eighteenth-century English coffeehouse where people can read newspapers and speak freely and truthfully. Instead, the men who gang up on Weiyang sheng after Yuxiang's death act out of a sense not of public violation but of private outrage. Rather than a just punishment meted out to a murderer who has offended public morals, Weiyang sheng's beating is administered out of a misplaced feeling of individual wrong because each man thinks of Yuxiang as his own wife. The narrator makes the point even more strongly when he compares her cunt to an "ancestral temple," a place where grandfathers, fathers, and sons might all meet. That temple, properly a place where ancestors and descendants are in their right places, instead stages a grotesque degree of *luanlun*, as men sleep with their brothers' wife—or their fathers', or grandfathers'.

Other moments, too, feature perverse mirror-image versions of orthodoxy. In their first long conversation, the master thief Sai Kunlun describes his work to Weiyang sheng: despite being a criminal, he considers himself an honorable man. He goes on to say, "I have some principles. I have always lived by the 'Five Do Not Steals.'" Five Do Not Steals—*wubutou* 五不偷 in Chinese—is a visual pun for *wulun* 五倫, the Five Normative Relations. Sai Kunlun lists his guidelines for theft: "Don't steal at an unpropitious time. Or a propitious one. Don't steal from someone you know. Don't steal from someone you've already stolen from. Don't steal from someone who is undefended."[8] In suggesting a framework to organize a society, these rules in fact substitute for the Five Normative Relations.

Sai Kunlun's Five Do Not Steals intimates something that becomes more and more apparent in the novel: any understanding of the whole community can emerge only out of behavior that is, to say the least, highly heterodox. Only by transgressing all the laws that guide normative behavior can one come truly to know the world. *Wubutou*—in which theft, not ownership, organizes the material world—is one alternative. Here is another. Instead of the *wulun*'s rigid hierarchical rules that separate people from one another by enforcing proper roles and behavior, a sexual free-for-all in which everyone has relations with everyone else might lead to something approaching a free exchange of knowledge, a world with no borders at all.

If, as ought to be the case in a Confucian society, women have sex only with their husbands, and if they do not appear in public, then how can a man—even one as concupiscent as *Jinpingmei*'s Ximen Qing, never mind a man with a more run-of-the-mill sex life—ever come to know the world of women? The novel's concern with the whole public is largely with the idea of public knowledge. How is one to know the world, as a whole, beyond Dunbar's number, beyond one's coincidental encounters with individuals? Does any such comprehensive understanding—necessarily beyond one's own limitations of birth—lie outside the capacity of the human mind? The rake Weiyang sheng sets out to debauch as many women as possible, but in some respects the sexual aspect of the quest is secondary. His initial ambitions would probably not seem so alien to the real-life explorer Xu Xiake, dead only fifteen years at the time of the novel's writing. Like the geographer who traveled across the empire meticulously describing his journeys, Weiyang sheng is motivated largely by a desire to know the world in its entirety. We are back where we began, with the shaman soaring over the landscape, capturing everything in a single glance.

The author gives only a few sparse details about locations (which is not inconsistent with the rest of his oeuvre, as Li Yu—though famously peripatetic and fascinated by the abstract concepts of distance and of travel—seems notably uninterested in cultural difference). We are told the name of the monk Gufeng's mountain base and the fact that Weiyang sheng is traveling in Zhejiang province, and at the end, Yuxiang is sold in the Yuan capital. Space in the novel is not mapped out geographically, and travel is utterly unrealistic. Probably no real-life rich man in the 1650s could have led the life Weiyang sheng does. Lacking any family, he is totally unrooted to any specific location and free to travel wherever he pleases, seeking pleasure wherever he finds it. For him, the empire is mapped out not geographically but sexually, so that each new location has sexual partners and experiences associated with it. In one specific way, the novel has more than a little in common with its contemporary, the enormously influential *Banqiao zaji* (Random notes of the wooden bridge) by Yu Huai (1616–96), which recounts in loving detail the pleasure quarters in Nanjing right before the fall of the Ming. That book nostalgically revisits the historical past through the prism of the sex trade; *Rouputuan*'s guide to travel is that of a sex tourist. Understanding the whole of the empire has more to do with experiencing the full range of sexual pleasures open to a man than it does to any map or genealogy or history.

Still, a certain kind of total knowledge may not be possible. Just as Balzac cannot include every Frenchman, Weiyang sheng cannot seduce every living beauty. But again and again, that thwarted desire for total knowledge returns in different forms throughout the novel, not just in Weiyang sheng but in other characters as well. Characters question how reality differs not only from books and received wisdom but also from their own narrow experience. How can a person transcend the limitations of personal experience to see in a disinterested way the entirety of humanity? One model is that of the voyeur Sai Kunlun, who has so left the normal, subjectively limited run of man that he is no longer even sexually aroused by the sight of beautiful naked women and is instead stirred only somewhat by watching other people engaged in the sexual act.

The relative size of a man's erection, his prowess and endurance, the special techniques that a courtesan brings to the bedroom—the novel points out that all of these clichéd pornographic tropes are actually based on how we understand (or are ignorant of) the human population as a whole. If everyone lived according to the strictures of common morality, no one would have any conception at all of any of these. At the beginning of the novel, the would-be lothario Weiyang sheng has no idea how well endowed or skilled he is. What heterosexual man does? He never has a chance to compare himself to his peers. He finally comes to some awareness of how he stands with regard to others only because Sai Kunlun (whose profession has allowed him to see great numbers of aroused penises) tells him. Without such a confidant, no man can know how well endowed he is compared to others. Later, his sheltered wife, Yuxiang, is curious as to how her husband measures up to others. Do other men really have so much more endurance? Are their penises really larger than his, which is "no greater than two inches in length, and no wider than two fingers' widths"?[9] Or do the pornographic books she draws on for knowledge exaggerate the truth? She gets an inkling of how Weiyang sheng stands when she takes on a lover, the virile Quan Laoshi, but of course she finds out precisely how her husband ranks only once she becomes a prostitute, with hundreds, perhaps thousands, of clients.

One of her early clients is dissatisfied with Yuxiang and urges her madam Gu Xianniang to impart to her Gu's own special technique, which has brought her (a middle-aged prostitute of unprepossessing appearance) lasting fame and fortune. The technique—a variant of woman-on-top with a few additional salacious but vague details—can only be taught in person, which leads to some more deviant behavior. Voyeurism, as well as a certain cold-blooded attitude to the sexual act, are built into the pedagogical process. The student attends to the teacher when she is at work; the teacher coaches the student in action. The master class proceeds thus: "When she herself was doing it with a customer, she had Yuxiang stand beside them, to look on carefully, so that Xianniang could instruct her right then and there. When Yuxiang was doing it with a customer, Xianniang herself would sit there, to look on carefully, so that Xianniang could remind her of the instruction."[10]

Afterwards, Woyun sheng and Yiyun sheng, beneficiaries of Yuxiang's newly mastered technique, rhapsodize about it to each other and to their wives. The women are suspicious that the men are lying to suit their own ends, perhaps to make their wives feel inadequate. As heterosexual women, they can never know how other women rank in bed. They can only guess about women's sexuality as a whole, since that whole field of knowledge is precisely obscured to them: "I don't believe there's a woman in the world who is such a freak."[11] But unlike virtuous women, however, they do possess a native informant, their shared lover, Weiyang sheng, whose own promiscuity allows him to make an educated guess and then to test these claims in person.

—

What ways are there to conceive of the whole world of people, other than as a sexual free-for-all? There is the double whose presence is so important in *Hongloumeng*. Identical twins are born at about the same frequency in all human societies; yet although they are frequent plot devices in Western literature, twins are virtually invisible in Chinese literature. But this novel does feature twins, the daughters born to Weiyang sheng of his concubine Yanfang, formerly the wife of Quan Laoshi.

We never catch a glimpse of these twin daughters, but elsewhere in the novel there are other hints of doubled people and doubled scenarios. Doubling is, as I have written elsewhere, rife in the literature of the period, but rather than relatedness, these non-twin doubles often meditate on the qualities of a stranger, for example, on whether true strangerhood is even possible. One might consider these musings displaced twinhood, since monozygotic twins might be the only people truly beyond any accusation of strangerhood to each other. This use of the double is in marked contrast to Western literature, in which the presence of the twin poses questions about the relation between nature and nurture. The appearance of the doppelgänger in literature after Dostoyevsky points primarily to an alienation from the self, whether symbolically or literally, as a criminal.

In *Rouputuan*, doubles almost appear, fleeting suggestions of worlds parallel to our own, momentary glimpses into something larger than our own ken. Throughout late imperial fiction and drama, the figure of the stranger and that of the double are closely related; the logic—suggested over and over—is that if true strangers, unrelated by any connection or set of connections, are in fact a possibility, then it stands to reason that there would also be people who were perfect doubles as well. In some sense, an unrelated double almost seems to prove the existence of strangers.

At first, when Weiyang sheng finds himself locked in the room with the dead prostitute who has just hanged herself, he is unsure whether she is actually his wife who happens to have become a prostitute or a prostitute who happens to look like Yuxiang. Weiyang sheng suffers from a momentary variant of Capgras Syndrome, the psychiatric diagnosis for the belief that someone familiar has been replaced by an identical impostor. Those afflicted by the syndrome see the world as basically filled with strangers, no matter how familiar they might seem. Even surrounded by family and friends, sufferers would claim that these people, despite all appearances, are impostors. Some argue that the syndrome is particular to modernity itself.

Which is this woman—wife or stranger? When Weiyang sheng left her, she was a proper young Confucian matron, not only safely ensconced at home but guarded by her notoriously strict father, Tiefei daoren (Iron Door), who later told Weiyang sheng that his daughter had died of illness. So how could she be here in the brothel? But then Weiyang sheng begins to doubt Yuxiang's father; perhaps his story of her death was meant to cover up some act of shameful behavior. Once that thought crosses Weiyang sheng's mind, he is almost positive that the dead woman must be his wife.

Nonetheless, even after he thinks he has figured out who she is, he still feels the need to confirm his hunch: "He worried that there might be a person in the world who resembled his wife to that extent; so he had to test it more carefully."[12] He recalls a tiny hairless patch on her scalp, and when the corpse shares that physical trait, he begins to feel confident in its identity. But what if that tiny hairless patch had not been there and it had been someone else? After all, to all of her other customers, she *was* someone else's wife. Without that hairless patch, she might not be his woman—but she is still someone else's, whether daughter or wife. Just as Jia Baoyu learns in *Hongloumeng*, the double suggests a world of strangers behaving in parallel ways, of other families just as important as one's own, but it also suggests a world of other minds, of other subjectivities just as important as one's own.

—

The novel's conclusion also suggests the possibility of a true stranger. At the end, Weiyang sheng has become an acolyte of the monk Gufeng. Another penitent arrives to confess his own sexual wrongdoings. He says his sins are unforgivable: out of a lust for revenge, he seduced the wife of the man who stole away his own wife. But even that did not slake his desire for vengeance; after the woman ran away with him, he then betrayed her and sold her into prostitution. The confession, of course, perfectly corresponds to Yuxiang's sorry tale:

> Weiyang sheng's heart was stirred. He said, "May I ask you, brother, what was the name of the woman whom you kidnapped and sold? Whose wife was she? Whose daughter was she? Where is she now?" The monk said, "She was the wife of Weiyang sheng and the daughter of Tiefei daoren. Her own name was Yuxiang. Her maidservant was called Ruyi, and now she is in the capital receiving customers. Do you know her?"[13]

This man is Quan Laoshi, and the two men are of course tied together by the same woman, Weiyang sheng's wife, Yuxiang. The men identify themselves; they embrace and forgive each other. With that, this particular karmic debt has been paid in full.

But the moment before the mutual identification is what interests me. Here is the possibility of another doppelgänger, not a physical twin, but someone who has had an identical set of experiences. What if this man had not been Quan Laoshi, but instead someone else entirely? Other men have been known to seduce and ruin their enemies' wives. Just like the unnamed mob that attacks Weiyang sheng, the moment before Quan Laoshi identifies himself suggests a society in which unknown others are behaving in parallel with oneself, identical in experience, but not the same individual. That double stands in as a means to imagine strangers in a society—a public beyond one's own experience, to be known demographically, rather than individually. When someone from one set of individuals (the complete number of types, and so the full range of human difference) encounters his equivalent in another set, that meeting can serve as one model for universality, Balzac's thousands repeated again and again to create France's millions. The novel's conclusion allows us to sustain two models, the world not only as a finite community of individuals, linked by a small set of connections, but also as a potentially infinite set of individuals, types behaving in parallel ways. The double—the deferred twin, the misidentified corpse—hints at all of this.

—

Even at the end of the novel, Weiyang sheng, so interested in statistics, does not waste much energy wondering about the odds of such an unusual punishment. Instead, he focuses on the disproportionate nature of his punishment.

> But now, when I add it up, the women I've slept with are no more than five or six. My own wife has done this thing where the men she's slept with, on the high end, we're talking thousands, on the low end, at least hundreds—definitely more than a few tens. Could there ever have been a higher rate of interest than this one?[14]

Weiyang sheng's language makes it seem as if he has been engaged not in adultery but in theft of property, just like his friend the burglar Sai Kunlun. When individual women are wrongfully taken, either seduced or kidnapped, men then accrue a debt that can be paid back only in kind, in the currency of their own women's virtue. The parallel between sexual thievery and thievery of goods only works if, as the novel suggests, men are sexual agents and women are essentially objects that are acted on.

Nowhere is this idea more shockingly expressed in the novel than in the fate of Weiyang sheng's only relatives by blood, the twin daughters born of his mistress Yanfang, Quan Laoshi's wife. Gufeng explains to Weiyang sheng that punishment for his sexual indiscretion will continue to be inflicted on the women of his household, no matter how innocent they might appear. In other words, the baby girls will one day exact a sexual revenge on their father—whether through incest, adultery, or prostitution—so that their very existence is a threat hanging over his head, a ticking time bomb. In his despair, Weiyang sheng chillingly refers to his daughters—the last of a line, whose survival would surely be a matter of supreme importance in another narrative—not as people, but as *xuekuai*, "blocks of blood."[15] They are things of flesh and blood that only appear to be his daughters.

In *Yu chanshi cuixiang yimeng* (Zen master Yutong), the second of the four plays in Xu Wei's highly influential *Sisheng yuan* (Four cries of the gibbon; ~1558), a monk takes revenge on a family by being reincarnated as a promiscuous daughter who ruins her family from within. In that play, female promiscuity seems to have the ability to transform a family member into a vessel for a fearsome alien force. More accurately, perhaps, female promiscuity does not radically transform but only reveals what is already the case. It is not that some daughters become strangers through their behavior, but that all daughters are fundamentally always alien. Weiyang sheng's interpretation of his daughters' place is simply the nature of all daughters brought to a natural conclusion. If, once married, daughters are strangers to their natal families, then even as children they are nothing but future aliens. What distinguishes Weiyang sheng's daughters from those of other people is not only that they are not true members of *his* family, but that he stops regarding them as part of the human family.

Weiyang sheng responds to the monk's warnings by repeatedly threatening to kill his children. On Buddhist grounds, Gufeng forbids him, at the same time that Gufeng comes close to exculpating such a murder: "Those two children aren't your daughters. After seeing how you sinned, the Heavenly Lord sent them down to pay back your debt." Eventually, Weiyang sheng's hopes for total forgiveness are realized when the two babies die—or perhaps more accurately, are essentially erased from existence. Sai Kunlun reports on how it happened:

> Those two girls didn't have smallpox or a respiratory infection. Just sleeping in their beds they died together. The night before they died, the two wet nurses both dreamed that they heard someone calling out, 'The family tab has been wiped clean. You're not needed anymore! Come back with me.' By the time they'd woken and touched the children, it was too late.[16]

Compare this conclusion to that of *Jinpingmei* in which characters never disappear; even after death, they are reincarnated, or their behavior is echoed by new characters. At *Rouputuan*'s conclusion, the root of deviant behavior has been extirpated. Weiyang sheng and Quan Laoshi—who each cuckolding the other had been intractable enemies—are now brought together as friends, but how can their enmity come to an end so long as the women are still around? The only way is for all the women involved to vanish: Yuxiang hangs herself; Sai Kunlun kills Yanfang and her lover; the baby daughters born of an adulterous union practically evaporate. Novels, as I have suggested, are drawn to theories of human nature—what a person really is, what a person's place is. Here, all women are aliens to the human community, nothing more than chits to mark value that passes through men's hands. Women—as lovers, as wives, even as descendants—turn out to be superfluous.

But it is not simply the gendered female body that can so easily be removed from the picture. Rather than being *rendao* 人道—"the way of humanity," central to and inseparable from human existence—sex itself by the end of the novel has been excised from human experience, and the only individuals left are sexless males. Human genitals in the novel are portable and detachable, like Gufeng's leather sack which is really a kind of displaced set of genitals. Long ago, when Gufeng left his life as a wealthy scholar to become a penniless monk, "he sewed a big leather sack and filled it with his wooden fish drum and sutras."[17] Like Yuxiang's vagina, it is capacious. Gufeng sighs when his first efforts to convert Weiyang sheng fail: "If I don't put him into my leather sack, he would certainly make his way into inner quarters and brew up some sexual mischief. Who knows how many women would be harmed by him?"[18] Unless the walking phallus that is Weiyang sheng is contained by the sack, he will enter other vaginas where he doesn't belong. At the same time, the sack is also a phallus of sorts. After Weiyang sheng rejects his efforts to save him, Gufeng is entirely dejected. He hangs the leather sack up on a tree and vows not to remove it until Weiyang sheng returns. Three years later, the sack has turned into something resembling an erection: "Not only had it not rotted at all, it had instead gotten hard and distended."[19] Both penis and vagina, the bag is offered to Gufeng, at which point it disappears, no longer important to the plot of the novel.

"Leather sack," or *pibudai* 皮布袋, might just as easily be rendered "skin sack." In *Hongloumeng*, when Baoyu dreams of the other Baoyu, he overhears his double making reference to *his* double, nothing but a *pi'nang*, a sack of skin; the dream, subjectivity without material, meets its match in the *pi'nang*, material without subjectivity. The Carnal Prayer Mat of the title refers to a presumably female body with nothing that marks it as an individual, on whom the male mind's progress toward enlightenment is sped as he copulates with it. The mat and the leather sack are both shells, human bodies emptied of content.

The disappearance of a literal set of genitals marks the end of the novel. Earlier, in the novel's most famous scene, Weiyang sheng—disgusted with the meagerness of his sexual endowment—undergoes a penis transplant, in which his is fused with that of a dog, producing a giant organ. That scene is paralleled by another at the end of the novel, when still disturbed by sexual desire even after enlightenment, Weiyang sheng castrates himself in a fit of self-loathing. As he does so, he addresses the penis as if it were an external object, "that root of evil."[20] Although he dreads the agony of castration, chopping the penis off turns out to be strangely painless. Genitals are attached and detached with relative ease. One might, in other words, conceive of the human subject as male, but essentially sexless, with a penis that is to be enlarged and detached at will.

This human body—unlike the mutilated one of a eunuch—has lost its genitals, but nothing essential to it. And similarly, at novel's end, families are not restored. Nor are they even destroyed with the hope that they will be recreated; in Weiyang sheng's case, his daughters gone, his penis removed, no family can ever be born of him. Instead, the elimination of the women (and Weiyang sheng's castration) allows for the family to be replaced by an asexual communion among the male characters—Gufeng, Sai Kunlun, Quan Laoshi, Weiyang sheng. Why does the novel choose such an unusual endpoint, not the family, not the state, nor any combination of the two? Instead, we conclude with a community of coolheaded subjectivities, of male subjects stripped of everything, even their very maleness.

—

Here, where the open-endedness of the novel meets the epistemological questionings of the age, the concerns of a historical moment and of a genre dovetail. (The novel, first circulated thirteen years after the fall of Beijing, seems in its tenor and themes mostly still to be a late Ming work.) Historians have noted that by the end of the Ming there was a widespread sense that earlier ways of making sense of knowledge—we might call them modes of coherence—no longer seemed to hold.

Weiyang sheng's own particular desire for knowledge (which expresses itself as the drive to sexual omniscience) emerges out of a sense of belatedness in which older forms of mastery are treated only ironically. When Gufeng asks Weiyang sheng about his ambitions, the young man says that under different circumstances he would have hoped for official success. In yet another attempt to grasp the whole of the situation through statistics and yet another dig at the way largeness eats away at Confucian orthodoxy, Weiyang sheng says that he gave up on that path because the odds of success are too daunting: "Those who get it are few, and those who don't are many."[21] A completist faith in classical knowledge—in which the literary, the ethical, and the philosophical are one, and simultaneous perfection in all these realms is possible—has been supplanted by a cold-blooded demographic assessment of one's odds of success. If that faith in classical learning had remained alive, the examination system would have provided coherence to Weiyang sheng's ambitions; nonetheless, even in its absence, he still fetishizes an elusive sense of completeness.

Weiyang sheng ultimately chooses an underground society of secret knowers. But he first rejects another career path, that of the author. Weiyang sheng concedes the real authority of writers but says that most men in Li Yu's position are nothing but fakers: "To be a true famous scholar (*mingshi* 名士), one needs to have read all the unusual books in the world, to have met all the unusual scholars of the world, and to travel to all the famous mountains of the world—and then to retire to one's own quarters to write and pass it on to the next generations."[22] Simply making a living off his pen would not be enough for Weiyang sheng, who values totality in all ambitions, even those he eschews. Whether it is the orthodox claims made by the examination system, a lothario's desire to know all women, or a writer's complete mastery of private life, the ethos of completeness underlies the novel.

The urbane Li Yu never seems seriously to have pursued a civil service career, but he still declaimed with matter-of-fact authority on the best foods, the best furniture, the best art, the best performances of opera, the best books. Some of his contemporaries who also never found success in the examination system nonetheless compiled annotated anthologies of successful examination essays that pronounced *ex cathedra* on their merits and failings. Who gave these men such authority, when the state had ruled their essays inadequate? In the late sixteenth century, a new class of *littérateurs* emerged, of whom Li Yu was one of the most famous: a public figure whose fame was established and perpetuated in print, a virtual realm in which writers commanded an authority that previously had been reserved for officials alone.[23]

Even as he disdains most writers as purveyors of fake knowledge, Weiyang sheng's own chosen field—total sexual knowledge, that is—possesses built-in limitations. At one point, Weiyang sheng wants to know how many women enjoy sex and how many have orgasms. Drawing on his unique experiences, his friend the thief Sai Kunlun, who sneaks into people's houses and observes them without their knowing, gives him definitive answers to these and other pressing questions (in answer to both questions, the vast majority do). Sai Kunlun describes the cries made by women in the throes of passion, some fake, some real, indistinguishable to their sexual partners, who are themselves not in a state to evaluate these cries objectively. As Sai Kunlun explains, "Only I can tell them apart clearly—in contrast, the men having sex don't know."[24] In other words, even the impossible feat of having sex with every woman in the world would not open up all knowledge to an individual man; the voyeur is singularly privileged with this information. Without him, such knowledge can never be achieved or circulated: one sexual partner is necessarily too engrossed to know, and the other has no inclination to share (and no chance to compare her experiences with those of her peers). Not only does Sai Kunlun know more than others, but his knowledge has also rendered him detached and objective about sex: naked women no longer have the effect of arousing him.

Sai Kunlun and the narrator, both privy to the sexual and the private, both possessed of inhuman knowledge, are parallel figures. Yuxiang's teacher, Gu Xianniang, who in the midst of the sex act calmly guides her pupil's attention, is related to them as well. *Rouputuan* valorizes this position, detached from human experience and hence all-seeing and all-understanding, unlike those bound by limited experience and prudery. We might call it the place of the writer.

One rhetorical pattern appears again and again in the novel: sex scenes are interrupted by long explanations. Take chapter 3, for example, which another novel would have turned into a straightforward erotic scene. Weiyang sheng stirs up his bride Yuxiang's passions by showing her a sex manual, and the two then have sex. In describing how Weiyang sheng removes his wife's clothing only *after* penetrating her, the narrator goes on at some length to explain this unconventional sequence. An experienced lover, Weiyang sheng does so to forestall any fake coyness. The commentator (also Li Yu, of course) remarks that these clever discursive interruptions to narrative flow are utterly characteristic of the novel and distinctive of the authorial voice:

> Only the writer of this book is able to keep calm amid the panic and cool amid the heat. In the middle of every tense passage of narrative, he will insert a piece of leisurely discourse, posing and answering his questions in an orderly way. . . . When the author has finished his discussion . . . one observes that his writing dovetails perfectly with what has gone before.[25]

These moments—when the narrator hits pause on the unfolding x-rated movie, as it were—seem always to involve the dispensing of knowledge: proper sex terminology, analysis of action, but above all else, demographics (as in how common or not any given behavior is in the population as a whole). For an erotic novel, there is something surprisingly distinctly restrained and detached about this repeated pattern. Rather than coming out of the blue, Weiyang sheng's conversion and castration at the end of the novel—or his transformation from a sexual participant to a permanently dispassionate observer—is simply the triumph of the narrator's voice.

The commentator hints at a comparison between the narrator and all the other characters who pursue knowledge, except that of course the narrator's knowledge (and his supremely dispassionate attitude toward all he knows) trumps that of all others. In other words, where we arrive at the end, the community of disembodied, objective men, hardly should surprise. The right kind of community, not the gang of hooligans at the brothel but the desexed men at the conclusion, takes place on a virtual level, without sex and without reproduction; with men like these, intercourse refers to discourse and exchange of knowledge.

The voice of the narrator, utterly individual in its appeal, urbane, all-seeing, all knowledgeable, holds secrets to information that are exclusively his, but that he will share, at the right price. This sort of knowledge belongs to the marketplace, not the examination hall or the yamen. In a novel full of theories of population, one of the commentator's critiques gives us another:

> This novel is most inviting to read. I know that once it is finished, all the world without exception will buy it and read it. Those who don't read it and buy it will only be those moralists. Of course, all real moralists will buy and read it. Only the fake ones who use the appearance of righteousness to deceive people will not dare to buy the book and read it. Or one could say, although they daren't buy it on their own, they might send someone else to buy it for them; even if they daren't read it in the open, they might well read it secretly.[26]

This is, of course, an advertisement, but one that also includes a definition of everyone—*tian* or *tianxia* (天下), that concept on which so much hinges in the novel and in the literature of the period as a whole. And what is *tianxia*? It ultimately refers to nothing more or less than people who will buy this novel and enjoy it, whether openly or on the sly. The world of everyone, however it is properly conceived, whether as community, society, or empire, has turned into a marketplace. The public has blurred into a readership that in turn is unmistakably part of a market.

Fredric Jameson argues that the money economy is antithetical to genre, inexorably wearing it down to brand-name specifications, a pale shadow of its former self. The end product sold here is in fact the voice of the narrator, cool and detached and all-knowing. But this particular thematizing of readership, in which participating in discussion as a reader is the ideal connection that human beings can make with one another, can take place only in the novel, and perhaps only in a novel like this one whose claims vis-à-vis the tradition are modest. Open-ended and messy, the novel finds another way to think of the human community, as a virtual plane with reader and writer the only people left, after the claims of family and state have dwindled down to nothing.

Reference Matter

Character List

Note: The entries are ordered letter by letter, ignoring syllable and word breaks with the exception of personal names, which are grouped first by surname and then ordered by given name.

Aina 艾衲

Bai Juanjuan 白娟娟
Ban'er 板兒
Banqiao zaji 板橋雜記
bao 報
Bao Jiejie 寶姐姐
Bao Yong 包勇
"Baowu sheng zhuan" 寶婺生傳
baoying 報應
bazi 八字
Beijing wang (Prince of Beijing) 北靜王
Beishu xuyan 北墅緒言
benye 本業
bunuo 卜儺
buzhong xiangyu 不中相與

Cai Jing 蔡京
Cai Yuanpei 蔡元培
caizi jiaren 才子佳人
Cao Baoer 曹保兒
Cao Xueqin 曹雪芹
Changsheng dian 長生殿
Chen Chen 陳忱
Chen Dalang 陳大郎
Chen Ding 陳鼎
Chen Jingji 陳敬濟
Chen Zilong 陳子龍
cheng 成
Cheng San 程三
chenghu 稱呼
Chibei outan 池北偶談
Chongzhen 崇禎
chuanqi 傳奇
Chuci 楚辭
cihua 詞話
"Cike liezhuan" 刺客列傳

da 達
Da an 大安
Daian 玳安
dan 旦
"Da'nan" 大男
Dang zijia gurou 當自家骨肉
Daqing tongli 大清通禮
Daxue 大學
dianguan 店官
Ding Yaokang 丁耀亢
Diyi qishu 第一奇書

Dongjing 東京
Dongqing shu 冬青樹
Doupeng xianhua 豆棚閒話
Du Bao 杜寶
Du Jingshan 杜景山
Du Liniang 杜麗娘
duanfa 短髮
dufa 讀法
Dugu Xiashu 獨孤遐叔

erchen 二臣
Erpai 二拍

fan 番
Fan Chengmo 范承謨
Fang Xiaoru 方孝孺
feifei 狒狒
Feng Menglong 馮夢龍
Feng Ziying 馮紫英
Fenggu 鳳姑
Fengyue baojian 風月寶鑑
fu 賦
fubi 伏筆
Fushe 復社
futao qisan 夫逃妻散
Fu Xi 伏羲
fuzi bugu 父子不顧

Gao E 高鄂
Gao Lian 高濂
Gaozong 高宗
gegan 割肝
gegu 割股
genben 根本
gongyang 供養
Gu Xianniang 顧顯娘
Gu Yanwu 顧炎武
Guangzhi yi 廣志繹
Gufeng 孤峰
Gui Zhuang 歸莊
guisu 歸宿
Gujin xiaoshuo 古今小說
guo 過
Guo Ju 郭巨
Guo Xiang 郭象
gutou shang zheng chulai 骨頭上掙出來

Han Aijie 韓愛姐
Han Daoguo 韓道國
He San 何三
Hong Qiufan 洪秋蕃
Hong Sheng 洪昇
Hongloumeng 紅樓夢
Hu Shi 胡適
Hu Tianyou 胡天遊
Hu Yinglin 胡應麟
Hua Xiren 花襲人
Hua Zixu 花子虛
huaben 話本
huafen liangtou 話分兩頭
Huang Bian 黃汴
Huang Xiangjian 黃向堅
Huangyu quantu 皇輿全圖
Huizong 徽宗
husun 猢猻

Ji Yun 紀昀
jia (false) 假
Jia (surname) 賈
Jia Baoyu 賈寶玉
Jia Daihua 賈代化
Jia Fan 賈範
Jia Hua 賈化
Jia Huan 賈環
Jia Lan 賈蘭
Jia Lian 賈璉
Jia Min 賈敏
Jia Qiaojie 賈巧姐
Jia Rong 賈蓉

Jia She 賈赦
Jia Tanchun 賈探春
Jia Xichun 賈惜春
Jia Yingchun 賈迎春
Jia Yuanchun 賈元春
Jia Yucun 賈雨村
Jia Yun 賈芸
Jia Zheng 賈政
Jiandeng xinhua 剪燈新話
Jiang Shiquan 蔣士銓
Jiang Xingge 蔣興哥
Jiaohong ji 嬌紅記
jiayu cunhua 假語村話
jiefu 節婦
jiemei 姐妹
Jiling 吉零
Jin Ding 金定
Jinghuan xiangu 警幻仙姑
Jinghua yuan 鏡花緣
Jingshi tongyan 警世通言
Jingzhong qi 精忠旗
Jinling 金陵
Jinpingmei 金瓶梅
Jinpingmei cihua 金瓶梅詞話
Jinpingmei dufa 金瓶梅讀法
jinzhong baoguo 盡忠報國
Jiuzhou 九州
Juqizi 菊畦子
juren 舉人

Kangxi 康熙
kaozheng 考證
Kongkong daoren 空空道人

Langxian 浪仙
Lechang 樂昌
Leng Zixing 冷子興
Li An 李安
Li Guijie 李桂姐
Li Jili 黎季犁
Li Ping'er 李瓶兒
Li Qi 李綺
Li Shengshan 李盛山
Li Wan 李紈
Li Wen 李紋
Li Yu 李漁
Li Yu 李玉
Li Zhi 李贄
liang 兩
Liangui 蓮貴
Liangshan 梁山
Liaozhai zhiyi 聊齋誌異
Lienü zhuan 烈女傳
Lin Daiyu 林黛玉
Lin Taitai 林太太
Lin Zhixiao 林之孝
Linchuan pai 臨川派
Ling Mengchu 陵濛初
Liu Cuicui 劉翠翠
Liu Laolao (Grannie Liu) 劉姥姥
"Liu xing" 劉姓
liyi 禮義
Lu Ciyun 陸次雲
Lu Shusheng 陸樹聲
luanlun 亂倫

man 蠻
Mao Qiling 毛奇齡
meipi 眉批
Meng Chengshun 孟稱舜
Miaoyu 妙玉
Mingwu 明悟
Mo Hao 莫昊
Mo Huaigu 莫懷古
Mudan ting 牡丹亭

nanxi 南戲
neiren 内人
Ni Er 倪二

niangjia 娘家
Ningguo fu 寧國府
Nü Wa 女媧

Paian jingqi 拍案驚奇
Pan Jinlian 潘金蓮
Pang Chunmei 龐春梅
pengyou 朋友
pibudai 皮布袋
Pima daixiao 披麻戴孝
pi'nang 皮囊
ping 平
Ping'er 平兒
Ping shi (Ms Ping) 平氏
Pu Songling 蒲松齡
Pujing 普靜

Qi Sanlang 戚三郎
qian 錢
Qiao tuanyuan 巧團圓
Qin Gui 秦檜
Qin Keqing 秦可卿
Qin Shifang 秦世芳
Qin Shiliang 秦世良
qing 情
Qinghe 清河
Qingping shantang huaben 清平山堂話本
Qingwen 晴雯
Qingzhong pu 清忠譜
qin shang jia qing 親上加親
qiqiao 七巧
qiqiao ban 七巧板
Qiu Jun 邱濬
Qiu Huzi 秋胡子
Qiu Weiping 邱維屏
Qu You 瞿佑
Quan Laoshi 權老實

rendao 人道
renlun 人倫
Rongguo fu 榮國府
Rouputuan 肉蒲團
ru 入
Ruan Dacheng 阮大鋮
Ruiyun 瑞雲
Ruizhu 瑞珠
Rulin waishi 儒林外史

Sai Kunlun 賽崑崙
Sanfoqi 三佛齊
Sanyan 三言
Shangcheng yilan 商程一覽
Shen Chun 申純
sheng 生
shengqi 聲氣
Shi Kefa 史可法
Shi Runzhang 施閏章
Shi Xiangyun 史湘雲
Shi diantou 石點頭
Shier lou 十二樓
Shitou daizi 石頭呆子
Shuangzhong ji 雙忠記
Shuihu houzhuan 水滸後傳
Shuihu zhuan 水滸傳
Shunzhi 順治
"Shu Qi Sanlang shi" 書戚三郎事
Siku quanshu 四庫全書
Sima Qian 司馬遷
Sisheng yuan 四聲猿
Suishi yiwen 隋史遺聞
suodi fa 縮地法
suoyin 索隱
Song Maocheng 宋懋澄
Sun Shaozu 孫紹祖
Sun Xue'e 孫雪娥

tanci 彈詞
Tang Xianzu 湯顯祖

Tao Qian 陶潛
Taohua shan 桃花扇
"Taohua yuan ji" 桃花源記
tianxia 天下
Tiefei daoren 鐵扉道人
Tihong ji 題紅記
titong 體統
tongyang xi 同養媳
Tusi nümeng 兔絲女夢
tuanyuan 團圓

waifan de guiju 外藩的規矩
waizhuan yeshi 外傳野史
Wanchou qu 萬愁曲
Wanli yuan 萬里緣
wanren de qi 萬人的妻
Wanshi 頑石
Wang Chaofeng 汪朝奉
Wang Furen (Lady Wang) 王夫人
Wang Jide 王繼德
Wang Jiaoniang 王嬌娘
Wang Jinnu 王進奴
Wang Liu'er 王六兒
Wang Ren 王仁
Wang Sanguan 王三官
Wang Sanqiao 王三巧
Wang Shixing 王士性
Wang Shizhen 王士禎
Wang Xifeng 王熙鳳
Wang Ziteng 王子騰
Wei Zhongxian 魏忠賢
Weiyang sheng 未央生
Wen Shi 文實
Wen Tianxiang 文天祥
Woyun sheng 臥雲生
wu 戊
Wu Da 武大
Wu Jie 吳傑
Wu Song 武松
Wu Ying'er 武迎兒
Wu Yueniang 吳月娘
wulun 五倫
Wulun quanbei 五倫全備
wusha 誤殺
Wusheng xi 無聲戲
wuwai 無外
"Wuzhong xiaozi" 吳中孝子

Xi Chenglie 奚成列
Xia Jingui 夏金桂
xianzheng 顯証
xiao 孝
Xiaoyu 小玉
xifu de er 媳婦的兒
Xihu erji 西湖二集
Xilou ji 西樓記
Ximen Guan'ge 西門官哥
Ximen Qing 西門慶
Ximen Xiaoge 西門孝哥
Xing furen (Lady Xing) 邢夫人
Xing Xiuyan 邢岫煙
xinghong 猩紅
Xingmeng pianyan 醒夢駢言
xingrong 猩絨
Xingshi hengyan 醒世恆言
xingxing (ape) 猩猩
xingxing (lucid) 惺惺
Xinhongxue 新紅學
xiuxiang 繡像
Xixiang ji 西廂記
Xu Aji 徐阿寄
Xu Hongzu 徐弘祖
Xu Jifang 許季芳
Xu Wei 徐渭
Xu Xiake 徐霞客
Xu Xin 徐信
Xue Baochai 薛寶釵
Xue Baoqin 薛寶琴
Xue Pan 薛蟠

Xue Yima (Aunt Xue) 薛姨媽
xuekuai 血塊
Xu Jinpingmei 續金瓶梅
xunfu 殉父
xushu 續書

Yan Shifan 嚴世蕃
Yan Song 嚴嵩
Yan Yuan 嚴元
Yanfang 艷芳
yang 養
Yang Baiwan (Millionaire Yang) 楊白萬
Yang Yuhuan 楊玉環
yanyu xiangfu 言語相符
Yanzi jian 燕子箋
Yao Dizhu 姚滴珠
Yao Ji 姚繼
Yao Maoliang 姚茂良
Yao Xie 姚燮
yaonü 妖女
yeshi 野史
Yesou puyan 野叟曝言
Yijing 易經
Yin Xiaolou 尹小樓
yinguo 因果
yinguo baoying 因果報應
yinyang 陰陽
yinyuan 因緣
Yipeng xue 一捧雪
yiwang 一望
Yiyun sheng 倚雲生
Yongfu si 永福寺
Yongzheng 雍正
You Erjie 尤二姐
You Ruilang 尤瑞郎
You Ruiniang 尤瑞娘
You Sanjie 尤三姐
Yu Huai 于懷
Yu Juan 于鵑
Yu Pingbo 俞平伯
Yuan Yuling 袁于令
Yuanyang 鴛鴦
yuanzu 遠族
Yu chanshi cuixiang yimeng 玉禪師翠鄉一夢
Yue Fei 岳飛
Yuewei caotang biji 閱微草堂筆記
Yun Lishou 雲理守
Yuxiang 玉香
Yuzan ji 玉簪記

zaju 雜劇
Zhang Hua 張華
Zhang Sheng 張勝
Zhang Xinzhi 張新之
Zhang Zhupo 張竹坡
zhanghui xiaoshuo 章回小說
Zhao 趙
Zhao Yiniang (Aunt Zhao) 趙姨娘
zhaoluo 著落
Zhaoshi bei 照世杯
"Zhao xiaozi zhuan" 趙孝子傳
zhen (true) 眞
Zhen (surname) 甄
Zhen Baoyu 甄寶玉
Zhen Shiyin 甄士隱
Zheng Yue'e 鄭月娥
zhi 至
zhiguai 志怪
Zhiyanzhai 脂硯齋
zhonghua titong 中華體統
Zhou Di 周迪
Zhou Lianggong 周亮工
Zhou Rui 周瑞
Zhou Shunchang 周順昌
Zhu 朱
Zhu Chunhui 朱春輝

Zhu Donglao 祝東老
Zhuangzi 莊子
Zhui baiqiu 綴白裘
Zhuoyuan ting zhu 酌元亭主
"Zhushan" 珠衫
Zhuzhu 朮朮
Zijuan 紫鵑
Zong Erniang 宗二娘
Zuixing shi 醉醒石
Zuozhuan 左傳

Notes

Chapter 1

EPIGRAPH: Jorge Luis Borges, *Collected Fictions*, trans. Andrew Hurley (New York: Viking, 1998), p. 325.

1. Pagden, *Lords of All the World*, p. 22.

2. Li Yu, *Qingzhong pu*, p. 86. Unless otherwise noted, all translations are mine. The playwright Li Yu (ca. 1591–ca. 1671; *zi* Xuanyu) should not be confused with his contemporary Li Yu (1611–80; *zi* Liweng), famous for his plays, short stories, criticism, and essays. Writings by Li Xuanyu feature in this chapter; writings by Li Liweng appear in many other chapters. I have differentiated the two by referring to the Suzhou playwright Li Yu by his *zi*, Xuanyu, and the belle-lettrist as Li Yu.

3. Hong Sheng, *Changsheng dian*, p. 236.

4. Ibid., p. 236.

5. In his introduction to *Zhui baiqiu*, an eighteenth-century anthology of *chuanqi*, the May Fourth intellectual Hu Shi expressed a common modern attitude when he wrote: "*Chuanqi* are long and bloated. Their length shows that their authors knew nothing about stagecraft. *Zaju* are just right in length; their brevity shows that they were properly edited. Selecting four or five acts from the greatest *chuanqi* reduces them to the scale of *zaju* and improves them."

6. Anderson, *Imagined Communities*, p. 24.

7. The state zealously guarded control over the calendar. Calendars lacking an official seal were considered to have been forged, a crime to be punished by beheading; a handsome fifty taels of silver was rewarded to informants for bringing such offenses to the authorities' notice.

8. Laura Hostetler (*Qing Colonial Enterprise*, p. 4) describes how central to the imperial enterprise cartography and ethnography were—and how international an enterprise early Qing mapmaking was, with Jesuit technology

helping to demarcate the border with the Russian empire. The practical implications of mapmaking help us ground the gadget collections of early modern monarchs; both Louis XIV and the Qianlong emperor shared, for example, a fascination with clocks, partly because the accurate measurement of time was critical to a proper measurement of longitude and to the construction of truly accurate maps.

9. Certainly, there is indirect evidence that this might have been the case; for example, during the literary inquisitions of the eighteenth century, books seem usually to have been classified as seditious more for who their authors were than for the ideas contained in them. Even the most seditious books questioned, not the entire dynastic system, but only the legitimacy of specific emperors. In "Censorship in Eighteenth-Century China," an article on Qianlong's campaign to purge the *Siku quanshu* of seditious texts and authors, Timothy Brook compares how the Catholic Church and the Chinese state legitimated their own dominance and concludes that the Chinese state relied on a much less complex structure of ideas.

10. When the Spanish Empire expanded into the New World, it faced a similar situation: a state legitimized by and representative of the Catholic Church also might spread infinitely, ruling the whole world. To Spanish political theorists, the seeming infinitude of the world was an enormous and intractable problem opening up the possibility of a *monarchia universalis*. But unlike the Chinese case, in the case of Spain, such positions had to be articulated—to rival institutions and states, the Church, and other Catholic states (Pagden, *Lords of All the World*, pp. 56–62).

11. Scholars traditionally have made much of another way in which late imperial writers engaged themselves with politics. Virtually every Ming writer of note was affiliated with a literary society, which in turn blurred into a political faction. Tang Xianzu, for example, perhaps the most influential of all playwrights, was embroiled in political controversy throughout his career; he was forced to leave office because of his opposition to the powerful minister Zhang Juzheng. Later, virtually all the pioneers in evidential learning had been supporters of the Revival Society, which was united in its condemnation of the eunuch Wei Zhongxian. But that is not the kind of political stand I am interested in, and the book that follows is not concerned with the political lives of authors.

12. Appadurai, "Introduction," p. 3.

13. Lévi-Strauss, "The Family," p. 277.

14. Meng Chengshun, *Jiaohong ji*, p. 107.

15. Carlitz, "Desire, Danger, and the Body," pp. 101–4.

16. Kang-i Sun Chang, *The Late-Ming Poet Ch'en Tzu-lung*, p. 16.

17. Mao Qiling, "Shen Yunying zhuan," in Zheng Shuruo, *Yu Chu xuzhi*, *juan* 4, p. 4.

18. *Jingzhong qi*, in *Zhongguo shida gudian beiju ji*, 2: 250.

19. Lu Shusheng, "Yan shi ji," in Shi Zhicun, *Wan Ming ershi jia xiaopin*, p. 18; trans. Ye Yang, *Vignettes from the Late Ming: A Hsiao-p'in Anthology* (Seattle: University of Washington Press, 1999), p. 12.

20. Appadurai, "Introduction," p. 24.

21. Kopytoff, "The Cultural Biography of Things," p. 87.

22. Ji Yun, *Yuewei caotang biji*, 9.14; trans. David L. Keenan, *Shadows in a Chinese Landscape: The Notes of a Confucian Scholar* (Armonk, NY: M. E. Sharpe, 1999), pp. 6–7.

23. Lewis, *Writing and Authority in Early China*, p. 365.

24. Jameson, *The Political Unconscious*, p. 106.

25. In the case of all three forms, it was members of the elite who were active gatekeepers, carefully managing these literary institutions. Compiling an anthology, whether a selection of Tang poems or a volume of classical tales on ghosts, allowed an editor to control access to texts. Sometimes the acts of surveillance and control are obvious. *Chuanqi*, the written form of southern drama (or *nanxi*), took off in popularity in the second half of the sixteenth century, and the genre's close association to the elite is evident in the prescriptive criticism for this new genre: how closely an aria ought to adhere to metrical guidelines and what the libretto's relationship to performance ought to be. Even the seemingly spontaneous appearance of a genre from popular roots can mask the guiding hand of members of the elite. The vernacular short story's flowering really began with Feng Menglong's three anthologies of the 1620s; scion of an educated family, possessed of scholarly and official ambitions, Feng Menglong authored, edited, or commissioned all 120 stories. At the same time, older forms that had never merited notice before were shoehorned into older categories, as, for example, when the wealthy sixteenth-century bibliophile Hu Yinglin tried to work out where classical fiction ought to fit according to the schema of the Siku, or Four Treasuries.

26. Ji Yun, *Yuewei caotang biji*, pp. 15–41.

Chapter 2

1. Mauss, *The Gift*, p. 24.

2. Moretti, *Atlas of the European Novel*, p. 20.

3. Ibid., p. 22.

4. Idema, "Time and Space in Traditional Chinese Fiction," p. 369.

5. Brook, "Guides for Vexed Travelers," p. 142.

6. Wang Shixing, *Guangzhi yi*, p. 135.

7. Tian Rucheng's version is probably the next most famous, after the *Sanyan*'s. Scholars also point out the version by Li Guochang, in *Chongxiu zhiyao* (1667).

8. Brook, *The Confusions of Pleasure*, p. 174. "You could 'hop a boat' outside the city of Yangzhou and sail down the Grand Canal to the north gate of Guazhou, the canal's port on the Yangzi River, for 3 copper cash. You walked through Guazhou to the south gate to catch another boat that for 2 cash would ferry you across the Yangzi and past Jin Mountain monastery to the wharf at Zhenjiang on the other side. From the wharf you entered the west gate of Zhenjiang, walked 1.5 kilometers down the Jiangnan portion of the Grand Canal. If you were traveling with baggage, a porter could be hired at the wharf for about 15 cash per carry. South from Zhenjiang, the rate for boat carriage was only 2 copper cash for every 20 *li* (11.7 kilometers). The day's journey from Zhenjiang down to Wujiang, one of Suzhou's counties on Lake Tai, involved a relay of six boats. From Wujiang you could take either a day or night boat to Jiaxing, and from there a day boat up to Songjiang or a day or night boat down to Hangzhou. From Hangzhou east to Ningbo, the route was well serviced to handle the pilgrims going out to the Buddhist island of Putuo, and commercial boats plied the route day and night. However, if your destination from Suzhou was westward into Huizhou prefecture, you could get a night ferry to Huzhou, and then another night ferry from Huzhou to Sian on the Zhejiang–South Zhili border."

9. Feng Menglong, *Xingshi hengyan*, p. 749.

10. Li Yu, *Wusheng xi*, p. 218.

11. Feng Menglong, *Xingshi hengyan*, p. 751.

12. Ling Mengchu, *Paian jingqi*, p. 7.

13. Ibid., pp. 7–8.

14. In another sense, however, it is important that the trader hails specifically from Persia. Victor Mair points out that this Persian trader is a late imperial version of a venerable *topos*, the Persian as financial wizard. See also Schafer, "Iranian Merchants in T'ang Dynasty Tales."

15. Feng Menglong, *Xingshi hengyan*, p. 22.

16. Mauss, *The Gift*, p. 45.

17. Hanan, "The Early Chinese Short Story," p. 307.

18. Song Maocheng, *Jiuyue ji*, p. 274.

19. Ibid.

20. A commentator writes, "The husband does not misuse the wife, although the wife misuses the husband. So, even though she is expelled, she

does not blame him and is ultimately able to expiate her sins against him. How she is able to requite (*chou*) him is marvelous" (ibid., p. 74).

21. Feng Menglong, *Xingshi hengyan*, p. 1.

22. Ibid., p. 3.

23. Ibid., p. 30.

24. The characters' names were added by the redactor of the *Gujin* version, probably Feng Menglong, and do not exist in Song Maocheng's version. Sanqiao's name, too, is significant. The third daughter of the family, ostensibly named after the holiday Qiqiao, Sanqiao also means "Three Coincidences": the first, the way she inadvertently catches Chen Dalang's eye; the second, Jiang Xingge and Chen Dalang's coincidental meeting; and the third, her fortuitous reunion with Jiang Xingge.

25. Feng Menglong, *Xingshi hengyan*, p. 23.

26. Ibid., p. 28.

27. Ibid., p. 23.

28. Charlotte Furth describes late Ming medical case studies featuring merchants just like Chen Dalang, who succumb to illness both because of the stresses of travel and because of the temptations of the road. To medical thinkers, at least, part of the price for travel's profits was paid in the cost to the traveler's health.

29. Hanan, "The Making of 'The Pearl-Sewn Shirt' and 'The Courtesan's Jewel Box,'" p. 136.

30. Feng Menglong, *Xingshi hengyan*, p. 31.

31. "Anyone who unintentionally kills or injures another (*this is comparatively less serious than killing in play*) will be sentenced as if it were killing or injuring in an affray" (Art. 290; "Anyone who, during an affray, strikes and kills another, regardless of whether he has struck with the hand, or the feet, or with another object, or with a metal knife, will be punished with strangulation") (*The Great Qing Code*, pp. 278, 276).

32. Feng Menglong, *Xingshi hengyan*, p. 32.

33. Ibid., p. 33.

34. Matthew Sommer, pers. comm.

35. Lévi-Strauss, "The Family," p. 284.

36. Li Yu, *Wusheng xi*, p. 103.

37. Ibid., p. 105.

38. Ibid., p. 126.

39. Ibid., p. 133.

40. Ibid., pp. 129–30.

41. Ibid., p. 128.

42. Ibid., p. 125.

43. Ibid.

44. The companion story to "Losing a Thousand Pieces of Gold," *Wusheng xi* 3 ("After a Change in Horoscope the Bitter Ends and the Sweet

Comes In"), also deals with the question of whether events can take place outside predictive frameworks, in this case, that of horoscope reading (*bazi*). It tells of Jiang Cheng, a poor government factotum, who with the legerdemain of a fortuneteller changes his own horoscope; in so doing, he also manages to change his own fortune. When he first comes into a little silver, he buys a new set of clothes that so changes his appearance that he marvels: "Could it be that in changing my horoscope, I have transformed my physiognomy too?" (ibid., p. 92).

45. Ibid., p. 112.

46. Ibid., p. 129.

47. Ibid., p. 136.

Chapter 3

1. Feng Menglong, *Jingshi tongyan*, p. 165.

2. In fact, even the restoration of proper family order can be the subject of a narrative. In *Shidian tou* 1 (also attributed to Langxian), all that is at stake in the reunion is family order: a father passes thirty-third in the *jinshi* examinations in the capital, and his long-lost son (whose pregnant mother had been abandoned by the father) passes thirty-fourth. The entire last section of the story concerns not just the reassembling of this family but its proper ranking (fully as much energy is spent describing the actual reunion as how the two women of the household—the concubine whose son is a successful examination candidate and the childless official wife—assume their proper positions within the family).

3. Feng Menglong, *Xingshi hengyan*, p. 514.

4. Ling Mengchu, *Erke paian jingqi*, p. 151.

5. Ling Mengchu, *Paian jingqi*, p. 42.

6. Ibid.

7. Shi Runzhang, "Wang Baihong qie Hu shi xiaozhuan," in Zhang Chao, *Yu Chu jizhi*, *juan* 7, p. 11.

8. Li Yu, *Shier lou*, p. 253.

9. Ibid., p. 227.

10. Ibid., p. 237.

11. Ibid.

12. Ibid., pp. 238–39.

13. Ibid., p. 239.

14. Ibid.

15. Shi Runzhang, who wrote of the dubious reunion between mother and daughter mentioned above, is said to have recorded this reunion in a long narrative poem, entitled *Tusi nü meng*. I was unable to locate a poem by this name in Shi Runzhang's collected works.

16. Lu Ciyun, "Baowu sheng zhuan," in *Qingdai xiaoshuo xuanyi*, p. 113.

17. Ibid.

18. Spence, *Death of Woman Wang*, p. 105, lists prices for women late in the seventeenth century; a night with a courtesan might cost 15 ounces of silver, but one of a lower caliber only 3 ounces. The outright purchase of a fancy prostitute might cost 1,000 ounces, a singing girl 200, and a "decent-looking" concubine 100; in contrast, a plain woman might cost a peasant only 3 ounces to marry. At an exchange ratio of 1:14 (von Glahn's estimate for 1650), 50 liang of gold comes to 700 taels of silver, a considerable price indeed and one approaching that of a fancy prostitute.

19. Sommer, *Sex, Law, and Society in Late Imperial China*, pp. 57–64, and pers. comm.

20. Munn, *The Fame of Gawa*, p. 57.

21. Ibid.

22. Ibid.

23. Ibid., p. 64.

24. Ibid.

25. Ibid., p. 63.

26. Ibid., p. 64.

27. Munn, *The Fate of Gawa*, p. 57.

28. Lu, *Persons, Roles, and Minds*, p. 187.

29. Qu You, "Cuicui zhuan," *Jiandeng xinhua*, p. 76.

Chapter 4

1. The collection's preface mentions a meeting in Hangzhou with Ding Yaokang (1599–1670), a well-known author who wrote, among other texts, *Xu Jinpingmei* (Continuation of *Plum in the Golden Vase*). Enough is known about Ding Yaokang's life to pinpoint when this meeting must have taken place.

2. Zhuoyuan ting zhu, *Zhaoshi bei* (hereafter cited as *ZSB*), p. 51.

3. McMahon, *Causality and Containment*, pp. 10 ff.

4. Wang Shizhen, *Chibei outan*, 2: 23.

5. Hostetler, *Qing Colonial Enterprise*, p. 127 and *passim*.

6. Widmer, *The Margins of Utopia*, p. 174 and *passim*.

7. *Qing zhigong tu xuan*, p. 16.

8. Not contiguous with the mainland, Taiwan, the author explains, has only recently become a part of the empire. Only in the 1680s, after Koxinga's death and his son's defeat—and only after heated debate at court as to the usefulness of this new territory—did Taiwan become considered a part of Fujian province, or, as the author puts it, "only in this dynasty has it entered the maps and records" (ibid., p. 23).

9. Ibid.

10. *ZSB*, p. 69.

11. Hegel, *The Novel in Seventeenth-Century China*, p. 118.

12. *ZSB*, p. 56.

13. *ZSB*, p. 55.
14. Ibid., p. 51.
15. Ibid.
16. Ibid., p. 52.
17. Ibid., p. 61.
18. Ibid., p. 65.
19. Ibid.
20. Ibid.
21. Ibid., p. 77.
22. Ibid., p. 65.
23. Ibid.
24. Shell, *Money, Language, and Thought*, p. 85.
25. Cavell, "Cover Letter to Emerson's 'Constitutional Amending,'" p. 101.
26. *ZSB*, p. 69.
27. Ibid., p. 71.
28. Ibid., p. 66.
29. Ibid.
30. Ibid.
31. Ibid., p. 67.
32. Ibid.
33. Ibid.
34. Ibid., p. 68.
35. Used in this particular way, *yan* and *yu* must split up some of the attributes of language. *Yu* might refer to a response to a *yan*; *yan* might imply speaking of one's own matters, and *yu* refers to the matters of others. Both the praise and the terms of the praise suggest that the apes possess claims to the values of civilization.
36. *ZSB*, p. 67.
37. Ibid., pp. 67–68.
38. Chen Ding, "Yiniu zhuan" in Zhang Chao, *Yu Chu xinzhi*, *juan* 11, p. 9.
39. McMahon, *Causality and Containment*, p. 140.
40. *ZSB*, p. 52.
41. Ibid., p. 73.
42. Ibid.
43. Ibid., p. 75.
44. Ibid., p. 76.
45. Ibid., p. 74.
46. Ibid., pp. 74–75.
47. Ibid., p. 82.
48. Carlitz, *The Rhetoric of "Chin P'ing Mei,"* p. 89.

Chapter 5

1. These journeys are a commonplace in Chinese literature, appearing in many texts, including such canonical ones as the eighteenth-century *Rulin waishi* (The unofficial history of the scholars).
2. Hu Tianyou, "Zhao xiaozi zhuan," in *Yu Chu xuzhi*, *juan* 10, p. 7.
3. Gui Zhuang, "Huang Xiaozi zhuan," in *Yu Chu xuzhi*, *juan* 3, p. 13.
4. Ibid.
5. Ibid., p. 14.
6. Ibid., p. 16.
7. Ibid., p. 17.
8. Ibid., p. 20.

9. In premodern China, only the very rare geographical speculation can escape an explicitly instrumental context, whether commercial, military, or administrative. In Gu Zuyu's early Qing geography, *Tushi fangyu jiyao*, for example, these three uses blur. See Peterson, "The Life of Ku Yen-wu," p. 136, for an example of the uses to which geography during the dynastic transition can be deployed.

10. Gui Zhuang, "Huang Xiaozi zhuan," p. 21.

11. Wakeman, "Romantics, Stoics, and Martyrs in Seventeenth-Century China," p. 650. This tie is made in numerous other contemporary texts as well, such as Wang Youding's "Xiaolie Zhang gong zhuan" (Biography of loyal and filial Sir Zhang).

12. Needless to say, Gu Yanwu was an adopted son—born of a different branch of the family, but raised by a virginal mother and performing sacrifices to a father who had died years before his birth.

13. Song Maocheng, "Wuzhong xiaozi," *Jiuyue ji*, p. 269.

14. Li Yu, *Wusheng xi*, p. 183.

15. Ibid., p. 185.

16. Mao Qiling, "Yang Xiaozi zhuan," in *Yu Chu xuzhi, juan* 9, p. 24.

17. Roy, "Introduction," 1: xxxix.

18. Ling Mengchu, *Paian jingqi*, p. 2.

19. Li Yu, *Wusheng xi*, p. 308.

20. Ibid., pp. 308–9.

21. Ibid., p. 309.

22. Ibid.

23. Ibid., p. 507.

24. Rousseau, *On the Origin of Language*, p. 33.

25. Ibid., p. 45.

26. Smith, "Liberating Animals in Ming-Qing China."

27. *Mencius* 5.4.

28. Li Zhi, *Li Zhi wenji: Fenshu*, p. 90.

29. Erik Zürcher ("'In the Beginning,'" p. 150) observes that the idea of a single primeval couple met with little resistance (other components of the Jesuit presentation of Genesis were not so readily accepted, however).

30. Ji Yun, *Rushi wowen*, in *Yuewei caotang biji*, p. xx.

31. Sometimes, loyalty to the state can also be expressed as cannibalism, as in the play *Shuangzhong ji*, discussed in Chapter 1. But such examples of virtuous cannibalism are unusual; and it should be noted that, like *gegu* and other cases of parental cannibalism, the concubine's and manservant's behavior is a matter of personal loyalty. Loyalty to the state is left to their master.

32. Knapp, *Selfless Offspring*, p. 114.

33. Carlitz, "Shrines, Governing-Class Identity," p. 623.

34. Zhou Ji, *Xiju erji*, p. 88.
35. Ibid., p. 89.
36. Fang Xiaoru, "Guo Ju lun."
37. Tianjan chisou, *Shi diantou*, p. 237.
38. Ibid.
39. Carlitz, "Desire, Danger, and the Body," p. 111.
40. Bynum, *Holy Feast and Holy Fast*, p. 269.
41. Tianjan chisou, *Shi diantou*, p. 237.
42. Ibid., pp. 237–38.
43. Pu Songling. *Liaozhai zhiyi*, p. 878.
44. Ibid.
45. Tianjan chisou, *Shi diantou*, p. 249.
46. Ibid., p. 255.
47. Ibid., p. 256.
48. Ibid., p. 257.
49. Ibid.
50. Ibid., p. 238.
51. Ibid., p. 250.
52. Ibid., p. 256.

Chapter 6

1. Robert E. Hegel, "Unpredictability and Meaning in Ming-Qing Literati Novels," p. 154.

2. Goldman, "Opera After the War."

3. Xiaoxiao sheng, *Zuben Jinpingmei*, p. 857.

4. Zhang Zhupo writes: "He depicts a Pan Jinlian and then goes on to depict a Li Ping'er. This could be described as repetitive, yet from first to last, whether they are together or apart, there is never the slightest confusion between them in their words or acts" (Zhang Zhupo, "Piping diyi qishu *Jinpingmei* dufa," in Hou Zhongyi and Wang Rumei, *Jinpingmei ziliao huibian*, p. 35 [*dufa* 45]). Andrew Plaks (*Four Masterworks*, p. 112) compares the entry of the two characters into the household and also observes: "In addition, certain other details of presentation, from clothing to sexual practices, further link the two as halves of an overlapping construction."

5. Xiaoxiao sheng, *Zuben Jinpingmei*, p. 997.

6. Plaks, *Four Masterworks*, p. 115.

7. Plaks ("Problem of Incest," p. 128) chooses another example, Chen Jingji's relationship to Pan Jinlian, as the "most obtrusive example of incest in the novel."

8. As Zhang Zhupo writes, "During the time when [Pan Jinlian] was a member of Imperial Commissioner Wang's establishment, if the male members of the household had shown respect for propriety and righteousness and the female members of the household had honored chastity and integrity so that obscene words and deeds were neither to be heard nor seen, then, even if she had been dissolute to begin with, she would have been transformed into a chaste girl" (Zhang Zhupo, in Hou Zhongyi and Wang Rumei, *Jinpingmei ziliao huibian*, pp. 29–30 [*dufa* 23]).

9. Hanan, "The Early Chinese Short Story," pp. 323–28.

10. Xiaofei Tian, "A Preliminary Comparison," p. 369.

11. Zhang Zhupo, *Zhang Zhupo pi ping Jinpingmei*, 2: 1569.

12. Ibid., p. 1572.

13. Ibid., p. 1578.

14. Ibid., p. 1572. See also Zhang Zhupo, in Hou Zhongyi and Wang Rumei, *Jinpingmei ziliao huibian*, p. 24 (*dufa* 2).

15. Zhang Zhupo, *Zhang Zhupo piping Jinpingmei*, 2: 1569.

16. Zhang Zhupo, in Hou Zhongyi and Wang Rumei, *Jinpingmei ziliao huibian*, p. 36 (*dufa* 47).

17. David T. Roy, trans., "How to Read the *Chin P'ing Mei*" in Rolston, *How to Read the Chinese Novel*, p. 235; Zhang Zhupo, in Hou Zhongyi and Wang Rumei, *Jinpingmei ziliao huibian*, p. 41 (*dufa* 76). Zhang Zhupo (*Zhang Zhupo piping Jinpingmei*, 2: 1561) makes much the same point again in his notes to Chapter 100.

18. Zhang Zhupo, *Zhang Zhupo piping Jinpingmei*, 2: 1579.

19. Ibid.

20. Zhang Zhupo, in Hou Zhongyi and Wang Rumei, *Jinpingmei ziliao huibian*, p. 24 (*dufa* 2).

21. Zhang Zhupo, *Zhang Zhupo piping Jinpingmei*, 2: 1572.

22. Ibid., p. 1560.

Chapter 7

1. One cannot exaggerate the political importance of proper nomenclature of any particular date; in one well-publicized legal case, one man's imprudent reference to the transitional year of 1644 according to its Ming name instead of as the first year of the Shunzhi era cost his own family and seventy other men their lives.

2. Cao Xueqin, *Bajia piping Honglou meng* (hereafter cited as *Bajia*), p. 2352. The comment is Zhang Xinzhi's.

3. Cao Xueqin and Gao E, *Honglou meng* (hereafter cited as *HLM*), p. 433.

4. *HLM*, p. 1102.

5. Theiss, *Disgraceful Matters*, p. 51.

6. Richards, *The Imperial Archive*, p. 6.

7. Elliott, *The Manchu Way*, p. 350.

8. *HLM*, p. 1283.

9. Ibid.

10. At the novel's beginning, various outsiders attempt to make sense of the Jia household: Lin Daiyu, through psychology; Grannie Liu, through economics; Jia Yucun, through the prism of genealogy.

11. *HLM*, p. 1416.
12. Ibid.
13. Ibid., p. 1450.
14. Ibid., p. 1588.
15. *Bajia*, p. 2566.
16. Ibid., p. 2500.
17. Ibid., p. 2581.
18. Ibid., p. 1416.
19. Ibid., p. 846.

20. In any group of 23 people—in other words, one much smaller than the Jia establishment—the odds that two of them share the same birthday are approximately 50 percent.

21. *HLM*, p. 846.
22. Ibid., p. 781.
23. *Bajia*, p. 1382.
24. *HLM*, p. 1138.
25. Ibid.
26. Ibid., pp. 1141–42.

27. In *Mapping Chengde*, Philippe Forêt discusses the Qing imperial residence built out of nothing in Mongolia, with fantastic gardens straight out of Jiangnan, Tibetan buildings, and a geomantically superior layout. One might see the Prospect Garden as sharing some of the magic of the imperial residences at Chengde, what Forêt calls "microcosmic interpretations of parallel universes" (p. 1)—which explains perhaps why the garden's dimensions seem so very changeable, sometimes small and sometimes large, sometimes porous, but at other times hermetically sealed. Like an imperial residence, it is at times the scene of magic, whereas at other times it is a quotidian residence. Sometimes nothing but the residence of a boy and his family, at other times the garden is the center of a drama whose stage is the cosmos itself.

28. *HLM*, p. 1138.
29. Ibid.
30. Ibid., p. 1495.
31. Cooper and Meng, "Patterns of Cousin Marriage," p. 91.
32. Hsu, "Observations on Cross-Cousin Marriage in China," p. 91.
33. Ibid., p. 84.
34. Kulp, *Country Life in South China.*
35. Hsu, "Observations on Cross-Cousin Marriage in China," p. 98.
36. Fei, *Peasant Life in China*, pp. 51–52.
37. Ibid.
38. *HLM*, p. 1376.
39. *Bajia*, p. 2496.
40. *HLM*, p. 1376.
41. Ibid., p. 1336.
42. Ibid., p. 1337.
43. Chuang and Wolf, "Marriage in Taiwan."
44. *HLM*, p. 1189.
45. *Bajia*, p. 2485.

46. Lévi-Strauss, *The Elementary Structures of Kinship*, p. 485.

47. Ibid.

48. Baoyu has tried once before to leave. In chapter 25, after Aunt Zhao has a curse put on Wang Xifeng and Baoyu, the two members of the family against whom she especially bears a grudge, both go into a delirium and come close to dying. As Baoyu worsens, he suddenly says to his grandmother: "From now on, I cannot stay in your household. Quickly send me off so I can go" (p. 344). To the heartbroken Grandmother Jia and the triumphant Aunt Zhao, Baoyu is simply euphemistically announcing his own death. But for Baoyu, clearly death itself seems at least partially subsumed by the greater issue of leaving the Jia household. The delirious rant foreshadows his eventual departure from the family—and the weightiness of staying or leaving.

49. *HLM*, p. 1579.

50. Ibid., p. 1197.

51. One hint, for example, is the picture that Baoyu sees in his dream in chapter 5 with Qiaojie: "a country cottage in a deserted village, with a beauty sitting inside spinning."

52. 小兒常情，遂成千里伏線。

53. *HLM*, p. 1437.

54. Ibid., p. 773.

55. Ibid., p. 774.

56. Ibid., p. 774.

57. Ibid., pp. 775–76.

58. *Bajia*, p. 1377.

59. Scholars have speculated that *Fengyue baojian* is the title of another novel that Cao Xueqin began but did not complete. Certain episodes in *Hongloumeng*—namely, the Jia Rui episode of chapters 11 and 12 and the story of the You sisters that extends from chapters 64 to 69—probably began as parts of the earlier novel. However, *Fengyue baojian* also appears as an alternative title for the novel—along with *Shitou ji* (The story of the stone), *Shier chai* 十二釵 (The twelve beauties of Jinling), and *Qingseng lu* 情僧錄 (The record of the monk of passion).

60. *Bajia*, p. 1369.

Epilogue

1. Li Yu, *Rouputuan*, p. 158.

2. Dunbar, *Grooming, Gossip, and the Evolution of Language*, p. 160.

3. Li Yu, *Rouputuan*, p. 162.

4. Ibid., p. 479.

5. Habermas, *Structural Transformation of the Public Sphere*, p. 36: "However exclusive the public might be in any given instance, it could never close itself off entirely and become consolidated as a clique; for it always

understood and found itself immersed within a more inclusive public of private people, persons who—insofar as they were propertied and educated—as readers, listeners, and spectators could avail themselves via the market of the objects that were subject to discussion."

6. Balzac, 1: xx ("Avant-propos de la *Comédie humaine*").

7. Li Yu, *Rouputuan*, p. 463.

8. Ibid., p. 198.

9. Ibid., p. 373.

10. Ibid., p. 463.

11. Ibid., p. 465.

12. Ibid., p. 476.

13. Ibid., p. 492.

14. Ibid., p. 480.

15. Ibid., p. 482.

16. Ibid., p. 496.

17. Ibid., p. 146.

18. Ibid., p. 151.

19. Ibid., p. 486.

20. Ibid., p. 489.

21. Ibid., p. 153.

22. Ibid., p. 154.

23. One can map these issues along other axes. During the late Ming, literary historians have explained, elite writers and readers assimilated the novel into high literary discourse, with its long-standing focus on authorship. Not coincidentally, the enterprise of fictional commentary also dates from the sixteenth century. Once authorial intent became a matter of high import, decoding it became the central enterprise in textual understanding. Before the end of the sixteenth century, no one asked what a novel really meant; but by the end of the Ming dynasty, it was widely assumed that deeper significances lay everywhere, and if one wanted to understand a novel, one had to figure out what the author had really meant—preferably with the assistance of a commentator.

The focus on the author as an individual had an impact on many novels written in the period; there, too, the author's voice became increasingly important. *Rouputuan*'s self-consciously clever plotting—with frequent discursive interruptions by a narrator whose urbane voice could be associated only with Li Yu's own and lavish praise by a commentator who again is almost certainly Li Yu himself—positions the novel squarely within this trend. What is exceptional here, however, is that in this novel, these trends are actually thematized. Both the author and the commentator distinguish themselves (advertise themselves, even) as voices of control and total knowledge. Reading the novel with commentary—one dimension of the author's voice praising another dimension of the same—has the effect of listening to a duet of coolheaded subjectivities, not unlike the fraternity of secret knowledge at novel's end.

24. 這些光景，惟有我們聽得清楚。那幹事的男子反不知道。

25. Li Yu, *Rouputuan*, p. 224–25.

26. Ibid., p. 142.

Works Cited

Primary Sources

Aina Jushi. *Doupeng xianhua*. Beijing: Renmin wenxue chubanshe, 1999.

Cao Xueqin. *Bajia piping Honglou meng*. Ed. and collated Feng Qiyong. Beijing: Wenhua yishu chubanshe, 1991.

Cao Xueqin and Gao E. *Honglou meng*. Beijing: Renmin wenxue chubanshe, 1998.

Da Qing huidian shili. Beijing: Zhonghua shuju, 1991.

Donglu gukuang sheng. *Zuixing shi*. Shanghai: Shanghai guji chubanshe, 1992.

Fang Xiaoru. "Guo Ju lun." In *Gujin tushu jicheng*. Shanghai: Zhonghua shuju, 1934.

Feng Menglong. *Gujin xiaoshuo*. 2 vols. Ed. Xu Zhengyang. Beijing: Renmin wenxue chubanshe, 1981.

———. *Jingshi tongyan*. 2 vols. Ed. Yan Dunyi. Beijing: Renmin wenxue chubanshe, 1995.

———. *Xingshi hengyan*. 2 vols. Ed. and annot. Gu Xueji. Beijing: Zhonghua shuju, 1987.

Hong Sheng. *Changsheng dian*. Ed. and annot. Xu Shuofang. Beijing: Renmin wenxue chubanshe, 1991.

Ji Yun. *Yuewei caotang biji*. Ed. Dong Guochao. Chongqing: Chongqing chubanshe, 1996.

Jiang Shiquan. *Dongqing shu*. Ed. and annot. Shao Haiqing. Shanghai: Shanghai guji chubanshe, 1988.

Juqi zi. *Xingmeng pianyan*. Ed. Wang Xiumei. Beijing: Zhonghua shuju, 2000.

Li Yu 李漁. *Li Yu quanji*. 20 vols. Hangzhou: Zhejiang guji chubanshe, 1992.

———. *Rouputuan*. Taibei: Taiwan da Ying baike, 1994.

———. *Shier lou*. Ed. Xiao Rongji. Shanghai: Shanghai guji chubanshe, 1986.

——. *Wusheng xi*. Taibei: Shuangdi guoji chubanshe, 1995.

Li Yu 李玉. *Qingzhong pu*. Beijing: Zhonghua shuju, 1959.

———. *Yipeng xue*. Ed. and annot. Ouyang Daifa. Shanghai: Shanghai guji chubanshe, 1989.

Li Zhi. *Li Zhi wenji: Fenshu, Xufenshu*. Ed. Li Wenling. Beijing: Beijing Yanshan chubanshe, 1998.

Ling Mengchu. *Erke paian jingqi*. 2 vols. Ed. and annot. Wang Gulu. Shanghai: Shanghai guji chubanshe, 1984.

———. *Paian jingqi*. Ed. Leng Shijun. Shanghai: Shanghai guji chubanshe, 1998.

Lu Ciyun. *Beishu xuyan*. Ji'nan: Qi Lu shushe chubanshe, 1997.

Meng Chengshun. *Jiaohong ji*. Ed. and annot. Ouyang Guang. Shanghai: Shanghai guji chubanshe, 1983.

Pu Songling. *Liaozhai zhiyi*. 3 vols. Ed. and annot. Zhu Qiqi. Beijing: Renmin wenxue chubanshe, 1989.

Qingdai xiaoshuo xuanyi. Ed. and annot. Jiang Dongfu and Xu Guiting. Shanghai: Shanghai guji chubanshe, 1990.

Qing zhigong tu xuan. Taibei: Taiwan yinhang, 1963.

Qu You. *Jiandeng xinhua: wai er zhong*. Ed. Zhou Yi. Shanghai: Gudian wenxue chubanshe, 1981.

Shi Zhicun, ed. *Wan Ming ershi jia xiaopin*. Taibei: Xin wenfeng chuban, 1977.

Song Maocheng. *Jiuyue ji*. Ed. Wang Liqi. Beijing: Zhongguo shehui kexue chubanshe, 1984.

Tang Xianzu. *Mudan ting*. Ed. and annot. Xu Shuofang and Yang Xiaomei. Beijing: Renmin wenxue chubanshe, 1998.

Tianran chisou. *Shi diantou*. Yangzhou: Jiangsu guji chubanshe, 1994.

Wang Shixing. *Guangzhi yi*. Ed. Lü Jinglin. Beijing: Zhonghua shuju, 1997.

Wang Shizhen. *Chibei outan*. 2 vols. Ed. Jin Siren. Beijing: Zhonghua shuju, 1982.

Xiaoxiao sheng. *Zuben Jinpingmei*. Ed. Liu Bendong. Hong Kong: Litong tushu, 1991.

Zhang Chao, ed. *Yu Chu xinzhi*. Shanghai: Shangwu yinshu guan, 1933.

Zhang Zhupo. *Zhang Zhupo piping Jinpingmei*. 2 vols. Ed. Wang Rumei, Li Zhaoxun, and Yu Fengshu. Ji'nan: Qi Lu shushe, 1991.

Zheng Shuruo, ed. *Yu Chu xuzhi*. Shanghai: Shanghai shudian chubanshe, 1986.

Zhongguo shida gudian beiju ji. 2 vols. Ed. Wang Jisi. Shanghai: Shanghai wenxue, 1982.

Zhou Ji. *Xiju erji*. Ed. Chen Meilin. Yangzhou: Jiangsu guji chubanshe, 1993.

Zhuibai qiu. Comp. Wanhua zhuren. 12 vols. Ed. Wang Xieru. Introduction by Hu Shi. Taibei: Taibei Zhonghua shuju, 1967.

Zhuoyuan ting zhu. *Zhaoshi bei*. Taibei: Tianyi chubanshe, 1974.

Secondary Literature

Anderson, Benedict. *Imagined Communities: Reflections on the Origin and Spread of Nationalism*. London: Verso Books, 1991.

Appadurai, Arjun. "Introduction: Commodities and the Politics of Value." In *The Social Life of Things: Commodities in Cultural Perspective*, ed. idem. Cambridge: Cambridge University Press, 1986.

Balzac, Honoré de. *La Comédie Humaine of Honoré de Balzac*, vol. 1. Introduced and trans. W. P. Trent. New York: Century, 1906.

Berling, Judith. "Religion and Popular Culture: The Management of Moral Capital in *The Romance of the Three Teachings*." In *Popular Culture in Late Imperial China*, ed. David Johnson, Andrew J. Nathan, and Evelyn S. Rawski. Berkeley: University of California Press, 1985.

Bernhardt, Kathryn. *Women and Property in China, 960–1949*. Stanford: Stanford University Press, 1999.

Brokaw, Cynthia. *Ledgers of Merit and Demerit: Social Change and Moral Order in Late Imperial China*. Princeton: Princeton University Press, 1991.

Brook, Timothy. "Censorship in Eighteenth-Century China: A View from the Book Trade." *Canadian Journal of History* 23 (Aug. 1988): 177–96.

———. *The Confusions of Pleasure: Commerce and Culture in Ming China*. Berkeley: University of California Press, 1999.

———. "Guides for Vexed Travelers: Route Books in the Ming and Qing." *Ch'ing-shih wen-t'i* 4 (June 1981): 130–40.

Bynum, Caroline Walker. *Holy Feast and Holy Fast: The Religious Significance of Food to Medieval Women*. Berkeley: University of California Press, 1988.

Cai Yuanpei. *Shitouji suoyin*. Ed. Hua Yun. Beijing: Beijing daxue chubanshe, 1989.

Cao Xueqin and Gao E. *The Story of the Stone*. 5 vols. Trans. David Hawkes and John Minford. London: Penguin Books, 1984.

Carlitz, Katherine. "Desire, Danger, and the Body: Stories of Women's Virtue in Late Ming China." In *Engendering China: Women, Culture, and the State*, ed. Christina K. Gilmartin, Gail Hershatter, Lisa Rofel, and Tyrene White. Cambridge: Harvard University Press, 1994.

———. *The Rhetoric of "Chin P'ing Mei."* Bloomington: Indiana University Press, 1986.

———. "Shrines, Governing-Class Identity, and the Cult of Widow Fidelity in Mid-Ming Jiangnan." *Journal of Asian Studies* 56, no. 3 (Aug. 1997): 612–40.

———. "The Social Uses of Female Virtue in Late Ming Editions of *Lienü zhuan*." *Late Imperial China* 12 (June 1991): 117–48.

Cavell, Stanley. "Cover Letter to Emerson's 'Constitutional Amending.'" In *The Translatability of Culture: Figurations of the Space Between*, ed. Sanford Budick and Wolfgang Iser. Stanford: Stanford University Press, 1996.

Chang, Kang-I Sun. *The Late-Ming Poet Ch'en Tzu-lung: Crises of Love and Loyalism.* New Haven: Yale University Press, 1991.

Chuang Ying-chang and Arthur P. Wolf. "Marriage in Taiwan, 1881–1905: An Example of Regional Diversity." *Journal of Asian Studies* 54, no. 3 (Aug. 1995): 781–95.

Clunas, Craig. *Fruitful Sites: Garden Culture in Ming Dynasty China.* London: Reaktion Books, 1996.

———. *Superfluous Things: Social Status and Material Culture in Early Modern China.* Cambridge: Cambridge University Press, 1991.

Cooper, Eugene. "Cousin Marriage in Rural China: More and Less Than Generalized Exchange." *American Ethnologist* 20 (Nov. 1993): 758–80.

Cooper, Eugene, and Meng Zhang. "Patterns of Cousin Marriage in Rural Zhejiang and in *Dream of the Red Chamber*." *Journal of Asian Studies* 52, no. 1 (Feb. 1993): 90–106.

Crossley, Pamela. *A Translucent Mirror: History and Identity in Qing Imperial Ideology*. Berkeley: University of California Press, 2002.

Dunbar, Robin. *Grooming, Gossip, and the Evolution of Language*. Cambridge: Harvard University Press, 1998.

Elliott, Mark. *The Manchu Way: The Eight Banners and Ethnic Identity in Late Imperial China.* Stanford: Stanford University Press, 2001.

Elvin, Mark. "Female Virtue and the State in China." *Past and Present* 104 (1984): 111–52.

Epstein, Maram. *Competing Discourses: Orthodoxy, Authenticity, and Engendered Meanings in Late Imperial Chinese Fiction.* Cambridge: Harvard University Asia Center, 2001.

Fei Hsiao-t'ung. *Peasant Life in China: A Field Study of Country Life in the Yangtze Valley*. New York: E. P. Dutton, 1939.

Fong, Grace. "Signifying Bodies: The Cultural Significance of Suicide Writings by Women in Ming-Qing China." In *Passionate Women: Female Sui-*

cide in Late Imperial China, ed. Paul Ropp, Paola Zamperini, and Harriet Zurndorfer. Leiden: Brill Academic Press, 2001.

Forêt, Philippe. *Mapping Chengde*. Honolulu: University of Hawai'i Press, 2000.

Furth, Charlotte. *A Flourishing Yin: Gender in China's Medical History, 960–1665*. Berkeley: University of California Press, 1999.

Godelier, Maurice. *The Engima of the Gift*. Trans. Nora Scott. Chicago: University of Chicago Press, 1999.

Goldman, Andrea. "Opera After the War: The Cultural Valence of Style at Court and at Large in the Post-Taiping Era." Paper presented at the annual meeting for the Association of Asian Studies, Atlanta, GA, Apr. 3–6, 2008.

The Great Qing Code: A New Translation with Introduction by William C. Jones. Trans. William C. Jones. Oxford: Clarendon Press, 1994.

Habermas, Jürgen. *The Structural Transformation of the Public Sphere: An Inquiry into a Category of Bourgeois Society*. Trans. Thomas Burger. Cambridge: MIT Press, 1991.

Hanan, Patrick. *The Chinese Vernacular Story*. Cambridge: Harvard University Press, 1981.

———. "The Early Chinese Short Story." In *Studies in Chinese Literary Genres*, ed. Cyril Birch. Berkeley: University of California Press, 1974.

———. *The Invention of Li Yu*. Cambridge: Harvard University Press, 1988.

———. "The Making of 'The Pearl-Sewn Shirt' and 'The Courtesan's Jewel Box.'" *Harvard Journal of Asiatic Studies* 33 (1973): 124–53.

Hegel, Robert. *The Novel in Seventeenth-Century China*. New York: Columbia University Press, 1981.

———. "Traditional Chinese Fiction—The State of the Field." *Journal of Asian Studies* 53, no. 2 (May 1994): 394–426.

Hevia, James. *Cherishing Men from Afar: Qing Guest Ritual and the Macartney Embassy of 1793*. Durham: Duke University Press, 1995.

Hostetler, Laura. *Qing Colonial Enterprise*. Chicago: University of Chicago Press, 2001.

Hou Zhongyi and Wang Rumei, eds. *Jinpingmei ziliao huibian*. Beijing: Beijing daxue chubanshe, 1985.

Hsieh, Andrew C. K., and Jonathan Spence. "Suicide and the Family in Pre-Modern Chinese Society." In *Normal and Abnormal Behavior in Chinese Culture*, ed. Arthur Kleinman and Tsung-yi Lin. Boston: Kluwer Boston, 1981.

Hsu, Francis L. K. "Observations on Cross-Cousin Marriage in China." *American Anthropologist* 47 (Jan. 1945): 83–103.

Idema, Wilt L. "Time and Space in Traditional Chinese Historical Fiction." In *Time and Space in Chinese Culture*, ed. Chun-chieh Huang and Erik Zürcher. Leiden: Brill Academic Press, 1995.

Jameson, Fredric. *The Political Unconscious: Narrative as a Socially Symbolic Act*. Ithaca: Cornell University Press, 1981.

Jardine, Lisa. *Ingenious Pursuits: Building the Scientific Revolution*. New York: Doubleday Press, 1999.

Knapp, Keith. *Selfless Offspring: Filial Children and Social Order in Medieval China*. Honolulu: University of Hawai'i Press, 2005.

Kopytoff, Igor. "The Cultural Biography of Things." In *The Social Life of Things: Commodities in Cultural Perspective*, ed. Arjun Appadurai. Cambridge: Cambridge University Press, 1986.

Kulp, Daniel Harrison. *Country Life in South China*. Taibei: Ch'eng-wen Publishing, 1966.

Kutcher, Norman. *Mourning in Late Imperial China*. Cambridge: Cambridge University Press, 2000.

Lévi-Strauss, Claude. *The Elementary Structures of Kinship*. Trans. James Harle Bell and John Richard von Sturmer. Boston: Beacon Press, 1969.

———. "The Family." In *Man, Culture, and Society*, ed. Harry L. Shapiro. New York: Oxford University Press, 1960.

Lewis, Mark Edward. *Writing and Authority in Early China*. Albany: State University of New York Press, 1999.

Li Chi. *The Travel Diaries of Hsü Hsia-k'o*. Hong Kong: Chinese University of Hong Kong Press, 1974.

Li Yu. *The Carnal Prayer Mat*. Trans. Patrick Hanan. New York: Ballantine Books, 1990.

Lu, Tina. *Persons, Roles, and Minds: Identity in "Peony Pavilion" and "Peach Blossom Fan."* Stanford: Stanford University Press, 2001.

Mann, Susan. Review of T'ien Ju-k'ang, *Male Anxiety and Female Chastity: A Comparative Study of Chinese Ethical Values in Ming-Ch'ing Times*. *Harvard Journal of Asiatic Studies* 52 (June 1992): 362–69.

Mauss, Marcel. *The Gift: The Form and Reason for Exchange in Archaic Societies*. Trans. W. D. Halls, with an afterword by Mary Douglas. New York: W. W. Norton, 1990.

McMahon, Keith. *Causality and Containment in Seventeenth-Century Chinese Fiction*. Leiden: Brill Academic Publishers, 1988.

Moretti, Franco. *Atlas of the European Novel, 1800–1900*. London: Verso Books, 1999.

Munn, Nancy D. *The Fame of Gawa: A Symbolic Study of Value Transformation in a Massim (Papua New Guinea) Society*. Chicago: University of Chicago Press, 1986.

Pagden, Anthony. *The Fall of Natural Man: The American Indian and the Origins of Comparative Ethnology*. Cambridge: Cambridge University Press, 1982.

———. *Lords of All the World: Ideologies of Empire in Spain, Britain and France c. 1500–c. 1850*. New Haven: Yale University Press, 1995.

———. *Spanish Imperialism and the Political Imagination: Studies in European and Spanish-American Social and Political Theory, 1513–1830*. New Haven: Yale University Press, 1990.

Peterson, Willard J. "The Life of Ku Yen-wu (1613–1682)." *Harvard Journal of Asiatic Studies* 28 (1968): 114–56.

Plaks, Andrew. *Archetype and Allegory in "The Dream of the Red Chamber."* Princeton: Princeton University Press, 1976.

———. *The Four Masterworks of the Ming Novel:* Ssu Ta Ch'i-shu. Princeton: Princeton University Press, 1987.

———. "The Problem of Incest in *Jin Ping Mei* and *Honglou meng*." In *Paradoxes of Traditional Chinese Literature*, ed. Eva Hung. Hong Kong: Chinese University Press, 1994.

Richards, Thomas. *The Imperial Archive: Knowledge and the Fantasy of Empire*. London: Verso Books, 1996.

Rolston, David. *How to Read the Chinese Novel*. Princeton: Princeton University Press, 1990.

——. *Traditional Chinese Fiction and Fiction Commentary*. Stanford: Stanford University Press, 1997.

Rousseau, Jean-Jacques. *On the Origin of Language*. Trans. John H. Moran. Chicago: University of Chicago, 1966.

Roy, David. "Introduction" to *The Plum in the Golden Vase or, Chin P'ing Mei*, Vol. 1, *The Gathering*, pp. xvii–xlviii. Princeton: Princeton University Press, 1993.

Schafer, Edward. "Iranian Merchants in T'ang Dynasty Tales." In *Semitic and Oriental Studies: A Volume Presented to William Popper, Professor of Semitic Languages, on the Occasion of His Seventy-Fifth Birthday, October 29, 1949*, pp. 403–22. Berkeley: University of California Press, 1951.

Shang Wei. *"Rulin Waishi" and Cultural Transformation in Late Imperial China*. Cambridge: Harvard University Asia Center, 2003.

Shell, Marc. *Money, Language, and Thought*. Baltimore: Johns Hopkins University Press, 1982.

Smith, Joanna Handlin. "Liberating Animals in Ming-Qing China: Buddhist Inspiration and Elite Imagination." *Journal of Asian Studies* 58, no. 1 (Feb. 1999): 51–84.

Sommer, Matthew. *Sex, Law, and Society in Late Imperial China.* Stanford: Stanford University Press, 2000.

Spence, Jonathan. *Death of Woman Wang.* New York: Penguin USA, 1979.

Stafford, Charles. *Separation and Reunion in Modern China.* Cambridge: Cambridge University Press, 2001.

Struve, Lynn. *Voices from the Ming-Qing Cataclysm: China in Tigers' Jaws.* New Haven: Yale University Press, 1998.

Sun Kaidi. *Zhongguo tongsu xiaoshuo shumu.* Beijing: Renmin wenxue chubanshe, 1991.

Tan Zhengbi, ed. *Sanyan liangpai ziliao.* Shanghai: Shanghai guji chubanshe, 1980.

Theiss, Janet. *Disgraceful Matters: The Politics of Chastity in Eighteenth-Century China.* Berkeley: University of California Press, 2004.

———. "Managing Martyrdom: Female Suicide and Statecraft in Mid-Qing China." In *Passionate Women: Female Suicide in Late Imperial China,* ed. Paul Ropp, Paola Zamperini, and Harriet Zurndorfer. Leiden: Brill Academic Press, 2001.

Tian Xiaofei. "A Preliminary Comparison of the Two Recensions of *Jinpingmei.*" *Harvard Journal of Asiatic Studies* 62 (Dec. 2002): 347–88.

T'ien Ju-k'ang. *Male Anxiety and Female Chastity: A Comparative Study of Chinese Ethical Values in Ming-Ch'ing Times.* Leiden: Brill Academic Press, 1998.

Vermeer, Eduard B. "Notions of Time and Space in the Early Ch'ing: The Writings of Ku Yen-wu, Hsü Hsia-k'o, Ku Tsu-yü and Chang Hsüeh-ch'eng." In *Time and Space in Chinese Culture,* ed. Chun-chieh Huang and Erik Zürcher. Leiden: Brill Academic Press, 1995.

von Glahn, Richard. *Fountain of Fortune: Money and Monetary Policy in China, 1000–1700.* Berkeley: University of California Press, 1996.

Wakefield, David. *Fenjia: Household Division and Inheritance in Qing and Republican China.* Honolulu: University of Hawai'i Press, 1998.

Wakeman, Frederic, Jr. "Romantics, Stoics, and Martyrs in Seventeenth-Century China." *Journal of Asian Studies* 43, no. 3 (Aug. 1984): 631–65.

Widmer, Ellen. *The Margins of Utopia: "Shui-hu hou-chuan" and the Literature of Ming Loyalism.* Cambridge: Harvard University Asia Center, 1987.

Wolf, Margery. "Women and Suicide in China." In *Women in Chinese Society,* ed. Margery Wolf and Roxane Witke. Stanford: Stanford University Press, 1975.

Yang Lien-sheng. "Economic Justification for Spending: An Uncommon Idea in Traditional China." In idem, *Studies in Chinese Institutional History*. Cambridge: Harvard University Press, 1963.

Zhou Ruchang. *"Hongloumeng" de zhengushi*. Beijing: Huayi chubanshe, 1995.

Zürcher, Erik. "'In the Beginning': Chinese Reactions to Christian Creationism." In *Time and Space in Chinese Culture*, ed. Chun-chieh Huang and Erik Zürcher. Leiden: Brill Academic Press, 1995.

Index

Harvard East Asian Monographs
(*out-of-print)

- *1. Liang Fang-chung, *The Single-Whip Method of Taxation in China*
- *2. Harold C. Hinton, *The Grain Tribute System of China, 1845–1911*
- 3. Ellsworth C. Carlson, *The Kaiping Mines, 1877–1912*
- *4. Chao Kuo-chün, *Agrarian Policies of Mainland China: A Documentary Study, 1949–1956*
- *5. Edgar Snow, *Random Notes on Red China, 1936–1945*
- *6. Edwin George Beal, Jr., *The Origin of Likin, 1835–1864*
- 7. Chao Kuo-chün, *Economic Planning and Organization in Mainland China: A Documentary Study, 1949–1957*
- *8. John K. Fairbank, *Ching Documents: An Introductory Syllabus*
- *9. Helen Yin and Yi-chang Yin, *Economic Statistics of Mainland China, 1949–1957*
- 10. Wolfgang Franke, *The Reform and Abolition of the Traditional Chinese Examination System*
- 11. Albert Feuerwerker and S. Cheng, *Chinese Communist Studies of Modern Chinese History*
- 12. C. John Stanley, *Late Ching Finance: Hu Kuang-yung as an Innovator*
- 13. S. M. Meng, *The Tsungli Yamen: Its Organization and Functions*
- *14. Ssu-yü Teng, *Historiography of the Taiping Rebellion*
- 15. Chun-Jo Liu, *Controversies in Modern Chinese Intellectual History: An Analytic Bibliography of Periodical Articles, Mainly of the May Fourth and Post-May Fourth Era*
- *16. Edward J. M. Rhoads, *The Chinese Red Army, 1927–1963: An Annotated Bibliography*
- *17. Andrew J. Nathan, *A History of the China International Famine Relief Commission*
- *18. Frank H. H. King (ed.) and Prescott Clarke, *A Research Guide to China-Coast Newspapers, 1822–1911*
- *19. Ellis Joffe, *Party and Army: Professionalism and Political Control in the Chinese Officer Corps, 1949–1964*

*20. Toshio G. Tsukahira, *Feudal Control in Tokugawa Japan: The Sankin Kōtai System*
*21. Kwang-Ching Liu, ed., *American Missionaries in China: Papers from Harvard Seminars*
*22. George Moseley, *A Sino-Soviet Cultural Frontier: The Ili Kazakh Autonomous Chou*
23. Carl F. Nathan, *Plague Prevention and Politics in Manchuria, 1910–1931*
*24. Adrian Arthur Bennett, *John Fryer: The Introduction of Western Science and Technology into Nineteenth-Century China*
*25. Donald J. Friedman, *The Road from Isolation: The Campaign of the American Committee for Non-Participation in Japanese Aggression, 1938–1941*
*26. Edward LeFevour, *Western Enterprise in Late Ching China: A Selective Survey of Jardine, Matheson and Company's Operations, 1842–1895*
27. Charles Neuhauser, *Third World Politics: China and the Afro-Asian People's Solidarity Organization, 1957–1967*
*28. Kungtu C. Sun, assisted by Ralph W. Huenemann, *The Economic Development of Manchuria in the First Half of the Twentieth Century*
*29. Shahid Javed Burki, *A Study of Chinese Communes, 1965*
30. John Carter Vincent, *The Extraterritorial System in China: Final Phase*
31. Madeleine Chi, *China Diplomacy, 1914–1918*
*32. Clifton Jackson Phillips, *Protestant America and the Pagan World: The First Half Century of the American Board of Commissioners for Foreign Missions, 1810–1860*
*33. James Pusey, *Wu Han: Attacking the Present Through the Past*
*34. Ying-wan Cheng, *Postal Communication in China and Its Modernization, 1860–1896*
35. Tuvia Blumenthal, *Saving in Postwar Japan*
36. Peter Frost, *The Bakumatsu Currency Crisis*
37. Stephen C. Lockwood, *Augustine Heard and Company, 1858–1862*
38. Robert R. Campbell, *James Duncan Campbell: A Memoir by His Son*
39. Jerome Alan Cohen, ed., *The Dynamics of China's Foreign Relations*
40. V. V. Vishnyakova-Akimova, *Two Years in Revolutionary China, 1925–1927,* trans. Steven L. Levine
41. Meron Medzini, *French Policy in Japan During the Closing Years of the Tokugawa Regime*
42. Ezra Vogel, Margie Sargent, Vivienne B. Shue, Thomas Jay Mathews, and Deborah S. Davis, *The Cultural Revolution in the Provinces*
43. Sidney A. Forsythe, *An American Missionary Community in China, 1895–1905*
*44. Benjamin I. Schwartz, ed., *Reflections on the May Fourth Movement.: A Symposium*
*45. Ching Young Choe, *The Rule of the Taewŏngun, 1864–1873: Restoration in Yi Korea*
46. W. P. J. Hall, *A Bibliographical Guide to Japanese Research on the Chinese Economy, 1958–1970*
47. Jack J. Gerson, *Horatio Nelson Lay and Sino-British Relations, 1854–1864*

48. Paul Richard Bohr, *Famine and the Missionary: Timothy Richard as Relief Administrator and Advocate of National Reform*
49. Endymion Wilkinson, *The History of Imperial China: A Research Guide*
50. Britten Dean, *China and Great Britain: The Diplomacy of Commercial Relations, 1860–1864*
51. Ellsworth C. Carlson, *The Foochow Missionaries, 1847–1880*
52. Yeh-chien Wang, *An Estimate of the Land-Tax Collection in China, 1753 and 1908*
53. Richard M. Pfeffer, *Understanding Business Contracts in China, 1949–1963*
*54. Han-sheng Chuan and Richard Kraus, *Mid-Ching Rice Markets and Trade: An Essay in Price History*
55. Ranbir Vohra, *Lao She and the Chinese Revolution*
56. Liang-lin Hsiao, *China's Foreign Trade Statistics, 1864–1949*
*57. Lee-hsia Hsu Ting, *Government Control of the Press in Modern China, 1900–1949*
*58. Edward W. Wagner, *The Literati Purges: Political Conflict in Early Yi Korea*
*59. Joungwon A. Kim, *Divided Korea: The Politics of Development, 1945–1972*
60. Noriko Kamachi, John K. Fairbank, and Chūzō Ichiko, *Japanese Studies of Modern China Since 1953: A Bibliographical Guide to Historical and Social-Science Research on the Nineteenth and Twentieth Centuries, Supplementary Volume for 1953–1969*
61. Donald A. Gibbs and Yun-chen Li, *A Bibliography of Studies and Translations of Modern Chinese Literature, 1918–1942*
62. Robert H. Silin, *Leadership and Values: The Organization of Large-Scale Taiwanese Enterprises*
63. David Pong, *A Critical Guide to the Kwangtung Provincial Archives Deposited at the Public Record Office of London*
*64. Fred W. Drake, *China Charts the World: Hsu Chi-yü and His Geography of 1848*
*65. William A. Brown and Urgrunge Onon, translators and annotators, *History of the Mongolian People's Republic*
66. Edward L. Farmer, *Early Ming Government: The Evolution of Dual Capitals*
*67. Ralph C. Croizier, *Koxinga and Chinese Nationalism: History, Myth, and the Hero*
*68. William J. Tyler, tr., *The Psychological World of Natsume Sōseki,* by Doi Takeo
69. Eric Widmer, *The Russian Ecclesiastical Mission in Peking During the Eighteenth Century*
*70. Charlton M. Lewis, *Prologue to the Chinese Revolution: The Transformation of Ideas and Institutions in Hunan Province, 1891–1907*
71. Preston Torbert, *The Ching Imperial Household Department: A Study of Its Organization and Principal Functions, 1662–1796*
72. Paul A. Cohen and John E. Schrecker, eds., *Reform in Nineteenth-Century China*
73. Jon Sigurdson, *Rural Industrialism in China*
74. Kang Chao, *The Development of Cotton Textile Production in China*

75. Valentin Rabe, *The Home Base of American China Missions, 1880–1920*
*76. Sarasin Viraphol, *Tribute and Profit: Sino-Siamese Trade, 1652–1853*
77. Ch'i-ch'ing Hsiao, *The Military Establishment of the Yuan Dynasty*
78. Meishi Tsai, *Contemporary Chinese Novels and Short Stories, 1949–1974: An Annotated Bibliography*
*79. Wellington K. K. Chan, *Merchants, Mandarins and Modern Enterprise in Late Ching China*
80. Endymion Wilkinson, *Landlord and Labor in Late Imperial China: Case Studies from Shandong by Jing Su and Luo Lun*
*81. Barry Keenan, *The Dewey Experiment in China: Educational Reform and Political Power in the Early Republic*
*82. George A. Hayden, *Crime and Punishment in Medieval Chinese Drama: Three Judge Pao Plays*
*83. Sang-Chul Suh, *Growth and Structural Changes in the Korean Economy, 1910–1940*
84. J. W. Dower, *Empire and Aftermath: Yoshida Shigeru and the Japanese Experience, 1878–1954*
85. Martin Collcutt, *Five Mountains: The Rinzai Zen Monastic Institution in Medieval Japan*
86. Kwang Suk Kim and Michael Roemer, *Growth and Structural Transformation*
87. Anne O. Krueger, *The Developmental Role of the Foreign Sector and Aid*
*88. Edwin S. Mills and Byung-Nak Song, *Urbanization and Urban Problems*
89. Sung Hwan Ban, Pal Yong Moon, and Dwight H. Perkins, *Rural Development*
*90. Noel F. McGinn, Donald R. Snodgrass, Yung Bong Kim, Shin-Bok Kim, and Quee-Young Kim, *Education and Development in Korea*
*91. Leroy P. Jones and Il SaKong, *Government, Business, and Entrepreneurship in Economic Development: The Korean Case*
92. Edward S. Mason, Dwight H. Perkins, Kwang Suk Kim, David C. Cole, Mahn Je Kim et al., *The Economic and Social Modernization of the Republic of Korea*
93. Robert Repetto, Tai Hwan Kwon, Son-Ung Kim, Dae Young Kim, John E. Sloboda, and Peter J. Donaldson, *Economic Development, Population Policy, and Demographic Transition in the Republic of Korea*
94. Parks M. Coble, Jr., *The Shanghai Capitalists and the Nationalist Government, 1927–1937*
95. Noriko Kamachi, *Reform in China: Huang Tsun-hsien and the Japanese Model*
96. Richard Wich, *Sino-Soviet Crisis Politics: A Study of Political Change and Communication*
97. Lillian M. Li, *China's Silk Trade: Traditional Industry in the Modern World, 1842–1937*
98. R. David Arkush, *Fei Xiaotong and Sociology in Revolutionary China*
*99. Kenneth Alan Grossberg, *Japan's Renaissance: The Politics of the Muromachi Bakufu*
100. James Reeve Pusey, *China and Charles Darwin*

101. Hoyt Cleveland Tillman, *Utilitarian Confucianism: Chen Liang's Challenge to Chu Hsi*
102. Thomas A. Stanley, *Ōsugi Sakae, Anarchist in Taishō Japan: The Creativity of the Ego*
103. Jonathan K. Ocko, *Bureaucratic Reform in Provincial China: Ting Jih-ch'ang in Restoration Kiangsu, 1867–1870*
104. James Reed, *The Missionary Mind and American East Asia Policy, 1911–1915*
105. Neil L. Waters, *Japan's Local Pragmatists: The Transition from Bakumatsu to Meiji in the Kawasaki Region*
106. David C. Cole and Yung Chul Park, *Financial Development in Korea, 1945–1978*
107. Roy Bahl, Chuk Kyo Kim, and Chong Kee Park, *Public Finances During the Korean Modernization Process*
108. William D. Wray, *Mitsubishi and the N.Y.K, 1870–1914: Business Strategy in the Japanese Shipping Industry*
109. Ralph William Huenemann, *The Dragon and the Iron Horse: The Economics of Railroads in China, 1876–1937*
*110. Benjamin A. Elman, *From Philosophy to Philology: Intellectual and Social Aspects of Change in Late Imperial China*
111. Jane Kate Leonard, *Wei Yüan and China's Rediscovery of the Maritime World*
112. Luke S. K. Kwong, *A Mosaic of the Hundred Days:. Personalities, Politics, and Ideas of 1898*
*113. John E. Wills, Jr., *Embassies and Illusions: Dutch and Portuguese Envoys to K'ang-hsi, 1666–1687*
114. Joshua A. Fogel, *Politics and Sinology: The Case of Naitō Konan (1866–1934)*
*115. Jeffrey C. Kinkley, ed., *After Mao: Chinese Literature and Society, 1978–1981*
116. C. Andrew Gerstle, *Circles of Fantasy: Convention in the Plays of Chikamatsu*
117. Andrew Gordon, *The Evolution of Labor Relations in Japan: Heavy Industry, 1853–1955*
*118. Daniel K. Gardner, *Chu Hsi and the "Ta Hsueh": Neo-Confucian Reflection on the Confucian Canon*
119. Christine Guth Kanda, *Shinzō: Hachiman Imagery and Its Development*
*120. Robert Borgen, *Sugawara no Michizane and the Early Heian Court*
121. Chang-tai Hung, *Going to the People: Chinese Intellectual and Folk Literature, 1918–1937*
*122. Michael A. Cusumano, *The Japanese Automobile Industry: Technology and Management at Nissan and Toyota*
123. Richard von Glahn, *The Country of Streams and Grottoes: Expansion, Settlement, and the Civilizing of the Sichuan Frontier in Song Times*
124. Steven D. Carter, *The Road to Komatsubara: A Classical Reading of the Renga Hyakuin*
125. Katherine F. Bruner, John K. Fairbank, and Richard T. Smith, *Entering China's Service: Robert Hart's Journals, 1854–1863*

126. Bob Tadashi Wakabayashi, *Anti-Foreignism and Western Learning in Early-Modern Japan: The "New Theses" of 1825*
127. Atsuko Hirai, *Individualism and Socialism: The Life and Thought of Kawai Eijirō (1891–1944)*
128. Ellen Widmer, *The Margins of Utopia: "Shui-hu hou-chuan" and the Literature of Ming Loyalism*
129. R. Kent Guy, *The Emperor's Four Treasuries: Scholars and the State in the Late Chien-lung Era*
130. Peter C. Perdue, *Exhausting the Earth: State and Peasant in Hunan, 1500–1850*
131. Susan Chan Egan, *A Latterday Confucian: Reminiscences of William Hung (1893–1980)*
132. James T. C. Liu, *China Turning Inward: Intellectual-Political Changes in the Early Twelfth Century*

*133. Paul A. Cohen, *Between Tradition and Modernity: Wang T'ao and Reform in Late Ching China*

134. Kate Wildman Nakai, *Shogunal Politics: Arai Hakuseki and the Premises of Tokugawa Rule*

*135. Parks M. Coble, *Facing Japan: Chinese Politics and Japanese Imperialism, 1931–1937*

136. Jon L. Saari, *Legacies of Childhood: Growing Up Chinese in a Time of Crisis, 1890–1920*
137. Susan Downing Videen, *Tales of Heichū*
138. Heinz Morioka and Miyoko Sasaki, *Rakugo: The Popular Narrative Art of Japan*
139. Joshua A. Fogel, *Nakae Ushikichi in China: The Mourning of Spirit*
140. Alexander Barton Woodside, *Vietnam and the Chinese Model: A Comparative Study of Vietnamese and Chinese Government in the First Half of the Nineteenth Century*

*141. George Elison, *Deus Destroyed: The Image of Christianity in Early Modern Japan*

142. William D. Wray, ed., *Managing Industrial Enterprise: Cases from Japan's Prewar Experience*

*143. T'ung-tsu Ch'ü, *Local Government in China Under the Ching*

144. Marie Anchordoguy, *Computers, Inc.: Japan's Challenge to IBM*
145. Barbara Molony, *Technology and Investment: The Prewar Japanese Chemical Industry*
146. Mary Elizabeth Berry, *Hideyoshi*
147. Laura E. Hein, *Fueling Growth: The Energy Revolution and Economic Policy in Postwar Japan*
148. Wen-hsin Yeh, *The Alienated Academy: Culture and Politics in Republican China, 1919–1937*
149. Dru C. Gladney, *Muslim Chinese: Ethnic Nationalism in the People's Republic*
150. Merle Goldman and Paul A. Cohen, eds., *Ideas Across Cultures: Essays on Chinese Thought in Honor of Benjamin L Schwartz*
151. James M. Polachek, *The Inner Opium War*
152. Gail Lee Bernstein, *Japanese Marxist: A Portrait of Kawakami Hajime, 1879–1946*

*153. Lloyd E. Eastman, *The Abortive Revolution: China Under Nationalist Rule, 1927–1937*
154. Mark Mason, *American Multinationals and Japan: The Political Economy of Japanese Capital Controls, 1899–1980*
155. Richard J. Smith, John K. Fairbank, and Katherine F. Bruner, *Robert Hart and China's Early Modernization: His Journals, 1863–1866*
156. George J. Tanabe, Jr., *Myōe the Dreamkeeper: Fantasy and Knowledge in Kamakura Buddhism*
157. William Wayne Farris, *Heavenly Warriors: The Evolution of Japan's Military, 500–1300*
158. Yu-ming Shaw, *An American Missionary in China: John Leighton Stuart and Chinese-American Relations*
159. James B. Palais, *Politics and Policy in Traditional Korea*
*160. Douglas Reynolds, *China, 1898–1912: The Xinzheng Revolution and Japan*
161. Roger R. Thompson, *China's Local Councils in the Age of Constitutional Reform, 1898–1911*
162. William Johnston, *The Modern Epidemic: History of Tuberculosis in Japan*
163. Constantine Nomikos Vaporis, *Breaking Barriers: Travel and the State in Early Modern Japan*
164. Irmela Hijiya-Kirschnereit, *Rituals of Self-Revelation: Shishōsetsu as Literary Genre and Socio-Cultural Phenomenon*
165. James C. Baxter, *The Meiji Unification Through the Lens of Ishikawa Prefecture*
166. Thomas R. H. Havens, *Architects of Affluence: The Tsutsumi Family and the Seibu-Saison Enterprises in Twentieth-Century Japan*
167. Anthony Hood Chambers, *The Secret Window: Ideal Worlds in Tanizaki's Fiction*
168. Steven J. Ericson, *The Sound of the Whistle: Railroads and the State in Meiji Japan*
169. Andrew Edmund Goble, *Kenmu: Go-Daigo's Revolution*
170. Denise Potrzeba Lett, *In Pursuit of Status: The Making of South Korea's "New" Urban Middle Class*
171. Mimi Hall Yiengpruksawan, *Hiraizumi: Buddhist Art and Regional Politics in Twelfth-Century Japan*
172. Charles Shirō Inouye, *The Similitude of Blossoms: A Critical Biography of Izumi Kyōka (1873–1939), Japanese Novelist and Playwright*
173. Aviad E. Raz, *Riding the Black Ship: Japan and Tokyo Disneyland*
174. Deborah J. Milly, *Poverty, Equality, and Growth: The Politics of Economic Need in Postwar Japan*
175. See Heng Teow, *Japan's Cultural Policy Toward China, 1918–1931: A Comparative Perspective*
176. Michael A. Fuller, *An Introduction to Literary Chinese*
177. Frederick R. Dickinson, *War and National Reinvention: Japan in the Great War, 1914–1919*

178. John Solt, *Shredding the Tapestry of Meaning: The Poetry and Poetics of Kitasono Katue (1902–1978)*
179. Edward Pratt, *Japan's Protoindustrial Elite: The Economic Foundations of the Gōnō*
180. Atsuko Sakaki, *Recontextualizing Texts: Narrative Performance in Modern Japanese Fiction*
181. Soon-Won Park, *Colonial Industrialization and Labor in Korea: The Onoda Cement Factory*
182. JaHyun Kim Haboush and Martina Deuchler, *Culture and the State in Late Chosŏn Korea*
183. John W. Chaffee, *Branches of Heaven: A History of the Imperial Clan of Sung China*
184. Gi-Wook Shin and Michael Robinson, eds., *Colonial Modernity in Korea*
185. Nam-lin Hur, *Prayer and Play in Late Tokugawa Japan: Asakusa Sensōji and Edo Society*
186. Kristin Stapleton, *Civilizing Chengdu: Chinese Urban Reform, 1895–1937*
187. Hyung Il Pai, *Constructing "Korean" Origins: A Critical Review of Archaeology, Historiography, and Racial Myth in Korean State-Formation Theories*
188. Brian D. Ruppert, *Jewel in the Ashes: Buddha Relics and Power in Early Medieval Japan*
189. Susan Daruvala, *Zhou Zuoren and an Alternative Chinese Response to Modernity*
*190. James Z. Lee, *The Political Economy of a Frontier: Southwest China, 1250–1850*
191. Kerry Smith, *A Time of Crisis: Japan, the Great Depression, and Rural Revitalization*
192. Michael Lewis, *Becoming Apart: National Power and Local Politics in Toyama, 1868–1945*
193. William C. Kirby, Man-houng Lin, James Chin Shih, and David A. Pietz, eds., *State and Economy in Republican China: A Handbook for Scholars*
194. Timothy S. George, *Minamata: Pollution and the Struggle for Democracy in Postwar Japan*
195. Billy K. L. So, *Prosperity, Region, and Institutions in Maritime China: The South Fukien Pattern, 946–1368*
196. Yoshihisa Tak Matsusaka, *The Making of Japanese Manchuria, 1904–1932*
197. Maram Epstein, *Competing Discourses: Orthodoxy, Authenticity, and Engendered Meanings in Late Imperial Chinese Fiction*
198. Curtis J. Milhaupt, J. Mark Ramseyer, and Michael K. Young, eds. and comps., *Japanese Law in Context: Readings in Society, the Economy, and Politics*
199. Haruo Iguchi, *Unfinished Business: Ayukawa Yoshisuke and U.S.-Japan Relations, 1937–1952*
200. Scott Pearce, Audrey Spiro, and Patricia Ebrey, *Culture and Power in the Reconstitution of the Chinese Realm, 200–600*
201. Terry Kawashima, *Writing Margins: The Textual Construction of Gender in Heian and Kamakura Japan*
202. Martin W. Huang, *Desire and Fictional Narrative in Late Imperial China*

203. Robert S. Ross and Jiang Changbin, eds., *Re-examining the Cold War: U.S.-China Diplomacy, 1954–1973*
204. Guanhua Wang, *In Search of Justice: The 1905–1906 Chinese Anti-American Boycott*
205. David Schaberg, *A Patterned Past: Form and Thought in Early Chinese Historiography*
206. Christine Yano, *Tears of Longing: Nostalgia and the Nation in Japanese Popular Song*
207. Milena Doleželová-Velingerová and Oldřich Král, with Graham Sanders, eds., *The Appropriation of Cultural Capital: China's May Fourth Project*
208. Robert N. Huey, *The Making of 'Shinkokinshū'*
209. Lee Butler, *Emperor and Aristocracy in Japan, 1467–1680: Resilience and Renewal*
210. Suzanne Ogden, *Inklings of Democracy in China*
211. Kenneth J. Ruoff, *The People's Emperor: Democracy and the Japanese Monarchy, 1945–1995*
212. Haun Saussy, *Great Walls of Discourse and Other Adventures in Cultural China*
213. Aviad E. Raz, *Emotions at Work: Normative Control, Organizations, and Culture in Japan and America*
214. Rebecca E. Karl and Peter Zarrow, eds., *Rethinking the 1898 Reform Period: Political and Cultural Change in Late Qing China*
215. Kevin O'Rourke, *The Book of Korean Shijo*
216. Ezra F. Vogel, ed., *The Golden Age of the U.S.-China-Japan Triangle, 1972–1989*
217. Thomas A. Wilson, ed., *On Sacred Grounds: Culture, Society, Politics, and the Formation of the Cult of Confucius*
218. Donald S. Sutton, *Steps of Perfection: Exorcistic Performers and Chinese Religion in Twentieth-Century Taiwan*
219. Daqing Yang, *Technology of Empire: Telecommunications and Japanese Expansionism, 1895–1945*
220. Qianshen Bai, *Fu Shan's World: The Transformation of Chinese Calligraphy in the Seventeenth Century*
221. Paul Jakov Smith and Richard von Glahn, eds., *The Song-Yuan-Ming Transition in Chinese History*
222. Rania Huntington, *Alien Kind: Foxes and Late Imperial Chinese Narrative*
223. Jordan Sand, *House and Home in Modern Japan: Architecture, Domestic Space, and Bourgeois Culture, 1880–1930*
224. Karl Gerth, *China Made: Consumer Culture and the Creation of the Nation*
225. Xiaoshan Yang, *Metamorphosis of the Private Sphere: Gardens and Objects in Tang-Song Poetry*
226. Barbara Mittler, *A Newspaper for China? Power, Identity, and Change in Shanghai's News Media, 1872–1912*
227. Joyce A. Madancy, *The Troublesome Legacy of Commissioner Lin: The Opium Trade and Opium Suppression in Fujian Province, 1820s to 1920s*

228. John Makeham, *Transmitters and Creators: Chinese Commentators and Commentaries on the Analects*
229. Elisabeth Köll, *From Cotton Mill to Business Empire: The Emergence of Regional Enterprises in Modern China*
230. Emma Teng, *Taiwan's Imagined Geography: Chinese Colonial Travel Writing and Pictures, 1683–1895*
231. Wilt Idema and Beata Grant, *The Red Brush: Writing Women of Imperial China*
232. Eric C. Rath, *The Ethos of Noh: Actors and Their Art*
233. Elizabeth Remick, *Building Local States: China During the Republican and Post-Mao Eras*
234. Lynn Struve, ed., *The Qing Formation in World-Historical Time*
235. D. Max Moerman, *Localizing Paradise: Kumano Pilgrimage and the Religious Landscape of Premodern Japan*
236. Antonia Finnane, *Speaking of Yangzhou: A Chinese City, 1550–1850*
237. Brian Platt, *Burning and Building: Schooling and State Formation in Japan, 1750–1890*
238. Gail Bernstein, Andrew Gordon, and Kate Wildman Nakai, eds., *Public Spheres, Private Lives in Modern Japan, 1600–1950: Essays in Honor of Albert Craig*
239. Wu Hung and Katherine R. Tsiang, *Body and Face in Chinese Visual Culture*
240. Stephen Dodd, *Writing Home: Representations of the Native Place in Modern Japanese Literature*
241. David Anthony Bello, *Opium and the Limits of Empire: Drug Prohibition in the Chinese Interior, 1729–1850*
242. Hosea Hirata, *Discourses of Seduction: History, Evil, Desire, and Modern Japanese Literature*
243. Kyung Moon Hwang, *Beyond Birth: Social Status in the Emergence of Modern Korea*
244. Brian R. Dott, *Identity Reflections: Pilgrimages to Mount Tai in Late Imperial China*
245. Mark McNally, *Proving the Way: Conflict and Practice in the History of Japanese Nativism*
246. Yongping Wu, *A Political Explanation of Economic Growth: State Survival, Bureaucratic Politics, and Private Enterprises in the Making of Taiwan's Economy, 1950–1985*
247. Kyu Hyun Kim, *The Age of Visions and Arguments: Parliamentarianism and the National Public Sphere in Early Meiji Japan*
248. Zvi Ben-Dor Benite, *The Dao of Muhammad: A Cultural History of Muslims in Late Imperial China*
249. David Der-wei Wang and Shang Wei, eds., *Dynastic Crisis and Cultural Innovation: From the Late Ming to the Late Qing and Beyond*
250. Wilt L. Idema, Wai-yee Li, and Ellen Widmer, eds., *Trauma and Transcendence in Early Qing Literature*
251. Barbara Molony and Kathleen Uno, eds., *Gendering Modern Japanese History*

252. Hiroshi Aoyagi, *Islands of Eight Million Smiles: Idol Performance and Symbolic Production in Contemporary Japan*
253. Wai-yee Li, *The Readability of the Past in Early Chinese Historiography*
254. William C. Kirby, Robert S. Ross, and Gong Li, eds., *Normalization of U.S.-China Relations: An International History*
255. Ellen Gardner Nakamura, *Practical Pursuits: Takano Chōei, Takahashi Keisaku, and Western Medicine in Nineteenth-Century Japan*
256. Jonathan W. Best, *A History of the Early Korean Kingdom of Paekche, together with an annotated translation of* The Paekche Annals *of the* Samguk sagi
257. Liang Pan, *The United Nations in Japan's Foreign and Security Policymaking, 1945–1992: National Security, Party Politics, and International Status*
258. Richard Belsky, *Localities at the Center: Native Place, Space, and Power in Late Imperial Beijing*
259. Zwia Lipkin, *"Useless to the State": "Social Problems" and Social Engineering in Nationalist Nanjing, 1927–1937*
260. William O. Gardner, *Advertising Tower: Japanese Modernism and Modernity in the 1920s*
261. Stephen Owen, *The Making of Early Chinese Classical Poetry*
262. Martin J. Powers, *Pattern and Person: Ornament, Society, and Self in Classical China*
263. Anna M. Shields, *Crafting a Collection: The Cultural Contexts and Poetic Practice of the* Huajian ji 花間集 *(Collection from Among the Flowers)*
264. Stephen Owen, *The Late Tang: Chinese Poetry of the Mid-Ninth Century (827–860)*
265. Sara L. Friedman, *Intimate Politics: Marriage, the Market, and State Power in Southeastern China*
266. Patricia Buckley Ebrey and Maggie Bickford, *Emperor Huizong and Late Northern Song China: The Politics of Culture and the Culture of Politics*
267. Sophie Volpp, *Worldly Stage: Theatricality in Seventeenth-Century China*
268. Ellen Widmer, *The Beauty and the Book: Women and Fiction in Nineteenth-Century China*
269. Steven B. Miles, *The Sea of Learning: Mobility and Identity in Nineteenth-Century Guangzhou*
270. Lin Man-houng, *China Upside Down: Currency, Society, and Ideologies, 1808–1856*
271. Ronald Egan, *The Problem of Beauty: Aesthetic Thought and Pursuits in Northern Song Dynasty China*
272. Mark Halperin, *Out of the Cloister: Literati Perspectives on Buddhism in Sung China, 960–1279*
273. Helen Dunstan, *State or Merchant? Political Economy and Political Process in 1740s China*
274. Sabina Knight, *The Heart of Time: Moral Agency in Twentieth-Century Chinese Fiction*

275. Timothy J. Van Compernolle, *The Uses of Memory: The Critique of Modernity in the Fiction of Higuchi Ichiyō*
276. Paul Rouzer, *A New Practical Primer of Literary Chinese*
277. Jonathan Zwicker, *Practices of the Sentimental Imagination: Melodrama, the Novel, and the Social Imaginary in Nineteenth-Century Japan*
278. Franziska Seraphim, *War Memory and Social Politics in Japan, 1945–2005*
279. Adam L. Kern, *Manga from the Floating World: Comicbook Culture and the* Kibyōshi *of Edo Japan*
280. Cynthia J. Brokaw, *Commerce in Culture: The Sibao Book Trade in the Qing and Republican Periods*
281. Eugene Y. Park, *Between Dreams and Reality: The Military Examination in Late Chosŏn Korea, 1600–1894*
282. Nam-lin Hur, *Death and Social Order in Tokugawa Japan: Buddhism, Anti-Christianity, and the* Danka *System*
283. Patricia M. Thornton, *Disciplining the State: Virtue, Violence, and State-Making in Modern China*
284. Vincent Goossaert, *The Taoists of Peking, 1800–1949: A Social History of Urban Clerics*
285. Peter Nickerson, *Taoism, Bureaucracy, and Popular Religion in Early Medieval China*
286. Charo B. D'Etcheverry, *Love After* The Tale of Genji*: Rewriting the World of the Shining Prince*
287. Michael G. Chang, *A Court on Horseback: Imperial Touring & the Construction of Qing Rule, 1680–1785*
288. Carol Richmond Tsang, *War and Faith:* Ikkō Ikki *in Late Muromachi Japan*
289. Hilde De Weerdt, *Competition over Content: Negotiating Standards for the Civil Service Examinations in Imperial China (1127–1279)*
290. Eve Zimmerman, *Out of the Alleyway: Nakagami Kenji and the Poetics of Outcaste Fiction*
291. Robert Culp, *Articulating Citizenship: Civic Education and Student Politics in Southeastern China, 1912–1940*
292. Richard J. Smethurst, *From Foot Soldier to Finance Minister: Takahashi Korekiyo, Japan's Keynes*
293. John E. Herman, *Amid the Clouds and Mist: China's Colonization of Guizhou, 1200–1700*
294. Tomoko Shiroyama, *China During the Great Depression: Market, State, and the World Economy, 1929–1937*
295. Kirk W. Larsen, *Tradition, Treaties and Trade: Qing Imperialism and Chosŏn Korea, 1850–1910*
296. Gregory Golley, *When Our Eyes No Longer See: Realism, Science, and Ecology in Japanese Literary Modernism*

297. Barbara Ambros, *Emplacing a Pilgrimage: The Ōyama Cult and Regional Religion in Early Modern Japan*
298. Rebecca Suter, *The Japanization of Modernity: Murakami Haruki between Japan and the United States*
299. Yuma Totani, *The Tokyo War Crimes Trial: The Pursuit of Justice in the Wake of World War II*
300. Linda Isako Angst, *In a Dark Time: Memory, Community, and Gendered Nationalism in Postwar Okinawa*
301. David M. Robinson, ed., *Culture, Courtiers, and Competition: The Ming Court (1368–1644)*
302. Calvin Chen, *Some Assembly Required: Work, Community, and Politics in China's Rural Enterprises*
303. Sem Vermeersch, *The Power of the Buddhas: The Politics of Buddhism During the Koryŏ Dynasty* (918–1392)
304. Tina Lu, *Accidental Incest, Filial Cannibalism, and Other Peculiar Encounters in Late Imperial Chinese Literature*